Corporate Financial Reporting and Analysis

Third Edition

Corporate Financial Reporting and Analysis

A Global Perspective

Third Edition

S. David Young and Jacob Cohen

WILEY

Library of Congress Cataloging-in-Publication Data

Young, S. David, 1955-
 Corporate financial reporting and analysis : a global perspective/S. David Young and Jacob Cohen. — 3rd Edition.
  pages cm
 Includes index.
 ISBN 978-1-118-47055-8 (pbk.) – ISBN 978-1-118-55873-7 (ebk.)
 ISBN 978-1-118-55884-3 (ebk.) – ISBN 978-1-118-55886-7 (ebk.)
  1. Financial statements. 2. Corporations—Accounting. 3. Corporation reports. I. Cohen, Jacob, 1973
 II. Title.
 HF5681.B2Y68 2013
 657'.3—dc23

                                                                                    2012048290

ISBN 978-1-118-47055-8 (pbk)
ISBN 978-1-118-55884-3 (ebk)
ISBN 978-1-118-55883-6 (ebk)

A catalogue record for this book is available from the British Library

Set in 10/12pt TrumpMediaevalLTStd by MPS Limited, Chennai, India.
Printed and bound in Great Britain by TJ International, Padstow, Cornwall.

To Diane – S. David Young

To my parents – Jacob Cohen

Contents

About the Authors

S. David Young is Professor of Accounting and Control at INSEAD, based in Fontainebleau (France) and Singapore. He has been there since 1989. Professor Young holds a PhD from the University of Virginia and is both a Certified Public Accountant (USA) and a Chartered Financial Analyst. His primary areas of expertise are corporate financial reporting and value-based management, with works published in a wide variety of academic and professional journals, including several articles in the *Harvard Business Review*.

Professor Young is the author or coauthor of several books, including *EVA and Value-Based Management: A Practical Guide to Implementation* (McGraw-Hill, 2001), *Profits You Can Trust: Spotting and Surviving Accounting Landmines* (Financial Times Prentice Hall, 2003), and *Attracting Investors: A Marketing Approach to Finding Funds for Your Business* (John Wiley & Sons, 2004). His most recent book is *The Blue Line Imperative: What managing for value really means* (John Wiley & Sons, 2013).

Professor Young is also the recipient of several Outstanding Teaching Awards from the INSEAD MBA program, and the Distinguished Alumni Scholar Award from his undergraduate alma mater, The George Washington University. He has consulted extensively for companies in Europe, the US and Asia, mainly on issues related to value-based management and financial analysis.

Jake Cohen is Associate Dean for Undergraduate and Masters' Programs at MIT Sloan School of Management and Senior Lecturer in Accounting and Law, where he has been since 2012. In his role he oversees strategy for eight programs. From 2003 to 2011, Jake was an Affiliate Professor of Accounting and Control at INSEAD and was based in France and Singapore. He served as Director of the INSEAD-PricewaterhouseCoopers Research Center from 2004 to 2008 and as Dean of the MBA Program from 2008 to 2011.

He teaches courses in financial and managerial accounting, financial statements analysis, mergers and acquisitions, corporate restructuring, and business law. Cohen is a recipient of Outstanding Teaching Awards from the INSEAD MBA for both core and elective courses.

Prior to joining INSEAD, Cohen was a Senior Teaching Fellow in the Accounting and Control group at the Harvard Business School, where he was a founding member of the MBA Analytics Program. Prior to teaching at Harvard, he taught at Syracuse University as an assistant professor and was named "Professor of the Year."

Jake Cohen received a Bachelor of Science degree in accounting from Lehigh University, where he graduated with honors, a Master of Science degree in accounting and a Juris Doctor degree in law from Syracuse University.

Prior to his academic career, he worked as a tax accountant at KPMG LLP in Philadelphia and as a mergers and acquisition consultant for PricewaterhouseCoopers LLP in New York City.

CHAPTER 1

An Introduction to Financial Statements

Imagine that you're a banker, and you have to determine which companies to lend to, and on what terms. Or you're an investor who wants to know which companies are likely to out-perform the market averages over the next year or two. In short, where should you invest your capital? To answer this question, investors turn to corporate financial statements.

Financial statements exist to provide useful information on businesses to people who have, or may have, an economic stake in those businesses. These statements should help:

- *investors*, to make more intelligent decisions on where to put their scarce capital;
- *bankers*, to determine whether or not a company will be able to service its debts;
- *suppliers*, to assess whether or not a potential customer is a good credit risk;
- *customers*, to determine whether or not the company is strong enough financially to deliver on long-term promises of service and warranty coverage;
- *tax authorities*, to determine whether or not a company is paying its fair share of taxes;
- *trade union representatives*, in forming their negotiating positions with management;
- *competitors*, to benchmark their performance;
- *courts of law*, to measure, for example, the damage caused by one firm to another as a result of alleged unfair trade practices;
- *antitrust regulators*, to measure market share and profits relative to competitors;
- *prospective employees*, to determine whether the company is worth pursuing as a long-term employer.

You may notice one important constituency missing from this list of financial statement users: corporate management. Financial statements are the responsibility of management, but are not designed to meet their own informational needs. Financial statements are a means for company managers to communicate the financial strength and profitability of their businesses to investors and other groups, but are not really intended for internal management use. To understand why, let's take a brief look at the financial statements (shown in Exhibits 1.1–1.3) of SAP Group, one of the world's largest software companies.

The three principal financial statements – the balance sheet, the income statement, and the statement of cash flows – are highly aggregated documents: masses of detail accumulated in a small number of line items. Without this aggregation, the statements would be unreadable; however, a lot of details are missing. While this lack of detail might be appropriate for potential investors, who have to compare financial data across many different companies, the information found in these financial statements is not sufficiently detailed to be of any practical use to managers in corporate decision-making.

This is not to say that managers shouldn't care about the financial statements. Managers must understand their financial statements because these are the most important sources of information used by the investing community to determine where to invest capital. Managers who don't understand the signals that their financial statements are sending to investors are not in a position to compete effectively in the global capital markets. However, internal decision-making and management control require data that are far more detailed (by product line, region, cost categories, etc.) than the data found in annual reports.

In addition, financial statements are mainly historical. The balance sheet reflects the financial position at a precise moment in the recent past. The income statement shows profits over a period of time in the recent past – for example, the year just completed. Similarly, the statement of cash flows reports on the sources and uses of cash over a period of time already past. But while appreciating the insights of these statements is critical to managers in understanding their business and its competitiveness in the capital markets, they need information systems that are forward-looking in nature. Managers plan, budget, and forecast – and they therefore need systems that help them to perform these critical functions.

Another problem with financial accounting from a management perspective is that accounting rules that are designed to measure costs or value assets can result in misleading figures, even when calculated in good faith by managers. For example, when a manufacturing company measures the cost of its inventory, it must include not only direct costs of production, such as labor and materials, but also manufacturing overhead (such as depreciation on equipment, power and electricity, and maintenance costs). In contrast with direct costs, overhead cannot be directly traced to individual units of production. Instead, they are assigned to individual products (and to inventory accounts) using an arbitrary allocation technique. The resulting inventory figures may be acceptable for the broad overview that an investor wants from the financial statements, but can be seriously misleading if management intends to use them to calculate product-line profitability, to set pricing policy, or to make product-mix decisions. In short, managers need cost-accounting systems that provide more accurate costing data.

The three principal financial statements

The corporate financial reporting process focuses on the three principal financial statements – the balance sheet, the income statement, and the statement of cash flows.

The balance sheet[1]

Take a glance at SAP Group's balance sheet (Exhibit 1.1). One of the first things you should notice is that the balance sheet reports on the company's financial position at a moment in time, in this case the end of 2008 and 2009. In other words, it's a snapshot, taken at the end of each period, of the assets owned by the company and the financing for those assets. Assets are economic resources with the ability or potential to provide future benefits to a business, such as profits or cash flow.

Exhibit 1.1   SAP Group consolidated balance sheet (in € millions)

	December 31	
	2009	**2008**
ASSETS		
Cash and cash equivalents	€1,884	€1,280
Other financial assets	486	588
Trade and other receivables	2,546	3,178
Other nonfinancial assets	147	126
Tax assets	192	399
Total current assets	5,255	5,571
Goodwill	4,994	4,975
Intangible assets	894	1,140
Property, plant, and equipment	1,371	1,405
Other financial assets	284	262
Trade and other receivables	52	41
Other nonfinancial assets	35	32
Tax assets	91	33
Deferred tax assets	398	441
Total noncurrent assets	8,119	8,329
TOTAL ASSETS	€13,374	€13,900
EQUITY AND LIABILITIES		
Trade and other payables	€638	€599
Tax liabilities	125	363
Financial liabilities	146	2,563
Other nonfinancial liabilities	1,577	1,428

(Continued)

Exhibit 1.1 Continued

	December 31	
	2009	**2008**
Provisions	332	248
Deferred income	598	623
Total current liabilities	3,416	5,824
Trade and other payables	€35	€42
Tax liabilities	239	278
Financial liabilities	729	40
Other nonfinancial liabilities	12	13
Provisions	198	232
Deferred tax liabilities	190	239
Deferred income	64	61
Total noncurrent liabilities	1,467	905
TOTAL LIABILITIES	€4,883	€6,729
Issued capital	€1,226	€1,226
Treasury shares	−1,320	−1,362
Share premium	317	320
Retained earnings	8,571	7,422
Other components of equity	−317	−437
Equity attributable to owners of parent	8,477	7,169
Noncontrolling interests	14	2
TOTAL EQUITY	€8,491	€7,171
EQUITY AND LIABILITIES	€13,374	€13,900

The accompanying notes are an integral part of these consolidated financial statements.

The financing of assets occurs in two basic forms: liabilities and shareholders' equity. Liabilities are the company's debts or obligations. They are the claims on the assets held by a firm's creditors. Shareholders' equity shows the amount of financing provided by owners of the business, both in the form of direct investment (when shareholders contribute cash in exchange for shares) and indirect investment (when profits are reinvested in the firm).

The organization of the balance sheet can thus be summarized like this:

$$\text{Assets} = \text{Liabilities} + \text{Shareholders' Equity}$$

The term "balance sheet" is derived from this equation. It simply reminds us that the right side and the left side must always equal, for all companies, in all industries, in all countries, without exception. Simply put, the balance sheet must balance. The reason why this is can be seen if we look at the right side of the equation. Liabilities and shareholders' equity don't just represent financing, they also represent claims on the assets from the left side. In the event of liquidation (i.e., when a company goes out of business), first claim on resources belongs to creditors. The claims held by shareholders are residual in nature, which means that they are entitled to whatever is left over after the creditors have been paid off. Because shareholders' equity represents a residual claim on the assets, it will be whatever size it needs to be in order to ensure that the two sides of the balance sheet are equal.

SAP Group's balance sheet confirms this equality. Total assets at the end of 2009 of €13 374 million equal the sum of liabilities, €4883 million, and shareholders' equity, €8491 million.

The income statement

The income statement reports on a company's profits, or revenues less expenses, during the accounting period. Unlike the balance sheet, it's not a snapshot, but rather reflects what a firm has accomplished over a period of time. In the case of SAP Group, the income statement (Exhibit 1.2)

Exhibit 1.2 SAP Group consolidated income statements (in € millions)

	Year Ended December 31		
	2009	**2008**	**2007**
Software and software-related service revenue	€8,198	€8,466	€7,441
Professional services and other service revenue	2,432	3,039	2,744
Other revenue	42	70	71
Total revenue	10,672	11,575	10,256
Cost of software and software-related services	−1,714	−1,743	−1,350
Cost of professional services and other services	−1,851	−2,285	−2,091
Research and development	−1,591	−1,627	−1,461
Sales and marketing	−2,199	−2,546	−2,173
General and administration	−564	−624	−499
Restructuring	−198	−60	−2
Other operating income/expense, net	33	11	18
Total operating expenses	−8,084	−8,874	−7,558
Operating profit	2,588	2,701	2,698
Other nonoperating income/expense, net	−73	−27	2
Financial income, net	−80	−50	124
Profit before tax	2,435	2,624	2,824
Income tax expense	−685	−776	−916
Profit after tax	€1,750	€1,848	€1,908

The accompanying notes are an integral part of these consolidated financial statements.

reports on the company's performance for the years 2007, 2008, and 2009. Notice that the accounting year (sometimes called the "fiscal year") is the same as the calendar year (1 January–31 December). This is not required, however. For example, most major retailers in the US have accounting years that end between late January and the end of March. This is done to avoid having to close the books and prepare financial statements at the busiest time of the year.

The top line of the income statement, *revenues* (also called "sales" or "sales revenues"), represents the monetary value of goods or services sold to customers. Expenses represent the cost of resources used by the company to earn revenues during the period.

Profit (also known as "earnings" or "income") is shown in several ways on an income statement. For example, gross profit, sometimes called "gross margin," measures revenues, net of manufacturing costs. For a nonmanufacturing company, such as a retailer or distributor, gross profit equals revenues net of the cost of merchandise sold during the year.

Operating income equals sales net of all operating expenses, excluding taxes. It measures how well the company has done in a given period from its normal, recurring, day-to-day activities of producing and selling its products. For SAP Group, gross profit and operating income in 2009 were €7107 million and €2588 million, respectively.

When taxes and the nonoperating sources of income and expense are added or subtracted from operating income, as appropriate, the result is net income, the "bottom line" of the income statement. For 2009, SAP Group reports net income of €1750 million.

The statement of cash flows

The statement of cash flows summarizes the inflows and outflows of cash that arise from the three primary activities of a typical business: operations, investing, and financing. For SAP Group, operating activities refer mainly (but not exclusively) to the routine, recurring actions involved in developing and selling software, software-related services, and professional services. Investing activities involve the buying and selling of long-term assets such as machinery and equipment, companies or parts of companies, and financial securities such as government bonds. Financing activities refer mainly to actions involving the capital markets such as borrowing, paying off loans, issuing shares, share buybacks, and the payment of dividends.

The statement is structured in such a way that the net cash flows during the period for all three activities must equal the change in cash. In other words, the net cash flows from operating, investing, and financing activities must equal the net increase or decrease in the cash balance for the year. You can easily confirm this reconciliation in SAP Group's statement of cash flows.

What makes this statement so interesting is not just that it summarizes cash flows, and in so doing reconciles beginning and ending cash, but that it also reveals the sort of activities that gave rise to those cash flows. In short, the statement reveals where a company's cash came from during the year, and what the company did with it.

For example, SAP Group's statement of cash flows (Exhibit 1.3) shows operating cash flow of nearly €3015 million. Most of this cash (€2303 million) was returned in the form of repayments of borrowings. We know this is true because negative financing cash flows (i.e., as shown in brackets or with a "minus" sign) mean that the company returned more cash to investors (bankers and shareholders combined) than it acquired. Some of the remaining cash in 2009, nearly 600 million, was distributed by SAP Group in the form of dividends.

Exhibit 1.3   SAP Group consolidated statements of cash flows (in € millions)

	Year Ended December 31		
	2009	**2008**	**2007**
Cash flows from operating activities			
Profit after tax	€1,750	€1,848	€1,908
Depreciation and amortization	499	539	262
Gains/losses on disposals of noncurrent assets	−11	11	1
Gains/losses on disposals of financial assets	−2	−16	−1
Impairment loss on financial assets recognized in profit	10	15	8
Decrease/increase in sales and bad debt allowances on trade receivables	64	76	0
Other adjustments for noncash items	14	52	45
Deferred income taxes	−39	−91	8
Decrease/increase in trade receivables	593	−48	−521
Decrease/increase in other assets	205	−12	−277
Decrease/increase in trade payables, provisions and other liabilities	−116	−277	375
Decrease/increase in deferred income	48	61	124
Net cash flows from operating activities	3,015	2,158	1,932
Cash flows from investing activities			
Purchase of noncontrolling interests	€0	€0	€−48
Business combinations, net of cash and cash equivalents acquired	−73	−3,773	−672
Repayment of acquirees' debt in business combinations	0	−450	0
Purchase of intangible assets and PP&E	−225	−339	−400
Proceeds from sales of intangible assets or PP&E	45	44	27
Cash transferred to restricted cash	0	−448	−550
Use of restricted cash	0	1,001	0
Purchase of equity or debt instruments of other entities	−1,073	−396	−788
Proceeds from sales of equity or debt instruments of other entities	1,027	595	1,040
Net cash flows from investing activities	−299	−3,766	−1,391
Cash flows from financing activities			
Dividends paid	€−594	€−594	€−556
Purchase of treasury shares	0	−487	−1,005
Proceeds from reissuance of treasury shares	24	85	156
Proceeds from issuing shares (share-based compensation)	6	20	44
Proceeds from borrowings	697	3,859	47
Repayments of borrowings	−2,303	−1,571	−48
Purchase of equity-based derivative instruments	0	−55	0
Proceeds from the exercise of equity-based derivative financial instruments	4	24	75
Net cash flows from financing activities	−2,166	1,281	−1,287

(Continued)

Exhibit 1.3   Continued

	Year Ended December 31		
	2009	**2008**	**2007**
Effect of foreign exchange rates on cash and cash equivalents	54	−1	−45
Net increase (decrease) in cash and cash equivalents	604	−328	−791
Cash and cash equivalents at the beginning of the period	1,280	1,608	2,399
Cash and cash equivalents at the end of the period	€1,884	€1,280	€1,608

The accompanying notes are an integral part of these consolidated financial statements.

How the financial statements relate to each other

Although each statement is a separate, discrete entity, it is also linked with the other two. For example, the net income from the income statement (e.g., €1750 million in 2009 for SAP Group) is reflected in both retained earnings (from the shareholders' equity section of the balance sheet) and in the operations section of the statement of cash flows. Also, the net cash flows from the statement of cash flows (see final line) plus beginning cash (on the balance sheet) must equal ending cash. These relationships should come as no surprise because, logically, we would expect a company's performance, as reflected in its income statement, to influence its cash flows, and for both profit and cash flows to influence its financial position (i.e., the balance sheet).

To illustrate these relationships, let's take another look at SAP Group's financial statements. Net income in 2009 was €1750 million. As revealed in the statement of cash flows, the company paid €594 million in dividends that year. Retained earnings (on the balance sheet in the shareholders' equity section) represent all of the net income a company has ever earned in its history that has not yet been paid to shareholders as a dividend. In other words, it measures all of the profits retained by the business for reinvestment. We would expect retained earnings to change each year by an amount equal to the year's net income, less any dividends paid in that year. In the case of SAP Group, we should see an increase of €1750 million minus €594 million, or €1156 million. And that is very close to the amount by which the company's retained earnings increased from the end of 2008 to the end of 2009 (€8571 million − €742 million, i.e., €1149 million).

Note also that cash flows from operating, investing and financing activities (plus effect of foreign exchange rates on cash and cash equivalent in 2009, i.e., €54 million) result in a net increase in cash of €604 million, which is exactly equal to the difference between the cash balance at the end of 2009 (€1884 million) and at the end of 2008 (€1280 million).

Other items in the annual report

As mentioned earlier, the balance sheet, income statement, and statement of cash flows are highly condensed. For this reason, firms are required to provide supplemental information in the form of supporting schedules and notes. An opinion on the truthfulness of the financial statements from a firm of independent public accountants must also be furnished. Depending on its country of origin, a company may also include a discussion and analysis of recent performance and future prospects.

The statement of changes in shareholders' equity

There is, in fact, a fourth financial statement presented in many annual reports, although it functions more like a supporting schedule, and thus is not usually accorded the same status as the other three. This schedule, called the statement of changes in shareholders' equity (although it sometimes goes under different names), explains changes to all accounts in the shareholders' equity section of the balance sheet.

The notes

In addition to the principal financial statements, companies must also provide extensive supplemental disclosures known as "notes" or "footnotes." You will see these at the back of any annual report. The importance of these notes can be seen from the statement at the bottom of each of SAP Group's financial statements: "The accompanying Notes are an integral part of these Consolidated Financial Statements." This reminds us that the financial statements cannot be fully understood without reading the notes. In fact, the term "footnotes" is some-what misleading, though widely used, because it may lead you to think that they serve the same function as footnotes in a book. This is not true because footnotes in the annual report are an indispensable part of the story. The story doesn't really hold together without them.

Most notes fall into either of two categories:

- The first type describes the accounting policies used by the company to prepare its financial statements. For example, the first note in most annual reports is a summary of key accounting principles and policies.
- The second type of note presents additional, clarifying detail about one or more financial statement line items. Examples of this type include notes that elaborate on debt balances, investments, pensions, and taxes. Companies are also expected to provide financial details on major business segments. SAP Group discloses data on revenues, profits, assets, and capital expenditures for each of the segments – Product (marketing and licensing the software products, performing custom software development services for customers, and providing support services for the software products), Consulting (various professional services, mainly implementation of the software products), and Training (educational services on the use of the software products).

The auditor's opinion

Annual reports must include an opinion from an independent public accounting firm, attesting to whether or not the financial statements were correctly prepared and can therefore

Exhibit 1.4 Independent auditor's report

We have audited the consolidated financial statements prepared by SAP AG, Walldorf, comprising the statement of financial position, the income statement, the statement of comprehensive income, the statement of changes in equity, the statement of cash flows and the notes to the consolidated financial statements, together with the review of group operations for the business year from January 1 to December 31, 2009. The preparation of the consolidated financial statements in accordance with IFRSs, as adopted by the EU, and the additional requirements of German commercial law pursuant to § 315a Abs. 1 HGB [Handelsgesetzbuch "German Commercial Code"] as well as the preparation of the review of group operations in accordance with § 315 HGB are the responsibility of the parent company's management. Our responsibility is to express an opinion on the consolidated financial statements and on the review of group operations based on our audit.

We conducted our audit of the consolidated financial statements in accordance with § 317 HGB and German generally accepted standards for the audit of financial statements promulgated by the Institut der Wirtschaftsprüfer [Institute of Public Auditors in Germany] (IDW), and in supplementary compliance with International Standards on Auditing (ISA) and the standards of the Public Company Accounting Oversight Board (United States). Those standards require that we plan and perform the audit such that misstatements materially affecting the presentation of the net assets, financial position and results of operations in the consolidated financial statements in accordance with the applicable financial reporting framework and in the review of group operations are detected with reasonable assurance. Knowledge of the business activities and the economic and legal environment of the Group and expectations as to possible misstatements are taken into account in the determination of audit procedures. The effectiveness of the accounting-related internal control system and the evidence supporting the disclosures in the consolidated financial statements and the review of group operations are examined primarily on a test basis within the framework of the audit. The audit includes assessing the annual financial statements of those entities included in consolidation, the determination of entities to be included in consolidation, the accounting and consolidation principles used and significant estimates made by management, as well as evaluating the overall presentation of the consolidated financial statements and the review of group operations. We believe that our audit provides a reasonable basis for our opinion.

Our audit has not led to any reservations.

In our opinion, based on the findings of our audit, the consolidated financial statements comply with IFRSs, as adopted by the EU, the additional requirements of German commercial law pursuant to § 315a Abs. 1 HGB and give a true and fair view of the net assets, financial position and results of operations of the Group in accordance with these requirements. The review of group operations is consistent with the consolidated financial statements and as a whole provides a suitable view of the Group's position and suitably presents the opportunities and risks of future development.

Mannheim, March 11, 2010   KPMG AG Wirtschaftsprüfungsgesellschaft

be relied on by investors and other parties in making decisions regarding the business. The opinion shown in Exhibit 1.4 follows a standard format, with occasional variations.

The first paragraph indicates the scope of the opinion and also states that the responsibility for the financial statements rests with management. This responsibility has been reinforced by recent legislation in the US (known as Sarbanes–Oxley) that requires chief executive officers and chief financial officers to certify, under oath, the truthfulness of their companies' financial statements. This means that while auditors attest to the reliability of the accounts, the ultimate responsibility rests with senior managers.[2] SAP produces a similar declaration, signed by each member of the Executive Board:

> To the best of our knowledge, and in accordance with the applicable reporting principles, the consolidated financial statements give a true and fair view of the assets, liabilities, financial position and profit or loss of the Group, and the management report of the Group includes a fair review of the development and performance of the business and the position of the Group, together with a description of the principal opportunities and risks associated with the expected development of the Group.

The second paragraph affirms that the auditor followed generally accepted auditing principles. In other words, the audit was conducted according to the standards of the auditing profession. The auditor then expresses the opinion in the final paragraph. It is here that the auditor states that the financial statements provide a "true and fair" view of the company's financial position, and results of operations for each of the years presented in the annual report.

Most opinions are unqualified, or "clean," which means that there are no exceptions, reservations, or qualifications. In effect, the auditor is telling you, the reader, that the financial statements can be trusted in making investment and other decisions related to this business. But while the overwhelming majority of audit opinions are clean, there are some exceptions.

A qualified opinion may arise because of serious uncertainties regarding the realization or valuation of assets (which can sometimes occur when companies are financially distressed), outstanding litigation, or tax liabilities that might compromise the firm's financial health. Inconsistencies between periods caused by changes in accounting rules or policy can also result in a qualified opinion.

An auditor may also disclaim an opinion (i.e., issue no opinion at all) or even issue an adverse opinion. Disclaimers may arise, for example, because of pending bankruptcy. The uncertainties regarding the truthfulness of financial statement numbers are so profound, the auditor is reluctant to issue any opinion on the financial statements. This happened to Parmalat, the Italian dairy company, after it was embroiled in a massive financial scandal. Adverse opinions are rare, because an auditor is likely to resign or be fired by a client before an adverse opinion would ever appear in a published annual report.

Management discussion and analysis

Some annual reports, especially for companies that trade on stock exchanges in the US, include a management discussion and analysis section, also called the MD&A.[3] SAP calls their version the "review of operations." This section is an extended letter from the firm's management that summarizes the significant factors affecting the firm's operating results, financial strength, and cash flows for the past three years. It also contains an extensive discussion of business risks and forward-looking statements regarding the company's expectations for future operations, earnings, and prospects.

The review of operations from SAP's 2009 Annual Report runs to 87 pages. Most of the discussion consists of detailed explanations for the company's performance and financial condition, with emphasis on changes from the previous year. Important events from 2009 are also discussed, including acquisitions and product development. Management contrasts financial figures from 2009 with 2008, explaining why these numbers improved or worsened. Considerable attention is also given to liquidity, which is defined here as the ability of the company to obtain the cash resources it needs for growth and debt repayment.

Generally Accepted Accounting Principles: the rules of the game

When auditors declare that financial statements "present fairly" a company's financial condition, profitability, and cash flows, what they really mean is that the statements were prepared in accordance with Generally Accepted Accounting Principles (hereafter, GAAP). GAAP comprises the rules and principles that guide managers in the preparation of their companies' accounts. These rules provide the filter through which potentially millions of data points pass to produce the highly summarized financial statements we see in corporate annual reports.

GAAP sets the "rules of the game" under which financial statements are prepared. When these rules are implemented in good faith, the chances are high, though far from assured, that the resulting financial statements can be relied on by users to make important economic decisions regarding the business.

Here, we focus on two GAAP regimes: the one that prevails in the US, otherwise known as US GAAP, and International Financial Reporting Standards (IFRS). Although many other accounting regimes exist around the world, capital markets have come to be dominated by these two approaches. Important differences exist between the two, but their primary objectives are the same. Moreover, there is a serious ongoing effort at convergence that should ultimately lead to a single set of global financial accounting standards.

US GAAP comes from a variety of sources, but the dominant player is the Financial Accounting Standards Board (FASB), based in Norwalk, Connecticut. The FASB is a private-sector body that is tasked with determining the appropriate financial reporting responses to an ever-changing business climate. Its official pronouncements are called "Financial Accounting Standards." In some cases, these standards are supplemented by "Interpretations" that augment or clarify key aspects of the standards.

IFRS is the product of the International Accounting Standards Boards (IASB), based in London. Since 2005, compliance with IFRS has been required for all publicly traded companies based in the European Union. It is also widely used in Asia. Today, over 100 countries either require or allow the use of IFRS.

The barriers to understanding financial statements

Businesses can be complex, and if annual reports are to capture economic reality, they too must be complex. Analyzing and interpreting financial statements can be highly rewarding for readers who take the time to understand this complexity and the nature of the problems they are likely to encounter. The following discussion introduces the major barriers you can expect to face in trying to make sense of corporate financial reports.

The volume of data

The most obvious problem encountered by the reader of financial statements is the sheer volume of information available, especially for businesses traded on a major stock exchange. In addition to the principal financial statements, footnotes, management discussion and analysis, and auditors' reports, there are also financial filings with stock exchange and regulatory authorities (such as the SEC in the US). The result can be a veritable mountain of information. Although capital markets run on information, the risk is that a reader can be easily overwhelmed.

A variety of analytical tools, such as financial statement ratios, exist to help readers overcome this problem. These tools are discussed in detail in later chapters.

Accounting choice

Although GAAP and IFRS prescribe a set of rules and guidelines for preparing financial statements, they also afford corporate executives a broad range of choice. From the viewpoint of the financial statement reader, accounting choice adds greatly to the complexity of the task at hand. To some extent this choice is a logical outcome of the diversity we observe in the business world. What might be an appropriate accounting treatment for a steel company might not be appropriate for a biotechnology firm or an internet service provider. GAAP/IFRS must be flexible enough to accommodate all sorts of businesses and all types of business models. But even within the same industry, significant differences across companies in their accounting policies are often observed. For example, Coca-Cola's approach to translating the financial statements of its foreign subsidiaries into US dollars is different from that of PepsiCo, its major industry competitor.

To get a flavor for the nature of accounting choice, consider the following example. A machine with an expected life of five years is purchased for $500 000. For long-term assets like this, we must decide on a depreciation method. Depreciation is the process by which the cost of an asset is allocated to the future periods that will benefit from its use. The most common method is called "straight-line." Under this approach, each of the next five years (the periods expected to benefit from the use of the asset), will be assigned $100 000 of depreciation ($500 000÷5). This means that in the first year, the income statement will include $100 000 of depreciation expense. The balance sheet will show machinery with a net book value of $400 000 at the end of the year, the acquisition cost net of the depreciation charge.

But suppose we elect to use another depreciation method, as GAAP and IFRS allow us to do. For example, we may choose the "double-declining balance" method, in which depreciation is charged to the income statement in an accelerated fashion. Under this approach, we take the straight-line rate of 20% (the annual rate of depreciation on the asset) and multiply it by 2. The resulting figure, 40%, is then multiplied by the net book value of the asset at the beginning of each year to determine that year's depreciation expense. This means that depreciation in the first year is $200 000, instead of the $100 000 recognized under the straight-line method. Therefore, as a result of choosing double declining balance, depreciation expense in the first year would be $100 000 higher, and operating income $100 000 lower. In addition, the net book value of the asset at the end of the first year would be $300 000, instead of $400 000.

What this example shows is that the simple choice of one depreciation method over another can have a profound impact on both the balance sheet and the income statement. Which set of numbers is better? It's hard to say. Under some conditions, the straight-line approach may be better, but under other conditions it might not be. What's important to recognize is that both methods are allowed. Indeed, other methods are allowed too. Now imagine having to decide how all of the company's long-term assets are to be depreciated. And imagine the range of choices offered to corporate executives in how they measure other balance sheet items – or how they measure any transaction that arises in the normal course of their business.

Quite simply, differences in accounting choice can yield huge differences in financial statement numbers. One of the ways that a reader copes with this challenge is by carefully scrutinizing the notes to the financial statements.

In most annual reports, the first note summarizes the significant principles and policies chosen by the company's managers, helping the reader to understand the context under which the financial statements were prepared and key transactions measured. These disclosures allow analysts and other interested parties to compare a company's accounting policies with industry competitors and to make judgments on the quality of the numbers produced in the annual report.

Earnings management

Accounting choice doesn't just make financial statements more complicated. It also provides a powerful weapon for managers who wish to mislead the capital markets, for whatever motive. Accounting policy requires judgment, and whenever there is scope for judgment, there is also scope for manipulation.

"Earnings management" is the term commonly used to describe efforts by corporate managers to distort or bias their companies' reported results. "Creative accounting" is also used. Both terms imply a conscious effort by managers to mislead readers of financial statements.

Although the opportunities for earnings management are practically limitless, the most serious efforts fall into either of two categories: faulty revenue recognition, and the improper recognition of losses and expenses. The Enron fiasco brought to light another area prone to mischief: off-balance-sheet financing. This accounting game also featured prominently in the global financial meltdown of 2008.

Incompleteness

SAP Group is the world's largest enterprise software company. The company's best known products are its SAP Enterprise Resource Planning (SAP ERP) and SAP BusinessObjects software. But while these brands obviously carry great value for SAP Group, you won't see them in the company's balance sheet. The same holds true for the company's other well-known brands. This fact may seem odd given that these brands are almost certainly the most valuable resources the company has.

The above example shows that important attributes of a business, attributes with potentially profound effects on financial performance, may not always find their way into corporate balance sheets, at least not directly.

Reliability is a key characteristic of financial statements. To be reliable, financial statements should be verifiable: auditors must be able to check the numbers to ensure an acceptable degree of accuracy. This is not to say that all numbers have to be perfectly accurate; such a standard is not feasible, especially in large businesses such as SAP Group. But it does require at least some degree of objectivity, otherwise there is little for the auditors to observe and verify. For an intangible asset, such as the SAP BusinessObjects software, the common accounting practice is to include it in the balance sheet only if the asset has been bought. In other words, intangibles acquired from other companies are included, but internally generated intangibles are not. This means that when SAP Group acquires another company, any brands acquired from that purchase can be valued and subsequently included in the consolidated balance sheet. But the SAP BusinessObjects software, which was developed internally over many years, is not.

A similar practice can be seen in companies such as General Electric or Novartis. When they develop a valuable patent internally (i.e., from their own research and development activities), the patent is not included in the balance sheet. The only patents included are those acquired from other businesses.

Sophisticated readers of financial statements are fully aware of this inconsistency, and of the need to cast a wide net when gathering information about a company. In short, they understand that not everything you need to know about a company in order to value its shares or to assess its creditworthiness is revealed in the accounts.

Key lessons from the chapter

- There are many users of financial statements including: investors, bankers, suppliers, customers, tax authorities, trade unions, competitors, courts of law, government regulators, and prospective employees. Capital providers (i.e., shareholders, bankers, bondholders, and prospective investors) are arguably the most important constituencies.
- Although financial accounting is not targeted to the needs of corporate managers per se, financial statements are the outside world's "window" on the company. Therefore, managers need to know what signals are being sent to investors about their companies and how those signals are interpreted. Otherwise, their companies will be at a competitive disadvantage in the global capital markets.
- The notes at the back of the annual report complement the three principal financial statements – the balance sheet, the income statement, and the statement of cash

flows – and provide extensive supplemental disclosures. The notes describe the accounting policies used by the company and present additional clarifying detail about financial statement line items.

- Annual reports must include an opinion from an independent public accounting firm, attesting to whether or not the financial statements were correctly prepared.
- US companies prepare their financial statements in accordance with Generally Accepted Accounting Principles (GAAP). GAAP sets the "rules of the game" under which financial statements are prepared. Most non-US companies prepare their financial statements in accordance with International Financial Reporting Standards (IFRS).
- A serious effort is under way to achieve convergence between US GAAP and IFRS.

Key terms and concepts from the chapter

Stakeholders	Notes to the financial	Generally Accepted
Investors	statements	Accounting Principles
Creditors	Audit opinion	(GAAP)
Balance sheet	Clean opinion	International Financial
Income statement	Management discussion	Reporting Standards
Statement of cash flows	and analysis	(IFRS)
Statement of share-		Earnings management
holders' equity		

Questions

1. What are "consolidated financial statements"?

2. What is meant by the term "group financial statements"?

3. The balance sheet (or statement of financial position) is often referred to as a "snapshot." Why?

 4. If the balance sheet is a snapshot, how would you describe the income statement and the statement of cash flows?

 5. Why must the statement of financial position (i.e., the balance sheet) balance?

 6. What is the purpose of the auditor's opinion?

 7. What is Sarbanes–Oxley, and how has it affected corporate financial reporting?

 8. Describe the limitations of the financial reporting process.

 9. Financial accounting = Economic truth + error + manipulation. Explain.

10. Can you think of instances in which the creation of bias or error in the financial statements might be justified?

11. Describe how the three principal financial statements are linked.

12. What role is played by the notes in the financial reporting process?

13. What is the primary purpose of the statement of changes in shareholders' equity?

14. What is meant by the term "accounting choice," and why is the concept so important in financial accounting?

15. What is meant by the term "earnings management"?

Problems

1.1   Balance sheet terminology

Below is the statement of financial position (balance sheet) for the global brewing company, AB InBev. Identify the major differences in format and terminology between this balance sheet and the one introduced in this chapter for SAP.

Consolidated statement of financial position

As at 31 December Million US dollar	2011	2010
ASSETS		
Noncurrent assets		
Property, plant and equipment	16,022	15,893
Goodwill	51,302	52,493
Intangible assets	23,818	23,359
Investments in associates	6,696	7,295
Investment securities	244	243
Deferred tax assets	673	744
Employee benefits	10	13
Trade and other receivables	1,339	1,700
	100,04	101,745
Current assets		
Investment securities	103	641
Inventories	2,466	2,409
Income tax receivable	312	366
Trade and other receivables	4,121	4,638
Cash and cash equivalents	5,320	4,511
Assets held for sale	1	32
	12,323	12,597
Total assets	112,427	114,342
EQUITY AND LIABILITIES		
Equity	1,734	1,733
Issued capital	17,557	17,535
Share premium	381	2,335
Reserves	17,820	13,656
Retained earnings	37,492	35,259
Equity attributable to equity holders of AB InBev	3,552	3,540
Noncontrolling interest	41,044	38,799
Noncurrent liabilities	34,598	41,961
Interest-bearing loans and borrowings	3,440	2,746
Employee benefits	11,279	11,909
Deferred tax liabilities	1,548	2,295
Trade and other payables	874	912
Provisions	51,739	59,823
Current liabilities	8	14
Bank overdrafts	5,559	2,919

As at 31 December Million US dollar	2011	2010
Interest-bearing loans and borrowings	449	478
Income tax payable	13,337	12,071
Trade and other payables	241	238
Provisions	19,644	15,720
Total equity and liabilities	112,427	114,342

1.2   Understanding balance sheet relationships

Stora Enso is a large pulp and paper company headquartered in Finland. The company uses IFRS and reports its results in millions of euros (€). Compute the missing balance sheet amounts for each of the three years.

	2011	2010	2009
Current assets	€4,610	€4,494	?[b]
Noncurrent assets	?	8,543	?
Total liabilities	?	?	?
Total assets	?	?	€11,593
Current liabilities	2,786	2,569	2,619
Noncurrent liabilities	4,253	?	?
Total shareholders' equity	?	?	5,183
Share capital	?	3,150	?
Retained earnings	3,301	?[a]	1,200
Total liabilities and shareholders' equity	12,999	?	?

[a]Net income for 2010 is €766 and dividends are €158.

[b]Current assets – Current liabilities = €1144.

1.3   Interpreting an auditor's opinion

Excerpts are provided below from the auditor's opinion in the 2011 Annual Report of Creative Technology, Ltd., a Singapore-based consumer electronics company.

Required

(a) Describe the audit opinion rendered by PwC. Is this opinion "unqualified" or "qualified"?

(b) What is meant by the term "true and fair"?

(c) What is the economic significance of this opinion for investors and other interested parties?

(d) In what ways does management's responsibility for the financial statements differ from that of the auditor's?

> We have audited the accompanying financial statements of Creative Technology Ltd (the "Company") and its subsidiaries (the "Group") . . . which comprise the consolidated balance sheet of the Group and the balance sheet of the Company as at 30 June 2011, the consolidated statement of comprehensive income, the consolidated statement of changes in equity and the consolidated statement of cash flows of the Group for the financial year then ended, and a summary of significant accounting policies and other explanatory information.

Management's responsibility for the financial statements

> Management is responsible for the preparation of financial statements that give a true and fair view in accordance with the provisions of the Singapore Companies Act (the "Act") and Singapore Financial Reporting Standards, and for devising and maintaining a system of internal accounting controls sufficient to provide a reasonable assurance that assets are safeguarded against loss from unauthorized use or disposition, that transactions are properly authorized and that they are recorded as necessary to permit the preparation of true and fair profit and loss accounts and balance sheets and to maintain accountability of assets.

Auditor's responsibility

> Our responsibility is to express an opinion on these financial statements based on our audit. We conducted our audit in accordance with Singapore Standards on Auditing. Those Standards require that we comply with ethical requirements and plan and perform the audit to obtain reasonable assurance about whether the financial statements are free from material misstatement.
>
> An audit involves performing procedures to obtain audit evidence about the amounts and disclosures in the financial statements. The procedures selected depend on the auditor's judgment, including the assessment of the risks of material misstatement of the financial statements, whether due to fraud or error. In making those risk assessments, the auditor considers internal controls relevant to the entity's preparation of financial statements that give a true and fair view in order to design audit procedures that are appropriate in the circumstances, but not for the purpose of expressing an opinion on the effectiveness of the entity's internal controls. An audit also includes evaluating the appropriateness of accounting policies used and the reasonableness of accounting estimates made by management, as well as evaluating the overall presentation of the financial statements.
>
> We believe that the audit evidence we have obtained is sufficient and appropriate to provide a basis for our audit opinion.

Opinion

In our opinion, the consolidated financial statements of the Group and the balance sheet of the Company are properly drawn up in accordance with the provisions of the Act and Singapore Financial Reporting Standards so as to give a true and fair view of the state of affairs of the Group and of the Company as at 30 June 2011, and the results, changes in equity and cash flows of the Group for the financial year ended on that date.

PricewaterhouseCoopers LLP
Public Accountants and Certified Public Accountants
Singapore

Case studies

1.1   Apple: an introduction to financial statement analysis*

Apple is a global leader in the computing industry, with an emphasis on personal computing, mobile communication devices, and portable digital music players. It designs, manufactures, and markets both hardware and software. At the time of this writing (autumn 2012), Apple is the largest company in history in terms of market capitalization (i.e., the market value of the company's equity).

As recently as the late 1990s, however, Apple was perceived as mainly a niche player in the personal computer business, where the emphasis was on commoditized, low-margin products. The return of Steve Jobs, ousted in the 1980s from the company he cofounded, is now legendary in corporate history. He is credited for refocusing the company on the customer experience with products that emphasize not only performance and technology, but also aesthetics.

The excerpts from the company's financial statements included in this case will give you a summary view of recent financial performance. As you review these disclosures, think about what information is *excluded*, and how the absence of this information affects the reports' ability to communicate the true value of Apple.

Required

Balance sheet
(a) What was the magnitude and direction of the change to total assets for 2010?
(b) What was the magnitude and direction of the change to total liabilities for 2010?

---

*This case was prepared by Daniel Bens, Associate Professor of Accounting and Control, INSEAD.

(c) What was the magnitude and direction of the change to total shareholders' equity for 2010?

(d) Verify that the sum of your answers to (b) and (c) equals your answer to (a).

(e) What specific accounts explain most of the change to total assets?

(f) Based on your own experience, think about what makes Apple a valuable company. Does this "asset" that you've imagined appear on Apple's balance sheet? Are you satisfied that the balance sheet accurately reflects this value? Why or why not?

Income statement ("consolidated statement of operations")

(a) What was the magnitude and direction of the change to net sales?

(b) What was the magnitude and direction of the change to net income?

(c) Do the changes above seem consistent with the changes in total assets you calculated previously?

(d) Based on your own experience, think about the various product lines that generate these revenues (i.e., "sales") for Apple. Do you see the revenue from the individual product lines on the statement? Are you satisfied that the income statement accurately reflects these revenues? Why or why not?

Statement of cash flows

(a) What are the names of the three subsections that present the different sources of cash flow for the year?

(b) Note that net income is the first figure used in calculating cash generated by operating activities. How does net income compare to cash generated by operating activities?

(c) What does Apple appear to be doing with the cash that it generates from its day-to-day operations? (Hint: review investing activities.)

(d) Does Apple appear to have significant financing activities to report?

The auditor's opinion

(a) Describe Ernst & Young's role as Apple's external auditor?

(b) How useful is this opinion in helping an investor to value Apple's shares?

Apple's financial statements: Consolidated statements of operations (in millions, except share amounts which are reflected in thousands and per share amounts), three years ended September 25, 2010

	2010	2009	2008
Net sales	$65,225	$42,905	$37,491
Cost of sales	39,541	25,683	24,294
Gross margin	25,684	17,222	13,197

	2010	2009	2008
Operating expenses			
Research and development	1,782	1,333	1,109
Selling, general and administrative	5,517	4,149	3,761
Total operating expenses	7,299	5,482	4,870
Operating income	18,385	11,740	8,327
Other income and expense	155	326	620
Income before provision for income taxes	18,540	12,066	8,947
Provision for income taxes	4,527	3,831	2,828
Net income	$14,013	$8,235	$6,119
Earnings per common share			
Basic	$15.41	$9.22	$6.94
Diluted	$15.15	$9.08	$6.78
Shares used in computing earnings per share			
Basic	909,461	893,016	881,592
Diluted	924,712	907,005	902,139

Consolidated balance sheets (in millions, except share amounts)

	September 25, 2010	September 26, 2009
ASSETS		
Current assets		
Cash and cash equivalents	$11,261	$5,263
Short-term marketable securities	14,359	18,201
Accounts receivable, less allowances of $55 and $52, respectively	5,510	3,361
Inventories	1,051	455
Deferred tax assets	1,636	1,135
Vendor nontrade receivables	4,414	1,696
Other current assets	3,447	1,444
Total current assets	41,678	31,555
Long-term marketable securities	25,391	10,528
Property, plant and equipment, net	4,768	2,954
Goodwill	741	206
Acquired intangible assets, net	342	247
Other assets	2,263	2,011
Total assets	$75,183	$47,501

(*Continued*)

	September 25, 2010	September 26, 2009
LIABILITIES AND SHAREHOLDERS' EQUITY		
Current liabilities		
Accounts payable	$12,015	$5,601
Accrued expenses	5,723	3,852
Deferred revenue	2,984	2,053
Total current liabilities	20,722	11,506
Deferred revenue – noncurrent	1,139	853
Other noncurrent liabilities	5,531	3,502
Total liabilities	27,392	15,861
Commitments and contingencies		
Shareholders' equity:		
Common stock, no par value; 1 800 000 000 shares authorized; 915 970 050 and 899 805 500 shares issued and outstanding, respectively	10,668	8,210
Retained earnings	37,169	23,353
Accumulated other comprehensive (loss)/income	(46)	77
Total shareholders' equity	47,791	31,640
Total liabilities and shareholders' equity	$75,183	$47,501

Consolidated statements of cash flows (in millions), three years ended September 25, 2010

	2010	2009	2008
Cash and cash equivalents, beginning of the year	$5,263	$11,875	$9,352
Operating activities:			
Net income	14,013	8,235	6,119
Adjustments to reconcile net income to cash generated by operating activities:			
Depreciation, amortization, and accretion	1,027	734	496
Stock-based compensation expense	879	710	516
Deferred income tax expense	1,440	1,040	398
Loss on disposition of property, plant and equipment	24	26	22
Changes in operating assets and liabilities:			
Accounts receivable, net	(2,142)	(939)	(785)

	2010	2009	2008
Inventories	(596)	54	(163)
Vendor non-trade receivables	(2,718)	586	110
Other current assets	(1,514)	163	(384)
Other assets	(120)	(902)	289
Accounts payable	6,307	92	596
Deferred revenue	1,217	521	718
Other liabilities	778	(161)	1,664
Cash generated by operating activities	18,595	10,159	9,596
Investing activities:			
Purchases of marketable securities	(57,793)	(46,724)	(22,965)
Proceeds from maturities of marketable securities	24,930	19,790	11,804
Proceeds from sales of marketable securities	21,788	10,888	4,439
Purchases of other long-term investments	(18)	(101)	(38)
Payments made in connection with business acquisitions, net of cash acquired	(638)	0	(220)
Payments for acquisition of property, plant, and equipment	(2,005)	(1,144)	(1,091)
Payments for acquisition of intangible assets	(116)	(69)	(108)
Other	(2)	(74)	(10)
Cash used in investing activities	(13,854)	(17,434)	(8,189)
Financing activities:			
Proceeds from issuance of common stock	912	475	483
Excess tax benefits from stock-based compensation	751	270	757
Taxes paid related to net share settlement of equity awards	(406)	(82)	(124)
Cash generated by financing activities	1,257	663	1,116
Increase/(decrease) in cash and cash equivalents	5,998	(6,612)	2,523
Cash and cash equivalents, end of the year	$11,261	$5,263	$11,875
Supplemental cash flow disclosure:			
Cash paid for income taxes, net	$2,697	$2,997	$1,267

Report of Ernst & Young LLP, Independent Registered Public Accounting Firm

The Board of Directors and Shareholders of Apple Inc.

We have audited the accompanying consolidated balance sheets of Apple Inc. as of September 25, 2010 and September 26, 2009, and the related consolidated statements of operations, shareholders' equity and cash flows for the years then ended. These financial statements are the responsibility of the Company's management. Our responsibility is to express an opinion on these financial statements based on our audits.

We conducted our audits in accordance with the standards of the Public Company Accounting Oversight Board (United States). Those standards require that we plan and perform the audit to obtain reasonable assurance about whether the financial statements are free of material misstatement. An audit includes examining, on a test basis, evidence supporting the amounts and disclosures in the financial statements. An audit also includes assessing the accounting principles used and significant estimates made by management, as well as evaluating the overall financial statement presentation. We believe that our audits provide a reasonable basis for our opinion.

In our opinion, the financial statements referred to above present fairly, in all material respects, the consolidated financial position of Apple Inc. at September 25, 2010 and September 26, 2009, and the consolidated results of its operations and its cash flows for the years then ended, in conformity with US generally accepted accounting principles.

We also have audited, in accordance with the standards of the Public Company Accounting Oversight Board (United States), Apple Inc.'s internal control over financial reporting as of September 25, 2010, based on criteria established in *Internal Control – Integrated Framework* issued by the Committee of Sponsoring Organizations of the Treadway Commission and our report dated October 27, 2010 expressed an unqualified opinion thereon.

/s/ Ernst & Young LLP

San Jose, California
October 27, 2010

1.2   PepsiCo: communicating financial performance*

The Chairman's letter to the shareholders from PepsiCo's 2007 Annual Report is presented below.

Delivering Performance with Purpose in 2007

Dear Shareholders:

We have titled this year's annual report "Performance with Purpose: The Journey Continues." That's because in 2007 PepsiCo made great progress toward the long-term corporate objectives we set for ourselves last year: To achieve business and financial success while leaving a positive imprint on society.

---

*Source: 2007 PepsiCo Annual Report

Once more, our extraordinary associates around the world delivered terrific performance, and I am delighted to share with you the following 2007 financial results:

- Net revenue grew 12%, roughly three times the rate of global GDP growth.
- Division operating profit grew 10%.
- Earnings per share grew 13%.
- Total return to shareholders was 26%.
- Return on invested capital was 29%.
- Cash flow from operations was $6.9 billion.

In 2007 PepsiCo took important steps to support future growth.
What makes me particularly proud is that our 2007 performance was strong – not just measured by these short-term metrics – but also with the long-term equally in mind:

- We increased capital expenditures in plant and equipment worldwide to enable growth of core brands and expand into new platforms such as baked and crisp-bread snacks and non-carbonated beverages.
- We added several tuck-in acquisitions in key markets and segments, and we further expanded our successful coffee and tea joint ventures.
- We created the Chief Scientific Officer position to ensure our technical capabilities keep pace with increasingly sophisticated consumer demand; and we funded incremental investment to explore breakthrough R&D opportunities.
- We maintained focus on building next-generation IT capabilities with Project One Up, to support our long-term growth prospects worldwide.

Our brands once again demonstrated competitive strength.
On the ground, in cities and towns around the world, good brand strategies were implemented with operational excellence. I'd like to share a few notable examples of the big marketplace wins we enjoyed in 2007:

- Our carbonated soft drink and savory snack brands gained market share in the United States and in many of our top international markets.
- In the United Kingdom, Baked Walkers crisps was named "New Product of the Year" by *Marketing Week* magazine.
- SunChips snacks delivered double-digit growth in the United States as a result of great, innovative marketing and in-store execution.
- 7UP H2Oh! was our fastest-growing brand in value and volume share in Brazil in its launch year.
- Pepsi Max came of age as a global brand, with outstanding performance in the United States as Diet Pepsi Max, after successes in Northern Europe and Australia and 2007 launches across Asia.

- PepsiCo beverage brands crossed the $1 billion mark in Russia retail sales.
- We posted double-digit volume growth in China beverages and high-single-digit beverage volume growth in India.

And we did all of this while battling increased commodity inflation and more macro-economic volatility than in previous years.

Required

In her review of PepsiCo's performance in 2007, Indra Nooyi, PepsiCo's Chairman and CEO, claims that, "Net revenue grew by 12%, roughly three times the rate of global GDP growth." What message is she trying to convey in this statement? After reviewing the disclosure "Results of Operation – Division Review," which is found in the notes to the financial statements, do you agree with Mrs. Nooyi's assertions about PepsiCo's growth?

Consolidated Statement of Income

PepsiCo, Inc. and Subsidiaries: Fiscal years ended December 29, 2007, December 30, 2006, and December 31, 2005

(in millions except per share amounts)	2007	2006	2005
Net Revenue	$39,474	$35,137	$32,562
Cost of sales	18,038	15,762	14,176
Selling, general and administrative expenses	14,208	12,711	12,252
Amortization of intangible assests	58	162	150
Operating Profit	7,170	6,502	5,984
Bottling equity income	560	553	495
Interest expense	(224)	(239)	(256)
Interest income	125	173	159
Income before Income Taxes	7,631	6,989	6,382
Provision for Income Taxes	1,973	1,347	2,304
Net Income	$5,658	$5,642	$4,078
Net Income per Common Share			
Basic	$3.48	$3.42	$2.43
Diluted	$3.41	$3.34	$2.39

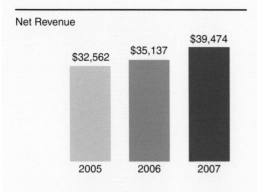

Net Revenue

$32,562 — 2005
$35,137 — 2006
$39,474 — 2007

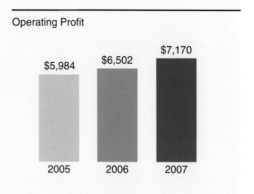

Operating Profit

$5,984 — 2005
$6,502 — 2006
$7,170 — 2007

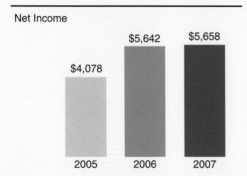

Net Income

$4,078 — 2005
$5,642 — 2006
$5,658 — 2007

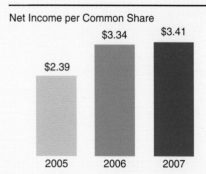

Net Income per Common Share

$2.39 — 2005
$3.34 — 2006
$3.41 — 2007

Results of Operations—Division Review

The results and discussions below are based on how our Chief Executive Officer monitors the performance of our divisions.

	FLNA	**PBNA**	**PI**	**QFNA**	**Total**
Net Revenue, 2007	**$11,586**	**$10,230**	**$15,798**	**$1,860**	**$39,474**
Net Revenue, 2006.........	$10, 844	$9,565	$12,959	$1,769	$35,137
% Impact of:..................					
Volume[a]	3%	(2)%	7%	2%	3%
Effective net pricing[b]	4	6	3.5	3	4
Foreign exchange...........	0.5	–	6	1	2

(*Continued*)

	FLNA	PBNA	PI	QFNA	Total
Acquisitions/divestitures	–	2	6	–	3
% Change[c]	7%	7%	22%	5%	12%
Net Revenue, 2006.........	$10,844	$9,565	$12,959	$1,769	$35,137
Net Revenue, 2005.........	$10,322	$9,146	$11,376	$1,718	$32,562
% Impact of:					
Volume[a]	1%	3%	6%	1%	3%
Effective net pricing[b]	3	1	4	2	3
Foreign exchange............	0.5	–	1	1	1
Acquisitions/divestitures	0.5	–	3	–	1
% Change[c]	5%	5%	14%	3%	8%

(a) Excludes the impact of acquisitions and divestitures. For PBNA and PI, volume growth varies from the amounts disclosed in the following divisional discussions due primarily to non-consolidated joint venture volume and temporary timing differences between BCS and CSE. Our net revenue for PBNA and PI excludes non-consolidated joint venture volume and is based on CSE.

(b) Include the year-over-year impact of discrete pricing actions, sales incentive activities and mix resulting from selling varying products in different package sizes and in different countries.

(c) Amounts may not sum due to rounding.

Notes

1. The balance sheet is also known as the statement of financial position. Although the latter is the official term, business people everywhere continue to use the term "balance sheet." We will do likewise in this book.
2. In some countries, such as the UK, principal responsibility for the financial statements rests with the board of directors.
3. A growing number of countries now require similar disclosures.

2

The Balance Sheet and Income Statement

In Chapter 1 we introduced the three principal financial statements – the balance sheet, income statement, and statement of cash flows – and the role they play in the financial reporting process. In this chapter, we discuss the first two statements in greater depth, focusing on the statements from SAP Group's 2009 Annual Report. (Cash flows are examined in Chapter 5.)

A further look at the balance sheet

The balance sheet reports the financial position of a company at a particular point in time. By "financial position" we mean the resources available to managers to run the business (i.e., "assets"), and the financing that made the acquisition of those resources possible (liabilities and shareholders' equity).

In Exhibit 1.1 you will have noticed the word "consolidated" at the top of SAP Group's balance sheet. This means that the document before you represents not just the balance sheet of SAP AG, the parent company, but also the balance sheet of any entity controlled by the parent. It's not the balance sheet of any one company, but rather that of a group of companies known to the investing world as "SAP."

To understand this idea, imagine that you buy shares in the company. What do you get for your investment? Not only do you obtain ownership rights over the legal entity whose shares you are buying, but you gain indirect ownership rights over any business or entity effectively controlled by that company. This means that when you want to know the financial position of SAP, it's not the balance sheet of the parent that you care about, but rather the balance sheet that includes all companies within the SAP Group. In fact, the standard practice in Europe and much of Asia is to refer to consolidated financial statements as "group accounts."

This example introduces us to an important concept in corporate financial reporting: *economic substance is more important than legal form*. Consider the above example. There is no legal entity anywhere that can rightly claim ownership of the SAP Group balance sheet because the document represents a consolidation, or aggregation, of many balance sheets. For a company of this size, the number of individual balance sheets included in the consolidated statement can easily run into the hundreds. But the consolidated balance sheet does correspond to an economic entity, namely, what you as an investor get when you buy shares in, or lend money to, this company. And from the investor's point of view, this economic perspective is more useful than the legal perspective. To put it another way, although the shareholders of SAP Group own shares only in the parent company, the parent's financial statements will tell them little about what they are really getting from their ownership interest. For this, they need consolidated accounts.

The SAP Group's balance sheets are dated 31 December 2008 and 2009. This tells us that financial position is measured at a specific point in time. In fact, balance sheets are sometimes referred to as "snapshots" in that they reflect financial position on a particular date; they say nothing directly about what the company did in the previous year. To find out how the company performed over a period of time, we need to look to the income statement and the statement of cash flows.

Assets

At the end of 2009, SAP Group reported total assets of €13 374 million (see Exhibit 1.1). This does not mean that the company's assets were worth this much. The market, or fair, value of a company's assets can be less than, or greater than, their balance sheet value. This divergence occurs for two reasons:

- Many assets, such as land and buildings, are recorded at their acquisition, or historical, cost (i.e., what the company paid for the assets when they were acquired). Over time, these costs can sharply diverge from market values. This is particularly true for real estate. In some countries companies are permitted periodically to restate real estate to market values. This treatment is permitted, though not required, under International Financial Reporting Standards (IFRS). American companies are constrained by the "historical cost rule," at least for nonfinancial assets. This is the valuation principle that says that assets should appear on the balance sheet at the price paid for them (historical or acquisition cost), less depreciation (if applicable). For property, plant and equipment, they deviate from this rule only when the value of assets is impaired (i.e., fair value is significantly less than acquisition cost).

- Some assets (especially those of an intangible nature) might not even appear on a balance sheet and, therefore, will not be reflected in total assets. For example, SAP's intellectual capital – arguably its most valuable asset – is missing from the balance sheet. Most intangibles appear on balance sheets only when acquired from other firms. This rule permits a reasonably objective valuation of the asset, but in knowledge-intensive companies such as SAP, important assets are left out. Although this treatment may seem inconsistent (reporting assets only when bought from other firms, and ignoring them if created internally), it is important to recognize the role it plays in causing a divergence between the book (or balance sheet) value of assets and what they are really worth.

Current assets

Current assets are short-term assets. An asset is short term if we expect to consume it or convert it into cash within one year or one operating cycle, whichever is longer. "Operating cycle" refers to the process of converting raw materials into finished products, selling them, and collecting cash from customers. In the case of SAP Group, this includes the process of software development, implementing software solutions, providing various professional and educational services, and collecting the cash owed on those sales. For the overwhelming majority of businesses, SAP included, the amount of time required for this cycle to turn is less than one year. Therefore, for SAP Group, the criterion for "current" is one year.

Total current assets at the end of 2009 are €5255 million. One way to interpret this figure is that it represents the sum of all SAP Group's assets that (1) were already in the form of cash, or (2) were expected to be consumed or converted into cash some time in 2010. All other assets are classified as "noncurrent."

SAP Group follows the American convention, also used in Canada and Japan, of listing current assets in descending order of liquidity ("liquidity" refers to the speed and ease with which an item can be converted into cash):

- Because it is already in the form of cash, cash is the most "current" or liquid of all assets and is the first to appear in the balance sheet.
- "Other financial assets" are comprised of financial securities held for short-term, cash management purposes. Government bond investments are common examples.
- Trade receivables (also known as "accounts receivable") are the amounts owed by the company's customers.
- SAP is not a manufacturing or retailing company. Therefore, it does not have inventories. If it did, we would see the balance for inventories below that of receivables. The reason is simple: in the case of inventories, sales have yet to take place. In fact, some of that inventory doesn't even exist as a finished product (raw materials and work in process for manufacturing companies). Therefore, receivables are closer than inventories to being realized as cash.
- "Other nonfinancial assets" consist mainly of prepaid expenses, such as rent and insurance. These are examples of current assets that will not be converted into cash, but rather are expected to be consumed in the short term.

Noncurrent (long-term) assets

Most of SAP's noncurrent assets fall into three broad categories:

- Investments ("other financial assets")
- Property, plant and equipment
- Intangibles (including "goodwill").

"Investments" are those that management intends to hold for the long term, including securities in other firms. For example, a company might acquire shares of stock in one of its suppliers to ensure continued availability of raw materials.

"Property, plant and equipment" (PP&E) are tangible, long-term assets used in a firm's operations over a period of years and generally not acquired for resale. This category includes land, buildings, machinery, equipment, vehicles, and computers. The notes reveal that half of PP&E is in the form of land and buildings; the other half is primarily IT capacity.

SAP records all such assets in the balance sheet at acquisition cost, net of accumulated depreciation. All tangible assets, apart from land, are depreciated because their service potential (i.e. their contribution to the firm's operations) gradually erodes over time. The notes to the company's financial statements reveal that plant and equipment at cost was €2562 million at the end of 2009. Accumulated depreciation, which represents all depreciation ever recognized on any asset still owned by the company, was €1191 million. This amount is offset against the acquisition cost to yield the net amount of €1371 million that you see on the balance sheet. This amount is sometimes called "net book value."

Accumulated depreciation is an example of a contra-account, in that its balance is offset against that of another account to yield a net amount that goes into the balance sheet total. Allowance for uncollectible accounts is another common example. Although we don't see any mention of this account in SAP's balance sheet, you can be sure it's there. The company reports €2546 million of accounts receivable at the end of 2009. Technically, this is not the amount of cash owed by the company's customers at that date, but rather the amount of cash owed that management believes will actually be paid. To illustrate, if we are owed €500 000 by our customers, but believe that only €460 000 will be collected, the balance sheet total should reflect the latter number. We would arrive at that figure by netting an allowance for uncollectable accounts of €40 000 (the contra-asset) against the €500 000 of gross receivables. For SAP, the allowance for doubtful accounts had a balance of €48 million, meaning that the gross amount of receivables owed to SAP at the end of 2009 was €2594 million, or €2546 million ("net" receivables) + €48 million.

"Intangible assets" are resources, apart from financial assets such as investments, that do not have any physical substance. Common examples include patents, copyrights, customer lists, brand names, and goodwill. The practice employed by most companies is that intangibles do not appear on balance sheets unless a market price has been paid for them. As a result, intangibles that are developed in-house typically are not included (with some exceptions), while intangibles that are bought from other firms are.

The term "goodwill" is often taken to represent reputation, management quality, and other qualitative aspects of a business firm that give rise to value but that cannot be directly observed and separately measured. But like most other intangibles, goodwill is not recognized unless it is bought. And it cannot be bought unless there is an acquisition of one company by another. Accountants assume that goodwill is acquired any time the purchase price for a company is greater than the sum of the fair value of all other assets (tangible, intangible, and financial), net of the fair value of the target company's debt. For example, if a company's assets (apart from goodwill) have a value of €10 million on the date it is acquired, and its debts have a fair value of €1.5 million, a purchase price of €12 million would require the buyer to recognize €3.5 million of goodwill [€12m – (€10m – €1.5m)].

SAP reports other noncurrent assets, including long-term trade receivables and deferred tax assets. We will discuss deferred taxes later in the chapter.

Liabilities

A liability arises when a firm receives benefits, and in exchange promises to pay the provider of those benefits a reasonably definite amount at a reasonably definite future date. Broadly speaking, liabilities fall into four broad categories:

- current liabilities
- debt ("financial liabilities")
- provisions
- deferred tax liabilities.

Current liabilities

Just as there are current assets, there are also current liabilities. These are obligations that must be paid within one year, or one operating cycle, whichever is longer. In the case of SAP, any liability listed as current as of the end of 2009 will have to be paid sometime in 2010.

"Trade payables" (also known as "accounts payable") shows the amount owed by the company to its suppliers.

"Other nonfinancial liabilities" consist mainly of employee-related liabilities such as earned but unpaid salaries, and other benefits.

"Deferred income" represents payments made by customers for products or services not yet delivered. For example, SAP may sell a software product with guaranteed upgrades for a specific period. If the customer pays not only for the software but also for future upgrades, a portion of the customer's payment represents unearned revenue. Until SAP delivers the promised upgrades, the unearned revenue is a liability.

"Tax liabilities" appear twice on the balance sheet. The difference between the two accounts is based on when the tax payments are due. Some payments (€125 million at the end of 2009) are due within the next year. The rest (€239 million) are due later. Similarly, some of SAP's trade payables are long term (€35 million).

The next several items on the balance sheet are noncurrent liabilities.

"Financial liabilities" indicate how much the company owes to its bankers and to holders of debt instruments (loans in the form of financial securities, such as notes and bonds) issued in the capital markets. Most of SAP's debt is long term (€729 million at the end of 2009); however, there is short-term debt too (€146 million).

"Deferred tax liabilities" arise because the amount of income that a company reports on its income statement differs from the amount of taxable income that appears on its income tax return. This account can be an asset or a liability, depending on the differences between book income (i.e., profit according to the income statement) and tax income (i.e., profit reported to tax authorities). Later in this chapter, we will explain the reason for these differences.

"Provisions" capture a broad range of long-term obligations that a firm may have to other parties. For example, suppose a company decides to close some of its facilities over the next two years. When companies restructure like this, they incur significant shutdown costs, such as the redundancy payments that must be made to employees. Accounting rules require firms to estimate what these shutdown costs might be in the period in which the decision is made, and to then recognize in that period an expense or loss on the income statement and a liability on the balance sheet. A firm does not wait until the actual payments are made to employees and other parties before acknowledging the financial effects of the restructuring decision.

Other common sources of provisions include the costs of environmental cleanup, and litigation. Most of SAP's provisions are comprised of unfunded pension obligations (i.e., employee pension benefits earned but not yet funded), restructuring, and product warranties.

Shareholders' equity

Shareholders' equity comprises the final section of the balance sheet. This section reports on the net amounts invested in the firm by its owners. Owners invest in their businesses in two ways: directly or indirectly.

Direct investment

This occurs when investors contribute cash or other consideration in exchange for shares of stock that represent ownership stakes in the business. A long-standing convention in some countries, such as the US, is to report this investment in two separate accounts:

- one that represents the "par value," "stated value," or "nominal value" of the shares (SAP calls it "issued capital") and
- a capital surplus amount (here, "share premium"), but sometimes called "capital in excess of par" or "additional paid-in capital."

To illustrate, imagine that a company issues shares for €10, with a par value of €1. For each share of stock sold the company would report common stock of €1 and additional paid-in capital of €9.

An alternative approach, common in European countries, is to combine these two accounts into a single-line item on the balance sheet. In such cases, the account may be called "share capital," "paid-in capital," or "contributed capital."

Indirect investment is made by owners in the form of "retained earnings." This account represents all earnings ever earned in the history of the business that have not yet been paid out as dividends (and, hence, have been "retained" in the business). Because earnings are the property of shareholders, any earnings that have been retained, and presumably reinvested, have been reinvested on the behalf of shareholders. In fact, some companies call this account "reinvested earnings."

"Treasury shares" are shares of SAP stock bought back by the company from its shareholders, and retained in corporate treasury for possible reissue. These shares may be reissued as part of an employee stock ownership plan, to provide shares to employees exercising stock options, or to raise additional equity finance.

SAP also reports an account titled "other components of equity." This account consists of gains and losses that, for reasons we discuss later in this book, bypassed the income statement and, therefore, retained earnings.

A further look at the income statement

The income statement reports on a company's performance during an accounting period. It is here that we find "net income" (or as SAP calls it, "profit after tax"). SAP's income statement (Exhibit 1.2) begins with two revenue figures, one related to the sale of software and the other to the sale of professional services. Revenue recognition will be explored in detail in Chapter 5.

The various expense categories that follow on the income statement represent the amounts, in monetary terms, of the resources used by the business to earn revenues during the period.

The first two major expense items are the cost of sales for the two revenue streams – software and professional services. These amounts (€1714 million and €1851 million) include all expenses incurred during 2009 to generate the revenues. Most of these expenses are employee related.

In a manufacturing, retail, or distribution company, the most prominent expense category is "cost of goods sold," or "COGS." This figure includes all of the costs incurred to manufacture or acquire the inventory sold to customers, including (in the case of manufacturers) labor, materials, and factory overhead. In the case of retailers, such as Wal-Mart or Carrefour, cost of sales comes from the merchandise inventory sold in stores.

One common profit measure is called "gross profit" and is calculated by subtracting cost of sales from revenues. Although SAP doesn't report gross profit, the figure is easily calculated: for software, we subtract the €1714 million cost of sales from the revenue of €8198 million, yielding €6484 million. For professional services, €2432 million − €1851 million = €581 million.

"Research and development," "sales and marketing," and "general and administration" also feature prominently among SAP's expenses. When all expenses are subtracted from revenue, the result is "operating profit," also known as "operating income." Operating profit is an important number because it reveals how successful the company has been in generating profit from its operating cycle (i.e., the process of producing and selling its goods and services). In other words, it tells us how much profit the company returns from its normal, day-to-day operating activities.

Operating profit is followed by "other non-operating income/expense," which is a catchall category consisting of many miscellaneous increases or decreases to profit from nonoperating sources, none of which were large enough to merit their own line item on the income statement. "Financial income, net" includes both interest expenses and interest income. The negative figure indicates that the former exceeds the latter.

After reporting "profit before tax," SAP subtracts its income tax expense of €685 million. "Profit after tax" (or net income) equals €1750 million. When we speak of the "bottom line" in the context of a company's financial performance, this is the number we are referring to. However, the analyst community tends to focus on net income on a per share basis, otherwise known as "earnings per share." When the net income is divided by the number of SAP shares outstanding (i.e., the number of shares of stock held by all owners), the result is €1.47. Because their point of reference is the price of a single share of stock, most securities analysts would say that SAP "earned €1.47 in 2009."

Other things you should know about the balance sheet and the income statement

Deferred taxes

SAP reports deferred tax liabilities of €190 million at the end of 2009. This liability arises because the amount that the firm reports as profit before tax (€2435 million for 2009) differs from the amount of taxable income that appears on its income tax return. This difference implies that the rules that SAP uses to calculate its earnings under IFRS may not be the same as the rules that govern how earnings are calculated for tax purposes. At first glance this difference may seem odd. Why doesn't the company simply use the same accounting for its income statement as it uses for its tax return? There is a logical reason why it doesn't.

The main purpose of IFRS (and US GAAP) is to help companies produce a set of accounts that captures the underlying economic reality of their businesses. In this way, it can guide investors and other relevant parties to make better, more value-enhancing decisions when they allocate resources, such as capital, or make any decisions related to the company. At its most basic, accounting exists to promote the efficient allocation of capital, and IFRS exists first and foremost to advance this goal.

In contrast, tax law exists mainly to allow governments to assess and collect tax revenues from businesses in a manner consistent with the public-policy priorities of the country's lawmakers. In the US, for example, tax law is made in the Congress. When tax laws are written and amended, the efficient allocation of capital may have been the last thing on the minds of the politicians responsible for them. They are moved by other priorities. For example, tax law may be written to encourage investment in capital goods or personnel hiring in an economically depressed region. Or it may be written to discourage excessive management pay. The point here is that politicians deliberately inject bias into tax law, and thus into the measurement of corporate performance under tax law, to promote public policy goals. While such efforts may be laudable (or not), we can say with certainty that the result is bias and distortion in profit measurement.

To cope with this problem, accountants came up with the idea of separating tax reporting from the financial reports used to raise funds in the capital markets. In short, this means that firms calculate their earnings in two ways:

- in accordance with tax law ("tax earnings") and
- in accordance with GAAP or IFRS (often called "book earnings").

As a result, companies can conform with tax law, with all of the bias and distortion therein, while at the same time producing financial statements that are true and fair for the investment community. Deferred tax assets and liabilities reconcile the two approaches.

In many countries, including the US and Britain, the biggest source of deferred tax liabilities is depreciation. Companies tend to use straight-line depreciation for book earnings, while using accelerated approaches for tax earnings. To illustrate, suppose a company buys a machine for $100 000, which it will depreciate over the next five years. In the first year, it will recognize $20 000 of depreciation expense for book earnings ($100 000÷5 years). Tax law in nearly all countries allows companies to depreciate assets using an accelerated approach, so that depreciation for tax purposes might be, say, $30 000. If the company's tax rate is 30%, income tax expense under IFRS will be $3000 greater than the taxes it owes to the government that year [($30 000 − $20 000) × 30%]. This $3000 of tax savings in the current year is not a permanent gift, but merely a temporary tax saving. The company will have to pay more tax in the future to make up the difference. That's why the $3000 is called a deferred tax *liability*. We expect that at some point in the future, the additional taxes will have to be paid. Any time a company uses an accounting method under IFRS that leads to such temporary differences between profits and taxes under IFRS and under tax law, the difference is reconciled using deferred tax.

As we noted earlier, SAP also has deferred tax *assets*. These assets arise when expenses are recognized for book purposes (per IFRS or GAAP) before they are recognized under tax law. The most common source of such assets is the provisioning for restructuring, litigation, warranties, etc. For example, when a company decides to restructure part of its business, the resulting loss is recognized immediately under IFRS. However, governments allow such losses to be deducted only after actual payments have been made. In effect, deferred tax assets represent future tax deductions on losses or expenses already recognized under IFRS. This topic is discussed in greater detail in Chapter 15.

Expenditure vs expense

To most people, these words are interchangeable, but not to accountants. When an expenditure is made, the firm can account for it in either of two ways: capitalization or expensing. To "capitalize" an expenditure is to record the amount as an asset. This treatment implies that the expenditure is expected to benefit a future period. For example, when a company buys a building, the cost appears as an asset on the balance sheet, only gradually finding its way into the income statement through the process of depreciation. When an expenditure is "expensed," the amount is charged in the current period to expense, and thus reduces earnings. The guiding principle is that if an expenditure is expected to benefit more than just the current period, it should be capitalized, thus appearing on the balance sheet. All other expenditures should be "expensed," that is, charged immediately to earnings on the income statement. However, as you proceed in your study of financial accounting, you will see that this guiding principle is sometimes violated.

Comprehensive income

A widely accepted axiom in accounting states that changes in shareholders' equity, from the beginning of a period to the end, should equal the change in retained earnings for the year, holding new share issues and share buybacks constant. To put it another way, assuming that a company is not issuing new shares or buying back old shares, the change in shareholders' equity during the period should equal earnings in that period, net of any dividends paid to shareholders. This relationship is known as "clean surplus accounting."

When earnings are defined as "profit after tax" or "net income," the final line item on the income statement, this relationship usually does not hold. You can see this with a quick glance at the balance sheet and income statement of SAP. Retained earnings increase from €7422 to €8571. Even if we control for changes in issued capital, changes in the share premium (i.e., additional paid-in capital), and changes in treasury shares, we can't reconcile the change in shareholders' equity (from €7171 million to €8491 million). This happens because companies sometimes recognize gains or losses that impact on shareholders' equity, but which bypass the income statement. To restore the clean surplus relationship, accounting regulators developed the concept of "comprehensive income." This measure includes net income, but also any gains or losses that, for whatever reason, were not included in the income statement and therefore are not reflected in retained earnings.

These other gains or losses are shown on the balance sheet as "other components of equity." This line item covers a variety of gains or losses that do not figure in net income calculations because their true impact on earnings is not yet certain, irreversible, or realized. Items that might appear in this account include:

- unrealized (or "paper") gains and losses on most investments in financial securities;
- some gains and losses on derivatives transactions (options, futures, swaps, etc.) used to hedge risks; and
- most gains or losses incurred when translating the financial results of subsidiaries from local currency to the parent company's currency.

Comprehensive income for the year equals net income, plus or minus changes in the "other components of equity" account. When income is defined in this way, clean surplus accounting is restored.

Key lessons from the chapter

- The balance sheet reports the financial position of a company at a particular point in time.
- The equation underlying the balance sheet is: Assets = Liabilities + Shareholders' Equity. This equation must hold for all companies.
- Most nonfinancial assets are carried on the balance sheet at their acquisition cost, net of accumulated depreciation (if applicable). Thus, the balance sheet does not necessarily reflect the true economic value of the company's assets.
- Total assets are classified into current and noncurrent assets. Current assets are expected to be consumed or converted into cash within one year or one operating cycle, whichever is longer. Noncurrent assets fall into three broad categories: investments, property plant and equipment, and intangibles.
- Liabilities fall into four broad categories: current liabilities, long-term debt, provisions, and deferred taxes.
- Shareholders' equity reports on the net amounts invested in the firm by its owners. It assumes that owners invest in the business directly and indirectly.
- Direct investment occurs when investors contribute cash or other consideration in exchange for shares of stock that represent ownership stakes in the business. The relevant amount is represented by "issued capital" or "share capital." The convention is some countries, such as the US, is to separate share capital into two accounts: one for par value, and another for additional paid-in capital.
- Indirect investment occurs in the form of retained earnings. Because earnings are the property of shareholders, any earnings that have been retained, and presumably reinvested, have been reinvested on the behalf of shareholders.
- When an expenditure is made, the firm can account for it either as an expense in the current period or as a capitalized asset on the balance sheet. Capitalized assets are future expenses.

Key terms and concepts from the chapter

Assets	Noncurrent assets	Expenses and
Liabilities	Current liabilities	expenditures
Stockholders' equity	Cost of goods sold	Gains and losses
Current assets	Revenues	Comprehensive income

Questions

1. Describe the difference between current assets and noncurrent assets.

2. True or false: The criterion that determines whether or not an asset is current is 12 months.

3. How are current assets listed on the balance sheet?

4. What is meant by "prepaid expenses" and why is this item classified as an asset?

5. What is the dominant valuation basis for property, plant and equipment?

6. Why is share capital described as "direct" investment and retained earnings as "indirect" investment?

7. What does the term "net" mean in the context of net sales or net revenues?

8. Why do deferred income taxes exist?

9. What is the difference between "expensing" an item and "capitalizing" it?

10. What is "comprehensive income" and what is it designed to achieve?

Appendix 2.1   The mechanics of financial accounting: the double-entry system

Financial statements are the primary end-products of the financial accounting process. To produce financial statements, all transactions that occur during a given period must be recorded and classified. The process of recording and classifying transactions is accomplished through journal entries prepared under the double-entry system. This chapter looks at how this system is used to prepare income statements and balance sheets. (Cash flow statements are addressed in Chapter 5.)

The origins of double-entry accounting have been traced as far back as the twelfth century. By the end of the fifteenth century, the system was widely used by Venetian merchants. In 1494, Luca Pacioli, a monk who traveled in the same circles as Leonardo da Vinci, formalized the double-entry system in the chapter of a book on mathematics. The system used today in practically every country of the world is nearly identical to that described by Pacioli over 500 years ago.

Under the double-entry system, every transaction recorded in the accounts has an equal amount, in monetary terms, of debits and credits. Each line item on the balance sheet and income statement has its own account. These accounts can be graphically depicted as a "T," hence the commonly used term, "T-account." For example,

Plant and machinery

Debit (+)   Credit (–)

Notice the space at the top for the account name (in this case, plant and machinery), a left side to record debits, and a right side to record credits. Asset accounts are increased by making debit entries, liabilities and shareholders' equity accounts are increased through credit entries. Because sales, all else being equal, increase earnings (and earnings enter retained earnings, a shareholders' equity account), sales are recorded as credits. Expenses, on the other hand, are debited. Similarly, gains (from, for example, the sale of assets at a price exceeding book value) are recorded as credits; losses are recorded as debits. These rules may appear arbitrary, but their simplicity has contributed to their constant use over the centuries. They are summarized in Table 2A.1.

When the debit–credit equality is satisfied for each transaction, the total amount in monetary terms (i.e., dollars, euro, etc.) for all accounts with debit balances should equal the total

Table 2A.1   Accounts

Accounts	Increase	Decrease
Assets		
Expenses and losses	Debit	Credit
Liabilities		
Shareholders' Equity Revenues and gains	Credit	Debit

for all accounts with credit balances. Also, when this equality holds, the balance sheet equation (Assets = Liabilities + Shareholders' Equity) is satisfied.

To illustrate the double-entry system, assume that plant and machinery is bought on credit for $55 000. The journal entry is recorded like this:

Plant and machinery $55,000
  Liability $55,000

Plant and achinery, an asset account, increases by $55 000 (debit), and a liability is recognized for the same amount (credit). Notice that while the debit entry appears on the left margin, the credit entry is indented. The debit and credit are then posted to the relevant T-accounts:

Plant and machinery		Liability	
$55,000			$55,000

At the end of each accounting period, and after every transaction that took place during the year is recorded, the balances in the T-accounts are posted to a "trial balance." This document lists every account in the balance sheet and income statement, and helps to ensure that total debit balances in the system equal total credit balances.

Adjusting entries are then posted, mainly to implement the matching principle. This principle says that any costs incurred to generate revenues must be recognized in the same period as the revenues. Revenues are "matched" with the costs that were incurred to generate them. Estimates are made of any revenues earned or expenses incurred for which cash has not yet been received or paid. The "accrual method" of accounting exists for the purpose of implementing this principle.

At the end of each accounting period, a standard set of accruals will be made before the financial statements are prepared. For example, nearly all companies must adjust for:

- interest income earned but not yet received;
- interest expense incurred but not yet paid;
- depreciation of tangible assets;
- amortization of intangibles;
- use of prepaid assets such as rent and insurance, and
- any unpaid benefits earned by employees (including salaries, bonuses, and pensions).

Other adjustments may also be needed. These entries are made whenever a company wishes to prepare a balance sheet and income statement.

After the adjustments, balances are recalculated for each account, and a postadjustment, preclosing trial balance is prepared. This document ensures that the system is still in balance, and is ready for the final steps in the process: the preparation of the financial statements.

The sequence works like this: the income statement is prepared from the preclosing trial balance. All income statement accounts (e.g., revenues, expenses, etc.) are then closed to retained earnings. The closing process performs two important functions. First, it transfers the company's profits (or losses) to the balance sheet. Second, it brings the balance of each account to 0, allowing the "slate to be wiped clean" for the next accounting period.

After the closing process is complete, a postclosing trial balance is prepared. Because all income statement accounts have zero balances, only balance sheet accounts appear in this version of the trial balance. The accounts can then be recast in the form of a proper balance sheet, and the accounting process is now completed.

The accounting process in practice

To see how the accounting process works, we draw on the example of Truly Books & Co.

1. Misha establishes Truly Books at the beginning of 2010, investing $100 000 in the business.

| Cash | $100,000 | |
| Share capital | | $100,000 |

Cash (A)			Share capital (SE)	
$100,000				**$100,000**
$100,000				$100,000

where (A) = assets, and (SE) = shareholders' equity.

2. A bank loans Truly Books $50 000, to be paid in five years with an interest rate of 10% payable annually. The funds are used to purchase inventory and shop equipment, and to cover rent on the shop.

| Cash | $50,000 | |
| Bank loan | | $50,000 |

Cash (A)			Bank loan (L)	
$100,000				
50,000				**$50,000**
$150,000				$50,000

where (L) = liability.

3. Misha signs a two-year lease for a store paying the full amount, $12 000, in advance.

Prepaid rent $12,000
    Cash $12,000

Prepaid rent (A)			Cash (A)	
$12,000			**$150,000**	**$12,000**
$12,000			$138,000	

4. In early January, Misha spends $1000 on bookshelves for her store.

Bookshelves $1,000
    Cash $1,000

Bookshelves (A)			Cash (A)	
$1,000			**$138,000**	**$1,000**
$1,000			$137,000	

5. Books are bought on credit for $50 000.

Inventory $50,000
    Accounts payable $50,000

Inventory (A)			Accounts payable (L)	
$50,000				**$50,000**
$50,000				$50,000

6. Before the end of 2010, Misha pays cash for half of the inventory purchased earlier in the year.

Accounts payable $25,000
    Cash $25,000

Accounts payable (L)			Cash (A)	
$25,000	$50,000		**$137,000**	**$25,000**
	$25,000		$112,000	

7. In 2010, the business sells books costing $40 000 for $100 000. By the end of the year, 90% of the sales have been paid in cash; the remaining 10% are still unpaid.

Cash	$90,000	
Accounts receivable	$10,000	
Revenues		$100,000

Cash (A)		Accounts receivable (A)	
$112,000		**$10,000**	
$90,000			
$202,000		$10,000	

Revenues (R)	
	$100,000
	$100,000

Cost of goods sold	$40,000	
Inventory		$40,000

Cost of goods sold (E)		Inventory (A)	
$40,000		$50,000	**$40,000**
$40,000		$10,000	

where (E) = expense.

8. Utilities expense for 2010 is $3600. By the end of the year, $2700 of the expense has been paid. The final quarterly bill is unpaid, but the cost is recognized as both an expense and an accrued liability.

Utilities expense	$3,600	
Cash		$2,700
Accrued utilities liability		$ 900

Utilities expense (E)		Cash (A)	
$3,600		$202,000	**$2,700**
$3,600		$199,300	

Accrued utilities liability (L)	
	$900
	$900

At year end, a trial balance is prepared listing the balances for each balance sheet and income statement account – see Table 2A.2. As expected, the total debits and total credits are equal.

Table 2A.2   Misha's trial balance: Preadjusted trial balance, 31 December 2010

Balances

Balance sheet accounts	Debit	Credit
Cash	$199,300	
Accounts Receivable	10,000	
Inventory	10,000	
Prepaid Rent	12,000	
Bookshelves	1,000	
Bank Loan		$50,000
Accounts Payable		25,000
Accrued Utilities Liability		900
Share Capital		100,000
Income statement accounts		
Cost of Goods Sold	40,000	
Utilities Expense	3,600	
Revenues		100,000
Total	**$275,900**	**$275,900**

After each transaction is posted to the relevant accounts, Misha makes a series of adjusting entries to implement the matching principle. Unlike the entries made up to this point, the following entries do not arise because of transactions. Instead they are adjustments required under accrual accounting. In this example, adjustments are required for the use of prepaid rent, unpaid interest on the bank loan Misha took out at the beginning of the year, and depreciation on the bookshelves.

9. Two years' worth of lease payments were made at the beginning of the year. An adjustment is required at the end of the year to acknowledge that half of the asset acquired (prepaid rent) has been consumed.

Rent expense $6,000
   Prepaid rent $6,000

Rent expense (E)	
$6,000	
$6,000	

Prepaid rent (A)	
$12,000	**$6,000**
$6,000	

10. Interest on the bank loan is acknowledged, even if actual payment will not take place until the beginning of the following year. Given the $50 000 loan, and a 10% interest rate, the following entry is required.

Interest expense	$5,000	
Accrued interest liability		$5,000

Interest expense (E)		Accrued interest liability (L)	
$5,000			**$5,000**
$5,000			$5,000

11. Depreciation on the bookshelves must be recognized. A common practice in retailing is to depreciate such assets over 4 years, using the straight-line method. Given the initial investment of $1000, the annual depreciation charge is $250.

Depreciation expense	$250	
Accumulated depreciation		$250

Depreciation expense (E)		Accumulated depreciation	
$250			**$250**
$250			$250

Accumulated depreciation is a contra-asset account. All contra-assets have a credit balance, which is then offset against the asset account (in this case, Bookshelves) to yield the asset's net book value. The postadjustment, preclosing trial balance can now be prepared – see Table 2A.3. The income statement emerges from this trial balance – see Table 2A.4.

Table 2A.3   The postadjusted, preclosing trial balance: Postadjusted, preclosing trial balance, 31 December 2010

Balances		
Balance sheet accounts	**Debit**	**Credit**
Cash	$199,300	
Accounts receivable	10,000	
Inventory	10,000	
Prepaid rent	6,000	
Bookshelves	1,000	
Accumulated depreciation		$ 250
Bank loan		50,000
Accounts payable		25,000

(*Continued*)

Table 2A.3 Continued

Balances

Balance sheet accounts	Debit	Credit
Accrued utilities liability		900
Accrued interest liability		5,000
Share capital		100,000
Income statement accounts		
Cost of goods sold	40,000	
Utilities expense	3,600	
Rent expense	6,000	
Interest expense	5,000	
Depreciation expense	250	
Revenues		100,000
Total	**$281,150**	**$281,150**

Table 2A.4 Misha's income statement: Truly Books & Co. Income statement for year ending 31 December 2010

Revenues		$100,000
Less cost of goods sold		(40,000)
Gross profit		60,000
Less expenses:		
Utilities expense	$3,600	
Rent expense	6,000	
Interest expense	5,000	
Depreciation expense	250	
		(14,850)
Net income		**$45,150**

12. The income statement accounts are closed to Retained Earnings. This process is accomplished with offsetting entries to each account. For example, because the Revenues account has a credit balance of $100 000, a debit for the same amount is required. The account balance is brought to zero, and the balancing entry is always to Retained Earnings.

Revenues	$100,000	
Retained earnings		$100,000

Revenues (R)		Retained earnings (SE)	
$100,000	$100,000		$100,000
	$ ___		$100,000

Similar entries are required for the expenses, only now the accounts are credited, and Retained Earnings is debited.

Retained earnings	$54,850	
Cost of goods sold		$40,000
Utilities expense		3,600
Rent expense		6,000
Interest expense		5,000
Depreciation expense		250

Retained earnings (SE)		Cost of goods sold (E)	
$54,850	**$100,000**	**$40,000**	**$40,000**
	$45,150	$___	

Utilities expense (E)		Rent expense (E)	
$3,600	**$3,600**	**$6,000**	**$6,000**
$ ___		$ ___	

Interest expense (E)		Depreciation expense (E)	
$5,000	**$5,000**	**$250**	**$250**
$ ___		$___	

A postclosing trial balance, consisting entirely of balance sheet accounts, is then prepared. This document will serve as the basis for the end-of-year balance sheet, and as the beginning trial balance for the next period – see Table 2A.5.

Finally, Misha can prepare the balance sheet for Truly Books and Co. – see Table 2A.6.

Table 2A.5 Postclosing trial balance as at 31 December 2010

Balances Account	Debit	Credit
Cash	$199,300	
Accounts receivable	10,000	
Inventory	10,000	
Prepaid rent	6,000	
Bookshelves	1,000	

(Continued)

Table 2A.5   Continued

Balances Account	Debit	Credit
Accumulated depreciation		$250
Bank loan		50,000
Accounts payable		25,000
Accrued utilities liability		900
Accrued interest liability		5,000
Share capital		100,000
Retained earnings		45,150
Total	**$226,300**	**$226,300**

Table 2A.6   Truly Books & Co. balance sheet: Truly Books and Co. Balance Sheet as at 31 December 2010

Assets		
Cash		$199,300
Accounts receivable		10,000
Inventory		10,000
Prepaid rent		6,000
Bookshelves	$1,000	
Less accumulated depreciation	(250)	750
Total assets		$ 226,050
Liabilities and stockholders' equity		
Bank loan		$50,000
Accounts payable		25,000
Accrued utilities liability		900
Accrued interest liability		5,000
Share capital		100,000
Retained earnings		45,150
Total liabilities and stockholders' equity		**$226,050**

Key terms and concepts from the appendix

Double-entry accounting	Credit	Adjusting entries
Accounts	Journal entry	Closing entries
T-account	Trial balance	General ledger
Debit	Transaction entries	

Key lessons from the appendix

- The process of recording and classifying transactions is accomplished through journal entries prepared under the double-entry system. This system has been in continuous use for over 500 years.
- Under the double-entry system, every transaction recorded in the accounts has an equal amount, in monetary terms, of debits and credits.
- The income statement accounts are "temporary," meaning that they are closed at the end of the accounting period to the retained earnings account on the balance sheet. The closing process achieves two purposes. First, it removes any balances from income statement accounts, allowing the income measurement process to start from zero at the beginning of the following period. Second, it transfers net income or net loss to the balance sheet.
- Balance sheet accounts are "permanent" in the sense that they are not closed at the end of the accounting period. Permanent simply means that account balances can straddle two accounting periods.

Problem

2.1   Preparing a balance sheet and an income statement

The following information is based on accounting data for 2011 and 2012 for PetroLim, a petrochemicals company based in Malaysia. It reports its results in thousands of Malaysian Ringgits.

| | 31 December | |
Statement of financial position items	2012	2011
Cash	177,178	108,140
Accounts receivable	36,838	16,976
Advances to suppliers	40,772	25,328
Inventories	176,934	152,076
Other current assets	40,734	26,914
Property, plant and equipment (net)	495,606	463,180
Oil and gas properties	652,656	540,992
Intangible assets	40,044	32,254
Other noncurrent assets	327,422	264,428

(Continued)

	31 December	
Statement of financial position items	**2012**	**2011**
Accounts payable	208,920	155,872
Advances from customers	24,866	23,180
Other current liabilities	169,522	181,878
Long-term debt	70,610	60,802
Other noncurrent liabilities	84,124	73,366
Common shares	889,054	708,680
Retained earnings	541,088	426,510

Income statement items	**2012**
Net operating revenues	1,670,074
Interest and other revenues	6,196
Cost of sales	974,224
Selling expenses	82,690
General and administrative expenses	98,648
Other operating expenses	129,320
Interest expense	5,738
Income taxes	98,662

Required

(a) Prepare an income statement for PetroLim for the year ending 31 December 2012.
(b) Prepare statements of financial position for PetroLim as of 31 December 2011 and 31 December 2012.

Case study

2.1   JanMar Fabrics: preparing the balance sheet and income statement*

The adjusted, postclosing trial balance of JanMar Fabrics on 30 June 2012 appears on the next page.

---

*Note that this case assumes that students are familiar with the double-entry system of accounting, the subject of this chapter's appendix.

JanMar Fabrics adjusted, postclosing trial balance June 30, 2012

Cash	$221,000	
Accounts Receivable	136,250	
Merchandise Inventory	340,750	
Prepaid Insurance	2,000	
Equipment	1,050,000	
Accumulated Depreciation		$420,000
Accounts Payable		165,500
Notes Payable		25,000
Salaries Payable		6,250
Common Stock		750,000
Retained Earnings		383,250
	$1,750,000	$1,750,000

The firm made the following transactions during July:

1. Sold merchandise on account for a total selling price of $425 000.
2. Purchased merchandise inventory on account from various suppliers for $231 500.
3. Paid rent for the month of July of $58 750.
4. Paid salaries to employees during July of $103 000.
5. Collected accounts receivable of $170 750.
6. Paid accounts payable of $194 750.
7. Paid miscellaneous expenses of $16 000.

Adjusting entries required at the end of July relate to the following:

8. The company paid the premium on a one-year insurance policy on 1 March 2012, with coverage beginning on that date. This is the only insurance policy in force on 30 June 2012.
9. The firm depreciates its equipment over a 10-year life. The equipment is not expected to have any residual value.
10. Employees earned salaries of $8000 during the last three days of July but were not paid. These are the only unpaid salaries at the end of July.
11. The note payable is a 90-day, 12% note issued on 30 June 2012.
12. Merchandise inventory on hand on 31 July 2012 was $389 750.

Required

Using a trial balance and T-accounts, prepare an income statement for the month of July 2012, and prepare a balance sheet dated 31 July 2012. Cross-reference entries in the T-accounts using the numbers of the transactions shown above.

3

A Brief Overview of GAAP and IFRS: the Framework for Financial Accounting

The primary objective of Generally Accepted Accounting Principles (GAAP) and International Financial Reporting Standards (IFRS) is to guide companies in producing economic information that helps external users make better decisions. To put it another way, the main purpose of corporate financial reporting from a broad economic perspective is to promote the efficient allocation of capital in the global capital markets. If accountants and auditors are doing their jobs properly, financial statements should facilitate the movement of capital to where it is likely to earn its highest risk-adjusted returns, thus maximizing wealth creation.

To achieve this goal, GAAP and IFRS are governed by a set of (1) core principles, (2) qualitative characteristics, (3) underlying assumptions, and (4) modifying conventions.

The core principles of GAAP and IFRS

Several principles exert a broad influence over the standards produced by the Financial Accounting Standards Board (FASB) and the International Accounting Standards Board (IASB) and on the way in which financial statements are prepared. The most important of these principles deal with: asset valuation, revenue recognition, and the matching principle.

Asset valuation

For an asset to appear on a balance sheet, some basis must be chosen for assigning a value to it. The default option, and the dominant approach for certain classes of assets, is known as "acquisition (or historical) cost." As the term implies, value is measured as the cash or cash-equivalent price of the asset on the date it was acquired. Assets such as buildings, machinery, equipment, and vehicles are usually valued on this basis.

What happens subsequent to acquisition depends on whether an asset's value increases or decreases, on whether the company uses US GAAP or IFRS, and on the nature of the asset. As of now, IFRS is more flexible than US GAAP in the valuation of nonmonetary assets, such as land. While companies such as SAP keep land and buildings on the balance sheet at acquisition price, businesses preparing balance sheets under IFRS have the option of using "fair value." Fair value is the price that would be received for an asset in an arm's-length (i.e. genuine market) transaction. It represents what the firm could get for the asset on the balance sheet date, assuming an orderly sale, not a fire sale or sale out of desperation. The assets are initially recorded at acquisition cost, but as market values change, so too will the balance sheet amounts. For example, if land acquired at $20 million is now worth $30 million, the latter amount might appear on the balance sheet. Although IFRS allows for this treatment, most IFRS-compliant companies do in fact use acquisition cost for such assets anyway.

What happens if the value of the asset falls below its acquisition cost? The rule that prevails under both accounting regimes is that if an asset's value is deemed to be permanently impaired (i.e., a decline in value below acquisition cost appears irreversible), the asset must be written down to its fair value. For example, if land bought for $20 million is now worth only $8 million, and recovery is unlikely, the balance sheet must now say $8 million. The $12 million reduction in value appears as a loss in the income statement for the period in which the asset impairment is recognized.

The nature of an asset also influences its measurement. For example, in the case of monetary assets – such as shares of stock, bonds, and positions in options and futures – fair value is the dominant measurement basis, under both US GAAP and IFRS. In other words, while nonmonetary assets, such as land and equipment, are usually measured at acquisition cost, most monetary assets appear on balance sheets at fair value.

Revenue recognition

Before companies are permitted to recognize revenue from the sale of goods or services to customers, three criteria must be met. The revenues must be: measurable, earned, and realizable.

"Measurable" implies that a reasonable basis exists for determining the amount of revenues earned. For routine sales, measurability is rarely a concern. But imagine a construction contract in which work is performed, and revenue earned, gradually over a period of years. The possibility of error, deliberate or otherwise, is far greater in such circumstances than in the software sales that comprise most of the revenues for SAP. However, SAP is not immune to measurement issues, particularly when a customer signs a contract that comprises not only software but also future upgrades and training. In such cases, the company must determine how much of the customer's total payments will be allocated to each of the products and services covered by the contract.

"Earned" implies that whatever the seller needs to do to generate the revenue (for example, produce the product and deliver it to the customer) has already been accomplished. Otherwise, the seller cannot rightfully claim that revenue has been earned, even if there is a willing buyer. For example, if a customer pays for a software package and future upgrades, SAP can recognize revenue only for the products already delivered. Future upgrades cannot be recognized as revenue until the upgrades have been produced and delivered, even if the customer pays for the upgrades in advance.

"Realizable" means that the seller can reasonably expect to get paid for the revenue earned. If there are serious doubts about the financial health of a customer, revenue shouldn't be recognized. Or if revenue is recognized, an adequate provision for bad debts should be included in the accounts.

The matching principle

This principle says that any costs incurred to generate revenues must be recognized in the same period as the revenues. Revenues must be "matched" with the costs that were incurred to generate them. Much of contemporary accounting practice is the direct result of applying this principle. So, too, are many of its controversies.

Notice that the word "cash" is missing from the above definition, because the expenditure of cash does not necessarily drive the recognition of expenses, just as the receipt of cash does not necessarily determine when revenue is recognized. To illustrate, imagine that employees are paid on the 10th of every month. If financial statements are prepared at the end of each month, the matching principle requires an estimate be made of any salaries and benefits earned by employees for the final three weeks. In short, expenses are recorded as incurred, regardless of when cash is paid.

The key characteristics of financial information

If the financial information produced by application of the above principles is to be of practical use to investors, it should possess certain characteristics, including:

Relevance

Information should be capable of making a difference in decisions. This implies that the information has at least some predictive value (i.e., it helps the reader to forecast the target company's future with more accuracy than if the information did not exist), and that it is released in a timely manner (i.e., quickly enough to help investors and other interested parties).

Reliability

Investors must be able to trust financial statements. This means that the statements should be "representationally faithful" (i.e., they capture economic reality), neutral (i.e., unbiased), and verifiable. The neutrality condition implies that while financial statement measurements may be incorrect, any errors that do arise are made in good faith and are not deliberately biased in one direction or the other. Verifiability implies that the information must be subject to audit by independent experts, such as a public accounting firm.

Consistency

To facilitate comparison of a company's performance over time, financial statement measurements must be consistent. This means that a company should employ the same measurement approaches from one year to the next. If there are changes in accounting methods, the effects of such changes must be discussed in detail in the notes to the financial statements. And if these changes are significant, a qualification of the auditor's opinion may be required. In addition, financial information should be comparable across firms, to enable comparison of performance between a company and its industry competitors.

The key assumptions of financial information

In addition to the above qualitative characteristics, there are several fundamental assumptions that underlie financial statements prepared under US GAAP and IFRS. For example, the entity assumption requires that the activities of a business be accounted for separately from those of its owners. This assumption is obvious enough for a corporation, because it operates as a legal person, separate and apart from its owners. But the entity assumption applies equally to nonincorporated businesses, such as partnerships, that may be considered inseparable from their owners from a legal or tax point of view.

There is also a "going concern" assumption, which states that the entity in question will remain in business for the foreseeable future. This doesn't mean that the business is expected to last forever, but there is no reason to believe that its immediate survivability is threatened. Much of contemporary financial reporting practice is based on this assumption. For example, when a long-term asset, such as land or a building, is reported on the balance sheet at its acquisition cost, the implication is that the company will be in business long enough to recover that cost in some way. In most cases, the cost will be recovered indirectly through the normal, day-to-day activities of the business in which materials and labor are converted into products, products into sales, and sales into cash. When this assumption is relaxed, as would be the case for a business on the verge of bankruptcy, the measurement rules for assets can change.

Modifying conventions

The financial reporting process is also governed by a set of "modifying conventions," or practical constraints. The two most important are "materiality" and "conservatism."

Materiality

This is the term accountants use to denote "significance." It means that relatively small amounts that are not likely to influence decisions should be recorded in whatever manner is most cost-efficient. For example, if a company were to buy office supplies the expenditure can be treated in either of two ways: as the acquisition of an asset or as an expense. If the former option is chosen, the cost of the supplies will be gradually transferred from an asset account on the balance sheet to an expense account on the income statement as the supplies are consumed. This is a lot of work for what may be a trivial sum of money. The materiality principle reminds us that because the amounts involved are small, the company should choose the approach that is most cost-efficient. This means that the expenditure would be charged immediately to the current year's income statement, even though (technically) an asset has been acquired.

It also means that accounts with insignificant balances (i.e., amounts that are not large enough to influence readers of the annual report) can be lumped together with other accounts. Typically, accounting systems include many more asset and liability accounts than we see in the balance sheet or income statement, but for the sake of convenience and readability these accounts are aggregated into broad summary accounts. Otherwise, the financial statements would be swamped by a mountain of useless detail.

Conservatism

This means that companies should exercise care not to overstate assets and revenues or to understate liabilities and expenses. This convention is applied to a wide range of measurement issues. For example, inventories are reported on the balance sheet at the lower of cost or net realizable value. In other words, inventories should be measured at acquisition cost, unless fair, or market, value is lower. But note that fair value is not used for balance sheet purposes if, as is usually the case, the inventory is worth more than acquisition cost. Applying the conservatism convention reduces the likelihood that an asset will be overvalued. The flip side, however, is that because fair value is ignored when greater than acquisition cost, conservatism increases the likelihood that an asset will be undervalued.

The future of financial reporting

In addition to the principles already discussed, other concepts of relatively recent vintage have emerged as part of an ongoing joint project of the IASB and the FASB. The project's aim is to establish a common standard that would improve how information is organized and presented in the financial statements. For this purpose, two principles have emerged, both of which have lurked in the background of standards setting for a long time, but only recently have been discussed in an explicit fashion: The *cohesiveness* principle and the *disaggregation* principle. Both are worth knowing because of the influence they are likely to exert on future changes to the presentation of financial information in corporate annual reports.

Cohesiveness

Cohesiveness refers to the use of consistent labeling and ordering of items *across* the financial statements. The aim is to enhance the usefulness and understandability of the financial statements, and to ensure that an entity's financial statements complement each other as much as possible. It reflects the idea that a company's traditional financial statements should be closely related, because they all contribute to the same goal of understanding its financial performance. For example, as we explore in a later chapter, the statement of cash flows is organized into three major sections – operations, investing, and financing. Because this statement is of more recent vintage than the balance sheet and income statement, these categories reflect contemporary thinking on how to categorize and order financial information. One practical consequence of the cohesiveness principle is that, in the not too distant future, the balance sheet and income statement could be reorganized into a format that more closely resembles that of the cash flow statement, providing a consistent and seamless view of an entity's performance.

Disaggregation

The financial statements already take highly aggregated items, such as total assets, and disaggregate them into smaller categories for display on the face of the statements. The idea behind the disaggregation principle is to extend this practice by providing a noticeably greater level of detail in the financial statements than before. The challenge is to ensure that the level of disaggregation for each component, such as property, plant, and equipment (PP&E), responds to user needs without distracting users from an overall view of performance. It's a delicate balancing act: greater detail vs. understandability, with appropriate consideration given to materiality and clarity. The goal is not disaggregation *per se*, but rather sufficient information to help the reader understand the company's financial performance. Also, we shouldn't forget the role of the notes, which allows further disaggregation of line items while maintaining the understandability and clarity of the financial statements. That's one reason why the application of this principle is controversial. To what extent should information traditionally relegated to the notes be brought into the financial statements proper? What this means to the financial statement reader is that, in future, some increased detail in the principal statements can be expected. The balance sheet, the income statement, and possibly the statement of cash flows, will almost certainly carry more account details than they do now. How much more is a matter of conjecture as of this writing.

Key lessons from the chapter

- The main purpose of corporate financial reporting from a broad economic perspective is to promote the efficient allocation of capital in the global capital markets.
- Historical (or acquisition) cost is the default valuation approach for nonfinancial assets.

- IFRS is more flexible in allowing fixed assets (PP&E) to be adjusted both upwards and downwards in value. US GAAP is more conservative and generally does not allow for an upward revaluation of fixed assets. However, most IFRS companies choose to rely on acquisition cost anyway.
- Before companies are permitted to recognize revenues from the sale of goods or services to customers, three criteria must be met. The revenues must be: measurable, earned, and realizable.
- The matching principle states that any cost incurred to generate revenues must be recognized in the same period as the revenues.
- The "going concern" assumption states that the entity in question will remain in business for the foreseeable future. This assumption has important implications for financial reporting practice.
- The materiality concept means that relatively small amounts that are not likely to influence decisions should be recorded in whatever manner is the most efficient.
- The conservatism principle (known as "prudence" in the UK) states that companies should exercise care not to overstate assets and revenues and not to understate liabilities or expenses.

Key terms and concepts from the chapter

Asset valuation	Reliability	Cohesiveness principle
Revenue recognition	Consistency	Disaggregation
The matching principle	Materiality	principle
Relevance	Conservatism	

Questions

1. Describe the basic criteria that must be met before revenue can be recognized under US GAAP or IFRS.

2. What is the "matching principle" and what role does it play in the financial reporting process?

3. True or false: The criteria describing the key characteristics of financial information (relevance, reliability, and consistency) are contradictory.

4. What is meant by the term "conservatism"? Doesn't it create biased financial reporting?

5. Describe the "materiality" concept and its influence on the financial statements.

6. What do the concepts of "cohesiveness" and "disaggregation" mean and what is their significance for the future of corporate financial reporting?

7. IFRS is often described as a "principles-based" system while US GAAP is described as "rules-based." What do these differences mean and what impact do they have on accounting and auditing practice?

8. Why did US GAAP evolve into a rules-based system?

CHAPTER 4

Revenue Recognition

Introduction

This chapter discusses revenue-recognition practices under US GAAP and IFRS. Revenue is one of the most important figures in a company's financial statements, and is often the largest. Not only is it the starting point for calculating profit, but sales forecasts are typically the first step in performing corporate valuations. But what exactly is "revenue" and how should companies measure and report it?

To begin, let's consider the operating cycle for a typical manufacturer. The cycle begins with the ordering of the raw materials, parts, and components needed to produce the company's products. These materials are then converted into finished products in the firm's manufacturing facilities. Meanwhile, orders are received from wholesalers, retailers, and other customers. The finished product is delivered and, usually a few weeks later, cash is collected from the customer.

So, when should revenue be recognized in this cycle? Perhaps when the order is received? Probably not, especially if the order is received before the product is produced. Common sense suggests that revenue should not be recognized from the sale of a product unless that product has already been manufactured.

Why not recognize revenue when the manufacturing process is complete? Again, too soon. Merely producing a product, without a willing buyer, is not sufficient to claim that revenue has been earned.

Perhaps we should go to the opposite end of the cycle and wait until the customer pays. This approach is more defensible because (1) the product has been made, (2) a willing buyer has already purchased the product, and (3) the buyer has paid for it. But this approach is too conservative. Also, it can be misleading in cases where the first two steps have occurred, and there is reasonable certainty that the third will too. Therefore, revenue is likely to be recognized after the product has been made and delivered to the customer (or is in the process of delivery), and receipt of cash can reasonably be expected. The point here is that all companies, regardless of their business model or how their operating cycle works, must have a revenue-recognition policy. This policy should state, explicitly, what steps must occur before revenue can appear in a given period's income statement.

In some businesses the revenue-recognition decision is fairly straightforward. But in many others, especially those with unique or unusual business models, the decision is not always so obvious. Even in relatively simple businesses, there may be enough latitude available to management to mislead investors on how much revenue has really been earned in a given year. One of the major tasks of the financial statement reader is to understand the chosen policy, to determine if that policy is reasonable given the underlying economics of the business, and if the reported revenue figures are supported by economic reality. For example, if a company reports 10% revenue growth in a stagnant industry, can this figure be defended?

Improper revenue recognition is often the cause of spectacular, high-profile financial reporting controversies. The Securities and Exchange Commission (SEC) reports that over half of all financial reporting frauds in the US involving publicly traded companies result from the deliberate overstatement of revenue. The practice has become so widespread that the chief accountant of the Commission's Enforcement Division felt compelled to say that improper revenue recognition is the "recipe of choice for cooking the books."[1]

Indeed, the problem is truly global. One of Japan's most prominent internet companies, Livedoor, was caught up in a major accounting scandal involving the inappropriate recognition of revenue. Lernout & Hauspie, a Belgian voice-recognition software company with a market capitalization of $9 billion at the peak of the dot-com boom, collapsed in 2001 when it was discovered that nearly all of its revenues resulted from fictitious transactions with Asian affiliates. The shares of India's Satyam Computer Services collapsed in January 2009 when it was discovered that most of the company's reported revenues were fictitious. Also, the notorious collapse of Parmalat, the Italian dairy company, was triggered in part by the discovery of fraudulent revenue-recognition practices.

Definition: what is revenue?

US GAAP and IFRS define revenue in a similar manner, although there are subtle differences in terminology. According to the former, revenue is the actual or expected cash inflow that has resulted, or will result, from a company's ongoing operations. IFRS defines revenue as the gross inflow of economic benefits during the period arising from the ordinary activities of an enterprise.

Both frameworks require measurement of revenues at fair value. In most cases, fair value is considered equal to the amount of cash or cash equivalents received or receivable. In cases where the inflow of cash is deferred, discounting to a present value is required under IFRS and, in limited situations, under US GAAP.

Revenue-recognition principles

IFRS describes specific revenue-recognition criteria for the sale of goods and services and for interest, royalties, and dividends. The criteria common to every form of revenue recognition include: the probability that the economic benefits associated with the transaction will flow to the company, and that the revenues and costs can be measured reliably. Also, in the case of goods, there should be evidence that the company has transferred to the buyer the significant risks and rewards of ownership and that the seller retains neither continuing managerial involvement nor effective control over the goods.

For example, Nokia, the Finnish telecommunications giant, reports the following from its 2009 Annual Report:

> Sales from the majority of the Group are recognized when the significant risks and rewards of ownership have transferred to the buyer, continuing managerial involvement usually associated with ownership and effective control have ceased, the amount of revenue can be measured reliably, it is probable that economic benefits associated with the transaction will flow to the Group and the costs incurred or to be incurred in respect of the transaction can be measured reliably.
>
> *Source*: Nokia 2009 Annual Report.

In contrast to IFRS, US GAAP focuses on whether or not revenues are *realized* (converted into cash or the likelihood of receipt being reasonably certain) and *earned* (the goods have been sold, or the service has been delivered, and no further action on the part of the seller is required). Both criteria must be met before revenue can be recognized.

Consider this disclosure from Microsoft, Inc. in its 2010 annual report:

> Revenue for retail packaged products, products licensed to original equipment manufacturers ("OEMs"), and perpetual licenses under certain volume licensing programs generally is recognized as products are shipped or made available. A portion of the revenue related to Windows XP is deferred due to the right to receive unspecified upgrades/enhancements of Microsoft Internet Explorer on a when-and-if-available basis. The amount of revenue allocated to the unspecified upgrade/enhancement rights for Microsoft Internet Explorer is based on the vendor-specific objective evidence of fair value for those elements using the residual method or relative fair value method and the deferred revenue is recognized ratably on a straight-line basis over the Windows XP life cycle. Revenue related to Windows Vista and Windows 7 is not subject to a similar deferral because there are no significant undelivered elements.
>
> *Source*: Microsoft 2010 Annual Report.

What Microsoft is saying is that not all of the cash received from the customer is recorded as revenue if the customer is paying for services, such as upgrades, that have yet to be delivered. For example, if the customer pays $1000 for a cluster of products and services, and Microsoft determines that $150 of the payment relates to future services, the company reports $850 as revenue. The remainder is treated as a liability (called "deferred revenue," "deferred income," or "unearned revenue").

When does revenue recognition occur?

In light of the above criteria, where revenue recognition actually occurs in a company's operating cycle depends entirely on its business model and on the ways in which it delivers products and services to customers. Broadly speaking, revenue recognition can occur:

- at point of sale
- at completion of production
- after the sale
- during production.

Point of sale is the dominant revenue-recognition practice in most industries, especially in the retail and manufacturing sectors. For example, a supermarket recognizes revenue as customers pass through checkout counters.

Revenue recognition can occur earlier in the operating cycle, for example, at the *completion of production*, but only if the product is immediately saleable at quoted market prices, the units are homogeneous, and no significant uncertainty exists regarding the costs of distributing the product. The most common examples are found in natural resources, such as oil and mining. Agricultural products sometimes qualify for this treatment too.

In some industries revenue is not recognized until *after the sale*, especially when there is extreme uncertainty regarding the amount of cash to be collected from customers. For example, customers may be in a precarious financial condition. Or contingencies in the sales agreement allow either party to terminate the exchange. Even more common is when the customer has the right to return the product within a given period and this right is frequently exercised. Examples include real estate development, where collection of the sales price occurs in protracted installments, and customers might choose to default on future payments if the real-estate market collapses. Another example is found in the sale of franchises in new or unproven products. In such cases, because the receipt of cash is highly uncertain, revenue is recognized only when cash is received, even if the actual sale occurs earlier.

Recognizing revenue *during production* is common in the construction industry, but can be found in other industries where products are produced or services delivered over extended periods. We treat this topic in more detail later in this chapter.

Revenue recognition: the journal entries

Regardless of when revenue is recognized, only three types of journal entries are possible:

1. Revenues have been earned and the customer has paid.

Cash	XX	
Revenue		XX

2. Revenues have been earned but the customer has not yet paid.

Accounts receivable	XX	
Revenue		XX

This entry assumes that the seller has reason to believe that the revenue is "realizable," meaning that cash collection is reasonably assured. Later, when cash is received, the following entry is made:

Cash	XX	
Accounts receivable		XX

3. Cash has been collected from the customer, but the product or service has not yet been provided.

Cash	XX	
Deferred revenue		XX

Deferred revenue is classified as a current liability. Later, when the company delivers the service or product to the customer, the following entry is made:

Deferred revenue	XX	
Revenue		XX

More on long-term contracts

Accounting for revenue during production is not only common in the construction industry, but in any sector characterized by long-term contracts. Shipbuilding is another prominent example. The operating process for a long-term contractor differs from that of a manufacturing firm in three important ways:

- The production period may span several accounting periods (even years).
- The firm identifies a customer and agrees on a contract price in advance.
- The buyer often makes periodic payments on the total contract price as work progresses.

Both US GAAP and IFRS require the use of the "percentage-of-completion method" for such contracts, if practicable. This method recognizes a portion of the contract price as revenue during each accounting period of construction. For example, if 40% of the total work was accomplished in a given year, 40% of the contract price is recognized as revenue. The proportion of total work carried out in any period is usually based on either engineers' estimates of the degree of completion (an output-based approach) or from the ratio of costs incurred to date to the total costs expected for the entire contract (an input-based approach).

The actual schedule of cash collections does not affect the revenue-recognition process under this method. In fact, percentage-of-completion can be used even in cases where the

Table 4.1 Revenues and expenses under the percentage-of-completion method

Year	% of completion	Revenue	Expense	Profit
1	$4m/$8m = 50%	$5.0m	$4m	$1.0m
2	$2m/$8m = 25%	2.5m	2m	0.5m
3	$2m/$8m = 25%	2.5m	2m	0.5m
		$10m	$8m	$2m

entire payment comes at the end of the contract, as long as the firm is able to reasonably estimate total revenues and total expenses over the life of the contract, the amount of work completed in any given period, and the collection of cash is reasonably assured.

To illustrate, assume that a firm has signed a three-year contract to construct a building. Total expected revenues are $10 million, and total expected costs are $8 million (with $4 million in the first year, and $2 million in each of the final two years). Revenue and expense recognition would look like this (assuming the work proceeds as expected) – see Table 4.1.

Suppose progress payments are made by the client as follows: $4.5 million at the end of the first year, $2.5 million at the end of the second year, and the remaining $3.0 million upon the project's completion. The contractor would make the following journal entries to record the progress payments:

Year 1

Cash	4.5	
Accounts receivable	0.5	
Revenue		5.0
Expenses	4.0	
Cash		4.0

Note that the difference between revenue and expenses is the amount of profit, or net income, for the year.

Year 2

Cash	2.5	
Revenue		2.5
Expenses	2.0	
Cash		2.0

Year 3

Cash	3.0	
Accounts rec.		0.5
Revenue		2.5
Expenses	2.0	
Cash		2.0

Note that the receipt of cash has no influence on the recognition of either revenues or expenses. It should also be noted that the above example was based on an input approach: the proportion of expenses incurred in a given year as a percentage of the total determined the percentage of work done. Alternatively, the firm could have chosen an output-based measure in which independent engineers certify a particular percentage of the total work as being completed. For example, if the engineers had certified that 55% of the total work was completed in the first year, the contractor could have recognized more revenue.

One factor to consider is the effect of cost overruns. For example, materials costs prove to be higher than budgeted, or inefficiencies result in higher labor costs. The important point here is to isolate the overruns and ensure that they have no influence on estimates of the percentage of work completed. If cost increases do not result from the performance of additional work, but rather from costs exceeding budgets, the increases should not result in the recognition of additional revenue. Many companies have found themselves in deep trouble because project managers obscured overruns, and maybe even theft, by citing higher percentages of completion, and therefore higher revenue. When the day of reckoning comes, and it must, the consequences can be devastating.

Another factor to note is what to do in the case of an *onerous contract*. This term refers to a contract in which losses are inevitable for the reporting entity. In such cases, the losses must be recognized immediately, even if the contract is far from being completed and the magnitude of the losses is not known with certainty. This treatment results from the conservatism principle.

Occasionally, there are instances in which it is not possible to determine with reasonable accuracy the percentage of work completed on a given project. For example, the reporting entity might not be able to estimate total costs at the beginning of the contract. In such cases, the percentage-of-completion method cannot be used. US GAAP and IFRS take different approaches to this issue, although this divergence is likely to be resolved within the next few years.

US GAAP requires the **completed contract method**. (As we discuss below, IFRS uses another method.) Under this approach, no revenues or expenses are recognized until the entire project is completed and ready to be turned over to the customer. Returning to the example above, the following entries would be made:

Year 1

Cash	4.5	
Deferred revenue		4.5

Remember that deferred revenue is a liability account. None of the cash received is recognized as revenue until the project is complete.

Construction in progress	4.0	
Cash		4.0

The expenses incurred *during* the project are accumulated in an asset account, construction in progress.

Year 2

Cash	2.5	
Deferred revenue		2.5
Construction in progress	2.0	
Cash		2.0

Year 3

Deferred revenue	7.0	
Cash	3.0	
Revenue		10.0
Expenses	8.0	
Cash		2.0
Construction in progress		6.0

The first entry acknowledges the final cash payment, the reversal of the deferred revenue account, and the recognition of the project's total revenues. The second entry acknowledges the cash paid in the final year to complete the project, reverses the construction in progress account, and recognizes the project's total expenses.

If percentage-of-completion is not practical, IFRS requires the cost recovery method. Consider this disclosure from Nokia:

> Revenue from contracts involving solutions achieved through modification of complex telecommunications equipment is recognized on the percentage of completion basis when the outcome of the contract can be estimated reliably. Recognized revenues and profits are subject to revisions during the project in the event that the assumptions regarding the overall project outcome are revised. Current sales and profit estimates for projects may materially change due to the early stage of a long-term project, new technology, changes in the project scope, changes in costs, changes in timing, changes in customers' plans, realization of penalties, and other corresponding factors.
>
> *Source:* Nokia 2009 Annual Report.

Nokia is informing us here that they normally use percentage-of-completion, but when the conditions required for its use are not met, a variant of the cost-recovery method is used instead.

The cost-recovery method works as follows: in each year, revenues are set equal to expenses, until all of the project's expected costs have been covered.

- In the first year, revenues and expenses are $4.0 million, meaning that no profit is recognized.
- In the second year, $2.0 million of revenues and expenses are recognized. Note that by the end of year 2, $6 million of expenses have been recognized, while the total expenses are expected to be $8 million. Therefore, profit still cannot be recognized.
- Only when all of the costs have been recovered can profit be acknowledged. All of the profit from the project ($2 million) is recognized in the final year (revenues equal $4 million, and expenses equal $2 million).

Revenue-recognition controversies

In this section, we address some of the more common issues and controversies that arise in revenue recognition.

Warranty and product maintenance contracts

Often companies sell extended warranties and product-maintenance contracts with their products. Under IFRS guidelines, the price received for an extended warranty is recognized gradually over the warranty period. Maintenance contracts are handled in a similar fashion. The treatment under US GAAP is similar: revenue is recognized on a straight-line basis over the contract period, unless the pattern of costs indicates otherwise. Also, consistent with IFRS, a loss must be recognized immediately if the expected cost of providing services during the warranty or maintenance period exceeds unearned revenue. The primary concern for the analyst is the temptation for reporting entities to report revenue from services covered by the contracts *before* the services are actually delivered.

Barter transactions

A barter arrangement exists when two companies enter into a noncash transaction to exchange goods or services. This issue became highly controversial during the dot-com boom of the late 1990s, as companies would exchange banner headlines and other forms of advertising on each others' websites and then report exaggerated amounts of revenue. Revenue recognition for barter transactions is allowed under IFRS and US GAAP, but only if strict criteria are met.

Under IFRS, revenue may be recognized on the exchange of dissimilar goods and services if the amount of revenue can be measured reliably. Note that the goods or services involved must be dissimilar, otherwise no revenue can be recognized. For example, an owner of several private cable and satellite television stations trading commercial air time for programming was deemed acceptable. But the exchange of inventory in different locations by petrol retailers was considered an exchange of similar goods and thus no revenue could be reported.

If a barter arrangement qualifies for recognition, the transaction must be measured at the fair value of goods or services received. In cases where the fair value of goods or services received cannot be measured reliably, the fair value of the goods and services given up is used. The fair value of advertising received or provided in a barter transaction is generally measured by reference to equivalent nonbarter transactions.

Under US GAAP, revenue and expense must be recognized at the fair value of the good or service given up. For example, in the case of advertising, fair value is based on the company's own historical practice of receiving cash for similar advertising services from unrelated entities. Also, similar transactions used as a guide to fair value must not be older than six months prior to the date of the barter transaction. If the fair value of the advertising given cannot be determined using these criteria, the carrying amount of the advertising surrendered, which is likely to be zero, must be used.

Multiple-element arrangements

Multiple-element contractual arrangements have become increasingly common in recent years, especially in software and other technology-driven industries. In such cases, multiple products or services are delivered under the same contract, over an extended period. Microsoft and its major industry competitors rely extensively on them.

US GAAP requires that arrangements with multiple deliverables should be divided into separate units of accounting. The arrangement's consideration should be allocated among the separate units of accounting based on their relative fair values. As goods or services are delivered to the customer, the fair value of each item is recognized as revenue.

In contrast, IFRS does not provide detailed guidance for multiple-element revenue arrangements. The recognition criteria are usually applied separately to each transaction in a manner similar to US GAAP.

Like product-maintenance contracts, the risk to the financial statement reader is that the reporting entity might abuse the uncertainties that sometimes arise under such arrangements by recognizing revenue before it has truly been earned.

As we discuss later in this chapter, the accounting for multiple-element contracts will undergo major changes in the near future, as the result of a joint FASB/IASB project on revenue recognition. In the meantime, the above-mentioned practices are expected to prevail.

Channel stuffing

Sometimes sellers use their power over customers to induce them to purchase more goods than is necessary to satisfy demand, thus allowing the sellers to report higher sales and profits. For example, automobile manufacturers have often been charged by dealers with pushing products through the distribution chain before the dealers really want them. The temptation for the automobile company to pursue such a strategy can be difficult to overcome when sales or profit figures for the year fall just short of targets. BristolMyers Squibb, a large pharmaceuticals company, was charged with boosting sales in 2000 and 2001 by offering discounts to wholesalers to purchase more drugs than patients needed. However, in early 2002, wholesalers stopped building up inventories, and the game was up. The company was forced to restate results, wiping out $2 billion of previously recognized revenue.

Although this practice is discouraged, US GAAP and IFRS are somewhat ambiguous on how to treat it. Generally, the seller can get away with it as long as there is no agreement for product returns. But even if the company gets away with it, and most do, channel stuffing catches up with them eventually because it effectively moves sales forward from future periods. At some point in the future, sales will take a hit because sales that should have been recognized in the current period had already been recognized in previous periods.

Gross vs. net

Some companies use their distribution systems or auction platforms to act as "go-betweens," or agents, for buyers and sellers. In effect, other companies' goods are sold at a slight markup. The reporting entity can easily inflate revenues by choosing to report the transactions on a gross basis, instead of reporting only the markup or commission. This practice became especially popular during the dot-com boom, as start-ups searched for ways to report the highest revenue numbers possible. One motive for such behavior was the belief that share prices are driven by revenue growth and not profitability. The dot-com meltdown in 2000 disproved this notion, but the temptation has not disappeared.

Although there is some ambiguity under IFRS regarding gross vs. net revenue treatment, the US Securities and Exchange Commission imposed regulations that have eliminated the most egregious abuses for companies reporting under US GAAP.

Round trips

This practice is similar to barter except that one company sells a product for cash to another company, which in turn sells an equivalent product back to the initial seller for a similar price. Each recognizes revenue on the sale. Although round trips are not allowed under US GAAP or IFRS, companies may try to disguise them by running transactions through a third party.

One variant is to sell inventory to third parties in one period, agreeing to buy it back in the next. Delphi, the troubled auto-parts company carved out of General Motors, was accused of this practice. Symbol Technologies, a maker of barcode readers and mobile computing equipment, was charged with pushing unwanted products on distributors, promising to buy them back at a 1% premium. The transactions were really loans, disguised as sales.

Deferred payments

In some industries, payments for goods sold are made over an extended period (sometimes lasting several years). Revenue can be recognized on a discounted cash-flow basis at the point of sale, but are collections reasonably assured and what discount rates are being used? For example, Xerox's Mexican subsidiary was found to use artificially low discount rates to boost present values, and thus the amount of revenue recognized from equipment leasing. The company was later forced to restate results.

Bill and hold

Here, the seller invoices the buyer but does not ship the product. In effect, it's a special case of channel stuffing. According to IFRS, revenue can be recognized under such circumstances, but only if certain criteria are met:

- delivery is delayed at the buyer's request;
- delivery is probable, and
- the item is available, ready for delivery, and cannot be used to satisfy other orders.

In extreme (i.e., criminal) cases, companies have been found to create false bill-and-hold letters from customers to justify premature revenue recognition.

Holding the books open

The idea here is to capture sales in one period that actually occur in the next. One variant of this practice: a company deliberately ships the wrong products at the end of the quarter or year when the products requested by the customer are not yet available. After booking the revenue, the company cancels the order in the next period, and ships the correct products. This practice is strictly forbidden under US GAAP and IFRS.

Revenue recognition: a checklist

What follows are the most important questions for analysts and other financial statement readers to consider when interpreting sales numbers and revenue-recognition practices:

- Are the revenue-recognition policies clearly described in the notes, or at least somewhere in the annual report?
- How is revenue defined? And what event triggers its recognition?
- Are the company's revenue-recognition policies consistent with those of its domestic and global competitors?
- Where revenue substantially exceeds cash received, are there clear business reasons that explain the divergence?
- Does the customer have a right of return? (Remember that risks and rewards of ownership must be transferred to the buyer before revenue can be recognized.) If revenue is recognized, has the right of return been properly provisioned? What percentage of goods tends to be returned, and has this percentage changed over time?
- Are the changes in revenue from quarter to quarter and year to year consistent with expectations and the industry environment? Is revenue growing at a time when the industry is stagnating or even declining?

The future of revenue recognition

In November 2011 the IASB and the FASB issued a joint exposure draft (ED) on revenue recognition. As of this writing, the ED has not yet been formally approved. However, the resulting standard is expected to become mandatory by 2015, or perhaps by the following year. The provisions of the ED will likely have a profound effect on how revenue-recognition practice unfolds over the coming years.

The motivation for the new standard was the widespread belief among standards setters and other interested parties that both US GAAP and IFRS have been seriously deficient in dealing with revenue-recognition issues. The rules-based nature of US GAAP has resulted in an overwhelming array of industry- and transaction-specific judgments that are often contradictory. For example, the treatment of hook-up fees in the cable television industry differs from that of the telecommunications business, despite the transactions being economically equivalent. US GAAP is full of such inconsistencies. The problem with IFRS is just the opposite – too little guidance and too much ambiguity.

One weakness shared by both regimes is their seeming inability to cope with changing business models, especially those that have emerged since the advent of the internet era. Examples include mobile phone contracts that come with a free phone, or sophisticated software products sold with training and future upgrades. The approach taken thus far, especially by the FASB and the US Securities and Exchange Commission, has been largely *ad hoc*, attacking revenue-recognition challenges as they emerge. This approach helps to explain some of the inconsistencies that currently exist under US GAAP and the confusion that often prevails in IFRS companies. The aim of the new standard is to develop a more robust framework for addressing not only current revenue-recognition issues, but those that may arise in future from business models we can't even conceive of today. The new standard will also remove inconsistencies from existing requirements, enhance disclosure, and improve comparability across companies, industries, and capital markets.

The core principle of the new standard can be expressed as follows: *a business should recognize revenue from contracts with customers when it transfers promised goods or services to the customers.*[2] On the surface, this statement does not appear to be a radical departure from current practice, but the emphasis on the word "transfer" will likely have significant consequences. In short, unless a good or service has been transferred to the customer (for example, a product has been shipped and is now the legal property of the customer), revenue cannot be recognized. Effects are likely to be felt in construction and real estate, and perhaps in other sectors as well.

Another important change is the emphasis on identifying all of the "separate performance obligations" in the contract between seller and buyer. To illustrate, consider the accounting for customer loyalty programs. Suppose a company has a loyalty program that rewards a customer with 1 point for every $10 of purchases.[3] Each point is redeemable for a $1 discount on any future purchases. During the year, customers purchase products for $100 000 and earn 10 000 points. The company expects 9500 points to be redeemed on the basis of past experience. The current approach would be to recognize $100 000 in revenue, and a provision (liability) for $9500. But under the proposed standard, the transactions would have to be treated as two distinct revenue streams.

The company would estimate a stand-alone selling price of $0.95 per point ($9500 in total) on the basis of the likelihood of redemption. It will then allocate the total revenue ($100 000) to the products sold and to the loyalty points on a relative stand-alone selling price basis. For the products, revenue recognized would equal [($100 000 × $100 000) ÷ $109 500], or $91 324. For the customer loyalty points, revenue would equal [$100 000 × $9500) ÷ $109 500], or $8676. The revenue from the loyalty points would be recognized gradually as customers redeem the points.

The above example is just one of many areas that are likely to be affected by the proposed standard.

Key lessons from the chapter

- Broadly speaking, revenue recognition can occur at point of sale, at completion of production, after a sale, or during production.
- Revenue recognition may seem like a straightforward exercise, but it is not always obvious when revenue should be recognized and in what amount. This concern is especially troublesome in accounting for long-term contracts.
- Percentage-of-completion is the preferred method for long-term contracts, such as those in the construction industry. The method's appeal lies in the fact that it's the only approach that has the possibility of conforming with the matching principle. However, substantial judgment is required to implement it. And where there is judgment, there is always the possibility of error and manipulation.
- Revenue recognition is probably the single greatest source of financial statement manipulation. The number of games that companies play is practically endless, but perhaps the most common is channel stuffing.
- A new revenue recognition is likely to take effect in 2015, or perhaps later. Its aim is to achieve consistency in revenue-recognition practices across companies, industries, and capital markets. Because it will eliminate current inconsistencies, the standard is expected to have a significant effect in revenue-recognition practices in a broad range of companies.

Key terms and concepts from the chapter

Revenue recognition	Cost-recovery method	Gross vs. net
Realized/realizable	Unearned revenue	Round trips
Percentage-of-completion	Barter transactions	Bill and hold
Completed contract method	Multiple-element arrangements	
	Channel stuffing	

Questions

1. Describe the criteria that must be met before revenue can be recognized.

2. Why do US GAAP and IFRS require, if practicable, the use of the percentage-of-completion method for long-term contracts?

3. Under what conditions might percentage-of-completion not be usable?

4. What should a company do if percentage-of-completion cannot be used?

5. Describe the differences between an "input-based" approach and an "output-based" approach to determining the percentage of work completed on a long-term construction project.

6. What is the major drawback of the percentage-of-completion method?

7. What is channel stuffing and how does it impact revenue recognition?

8. Describe the "gross vs. net" controversy. Why might a company prefer to recognize revenues on a gross basis?

Problems

4.1   Revenue recognition at and after time of sale

Suite Novotel is an all-suites hotel chain owned and operated by the Accor Group. Most of the hotels in this chain are found in France, Spain, and Germany.

On the company website, customers are offered a nonrefundable special rate at €160 per night, or a refundable rate at €225 per night. In either case, the entire amount is charged to the customer's account at the time of booking. For the refundable room, if the reservation is cancelled prior to 16.00 on the date of arrival, a full refund of the amount charged is made. If the cancellation occurs after 16.00 the customer forfeits one day at the reserved rate (€225).

Required

Determine the appropriate journal entries for each of the following transactions:

(a) On 6 March a customer makes a nonrefundable reservation for three nights beginning 24 March. The customer arrives as scheduled and checks out on 27 March.
(b) On 6 March a customer makes a reservation identical to the one in part (a). On 21 March, the customer cancels the reservation.
(c) On 6 March a customer makes a refundable reservation for three nights beginning 24 March. The customer arrives as scheduled and checks out on 27 March.

(d) On 6 March, a customer makes a reservation identical to the one in part (c). On 21 March the customer cancels the reservation.

(e) On 6 March, a customer makes a reservation identical to the one in part (c). On 24 March, at 19.30, the customer cancels the reservation.

4.2 The percentage-of-completion method

On 1 April 2011, Roller Construction entered into a fixed-price contract to construct an office building for €18 million. Roller uses the percentage-of-completion method. Information related to the contract appears below.

	December 31, 2011	December 31, 2012
Percentage completed	20%	60%
Estimated total cost	€ 13,500,000	€ 14,400,000
Profit recognized to date	€ 900,000	€ 2,160,000

Required

(a) Calculate the revenues and expenses recognized for both 2011 and 2012.

(b) What impact did the €900 000 increase in estimated total cost in 2012 have on revenue recognition in that year?

4.3 Journal entries for gift cards

Subway is a global food retailer with stores located throughout the world. Suppose a customer at one of its Paris stores purchases a sandwich for €5.00, a brownie for €2.00 and a soft drink for €1.50. The customer pays with cash.

Required

(a) What journal entry will Subway record for this transaction? (Ignore expenses.)

(b) Suppose that in addition to the above items, the customer buys a Subway gift card for €50.00. What journal entry would Subway record for this transaction?

(c) Now suppose that the customer buys the same items listed above, but uses a previously purchased gift card to pay for the purchases. Also assume that there is a sufficient balance on the card to cover the entire cost. What journal entry would Subway make now to record the transaction?

4.4   The percentage-of-completion method

On 1 September 2009, Tan Construction Company contracted to build a shopping complex on the east coast of Singapore. The total contract price was $90 million. As required by Singapore's Financial Reporting Standards (which are based on IFRS), Tan Construction uses the percentage-of-completion method in accounting for long-term contracts. The Company uses an input-based (i.e., cost-based) approach to determine the percentage of completion.

The schedule of expected and actual cash collections and contract costs is follows:

Year	Cash collections from customer	Estimated and actual cost incurred
2009	$18.0 million	$6.0 million
2010	22.5 million	18.0 million
2011	22.5 million	24.0 million
2012	27.0 million	12.0 million
	$90.0 million	$60.0 million

Required

(a) Calculate the amount of revenue, expense, and net income for each of the four years.
(b) Show the journal entries that Tan Construction will make in 2009, 2010, 2011, and 2012 for this contract. Tan accumulates contract costs in a Construction in Progress account. The costs involve a mix of cash payments, credits to various other asset accounts, and credits to liability accounts. But for the sake of simplicity, assume that all costs are credited to Accounts Payable.

4.5   Revenue recognition in different types of businesses

Determine when each of the following types of businesses is likely to recognize revenue:

(a) A bank lending money for home mortgages.
(b) A firm that grows and harvests oranges.
(c) A hair salon.
(d) A professional football team that sells season tickets before the season begins.
(e) A dress shop.
(f) A cattle rancher.
(g) An airline. Customers can accumulate frequent flyer miles, which earn them a free flight if enough miles are accumulated.
(h) A producer of port wine that is aged from 10 to 15 years.
(i) A real estate developer selling lots on long-term contracts with down payments equal to 10% of the selling price.
(j) A real estate developer who constructs houses and then sells them near or at completion.
(k) A printer who prints custom-order announcements (for weddings, etc.) and brochures.
(l) A military contractor constructing fighter aircraft.

Case studies

4.1   Kiwi Builders, Ltd.

In May 2001, Kiwi Builders, Ltd. was employed by the government of Hamilton, New Zealand, to erect a municipal office building on the outskirts of the city. The contract called for work to begin a few weeks later. Kiwi took on the role of general contractor. Most of the work would be done by subcontractors.

Under the terms of the contract, Kiwi Builders was to receive $24 million in cash payments to be paid as follows: 25% when the work was 30% complete, another 25% when the work was 60% complete, and the remaining 50% when the work was fully completed. The contract stipulated that completion percentage estimates had to be certified by an independent engineering consultant before progress payments would be made.

In preparing its bid, the company estimated that the total cost to complete the project would be $21.6 million, assuming no cost overruns. Hence, the company expected a profit of $2.4 million.

During the first year of the contract, the company incurred costs of $6.48 million. In late June 2002, the engineering consulting firm of C. McMillan & Associates determined that the project was at least 30% complete, and on 30 June the first progress payment was made.

In the following year, the company incurred additional costs of $7.02 million. In late June 2003 the engineers certified that at least 60% of the project had been completed, and the second progress payment was made at the end of the month.

In their report, the engineers noted that the company might be facing significant cost overruns. The directors of Kiwi Builders responded by saying that anticipated efficiency improvements in the final phases of construction would offset any prior cost overruns. Subsequent results suggest that some, but not all, of the cost overruns were recovered.

By the end of May 2004, Kiwi's work was done. Actual costs incurred during the fiscal year ending 30 June 2004 were $8.4 million. The firm received certification for the fully completed building, and the final cash payment was made.

Required

(a) Ignoring any other sources of revenues and expenses, determine the level of profits to be reported by Kiwi Builders, Ltd. for the years ended 30 June 2002, 2003, and 2004, using the following revenue recognition methods:

    (1) Percentage-of-completion. (Note that Kiwi uses an output-based approach.)
    (2) Completed contract.

(3) Cost recovery.

(4) Cash basis.

(b) Kiwi experienced cost overruns in the second year of the project. In hindsight, the overruns proved modest. But assume that the magnitude of the problem was severe enough so that by the end of fiscal year 2003 it was apparent that Kiwi would suffer a loss on the project of approximately $700 000. What impact would such information have had on the accounting for the project under the percentage-of-completion method?

(c) Which set of results from part (a) best reflects the economic performance of Kiwi during the three-year period, and what is the basis for your assessment?

4.2   Revenue recognition at Starbucks Corporation*

Introduction

On 2 February 2005, Starbucks Corporation's stock price plummeted 8.2% after the company released its latest revenue numbers (see Exhibit 4.1 for the company's stock graph). In a press statement, the specialty coffee company said sales rose 23% to $452 million from $368 million[4] for the four-week period ended 30 January 2005. Moreover, consolidated net revenues for the quarter were $2 billion, a 24% increase from $1.6 billion a year earlier.[5] Same-store sales, however, rose a disappointing 7%.[6] Starbucks' financial statements are shown in Exhibits 4.2–4.4.

Background

In 1971, Starbucks Coffee, Tea and Spice opened its first location in Seattle's Pike Place Market. In 1982, Howard Schultz joined the company as director of retail operations and marketing. Inspired by the popularity of espresso bars in Italy, he developed and launched a plan to bring the coffeehouse concept to the United States. In 1987, Schultz and other investors acquired the company's assets and renamed it Starbucks Corporation. The company went public in 1992 on the NASDAQ listed under the ticker symbol SBUX.

Starbucks' business consisted of purchasing, roasting, and selling high-quality whole bean coffees and coffee drinks, primarily through company-operated retail stores. The

---

*This case was adapted by S. David Young, Professor of Accounting and Control, INSEAD, from a case written by Jacob Cohen, Affiliate Professor of Accounting & Control and Business Law and Chad Myers, Research Associate. This case is intended to be used as a basis for class discussion rather than to illustrate either effective or ineffective handling of an administrative situation.

Exhibit 4.1 Starbuck stock graph performance compared to the NASDAQ

Stock performance for the week ending February 4, 2005

Stock performance for the year ending February 4, 2005

Source: www.BigChart.com, a service of Market Watch.

Exhibit 4.2 Starbucks Corp. balance sheet

Diluted (In millions US$)	2004	2003
ASSETS		
Current assets:		
Cash and cash equivalents	$299.13	$200.91
Short-term investments – available-for-sale securities	329.08	128.91
Short-term investments – trading securities	24.80	20.20
Accounts receivable, net of allowances of $2.2 and $4.8, respectively	140.23	114.45
Inventories	422.66	342.94
Prepaid expenses and other current assets	71.35	55.17
Deferred income taxes, net	81.24	61.45
Total current assets	1,368.49	924.03
Long-term investments – available-for-sale securities	135.18	136.16
Equity and other investments	171.75	144.26
Property, plant and equipment, net	1,471.45	1,384.90
Other assets	85.56	52.11
Other intangible assets	26.80	24.94
Goodwill	68.95	63.34
TOTAL ASSETS	$3,328.17	$2,729.75
LIABILITIES AND SHAREHOLDERS' EQUITY		
Current liabilities:		
Accounts payable	$199.35	$168.98
Accrued compensation and related costs	208.93	152.61
Accrued occupancy costs	65.87	56.18
Accrued taxes	63.04	54.93
Other accrued expenses	123.68	101.80
Deferred revenue	121.38	73.48
Current portion of long-term debt	0.74	0.72
Total current liabilities	782.98	608.70
Deferred income taxes, net	46.68	33.22
Long-term debt	3.62	4.35
Other long-term liabilities	8.13	1.05
Shareholders' equity:		
Common stock and additional paid-in capital	956.69	959.10
Other additional paid-in-capital	39.39	39.39
Retained earnings	1,461.46	1,069.68
Accumulated other comprehensive income	29.22	14.25

Source: Starbucks Corp. 10-K filing with Securities and Exchange Commission for fiscal year ended 3 October 2004.

Exhibit 4.3 Starbucks Corp. income statement

(In millions US$)	2004	2003	2002
Net revenues:			
Company-operated retail	$4,457.38	$3,449.62	$2,792.90
Specialty:			
Licensing	565.80	409.55	311.93
Foodservice and other	271.07	216.35	184.07
Total specialty	836.87	625.90	496.00
Total net revenues	5,294.25	4,075.52	3,288.91
Cost of sales including occupancy costs	2,198.65	1,685.93	1,350.01
Store operating expenses	1,790.17	1,379.57	1,109.78
Other operating expenses	171.65	141.35	106.08
Depreciation and amortization expenses	280.02	237.81	205.56
General and administrative expenses	304.29	244.55	234.58
Subtotal operating expenses	4,744.79	3,689.21	3,006.02
Income from equity investees	60.66	38.40	33.45
Operating income	610.12	424.71	316.34
Interest and other income, net	14.14	11.62	9.30
Gain on sale of investment	-	-	13.36
Earnings before income taxes	624.26	436.34	339.00
Income taxes	232.48	167.99	126.31
Net earnings	$391.78	$268.35	$212.69
Weighted average shares outstanding:			
Basic	397.17	390.75	385.58
Diluted	411.47	401.65	397.53

Source: Starbucks Corp. 10-K filing with Securities and Exchange Commission for fiscal year ended 3 October 2004.

Exhibit 4.4 Starbucks Corp. statement of cash flows

(In millions US$)	2004	2003	2002
OPERATING ACTIVITIES			
Net earnings	$391.78	$268.35	$212.69
Adjustments to reconcile net earnings to net cash provided by operating activities:	0.00	0.00	0.00
Depreciation and amortization	304.82	259.27	221.14
Gain on sale of investment	-	-	(13.36)
Provision for impairments and asset disposals	13.57	7.78	26.85
Deferred income taxes, net	(3.07)	(5.93)	(6.09)

(*Continued*)

Exhibit 4.4 Continued

(In millions US$)	2004	2003	2002
Equity in income of investees	(33.39)	(22.81)	(19.58)
Tax benefit from exercise of nonqualified stock options	63.41	36.59	44.20
Net accretion of discount and amortization of premium on marketable	11.60	6.00	-
Securities			
Cash provided/(used) by changes in operating assets and liabilities:			
Inventories	(77.66)	(64.77)	(41.38)
Prepaid expenses and other current assets	(16.62)	(12.86)	(12.46)
Accounts payable	27.95	24.99	5.46
Accrued compensation and related costs	54.93	42.13	24.09
Accrued occupancy costs	8.90	4.29	15.34
Deferred revenue	47.59	30.73	15.32
Other accrued expenses	16.47	9.47	31.90
Other operating assets and liabilities	(16.41)	(16.78)	(26.44)
Net cash provided by operating activities	$793.85	$566.45	$477.69
INVESTING ACTIVITIES			
Purchase of available-for-sale securities	(566.65)	(323.33)	(339.97)
Maturity of available-for-sale securities	163.81	180.69	78.35
Sale of available-for-sale securities	190.75	88.89	144.76
Acquisitions, net of cash acquired	(7.52)	(69.93)	-
Net additions to equity, other investments and other assets	(64.75)	(47.26)	(15.84)
Distributions from equity investees	38.33	28.97	22.83
Net additions to property, plant and equipment	(386.18)	(357.28)	(375.47)
Net cash used by investing activities	($632.19)	($499.26)	($485.34)
FINANCING ACTIVITIES			
Proceeds from issuance of common stock	137.59	107.18	107.47
Principal payments on long-term debt	(0.72)	(0.71)	(0.70)
Repurchase of common stock	(203.41)	(75.71)	(52.25)
Net cash provided/(used) by financing activities	($66.55)	$30.76	$54.52
Effect of exchange rate changes on cash and cash equivalents	3.11	3.28	1.56
Net increase in cash and cash equivalents	98.22	101.23	48.43
CASH AND CASH EQUIVALENTS			
Beginning of period	200.91	99.68	51.25
End of period	$299.13	$200.91	$99.68
SUPPLEMENTAL DISCLOSURE OF CASH FLOW INFORMATION			
Cash paid during the year for:			
Interest	0.37	0.27	0.30
Income taxes	172.76	140.11	105.34

Source: Starbucks Corp. 10-K filing with Securities and Exchange Commission for fiscal year ended 3 October 2004.

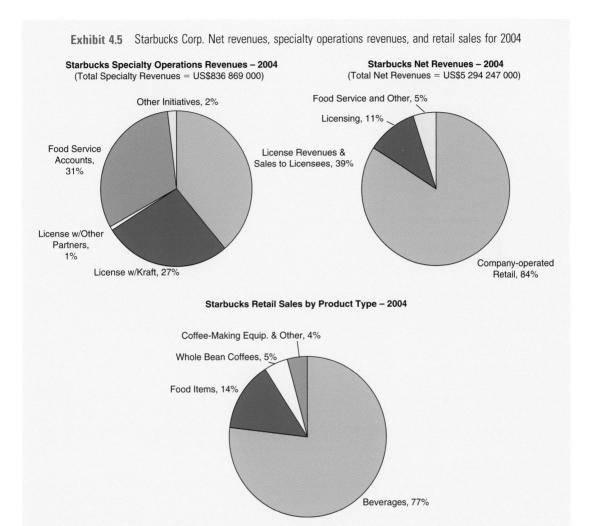

Exhibit 4.5 Starbucks Corp. Net revenues, specialty operations revenues, and retail sales for 2004

Starbucks Specialty Operations Revenues – 2004
(Total Specialty Revenues = US$836 869 000)

Other Initiatives, 2%

Food Service Accounts, 31%

License Revenues & Sales to Licensees, 39%

License w/Other Partners, 1%

License w/Kraft, 27%

Starbucks Net Revenues – 2004
(Total Net Revenues = US$5 294 247 000)

Food Service and Other, 5%

Licensing, 11%

Company-operated Retail, 84%

Starbucks Retail Sales by Product Type – 2004

Coffee-Making Equip. & Other, 4%

Whole Bean Coffees, 5%

Food Items, 14%

Beverages, 77%

Source: Starbucks Corp. 10-K filing with Securities and Exchange Commission for fiscal year ended 3 October 2004.

company also sold noncoffee beverages, a variety of complementary food items, value cards, coffee-related accessories and equipment, and a line of compact discs (CDs) (see Exhibit 4.5). In addition, Starbucks sold coffee and tea products through its equity investees and other channels.

The company's objective was to establish Starbucks as the most recognized and respected brand in the world. To achieve this goal, the company's strategy was threefold. First, it would continue rapid expansion of its retail operations. Secondly, it planned to grow its specialty operations (licensing, foodservices, and other initiatives). Finally, it would selectively pursue other opportunities, aiming to leverage the Starbucks brand

Exhibit 4.6 Starbucks Corp. company-owned retail stores categorized by region

Company-operated stores	
United States	4,293
International:	
United Kingdom	422
Canada	372
Thailand	49
Australia	44
Singapore	35
Total International	922
Total Company-operated	**5,215**

Source: Starbucks Corp. 10-K filing with Securities and Exchange Commission for fiscal year ended 3 October 2004.

through the introduction of new products and the development of new distribution channels. By the end of 2004, the company had over 8500 stores worldwide, strong alliances with established corporations, and one of the world's strongest brands.

Revenue recognition

Starbucks reported net revenues of $5.2 billion in 2004. The company derived that figure from five distinct revenue streams: company-operating retail stores, specialty operations, licensing, foodservice accounts, and a catch-all category called "other initiatives."

Company-operated retail stores

By the end of fiscal 2004, Starbucks had 5215 company-operated retail stores. These stores were typically situated in high-traffic, high-visibility locations in countries such as the United States, United Kingdom, Singapore, and Thailand (see Exhibit 4.6) and sold beverages, food, CDs, and coffee-related equipment.

In November 2001, Starbucks introduced the Starbucks card, which allowed customers to purchase prepaid cards that ranged in value from $5 to $500. These cards were intended to provide quicker, convenient transactions; build loyalty; reduce company costs; increase revenues; and improve customer data.

In fiscal 2004, the company opened the Starbucks Hear Music™ Coffeehouse, a first-of-its-kind music store, in Santa Monica, California. This café/music-store concept combined the Starbucks coffeehouse experience with an innovative retail environment. In addition to offering the usual Starbucks products, the store gave customers a hands-on guide to music discovery with an interactive listening bar and allowed customers access to CD burning technology to create personalized CDs from a digital music library.

Specialty operations

The company's specialty operations aimed to develop the Starbucks brand outside the company-operated retail store environment. Starbucks' strategy was to reach customers where they worked, traveled, shopped, and dined by establishing relationships with prominent and reputable third parties. These relationships took various forms, including licensing arrangements, foodservice accounts, and other initiatives related to the company's core businesses. In some cases, Starbucks had an equity ownership interest in the licensee operations. During fiscal 2004, specialty revenues, which included royalties and fees from licensees and product sales derived from specialty operations, accounted for 16% of total net revenues (see Exhibit 4.5).

Licensing

Starbucks did not franchise or generally relinquish operational control of its retail stores in the United States, nor did it plan to in the foreseeable future. However, in situations where a master concessionaire or another company controlled or could provide improved access to desirable retail space, the company licensed its operations.[7]

As part of these arrangements, Starbucks sold coffee and related products in the licensed locations and received license fees and royalties. Employees working in the locations were required to follow Starbucks' detailed store operating procedures and attend training classes similar to those given to company-operated store managers and employees.

In 2004, Starbucks had 1839 licensed stores in the United States. Internationally the company's licensed stores totaled 1515, arranged primarily with prominent local retailers.

Starbucks' licensing operations generated a number of revenue streams, including product sales, royalties, and license fees. In total, these stores accounted for 39% of specialty revenues in fiscal 2004 (see Exhibit 4.5).

In 2004, the company expanded its licensing agreement with Kraft Foods, Inc. ("Kraft") to provide a larger selection of Starbucks whole bean and ground coffees, Seattle's Best Coffee and Torrefazione Italia branded coffees, and a selection of premium Tazo teas in grocery and warehouse club stores throughout the United States. Kraft managed all distribution, marketing, advertising, and promotion and paid a royalty to Starbucks. Revenues from this category accounted for 27% of specialty revenues in fiscal 2004.

Foodservice accounts

Starbucks sold whole bean and ground coffees, including the Starbucks, Seattle's Best Coffee, and Torrefazione Italia brands, as well as a selection of premium Tazo teas, to institutional foodservice companies that serviced business, industry, education and healthcare accounts, office coffee distributors, hotels, restaurants, airlines, and other retailers. At the start of fiscal 2003, the company transitioned the majority of its US foodservice accounts to SYSCO Corporation's national broad line distribution network, aligning its foodservice sales, customer service, and support resources with those of SYSCO Corporation. This alliance greatly improved customer service levels and was expected to continue to generate new foodservice accounts over several years. The company's revenues from these accounts accounted for 31% of total specialty revenues (see Exhibit 4.5).

Other initiatives

The company maintained a website at www.starbucks.com where customers could purchase, register, or reload Starbucks stored value cards as well as apply for the Starbucks Card Duetto Visa, issued through an agreement with Bank One Corporation and Visa. The Duetto card was the first of its kind, combining the functionality of a credit card with the convenience of a reloadable Starbucks card. The website also contained information about the company's coffee products, brewing equipment, and store locations.

In fiscal 2004, Starbucks entered into a strategic marketing alliance with XM Satellite Radio, debuting the 24-hour Starbucks Hear Music channel 75 for all XM Satellite Radio subscribers. Starbucks started providing the Hear Music satellite channel in more than 4000 company-operated locations in the United States during fiscal 2005. Collectively, the operations of these other initiatives accounted for 2% of specialty revenues in fiscal 2004 (see Exhibit 4.5).

Required

(a) In terms of timing for the recognition of revenue relative to the receipt of cash, three revenue-recognition models are possible. In the first, revenue is recognized as cash is received. In the second, revenue is recognized before cash is received (hence, accounts receivable, or A/R). In the third, cash is received before the revenue is recognized (hence, the deferred revenue account). These models are summarized by the journal entries below.

(1)	Cash	x					
	Revenue		x				
				Later			
(2)	A/R	x		Cash	x		
	Revenue		x	A/R		x	
(3)	Cash	x		Dfd. rev	x		
	Dfd. revenue		x	Revenue		x	

Your task is to determine which of the above models is most appropriate for each of the following revenue streams:
- retail sales
- the "Starbucks" card

- the "Duetto" card
- food service operations
- licensing.

(b) Assume that Starbucks creates a loyalty card. Any customer can get the card free of charge. The way it works is that every time a customer buys a cup of coffee, the purchase is registered on the card. After 10 cups are purchased, the card can be turned in for a free cup of coffee. Assuming that the selling price for a cup of coffee is $3.30, how would you account for the loyalty program?

4.3 Network Associates (McAfee): a case of "channel stuffing"*

Network Associates (hereafter, NA, later renamed McAfee) designed computer hardware and software to combat viruses, improve network security, and manage network operations.

Like many other high-tech companies of that era, NA rode a wave of high stock market valuation in the late 1990s (see Exhibit 4.7). The company achieved high revenue growth through 1998, some of it organic, some via acquisitions (see Exhibit 4.8).

However, in early 1999 the stock price took a big hit. After peaking at a split-adjusted $335.39 per share in December 1998, the first four months of 1999 saw significant declines: –21% in January; –10% in February; –35% in March; and –57% in April. The closing price at the end of April was $67.08, or an 80% drop in just four months.

In its prerelease of 1998 earnings (made in January 1999 for the purpose of providing guidance to the analyst community), management gave no indication of sales declines on the horizon. On the contrary, they stated that they were on track to meet analysts' expectations for the year. Yet three months later they reversed their previous announcement. In April 1999 several shareholder lawsuits against the company and its senior management were filed.

Management's explanation for the reduced forecasts of future sales blamed a shift in customer preferences, as explained in this 7 April 1999 article from *Dow Jones Business Service*:

> "Our sales cycle is more complex," said Network Associates' Chairman and Chief Executive Officer William Larson. Only a year or so ago, corporations would buy security software by picking a so-called firewall, encryption software and then cobbling their purchases together as a security umbrella. Today, companies are seeking integrated suites of security products, taking longer periods of time to evaluate the product and paying more attention to price.
>
> Network Associates has begun integrating offerings from its many acquisitions into a suite. But the move toward a broader, enterprise-wide sales posture has meant longer evaluation cycles. "Be careful what you ask for, you just might get it," Larson said of its enterprise focus.

*This case was prepared by Professor Daniel Bens, INSEAD.

Yet at the time management was making these claims to the investing community, they were actually dealing with the effects of several quarters of channel stuffing. Inventory was backing up at the distributor level, and distributors could not pay off the amounts owed to NA.

On 26 December 2000 the CEO (Larson) resigned without explanation, as did the CFO and President. The company's share price fell by 68% that month, which followed a loss of 32% in November.

Eventually, the SEC filed a complaint in the US federal court system which sought monetary penalties from the company. Among other charges, the Commission claimed that the company:

- created a subsidiary to buy back inventory it had previously sold to distributors, in order to avoid characterizing the transaction as a return of merchandise;
- secretly paid distributors significant amounts so that funds could be cycled back to the company and be portrayed as "payments";
- used other unrelated reserve accounts to draw upon (i.e., debit) when transferring cash to the distributors as mentioned above;
- timed sales with a significant customer (Ingram Micro) with a fiscal quarter date that often followed McAfee's by several days – McAfee would pass the inventory along at the end of its quarter as a "sale," yet Ingram would return it after McAfee's new quarter started but before Ingram's current quarter ended;
- sold inventory to distributors *on consignment*, where the distributor only paid for the receivable when the product was passed along to an end customer; and
- conducted sham sales of its accounts receivable by transferring them to a financial institution for up-front cash, yet guaranteeing the institution that the receivables would be paid (thus McAfee retained the risk of collection).

NA, now called McAfee, settled these claims, without admitting or denying the allegations, in early 2006, by paying a fine of $50 million.[8]

Before the settlement, the company recorded a series of accounting restatements related to the above issues, most notably in June 2002 and October 2003. Those two restatements focused on the year 1998, and resulted in a reduction in revenues in that year of $562 million as well as a reduction in net income of $356 million. Overall, cumulative restatements during the early 2000s reduced revenue by $622 million and net income by $353 million over the period 1998 to 2000.

Required

(a) Describe in one or two sentences the concept of "channel stuffing."
(b) Can a company stuff its distribution channels forever? If not, how does the practice come to an end?

(c) After McAfee restated their accounts, what was the "true" number for 1998 sales?

(d) What indicators can you find in Exhibit 4.8 that might indicate channel stuffing?

(e) Not all of the allegations made by the SEC are easily detected from the analysis of financial statements. Which ones might be more difficult to detect?

(f) What is the pattern of operating cash flows that is likely to occur when a company stuffs its channel? In NA's (McAfee's) case, where was it getting the cash that enabled it to carry out the strategy?

(g) What sort of forces do you suppose pressure managers into opting for a strategy of channel stuffing?

Selected financial information and ratios from 1996 to 2001

Exhibit 4.7   Cumulative stock returns: McAfee vs. S&P 500

Cumulative Stock Returns 1995-2001

Source: Center for Research in Security Prices (University of Chicago).

Exhibit 4.8   Selected financial data for McAfee

	1996	1997	1998	1999	2000	2001
Revenue and income statement data						
Sales	181,126	612,193	990,045	683,668	745,692	834,478
Pre-tax Operating Income	67,269	18,221	119,966	−138,199	−151,967	−81,966
NOPAT	40,361	10,933	71,980	−82,919	−91,180	−49,180
Net Income	39,017	−28,356	36,438	−159,901	−102,721	−102,381
Balance sheet data						
Net A/R	25,930	125,284	260,784	174,646	122,315	136,366
Allowance	3,027	3,662	11,682	16,249	15,332	8,394
Gross A/R	28,957	128,946	272,466	190,895	137,647	144,760
Allowance % of Gross A/R	0.105	0.028	0.043	0.085	0.111	0.058
A/R turnover	7.737	8.097	5.129	3.140	5.022	6.452
Days A/R outstanding	47	45	71	116	73	57
Total Assets	194,485	601,931	1,536,721	1,479,394	1,384,848	1,627,132
Cash Flow Statement Data						
Cash from Operations	46,530	90,686	52,466	−23,335	26,672	145,706
Cash from Investing	−46,863	−134,704	−318,823	−168,549	10,443	20,775
Cash from Financing	46,397	43,391	533,330	96,597	−39,403	158,904
Significant financing items:						
Cash from exercise of employee stock options	14,290	43,188	151,099	27,471	46,548	51,067
Cash from tax benefits of employee stock options	32,107	39,941	43,500			
Cash used in repurchasing shares		−39,738		−12,443	−100,416	−53,800
Cash from issuance of convertible debt			337,624			335,081
Cash from IPO of subsidiary				78,945		
Cash used in repurchasing convertible debt						−173,708

Source: Company SEC filings

Notes

1. *Fact Sheet: Staff Accounting Bulletin No. 101 – Revenue Recognition*, US Securities and Exchange Commission, 3 December 1999.
2. Leases, insurance contracts, financial instruments, and biological assets are expressly excluded from the proposed standard.
3. The following example is taken from the joint FASB/IASB Exposure Draft.
4. All dollar amounts are in US$.
5. Anjali Cordeiro, "Starbucks Jan Same-Store Sales Rose 7%," *CNN Money*, 2 February 2005.

6. Same-store sales, which compare sales performance at stores open for at least one year, are an important metric in the retail industry.
7. Attractive retail real estate in the United States that would have otherwise been unavailable included airports, national grocery chains, major food services corporations, college and university campuses, and hospitals. Internationally, Starbucks employed three business strategies: joint ventures, licenses, and company-owned operations.
8. After the name change, in April 2004, McAfee divested its computer network management division. From that point onward, its strategic focus would be on the antivirus software business.

CHAPTER 5

The Statement of Cash Flows

Introduction

The accrual method of accounting is a fundamental feature of corporate financial reporting. Under this method, revenues are recognized when earned and expenses when incurred, even if cash is received or paid at some other time. But determining precisely when revenues are earned and expenses incurred requires judgment, and where there is judgment there is also the possibility of manipulation. One way for financial statement readers to deal with the possibility of manipulation is to analyze performance with the effects of accruals stripped from the accounts. That's what the statement of cash flows is for.

The statement of cash flows provides a view of the firm's performance independent of accruals. It summarizes cash inflows and cash outflows and, in so doing, reconciles beginning and ending cash. But the statement does more than just summarize cash flows. It reveals the nature of the activities that gave rise to those cash flows. To understand how this works, let's examine how the statement is organized. Once again, we'll use SAP Group as an example (see Exhibit 1.3).

The cash flow statement is prepared on the assumption that all cash flows result from just three types of activities—operating, investing, and financing.

The reporting of cash flows from operations

Cash flows from operating activities are reported in either of two equivalent ways: the direct method or the indirect method.

The direct method

Under the direct method, the firm reports gross cash receipts and cash payments related to operations. Receipts include cash received from customers, dividends, and interest. Payments include cash paid to employees and suppliers, interest paid to banks, and income taxes. This approach is shown in Exhibit 5.1 for Northrop Grumman, a large defense and aerospace company. The sources of operating cash reported by the company consist entirely of actual cash receipts from customers and other parties, just as the uses of operating cash consist entirely of cash actually paid out to suppliers, employees, and others.

The indirect method

Under the more popular indirect method, operating cash flows are calculated by removing all noncash items that went into the calculation of net income. In effect, all of the accruals embedded in net income are reversed through a series of adjustments. The end result should be the same figure calculated using the direct method. For example, notice that cash flow from operating activities for Northrop Grumman is $2133 million in 2009 under both methods.[1]

Exhibit 5.1(a)   Northrop Grumman Corporation operating cash flows: Direct method

	Year ended December 31		
($ in millions)	2009	2008	2007
Operating activities			
Sources of cash – continuing operations			
Cash received from customers			
Progress payments	**$8,561**	$6,219	$5,860
Collections on billings	**25,099**	26,938	24,570
Insurance proceeds received	**25**	5	125
Other cash receipts	**37**	83	34
Total sources of cash – continuing operations	**33,722**	33,245	30,589
Uses of cash – continuing operations			
Cash paid to suppliers and employees	**(29,250)**	(28,817)	(26,144)
Pension contributions	**(858)**	(320)	(342)
Interest paid, net of interest received	**(269)**	(287)	(334)
Income taxes paid, net of refunds received	**(774)**	(712)	(853)
Income taxes paid on sale of businesses	**(508)**	(7)	—
Excess tax benefits from stock-based compensation	**(2)**	(48)	(52)
Other cash payments	**(30)**	(16)	(52)
Total uses of cash – continuing operations	**(31,691)**	(30,207)	(27,777)
Cash provided by continuing operations	**2,031**	3,038	2,812
Cash provided by discontinued operations	**102**	173	78
Net cash provided by operating activities	**$2,133**	$3,211	$2,890

The accompanying notes are an integral part of these consolidated financial statements.

A brief glance at SAP Group's statement shows that it uses the indirect method. The line items that follow net income in the operating activities section show the common set of adjustments you can expect to see in nearly any cash flow statement. We'll discuss them in more detail later in this chapter.

Investing activities involve the buying and selling of (1) long-term assets such as machinery and equipment, (2) companies or parts of companies, and (3) financial securities, such as government bonds.

Financing activities cover actions involving the capital markets such as (1) borrowing, (2) paying off loans, (3) issuing shares, (4) buying them back, and (5) paying dividends. A cash flow statement should explain:

- why a company's cash balance increased or decreased during the year;
- how the company acquired cash, and
- what it did with the cash.

Exhibit 5.1(b)   Northrop Grumman Corporation operating cash flows: Indirect method

($ in millions)	Year ended December 31		
	2009	**2008**	**2007**
Reconciliation of net earnings (loss) to net cash provided by operating activities			
Net earnings (loss)	**$1,686**	$(1,262)	$1,790
Net earnings from discontinued operations	**(95)**	(91)	(39)
Adjustments to reconcile to net cash provided by operating activities			
Depreciation	**585**	567	570
Amortization of assets	**151**	189	152
Impairment of goodwill	—	3,060	—
Stock-based compensation	**105**	118	196
Excess tax benefits from stock-based compensation	**(2)**	(48)	(52)
Pretax gain on sale of businesses	**(446)**	(58)	—
Pretax gain on sale of investments	—	—	(23)
(Increase) decrease in			
Accounts receivable	**(6,313)**	(378)	(6,439)
Inventoried costs	**(291)**	(521)	4
Prepaid expenses and other current assets	**(6)**	(20)	9
Increase (decrease) in			
Progress payments	**6,655**	764	6,513
Accounts payable and accruals	**(151)**	383	(2)
Deferred income taxes	**112**	167	195
Income taxes payable	**65**	241	(59)
Retiree benefits	**(20)**	(167)	(50)
Other noncash transactions, net	**(4)**	94	47
Cash provided by continuing operations	**2,031**	3,038	2,812
Cash provided by discontinued operations	**102**	173	78
Net cash provided by operating activities	**$2,133**	$3,211	$2,890

The accompanying notes are an integral part of these consolidated financial statements.

From its statement, we see that SAP Group generated €3015 million of cash from operating activities in 2009. Most of that cash flow was used for financing activities such as repayments of borrowings and dividends (€2303 million and €594 million, respectively).

Preparing the statement of cash flows

Corporate accounting systems are designed to accumulate the information needed to prepare balance sheets and income statements. In other words, accounting systems are geared to the accrual method of accounting, not the cash basis. Therefore, companies must find a way to transform information from the balance sheet and the income statement into a cash flow statement. We illustrate how this process works using the T-accounts introduced in the appendix to Chapter 1.

In essence, the statement is prepared by showing how cash changes in relation to changes in noncash accounts. To understand this point, consider the basic accounting equation:

$$\text{Assets (A)} = \text{Liabilities (L)} + \text{Shareholders' Equity (SE)}$$

It therefore follows that

$$\Delta A = \Delta L + \Delta SE$$

where Δ, or delta, is the change in an item. This equation tells us that changes in assets during the period must equal the sum of changes in liabilities and changes in shareholders' equity.

If we divide assets into two categories, cash and noncash assets (NCA),

$$\Delta \text{ Cash} + \Delta NCA = \Delta L + \Delta SE$$

Rearranging the terms in this equation, we get the equation for changes in cash (or "delta cash"):

$$\Delta \text{Cash} = \Delta L + \Delta SE - \Delta NCA$$

This equation tells us that changes in cash can be explained by reference to changes in all other balance sheet accounts, and thus provides the underlying logic for preparing the statement of cash flows. Any transaction that changes cash must be accompanied by a change in liabilities, shareholders' equity, or noncash assets.

The preparation of the cash flow statement is shown using information for a company we call Morris Distributors Corporation. Exhibit 5.2(a) presents the balance sheets for the

Exhibit 5.2(a)   Morris Distributors, Inc. balance sheets for December 31, 2008 and 2009

	December 31	
	2008	2009
ASSETS		
Current assets		
Cash	$90,000	$18,000
Accounts receivables	60,000	165,000
Inventories	120,000	150,000
Total Current assets	$270,000	$333,000
Noncurrent assets		
Property, plant and equipment	$300,000	$675,000
Accumulated depreciation	90,000	120,000
Total Noncurrent assets	$210,000	$555,000
Total Assets	$480,000	$888,000
LIABILITIES and SHAREHOLDERS' EQUITY		
Current liabilities		
Accounts payable	$90,000	$150,000
Salaries payable	15,000	18,000
Other short-term payables	30,000	36,000
Total Current liabilities	$135,000	$204,000
Noncurrent liabilities		
Long-term loans	$0	$300,000
Shareholders' equity		
Common stock	$300,000	$300,000
Retained earnings	45,000	84,000
Total Shareholders' equity	$345,000	$384,000
Total Liabilities and shareholders' equity	$480,000	$888,000

beginning and the end of 2009, and Exhibit 5.2(b) the income statement for 2009. Morris Distributors declared and paid $21 000 in dividends during the year.

We begin with the T-account worksheet from Exhibit 5.3(a). At the top of the worksheet is a master T-account for Cash. This account is divided into three sections – operations, investing, and financing – to correspond to the three sections of the cash flow statement.

The beginning and ending balances have been recorded for each balance sheet account, including cash. The beginning balance is found at the top of each T-account; the ending balance is shown on the bottom.[2] Morris Distributors' beginning and ending cash balances were $90 000 and $18 000, respectively. For the statement of cash flows to balance, this $72 000 reduction in cash must be reconciled.

Exhibit 5.2(b) Morris Distributors Inc. income statement for 2009

Sales revenue	$375,000
Cost of goods sold	180,000
Depreciation expense	30,000
Salary expense	60,000
Operating income	$105,000
Interest expense	12,000
Income before taxes	$93,000
Income taxes	33,000
Net Income	$60,000
Statement of retained earnings, 2009	
Retained earnings, beginning	$45,000
Net income	$60,000
Dividends, declared and paid	$21,000
Retained earnings, ending	$84,000

All changes in the master T-account are explained by accounting for the changes during the year in each noncash account. In essence, the entries originally recorded in the accounts during the year are reconstructed and entered into the same accounts on the T-account worksheet. This process may seem complicated at first, but you will soon see that it's really quite easy.

The only additional requirement is that each entry in the cash T-account must be classified as operating, investing, or financing. Once the net change in each noncash account has been accounted for, all of the data are there to prepare a complete and proper cash flow statement.

We begin by recording net income:

(1)	Cash (operations)	60,000	
	Retained earnings		60,000

As shown in Exhibit 5.3(b), both the debit to cash and the credit to retained earnings are cross-referenced by a (1) to indicate that this is the first reconciling entry.

However, after this entry is recorded, the ending balance of retained earnings ($84 000) has not yet been reconciled to the beginning balance. What's missing is a $21 000 debit that corresponds to the dividends declared and paid in 2009:

(2)	Retained earnings	21,000	
	Cash (financing)		21,000

At this point, the difference between the beginning and ending balances for retained earnings has been explained. We signal this reconciliation with a check mark on the top line of the T-account.

Exhibit 5.3(a)   T-account worksheet for Morris Distributors

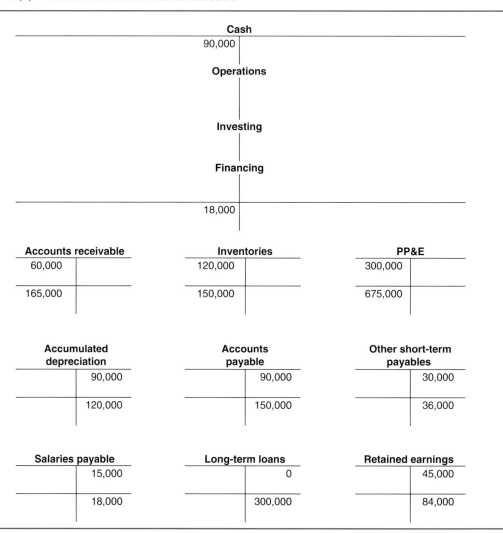

The next set of entries, shown in Exhibit 5.3(c), adjusts net income for the effects of items that reflect differences in the timing of the accrued-based net income figure and cash flows. For example, net income is adjusted for depreciation and amortization expense. This expense is subtracted in computing net income but does not involve an outlay of cash (the outlays occurred in previous years when the assets were acquired). Therefore, if we are to convert net income into its cash flow equivalent, depreciation and amortization expense must be added back. In this case, the effect of depreciation expense is removed by adding back $30 000 to net income:

Exhibit 5.3(b)   T-account worksheet for Morris Distributors (after the first two entries)

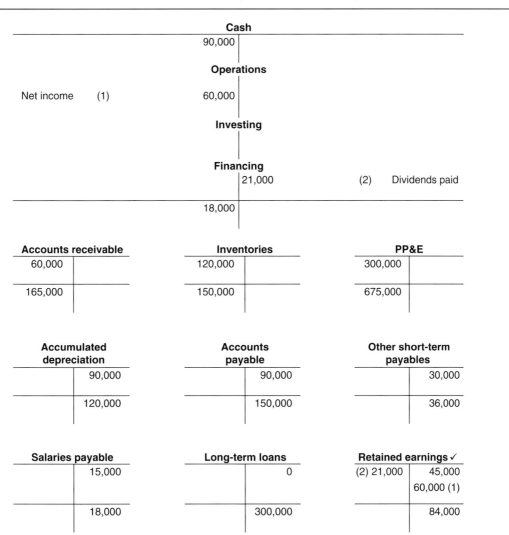

		Cash		
		90,000		
		Operations		
Net income	(1)	60,000		
		Investing		
		Financing		
		21,000	(2)	Dividends paid
		18,000		

Accounts receivable	
60,000	
165,000	

Inventories	
120,000	
150,000	

PP&E	
300,000	
675,000	

Accumulated depreciation	
	90,000
	120,000

Accounts payable	
	90,000
	150,000

Other short-term payables	
	30,000
	36,000

Salaries payable	
	15,000
	18,000

Long-term loans	
	0
	300,000

Retained earnings ✓	
(2) 21,000	45,000
	60,000 (1)
	84,000

Exhibit 5.3(c)   T-account worksheet for Morris Distributors (completed version)

		Cash			
		90,000			
		Operations			
		105,000		(4)	Increase in accounts
Net income	(1)	60,000			
			Receivable		
Depreciation Expense	(3)	30,000	30,000	(5)	Increase in merchandise Inventory
Increase in accounts payable	(6)	60,000			
Increase in other suppliers payables	(7)	6,000			
Increase in salaries payable	(8)	3,000			
		Investing			
		375, 000		(9)	Acquisition of buildings and equipment
		Financing			
Long-term bond Issue	(3)	300,000	21,000	(2)	Dividends paid
Ending balance		18,000			

Exhibit 5.3(c)   Continued

Accounts receivable ✓		Inventories ✓		PP&E ✓	
60,000		120,000		300,000	
(4) 105,000		(5) 30,000		(9) 375,000	
165,000		150,000		675,000	

Accumulated depreciation ✓		Accounts payable ✓		Other short-term payables ✓	
	90,000		90,000		30,000
	30,000 (3)		60,000 (6)		6,000 (7)
	120,000		150,000		36,000

Salaries payable ✓		Long-term loans ✓		Retained earnings ✓	
	15,000		0	(2) 21,000	45,000
	3,000 (8)		300,000 (10)		60,000 (1)
	18,000		300,000		84,000

(3) Cash (operations)	30,000	
Accumulated depreciation		30,000

Net income is then adjusted for changes in all current assets and current liabilities, apart from cash (which is already accounted for in delta cash) and short-term debt (which is accounted for as a financing cash flow). When converting net income to its cash flow equivalent, we apply the following general rules:

> Add the change when a current asset decreases or current liability increases; and subtract the change when a current asset increases or current liability decreases.

If you follow the logic and mechanics of the T-account approach, these rules will be implemented automatically. (In our later discussion on the analysis of cash flow statements, we elaborate on the economic reasoning behind these rules.)
For example:

(4) Accounts receivable	105,000	
Cash (operations)		105,000

To understand the logic behind this entry, remember that the sales revenues shown on the income statement are recognized when earned, not necessarily when cash is paid. For cash flow purposes, however, cash collected from customers is what matters. Sales revenues were $375 000 in 2009 (see Exhibit 5.2(b)). When these revenues were earned (from the sale of products), two entries were made: a credit to sales revenue and a debit to accounts receivable. Accounts receivable is then credited as collections are made. The fact that accounts receivable increased by $105 000 in 2009 means that debits to the account must have exceeded credits by the same amount. To put it another way, sales revenues recognized in 2009 must have exceeded cash collected from customers by $105 000. This amount is subtracted from net income (hence the credit to cash, under operations) to convert it into its cash flow equivalent.

The same logic is used to adjust for the other current assets and liabilities. For example, the $30 000 increase in inventories implies that purchases of inventory in 2009 (debits to the inventory account) must have exceeded the amount of inventory sold (credits to the account). This increase must be subtracted from net income to convert it into operating cash flow:

(5) Inventories   30,000
        Cash (operations)   30,000

Now consider accounts payable. Cash flow from operations must reflect cash purchases, but not all purchases are for cash. The $60 000 increase in accounts payable for 2009 means purchases on account (credits to accounts payable) must have exceeded payments to suppliers (debits to the account). In other words, the purchases amount that went into the calculation of costs of goods sold includes $60 000 of purchases for which cash payment has not yet been made. This amount must be *added* to net income:

(6) Cash (operations)   60,000
        Accounts payable   60,000

The increases in the next two current liability accounts, Other short-term payables and salaries payable, imply that accrued-based expenses exceeded cash paid for the expenses, and must be added back to net income:

(7) Cash (operations)   6,000
        Other short-term payables   6,000

(8) Cash (operations)   3,000
        Salaries payable   3,000

Two accounts remain to be reconciled: property, plant, and equipment (PP&E) and long-term loans. The $375 000 increase in PP&E means that assets were acquired during the year. Of course, it is possible that the company bought, say, $400 000, while raising $25 000 in cash from disposing of other assets. In other words, $375 000 is a net increase. But in the absence of additional information, it is reasonable to assume that the company must have invested that amount in property, plant and equipment. The credit to cash is under the investing section:

(9) Property, plant, and equipment   375,000
        Cash (investing)   375,000

The increase in long-term loans tells us that the company borrowed $300 000 from its bankers. This cash flow is debited to cash, under financing:

(10) Cash (financing)   300,000
            Long-term loans   300,000

As we can see from Exhibit 5.3(c), after recording entry 10, all of the balance sheet accounts have been reconciled.

   The final step is to take the information provided in the cash T-account and prepare a formal statement of cash flows, which is shown in Exhibit 5.4. The completed master T-account is a worksheet that provides us with all of the information needed to prepare the statement. In effect, the master T-account performs the same function for the statement of cash flows as the adjusted, preclosing trial balance does for the balance sheet and income statement.

Does the statement of cash flows tell us anything new?

You may think that because the data used to prepare the statement of cash flows come from the income statement and the balance sheet, they merely represent a reordering of information already available. Not quite. In fact, if you were to take the income statement and balance sheets for SAP Group and try to create your own cash flow statement, the results would be very different than the one shown in Exhibit 1.3. It might balance, but the amounts for

Exhibit 5.4   Morris Distributors statement of cash flows for the year ended December 31, 2009

Net income	$60,000	
Add: Depreciation	30,000	
Adjustments for working capital		
Increase in accounts receivable	−105,000	
Increase in inventories	−30,000	
Increase in accounts payable	60,000	
Increase in salaries payable	3,000	
Increase in other short-term payables	6,000	
Cash flow from operating activities		**$24,000**
Acquisition of buildings and equipment	−$375,000	
Cash flow used in investing activities		**− $375,000**
Borrowings	$300,000	
Dividends paid	−21,000	
Cash flow from financing activities		**$279,000**
Net change in cash		**− $72,000**

operating, investing, and financing activities would be wrong. The discrepancies would arise mainly because of how changes in short-term operating assets and liabilities (receivables, inventories, and payables) are classified by SAP Group. Most such discrepancies arise from the effects of acquisitions and divestitures.[3]

To illustrate, suppose your company acquires another company in the current year. The acquisition involves all of the company's assets, including working capital components such as receivables. Now imagine that the receivables for our own business, independent of the acquisition, did not change during the year, but consolidated receivables increased by $15 million because of the receivables acquired from the other company. If we were to prepare a cash flow statement based on reported account balances, the increase in receivables would be classified as an increase in working capital, and thus as a decrease in cash flow from operations. The problem with this treatment is that the increase in receivables did not arise from operating activities, but from an investing transaction.[4] Therefore, the $15 million increase in receivables should appear in the investing activities section.

Such details are not normally part of the financial information released by companies to the investing public. By omitting such details, the $15 million increase in receivables would be misclassified as an operating cash outflow. Therefore, the cash flow statement reveals information about operating, investing, and financing cash flows that cannot be discerned simply by reordering information already available from the balance sheet and the income statement.

IFRS and the statement of cash flows

The IFRS approach to preparing the statement is largely the same as the format presented in this chapter, although there can be differences. The most important difference is that IFRS is more flexible in defining operating, investing, and financing cash flows than US GAAP. For example, interest and dividends received can be classified as operating cash flows (as under US GAAP) *or* as investing cash flows. Interest paid can be classified as operating *or* financing cash flows. Dividends paid may be shown as operating *or* financing cash flows.

Generally speaking, if a cash flow statement is prepared in accordance with US GAAP, it is likely to be IFRS-compliant. However, the reverse is not necessarily true.

Analyzing the statement of cash flows

The analysis of the cash flow statement focuses on two fundamental issues:

- the relationship between net income and cash flow from operations, and
- the relationship between operating, investing, and financial cash flows.

We'll examine these issues by drawing again on the cash flow statements of SAP Group (Exhibit 1.3).

Net income and cash flow from operations

The operating activities section focuses on the firm's ability to generate cash internally from its recurring, day-to-day operating activities. To put it another way, it addresses how successful the company has been at generating cash from producing and selling its products and services.

Consider SAP Group. The operating activities section shows in Table 5.1 reveals that €3 billion of cash was provided by operations, an improvement of about €850 million from 2008 and almost €1.1 billion from 2007. Because SAP Group uses the indirect method, the starting point for the calculation of cash flow from operations (CFFO) is the profit after tax from the income statement. One of the most important tasks for the analyst is to understand how these two figures – net income and CFFO – are reconciled.

The reconciliation of the accrual-basis profit figure (net income) and CFFO begins with the adding back of depreciation and amortization.[5] As noted earlier in this chapter, these expenses are added back to net income because they are not the result of a cash outlay.

For the same reason, increases in provisions are added back to net income, while reductions are subtracted.[6] To illustrate, if a company reports provisions of $800 million at the beginning of the year and $720 million at the end, the implication is that $80 million of provisions taken in previous years were paid off in the current year, and therefore this amount must be subtracted from net income if we are to convert it into a cash flow.

The final major adjustment to net income is for changes in working capital. To understand how to interpret these changes, consider a typical manufacturing company.[7] As shown in Figure 5.1, the operating cycle begins with the acquisition of the materials used in the company's products. These materials are transferred to production facilities, where workers and various elements of manufacturing overhead (such as public utilities and maintenance) combine to convert the materials to a finished product.

Table 5.1   The operating activities section of SAP Group's statement of cash flows

	2009	**2008**	**2007**
Cash flows from operating activities			
Profit after tax	€1,750	€1,848	€1,908
Depreciation and amortization	499	539	262
Gains/losses on disposals of noncurrent assets	−11	11	1
Gains/losses on disposals of financial assets	−2	−16	−1
Impairment loss on financial assets recognized in profit	10	15	8
Decrease/increase in sales and bad debt allowances on trade receivables	64	76	0
Other adjustments for noncash items	14	52	45
Deferred income taxes	−39	−91	8
Decrease/increase in trade receivables	593	−48	−521
Decrease/increase in other assets	205	−12	−277
Decrease/increase in trade payables, provisions and other liabilities	−116	−277	375
Decrease/increase in deferred income	48	61	124
Net cash flows from operating activities	3,015	2,158	1,932

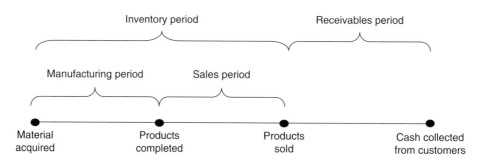

Figure 5.1   The operating cycle

The length of time from acquisition of raw materials to finished product is the manufacturing period. A sales period marks the time from completion of the manufacturing process to sale of the product.

The operating cycle does not end with the sale of the product, however. Most companies extend credit to their customers. The length of a company's operating cycle is thus the sum of its manufacturing period, sales period, and receivables period. We call this process a "cycle" because a portion of the cash collected from customers is used to pay suppliers and acquire more materials, which in turn enables the process to repeat itself.

Getting this cycle to turn requires investment, mainly in receivables and inventory. Other types of investment may be needed too, such as prepaid rent and insurance. Also, companies must maintain a certain level of cash to support their day-to-day operations. For example, retailers need to keep some cash in the register. We call this type of investment "operating cash" to distinguish it from more discretionary balances, or excess cash.

Therefore, we can think of the total investment in a company's operating cycle as the sum of inventories, receivables, prepaid expenses and other current assets, and operating cash. It is crucial to note, however, that this amount does not represent the company's own investment in the cycle, but rather the total investment made by the company and others, including suppliers, employees, and the government. The extent to which other parties invest in the company's operating cycle is the extent to which the company itself does not have to.

When suppliers grant credit to a company, they are really investing in its operating cycle. The same can be said for employees when they have not yet been paid for work already performed, for the government, in the form of owed but unpaid taxes, and for customers when they make advance payments. We can estimate the company's *net* investment in the operating cycle by subtracting the sum of accounts payable (supplier finance), accrued liabilities (which include unpaid wages and taxes), and advance payments, from the *total* investment in the operating cycle. We call this net investment the **working capital requirement (WCR)**:

$$\text{WCR} = (\text{inventories} + \text{receivables} + \text{other current assets} + \text{operating cash}) -$$
$$(\text{accounts payable} + \text{accrued liabilities} + \text{advances from customers})$$

Increases in the WCR reflect increases in the cash tied up in the operating cycle, and are therefore subtracted from net income in calculating CFFO. Decreases in the WCR have the opposite effect.

In the case of SAP in 2009 its working capital adjustments for receivables, other current assets, and all other working capital components were €593 million, €205 million, and -€116 million, respectively. The net effect was €682 million.

SAP's positive adjustment of €682 million means that the WCR must have declined in 2009. The effect of a decline is to release cash from the operating cycle, thus increasing CFFO. This results contrasts sharply with the previous year. The WCR actually increased in that year by €337 million (the sum of €48 million, €12 million, and €277 million).

One of the main challenges in analyzing the cash flow statement is assessing the sustainability of operating cash flow. A convenient starting point for this assessment is to look for any changes in the relationship between CFFO and net income.

For example, the trend in the *ratio of CFFO to net income* can be observed. Declines in this ratio (i.e., less cash flow relative to net income) are potentially troubling, indicating possible deterioration in the management of working capital or more aggressive revenue-recognition practices.[8] The ratio of CFFO to net income (or profit before tax) for SAP has improved since 2007 (1.72 in 2009; 1.17 in 2008; 1.01 in 2007). This is clearly a positive trend for SAP.

Nevertheless, we can question the sustainability of SAP's CFFO. While the decrease in the WCR suggests that SAP has become more efficient in managing its operating cycle, is it realistic to expect that the company can generate cash savings from further working capital reductions? Probably not, especially if SAP has an aggressive growth strategy. Sales growth becomes impossible without more receivables. Not only is the positive contribution from WCR reductions likely to cease in the near future, but it could actually reverse. As the WCR begins to rise again (as it did in 2007 and 2008), it will be a drag on SAP's operating cash flow.

Operating, investing, and financing cash flows

The second major area of interest in the analysis of cash flow statements centers on the relationship between operating, investing, and financing cash flows. This relationship is most conveniently expressed using the notion of **free cash flow**. Free cash flow can be defined in many ways, but perhaps the easiest way is to add cash flow from investing (CFFI) to CFFO. Because CFFI is usually a negative number (in most years, companies buy more fixed assets than they sell), the effect of adding CFFI is to subtract investment.

Free cash flow for SAP in 2009 equals €3015 million – €299 million, or €2716 million. This figure tells us how much operating cash the company has left over, net of all investing activities, and therefore the amount of cash flow generated in that year available for either financing activities or increasing cash balances. Because SAP's free cash flow is positive, the company is in a position to return cash to its investors, which it does in the form of dividend payments. In the two previous years, SAP also returned cash through share buybacks (€487 million in 2008 and €1005 million in 2007). Notice that free cash flow was negative in 2008, caused mainly by several acquisitions (resulting in cash outflows of €3773 million). SAP made up the shortfall with borrowings of €3859 million.

An alternative definition of free cash flow, known as **free operating cash flow**, deducts only capital expenditures from CFFO, ignoring other investing transactions such as company acquisitions and the sale or purchase of financial securities. The appeal of this approach is that these other types of investing transactions are more discretionary in nature. To include them is to produce free cash flow figures that are not truly reflective of the company's success in generating cash from its ongoing business activities. In the case of SAP, operating free cash flow for 2009 is marginally higher than the free cash flow figures reported earlier. However, operating free cash flows for 2007 and 2008 are much higher than raw free cash flows. For 2007, free cash flow is €1932 million – €1391 million = €541 million. Operating free cash flow is €1932 million – €373 million (purchase of intangible assets and PP&E, net of proceeds from sales of intangible assets and PP&E) = €1559 million. For 2008, free cash flow is €2158 million −€3766 million = −€1608 million. Operating free cash flow is €2158 million – €295 million = €1863 million. The operating free cash flow for 2009 is €3015 million – €180 million = €2835 million. The trend of this cash flow measure (from €1559 million in 2007 to €1863 million in 2008 to €2835 million in 2009) is almost certainly a better indicator of how performance evolved over the period than the unadjusted free cash figures (modestly positive in 2007 to hugely negative in 2008 and hugely positive in 2009).

A critical assumption underlying the above analysis is that operating, investing, and financing cash flows are easily and neatly defined. Unfortunately, cash flows do not always fit clearly into one of the three categories. For example, there is some ambiguity over the proper treatment of securitized receivables. Many companies package their receivables and sell them in the capital markets as securities, hence the term "securitized." In essence, a firm that securitizes its receivables is borrowing from investors, using the receivables as collateral for the loan. Given the financial nature of this transaction, it should be treated as a financing cash flow. But if the transaction is structured in the right way, securitization can be treated as a reduction in receivables (and in the working capital requirement), and thus as an increase in cash flow from operations. What this example teaches us is that cash flow statements can be manipulated, principally by redefining the boundaries that separate operations from investing and financing activities.

Key lessons from the chapter

- The statement of cash flows provides a view of the firm's performance independent of accruals.
- The statement summarizes cash inflows and outflows and, in so doing, reconciles beginning and ending cash. Because the statement is grounded in beginning and ending cash, two figures that are easy to verify, it is thought that the cash flow statement is harder to manipulate than the income statement or the balance sheet.
- The cash flow statement is prepared on the assumption that all cash flows result from three types of activities: operating, investing, and financing.

- Cash flows from operating activities are reported in either of two equivalent ways: the direct method or the indirect method. As of this writing, the overwhelming majority of companies use the indirect approach.
- The analysis of the statement of cash flows focuses on two fundamental issues: the relationship between net income and cash flow from operations, and the relationship between operating, investing, and financing cash flows.
- An alternative definition of free cash flow, known as free operating cash flow, deducts only capital expenditures from CFFO, ignoring other investing transactions. This metric is generally preferred to free cash flow for internal control purposes.
- Although beginning and ending cash must be reconciled, the cash flow statement can be manipulated. Efforts to manipulate focus on redefining the boundaries between operating cash flows on one hand, and investing or financing cash flows on the other.

Key terms and concepts from the chapter

Direct method	Financing cash flows	Working capital
Indirect method	Operating cycle	requirement
Operating cash flows	Cash to cash cycle	Free cash flows
Investing cash flows		

Questions

1. What are the primary uses of the statement of cash flows? Why aren't the statement of financial position (or balance sheet) and the income statement sufficient?

2. Define operating, investing, and financing cash flows.

3. Describe the major elements of a "cash flow profile."

4. What is the indirect method for determining CFFO, and how does it differ from the direct method? Which method is more common?

5. What are the primary causes for differences between net income and CFFO?

6. How can a company report positive net income, but CFFO for the same year is negative?

7. How can a company report a net loss, but CFFO for the same year is positive?

8. Which figure would you expect to be higher for most companies most of the time: net income or CFFO? Why?

9. One argument given for the statement of cash flows is that it is less subject to manipulation than the income statement. Do you agree with this view?

10. Under US GAAP, cash spent on interest is classified as an operating activity but cash spent on dividends is classified as a financing activity. Explain the paradox.

11. What is meant by the terms "negative free cash flows"and "positive free cash flows"? What are the managerial implications in either case?

12. True or false: a firm in a strong growth stage of development is more likely to have negative free cash flow than a more mature firm.

13. Why might an investor not put much weight on a firm's current free cash flow as an indicator of future free cash flow?

14. Why might changes in provisions appear as an item in the operations section of the statement?

15. What does "working capital requirement" mean, and what impact does it have on the statement of cash flows?

16. When total cash inflows exceed total cash outflows, or vice versa, how is the difference reflected on the statement of cash flows?

Problems

5.1   Interpreting the statement of cash flows

Exhibit 5.5 contains three years of cash flow statements from Massa Corporation.

Exhibit 5.5   Massa Corporation consolidated statements of cash flows ($millions)

	2011	2010	2009
Operating activities			
Loss from continuing operations	$(377.9)	$(623.5)	$(320.6)
Depreciation	168.4	220.1	263.4
Amortization of capitalized software	41.4	58.2	39.1
Gain from sale of investments and other assets	(16.6)	(119.0)	–
Restructuring and other unusual items, net	135.5	384.1	125.3
Changes in other accounts affecting operations			
Accounts receivable	160.8	73.4	(45.2)
Inventory	80.2	100.9	(3.0)
Other current assets	17.0	(1.2)	(13.0)
Accounts payable and other current liabilities	(91.3)	(21.3)	41.0
Other	2.8	14.1	(10.5)
Net cash provided by continuing operations	120.3	85.8	76.5
Net cash provided by (used in) discontinued operations	4.9	3.5	(29.7)
Net cash provided by operating activities	125.2	89.3	46.8
Investing activities			
Investment in depreciable assets	(129.7)	(174.4)	(303.6)
Proceeds from disposal of depreciable and other assets	157.0	242.0	94.1
Proceeds from the sale of discontinued operations	25.3	407.3	–
Investment in capitalized software	(27.8)	(43.1)	(59.5)
Other	(6.0)	(13.0)	14.2
Net cash provided by (used in) investing activities	18.8	418.8	(254.8)
Financing activities			
(Decrease) increase in short-term borrowings	(2.6)	(222.6)	139.8
Proceeds from long-term debt	44.4	167.7	305.0
Payments of long-term debt	(126.5)	(544.8)	(91.7)
Proceeds from sale of common stock	5.0	8.7	17.5
Purchase of treasury stock	(0.3)	(0.6)	(18.8)

(*Continued*)

Exhibit 5.5   Continued

	2011	2010	2009
Dividends paid	–	(7.2)	(26.0)
Net cash provided by (used in) financing activities	(80.0)	(598.8)	(325.8)
Effect of changes in foreign exchange rates	0.1	1.1	(3.9)
Increase (decrease) in cash equivalents	64.1	(89.6)	113.9
Cash and equivalents at beginning of year	169.1	258.7	144.8
Cash and equivalents at end of year	$233.2	$169.1	$258.7

Required

Answer the following questions:

(a) For each year:
1. What were the firm's major sources of cash? Its major uses of cash?
2. Was cash flow from operations greater or less than net income? Explain in detail the major reasons for the difference between these two figures.
3. Was the firm able to generate enough cash from operations to pay for all of its capital expenditures?
4. Did the cash flow from operations cover both the capital expenditures and the firm's dividend payments, if any?
5. If it did, how did the firm invest its excess cash?
6. If not, what were the sources of cash the firm used to pay for the capital expenditures and/or dividends?
7. Were the working capital accounts primarily sources of cash, or users of cash?
8. What other major items affected cash flows?

(b) What was the trend over the three years in:
9. Net income?
10. Cash flow from (continuing) operations?
11. Capital expenditures?
12. Dividends?
13. Net borrowing (proceeds less payments of short- and long-term debt)?
14. Working capital accounts?

(c) Based on the evidence in the statement of cash flows alone, what is your assessment of the financial strength of this business? Be as specific as possible in your assessment.

5.2   Adjustments on the statement of cash flows

The 2003 Annual Report of McDonald's includes the following note:

> In 2003, the $272.1 million of charges consisted of: $237.0 million related to the loss on the sale of Donatos Pizzeria, the closing of Donatos and Boston Market restaurants outside the US and the exit of a domestic joint venture with Fazoli's; and $35.1 million related to the revitalization plan actions of McDonald's Japan, including headcount reductions, the closing of Pret A Manger stores in Japan, and the early termination of a long-term management services agreement.
>
> In 2002, the $266.9 million of net charges consisted of: $201.4 million related to the anticipated transfer of ownership in five countries in the Middle East and Latin America to developmental licensees and ceasing operations in two countries in Latin America; $80.5 million primarily related to eliminating approximately 600 positions (about half of which were in the US and half of which were in international markets), reallocating resources and consolidating certain home office facilities to control costs; and a $15.0 million favorable adjustment to the 2001 restructuring charge due to lower employee-related costs than originally anticipated.

Required

(a) McDonald's reports cash flows from operating activities using the indirect method. How would the $237.0 million loss in 2003 for the sale of Donatos and other be reported on the company's statement of cash flows? Why?

(b) Explain how the $15.0 million favorable adjustment to the 2001 restructuring charge is accounted on each of the three principal financial statements for 2002.

5.3   Preparing and analyzing a statement of cash flows

Allen Company produces roofing supplies and insulation materials for use in home and commercial construction. Although Allen has been growing, recent lack of production capacity has caused production delays, some stockouts of finished goods, and a shift in the inventory mix from finished goods to raw materials and work in process. Allen Company's comparative balance sheet data and additional information follow (note that 2012 is the year listed first in the presentation):

Allen Company comparative balance sheet		
	2012	**2011**
Assets		
Cash	$108,000	$60,000
Accounts receivable, net	320,000	235,000

(*Continued*)

Allen Company comparative balance sheet

	2012	2011
Inventory	450,000	510,000
Prepaid expenses	27,000	30,000
Total current assets	905,000	835,000
Investments in affiliates	200,000	100,000
Property, plant, and equipment	1,100,000	950,000
Less accumulated depreciation	(440,000)	(370,000)
Intangible assets	35,000	45,000
Total assets	$1,800,000	$1,560,000
Liabilities and shareholders' equity		
Accounts payable	$554,000	$400,000
Accrued liabilities	36,000	38,000
Total current liabilities	590,000	438,000
Long-term notes payable	380,000	100,000
Contributed capital	710,000	750,000
Retained earnings	120,000	272,000
Total liabilities and shareholders' equity	$1,800,000	$1,560,000

The following additional information is available:

- The company's stock has no par or stated value. Contributed capital is shown as one amount (i.e., no distinction between common stock and capital in excess of par).
- Net loss for the year was $110 000.
- The intangible assets have limited lives and were amortized by $10 000 during the year.
- Investment in affiliates represents equity method investments. The income statement reported $80 000 income from equity method investments. $10 000 dividends were received from affiliates. Remaining changes in the account relate to additional investments.
- Less efficient equipment with an original cost of $200 000 was sold during the year for $40 000. The accumulated depreciation on that equipment was $130 000.
- Cash dividends of $12 000 were declared and paid during the year. The company also declared and distributed a $30 000 stock dividend during the year.
- The company repurchased the stock of a dissident shareholder during the year and retired the shares. The company paid $70 000 (which was the original issue price of the shares).
- No long-term notes were retired during the year.

Required

(a) Prepare a statement of cash flows for 2012.
(b) Discuss the relationship between net income and cash flow from operations and the relationship among cash flow from operating, investing, and financing activities during the two years. Be as specific as the data allow.
(c) Identify two conditions in the operating section of the statement which point to the possibility that cash flow from operations might decline next year.

5.4 Interpreting the role of accounts payable in cash flow from operations

AB InBev is the world's largest brewer. An abbreviated version of the operating activities section of the company's statement of cash flows appears below:

Cash flows from operating activities (million US dollars)	**2011**	**2010**
Profit	7,959	5,762
Interest, taxes and noncash items included in profit	7,420	8,503
Cash flow from operating activities before changes in working capital and use of provisions	15,379	14,265
Change in working capital	1,409	226
Pension contributions and use of provisions	(710)	(519)
Interest and taxes (paid)/received	(3,998)	(4,450)
Dividends received	406	383
Cash flow from operating activities	12,486	9,905

Elsewhere in the annual report, management reveals that trade payables increased in 2011 because of higher capital expenditures. Also, these payables have, on average, longer payment terms than payables from previous years.

Required

Explain why the increase in payables and the change in payment terms contributed to the increased in cash flow from operations in 2011. What other factors contributed to the increase?

5.5   Manipulating the statement of cash flows

You are the company's chief financial officer. It is early December, and your accountants have produced financial statements showing provisional results for the year. (Your company's fiscal year ends on 31 December.) You show these to the CEO who then expresses concern about several figures. One figure in particular, cash flow from operations (CFFO), appears low. The CEO wonders if anything can be done before the end of the year to increase it.

Which of the following actions will increase CFFO this year? Which of these actions do you consider appropriate, which are inappropriate, and why?

(a) The company sells €2 million of accounts receivable for 97% of face value to a bank. The receivables are sold "with recourse," which means that the company must reimburse the bank for any amount not collected beyond 3% of total receivables.

(b) Social charges are due on employees' wages at the end of the year. The firm can delay these payments by a few days so that they are made at the beginning of the following year.

(c) The company can work out a deal with some of its customers in which the customers buy goods now, for cash, but they can receive a full refund after the beginning of the next year.

(d) A training program is moved from the final month of the current year to the first month of the following year.

(e) Routine maintenance is delayed on machinery and equipment until early next year.

(f) The company delays the purchase of a new forklift until the beginning of next year.

5.6   Analysis of the statement of cash flows

The statements of cash flows shown below are from an anonymous IFRS-compliant Swedish company:

	Notes	2008 SKK 000s	2007 SKK 000s
Profit before tax		3,398,589	8,280,786
Adjustments to reconcile profit before tax to net cash provided by operating activities			
Depreciation, depletion, amortization and impairment		2,960,276	3,044,376

	Notes	2008 SKK 000s	2007 SKK 000s
Amortization of government grants and assets acquired free-of-charge	19	(38,395)	(52,375)
Write-off of inventories and reversal of impairment of inventories		(42,350)	11,844
Increase/(decrease) in provisions for liabilities and charges, net		8,885	(334,580)
Profit from the sale of intangible assets and property, plant and equipment	19	(18,452)	(334,412)
Write-off of receivables		10,727	14,998
Profit from the sale of available-for-sale financial assets and subsidiaries		–	(108,503)
Impairment of available-for-sale financial assets	23	826,305	–
Unrealized foreign exhcnage gain on receivables and payables		(70,332)	(35,702)
Other unrealized foreign exchange losses	23	138,509	128,892
Interest revenue	23	(63,913)	(148,142)
Interest expense on borrowings	23	42,267	9,481
Other financial (profit)/loss, net		(39,127)	21,865
Dividends received	23	(1,063,522)	(70,165)
Other non cash terms		(20,458)	10,030
Operating cash flow before changes in working capital		**6,029,009**	**10,438,393**
Decrease/(increase) in inventories		1,970,942	(418,799)
Decrease/(increase) in trade receivables		4,156,154	(1,013,185)
Decrease/(increase) in other current assets		784,466	(1,614,350)
(Decrease)/increase in trade payables		(4,702,919)	2,015,695
Increase in other current liabilities		57,158	182,186
Corporate income tax paid		(1,563,485)	(536,326)
Net cash provided by operating activities		**6,731,325**	**9,053,614**
Capital expenditures		(4,227,547)	(2,891,865)
Proceeds from disposals of intangible assets and property, plant and equipment		34,168	395,845
Acquired subsidiaries	4	(200)	(263,856)
Acquired associated companies and joint ventures	5	–	(29,679)
Purchase of available-for-sale financial assets	6	(2)	–
Net cash inflow on sale of subsidiary undertakings		–	7,229
Short-term loans repaid, net		876,116	1,377,293

(Continued)

	Notes	2008 SKK 000s	2007 SKK 000s
Interest received and other financial income		68,293	154,345
Dividends received and income from the decrease of share capital		1,526,861	105,973
Net cash used in investing activities		**(1,722,311)**	**(1,144,715)**
Proceeds from long-term bank borrowings		2,000,000	–
Repayments of long-term bank borrowings		(2,000,000)	–
Proceeds from/(repayments of) short-term bank borrowings, net		32,763	(85,200)
Net proceeds from short-term nonbank borrowings		–	6,698
Net proceeds/(payments) from derivative transactions	23	39,125	(20,542)
Interest paid and other financial costs		(40,118)	(8,051)
Dividends paid to shareholders of the parent company		(5,419,287)	(7,367,795)
Dividends paid to minority shareholders		(83,422)	(112,735)
Net cash used in financing activities		**(5,470,939)**	**(7,587,625)**
(Decrease)/increase in cash and cash equivalents		**(461,925)**	**321,274**
Cash and cash equivalents at the beginning of the period	11	1,935,789	1,672,716
Effects of exchange rate changes		(66,064)	(58,201)
Cash and cash equivalents at the end of the period	11	1,407,800	1,935,789

Required

(a) What are the company's major sources of cash?

(b) What are the company's major uses of cash?

(c) Were "depreciation, depletion, amortization and impairment" sources or uses of cash in each of the two years shown? Explain.

(d) Does the company's productive capacity appear to be increasing or declining in each of the two years depicted on the statement? Support your answer.

(e) Were the components of the working capital requirement a net source or use of cash in the most recent year? Support your answer.

(f) What does the amount (42 350) shown in the 2008 column (i.e., the fourth line item) refer to? Explain.

(g) What is your overall assessment of the company's situation (e.g., its apparent life-cycle stage, recent performance, changes to its financial structure, etc.) for the years presented?

5.7   Cash flow and credit risk

Taipei-based Tang Manufacturing has a $1.45 million bank loan that starts coming due in a year, and the loan officer at the local bank has asked for cash budgets to be reassured that the company can repay the debt on schedule. Management has prepared quarterly cash flow forecasts for each of the next six quarters, excerpts of which are produced in the table below. Also worth noting is that much of Tang's equipment and machinery is dated, and therefore long overdue for replacement.

	Q1	Q2	Q3	Q4	Q5	Q6
Scheduled loan payments					$725,000	$725,000
Forecasted cash flows						
Cash flow from operations	$290,000	$362,500	$435,000	$348,000	$290,000	$319,000
Capital expenditures	217,500		217,500		253,750	
Dividends					72,500	

Required

(a) Why might Tang's loan officer be concerned about the company's ability to repay the loan?
(b) What steps can Tang management take to reduce the bank's risk on the loan?

5.8   Preparing and interpreting the statement of cash flows

The annual reports from Year 7 and Year 8 of The GAP, a global clothing retailer, indicate the following changes in its balance sheet accounts (amounts in millions):

	Year 7	Year 8
Cash	$ 2 decrease	$428 increase
Marketable securities (current asset)	46 decrease	46 decrease
Merchandise inventories	96 increase	154 increase
Prepaid expenses	1 increase	56 increase
Property, plant and equipment (at cost)	372 increase	466 increase

(*Continued*)

	Year 7	Year 8
Accumulated depreciation	215 increase	270 increase
Other noncurrent assets	51 increase	15 increase
Accounts payable	114 increase	134 increase
Notes payable to banks (current liability)	18 increase	45 increase
Income taxes payable	26 increase	7 decrease
Other current liabilities	90 increase	123 increase
Bonds payable	—	577 increase
Common stock	360 decrease	524 decrease
Retained earnings	369 increase	455 increase

Abbreviated income statements for The GAP appear below:

	Year 7	Year 8
Sales	$5,284	$6,508
Cost of goods sold	−3,285	−4,022
Selling and administrative expenses	−1,250	−1,632
Income tax expense	−296	−320
Net income	$453	$534

Additional data:

- The cash balance was $486 at the end of Year 7 and $914 at the end of Year 8.
- The firm did not sell property, plant and equipment in either year.
- Changes in other noncurrent assets resulted from investing activities.

Required

(a) Prepare statements of cash flows for Year 7 and Year 8.
(b) Comment on the relationship between net income and cash flow from operations, and on the relationship between operating, investing, and financing cash flows. Compare Year 7 with Year 8.

Case studies

5.1   Blockbuster Inc.: movie rentals, profits, and operating cash

Ronald Baker, a US equities analyst in the London office of Homeguard Investments, has a problem. The stock of Blockbuster, Inc., the video rental chain, has done well over the last six months. (See Exhibit 5.6.) Because this company is not one that Ronald tracks on a routine basis, he barely noticed the move. But a brief correction over the past two weeks has led several clients to ask if the recent dip in price created a good buying opportunity.

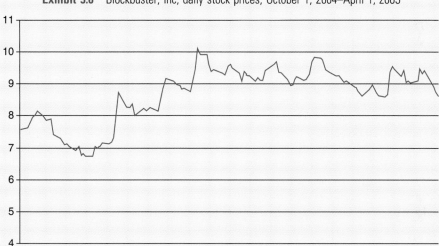

Exhibit 5.6   Blockbuster, Inc, daily stock prices, October 1, 2004–April 1, 2005

   Ronald's dilemma is caused by one simple fact: Blockbuster is not a profitable company, and hasn't been for years. (See Exhibit 5.7.) Still, the operating cash flows are positive and, from first appearances, strongly so. Blockbuster's cash flow performance is what appears to be supporting the share price. But Ronald's intuition is telling him that negative earnings and positive operating cash cannot go on forever. If earnings incorporate cash flows and accruals, and accruals are really nothing more than future cash flows, shouldn't we be seeing negative cash flows too? Or are the losses the result of excessively conservative accounting? Either way, Ronald needs an answer.

Blockbuster: a general overview

Blockbuster (NYSE: BBI) is the world's largest video rental chain with about 9000 company-owned and franchised stores in 25 countries. Founded in 1982, and head-quartered in Dallas, Texas, the company rents more than 1 billion videos, DVDs, and video games each year. In 2004, the company launched Blockbuster Online, in response to the growing popularity of Netflix. Later that year, entertainment giant Viacom, Blockbuster's majority shareholder, spun off its entire stake in a public sale.[9] But where Viacom had seen only chronic unprofitability, others saw value. Carl Icahn, the well-known financier, still owns about 9% of the company. Ronald thought that if a famously uncompromising investor like Icahn had retained a large stake, there must be something positive about Blockbuster. But the closer he looked the more worried he became.

In December 2004, Blockbuster announced the "end of late fees," effective 1 January 2005, which means no more extended viewing fees on any movie or game rental at more than 4500 company-operated stores and approximately 550 participating franchise stores in the US. A similar program was planned for its 426 stores in Canada. Ronald viewed this move with some skepticism, believing that it was unlikely to improve the company's operating margins. First, the marketing campaign was costly. Second, late fees have been an important source of revenue. In fact, the company admits that between $250 million and $300 million of operating income would be lost as a direct result of the move. Ronald thought that the figure might even be higher. Of course, Blockbuster hoped the loss would be partially offset by growth in other revenues. Third, Ronald was concerned about the effect of the move on Blockbuster's relations with franchisees. If late fees were an important source of revenue for Blockbuster, the same must be true for franchise stores. Will franchisees continue to offer their cooperation in an effort that will clearly affect, in a significantly negative way, their own bottom line? Ronald suspects that many will opt out, including some who have already agreed to participate.

In Ronald's view, the end-of-late-fees initiative was a sign of weakness, prompted by stagnating sales in the US. In addition, sales have declined in several international markets. On the plus side, video game rentals are growing, but the market is highly cyclical and prone to changes in technology. Also, video games have significantly higher prices than DVDs, which means that even hit game titles generate much lower volume than hit movies. These observations imply that game rentals are unlikely to make up for the flat growth in movie rentals.

Exhibit 5.7   Financial statements Blockbuster, Inc.: From the 2004 Annual Report

BLOCKBUSTER INC.

CONSOLIDATED STATEMENTS OF OPERATIONS

(In millions, except per share amounts)

	Year Ended December 31,		
	2004	**2003**	**2002**
		Restated	**Restated**
Revenues:			
Base rental revenues...	$3,806.2	$3,811.4	$3,720.9
Extended viewing fee revenues...	622.4	722.1	739.5
Total rental revenues...	4,428.6	4,533.5	4,460.4
Merchandise sales	1,532.6	1,281.6	1,019.7
Other revenues	92.0	96.6	85.8
	6,053.2	5,911.7	5,565.9
Cost of sales:			
Cost of rental revenues..	1,250.7	1,362.1	1,513.8
Cost of merchandise sold	1,190.7	1,027.7	844.9
	2,441.4	2,389.8	2,358.7
Gross profit	3,611.8	3,521.9	3,207.2
Operating expenses:			
General and administrative...	2,835.2	2,605.9	2,369.5
Share-based compensation...	18.3	—	—
Advertising..	257.4	179.4	249.2
Depreciation..	247.4	266.0	239.1
Impairment of goodwill and other long-lived assets..............................	1,504.4	1,304.9	—
Amortization of intangibles	2.3	2.4	1.7
	4,865.0	4,358.6	2,859.5
Operating income (loss)	(1,253.2)	(836.7)	347.7
Interest expense..	(38.1)	(33.1)	(49.5)
Interest income...	3.6	3.1	4.1
Other items, net	1.6	(0.4)	2.9

(Continued)

Exhibit 5.7 Continued

	Year Ended December 31,		
	2004	**2003**	**2002**
		Restated	**Restated**
Income (loss) before income taxes	(1,286.1)	(867.1)	305.2
Benefit (provision) for income taxes	37.3	(106.5)	(107.1)
Equity in loss of affiliated companies, net of tax	—	(0.7)	(2.2)
Income (loss) before cumulative effect of change in accounting principle	(1,248.8)	(974.3)	195.9
Cumulative effect of change in accounting principle, net of tax	—	(4.4)	(1,817.0)
Net loss	$(1,248.8)	$(978.7)	$(1,621.1)
Income (loss) per share before cumulative effect of change in accounting principle:			
Basic	$(6.89)	$(5.41)	$1.10
Diluted	$(6.89)	$(5.41)	$1.08
Cumulative effect of change in accounting principle per share:			
Basic	$—	$(0.02)	$(10.17)
Diluted	$—	$(0.02)	$(10.01)
Net loss per share:			
Basic	$(6.89)	$(5.43)	$(9.08)
Diluted	$(6.89)	$(5.43)	$(8.93)
Weighted average shares outstanding:			
Basic	181.2	180.1	178.6
Diluted	181.2	180.1	181.6
Recurring cash dividends per common share	$0.08	$0.08	$0.08
Special distribution per common share	$5.00	$—	$—

BLOCKBUSTER INC.
CONSOLIDATED BALANCE SHEETS
(In millions, except per share amounts)

	December 31,	
	2004	**2003**
		Restated
Assets		
Current assets:		
Cash and cash equivalents	$330.3	$233.4
Receivables, less allowances of $14.5 and $13.0 for 2004 and 2003, respectively	177.8	183.7
Merchandise inventories	516.6	415.1
Prepaid and other current assets	193.0	128.1
Total current assets	1,217.7	960.3
Rental library	457.6	354.4
Receivable from Viacom, net	2.6	3.5
Property and equipment, net	854.0	787.3
Deferred tax asset	87.0	—
Intangibles, net	34.5	34.4
Goodwill	1,138.5	2,627.7
Other assets	71.5	54.4
	$3,863.4	$4,822.0
Liabilities and Stockholders' Equity		
Current liabilities:		
Accounts payable	$721.8	$565.1
Accrued expenses	697.3	610.2
Current portion of long-term debt	5.8	124.1
Current portion of capital lease obligations	19.7	20.7
Deferred taxes	4.8	3.3
Total current liabilities	1,449.4	1,323.4
Long-term debt, less current portion	1,044.9	0.7
Capital lease obligations, less current portion	74.8	74.4
Deferred taxes	—	9.3
Deferred rent liability	69.2	71.1
Other liabilities	162.2	154.7
	2,800.5	1,633.6

Commitments and contingencies (Note 9)

(Continued)

	December 31,	
	2004	**2003**
		Restated
Stockholders' equity:		
Preferred stock, par value $0.01 per share: 100.0 shares authorized; no shares issued or outstanding	—	—
Class A common stock, par value $0.01 per share; 400.0 shares authorized; 111.7 and 36.9 shares issued and outstanding for 2004 and 2003, respectively	1.1	0.4
Class B common stock, par value $0.01 per share; 500.0 shares authorized; 72.0 and 144.0 shares issued and outstanding for 2004 and 2003, respectively	0.7	1.4
Additional paid-in capital	5,336.7	6,227.3
Retained deficit	(4,248.3)	(2,999.5)
Accumulated other comprehensive loss	(27.3)	(41.2)
Total stockholders' equity	1,062.9	3,188.4
	$3,863.4	$4,822.0

BLOCKBUSTER INC.
CONSOLIDATED STATEMENTS OF CHANGES IN STOCKHOLDERS'
EQUITY AND COMPREHENSIVE LOSS
(In millions)

	Year Ended December 31,					
	2004		**2003**		**2002**	
	Shares	**Amount**	**Shares**	**Amount**	**Shares**	**Amount**
			Restated		**Restated**	
Class A common stock:						
Balance, beginning of year	36.9	$0.4	35.6	$0.4	32.8	$0.3
Exercise of stock options	0.3	—	1.3	—	2.8	0.1
Issuance upon vesting of restricted shares....................................	2.5	—	—	—	—	—
Conversion from Class B common stock	72.0	0.7	—	—	—	—
Balance, end of year	111.7	1.1	36.9	0.4	35.6	0.4

	Year Ended December 31,					
	2004		**2003**		**2002**	
	Shares	**Amount**	**Shares**	**Amount**	**Shares**	**Amount**
				Restated		**Restated**
Class B common stock:						
Balance, beginning of year..................	144.0	$1.4	144.0	$1.4	144.0	$1.4
Conversion to Class A common stock..................................	(72.0)	(0.7)	—	—	—	—
Balance, end of year	72.0	$0.7	144.0	$1.4	144.0	$1.4
Additional paid-in capital:						
Balance, beginning of year..................		$6,227.3		$6,220.8		$6,181.1
Issuance of class A common stock.....		0.1		0.1		0.1
Exercise and expense of share-based compensation, net of tax benefit........		10.0		20.8		53.9
Net issuance of Class A common stock upon vesting of restricted shares...		10.7		—		—
Acceleration of Viacom stock options...		1.7		—		—
Viacom capital contribution		7.0		—		—
Recurring cash dividends.....................		(14.5)		(14.4)		(14.3)
Special distribution		(905.6)		—		—
Balance, end of year		$5,336.7		$6,227.3		$6,220.8
Accumulated other comprehensive loss:						
Balance, beginning of year..................		$(41.2)		$(100.9)		$(107.0)
Other comprehensive income (loss):						
Change in fair value of interest rate swaps, net of taxes............................		—		6.3		2.0
Foreign currency translation............		13.9		53.4		4.1
Balance, end of year		$(27.3)		$(41.2)		$(100.9)
Retained deficit:						
Balance at December 31, 2001, as previously reported..........................						$(327.1)
Cumulative effect of restatement for lease accounting (see Note 1)........						(72.6)
Balance, beginning of year, as restated..		$(2,999.5)		$(2,020.8)		$(399.7)

(Continued)

	Year Ended December 31,					
	2004		**2003**		**2002**	
	Shares	**Amount**	**Shares**	**Amount**	**Shares**	**Amount**
				Restated		**Restated**
Net loss		$(1,248.8)		$(978.7)		$(1,621.1)
Balance, end of year		$(4,248.3)		$(2,999.5)		$(2,020.8)
Total stockholders' equity		$1,062.9		$3,188.4		$4,100.9
Comprehensive loss:						
Net loss		$(1,248.8)		$(978.7)		$(1,621.1)
Other comprehensive income (loss): Change in fair value of interest rate swaps, net of taxes		—		6.3		2.0
Foreign currency translation............		13.9		53.4		4.1
Total comprehensive loss...................		$(1,234.9)		$(919.0)		$(1,615.0)

BLOCKBUSTER INC.
CONSOLIDATED STATEMENTS OF CASH FLOWS
(In millions)

	Year Ended December 31,		
	2004	**2003**	**2002**
		Restated	**Restated**
Cash flows from operating activities:			
Net loss	$(1,248.8)	$(978.7)	$(1,621.1)
Adjustments to reconcile net loss to net cash flow provided by operating activities:			
Depreciation and amortization.....................................	249.7	268.4	240.8
Impairment of goodwill and other long-lived assets ..	1,504.4	1,304.9	—
Rental library amortization	748.0	954.8	1,024.3
Non-cash share-based compensation expense	17.0	—	—
Excess tax benefit from share-based compensation ...	(5.1)	—	—
Cumulative effect of change in accounting principle, net of tax...	—	4.4	1,817.0
Deferred taxes and other	(94.3)	(73.5)	18.3

	Year Ended December 31,		
	2004	**2003**	**2002**
		Restated	**Restated**
Change in operating assets and liabilities:			
(Increase) decrease in receivables	8.6	5.9	(27.8)
Decrease in receivable from Viacom	0.8	14.0	82.9
(Increase) decrease in merchandise inventories	(84.2)	55.1	(221.8)
Increase in prepaid and other assets	(97.5)	(4.8)	(38.7)
Increase (decrease) in accounts payable	125.4	(221.9)	187.6
Increase in accrued expenses and other liabilities	91.4	101.7	0.8
Net cash flow provided by operating activities	1,215.4	1,430.3	1,462.3
Cash flows from investing activities:			
Rental library purchases	(798.4)	(836.6)	(1,060.9)
Capital expenditures	(289.1)	(191.0)	(151.7)
Cash used for acquisitions	(25.5)	(3.4)	(106.0)
Proceeds from notes receivable and other	1.2	4.5	3.6
Investments in affiliated companies	(0.5)	1.9	0.4
Net cash flow used for investing activities	(1,112.3)	(1,024.6)	(1,314.6)
Cash flows from financing activities:			
Proceeds from credit agreements	820.0	140.0	170.0
Proceeds from senior subordinated notes	300.0	—	—
Repayments on credit agreements	(170.0)	(450.0)	(360.0)
Net repayments on other notes and lines of credit	(23.8)	(5.8)	(10.1)
Net proceeds from the exercise of stock options	2.8	18.1	39.3
Cash dividends	(920.1)	(14.4)	(14.3)
Payment of debt financing costs	(18.7)	—	—
Capital lease payments	(21.0)	(23.4)	(24.1)
Capital contributions received from Viacom	6.9	—	—
Excess tax benefit from share-based compensation	5.1	—	—
Net cash flow used for financing activities	(18.8)	(335.5)	(199.2)
Effect of exchange rate changes on cash	12.6	10.7	3.8
Net increase (decrease) in cash and cash equivalents	96.9	80.9	(47.7)
Cash and cash equivalents at beginning of year	233.4	152.5	200.2
Cash and cash equivalents at end of year	$330.3	$233.4	$152.5
Supplemental cash flow information:			
Cash payments for interest	$23.2	$34.3	$45.8
Cash payments for taxes	44.4	98.1	12.6
Non-cash financing and investing activities:			
Retail stores acquired under capital leases	20.4	15.4	15.3

Blockbuster's rental library

Ronald figured that if he was to understand the true profitability and cash flow generation of Blockbuster, he would have to learn something about Blockbuster's core product – namely, the video library that served as the basis for its rental income.

The company purchases its movie rental inventory directly from the film studios or from third-party distributors on both a title-by-title basis and through various revenue-sharing arrangements. The number of domestic movie rental inventory units purchased under revenue sharing increased during 2004 to approximately 2/3 of total units purchased, up from half in 2003.

Revenue sharing requires the company to share an agreed-upon percentage of rental revenues with a studio for a limited period of time. The advantage to Blockbuster is the low initial price for the product. In effect, the studio's price is paid gradually as customers rent the film. Without revenue sharing, Blockbuster, and its franchisees, would struggle to purchase enough copies of popular films to satisfy customer demand. The upfront cost would create major cash flow problems, because the cost would have to be paid immediately to the studio while the revenues earned from customers would be generated over the ensuing months.

The rental library is reported on the balance sheet as a long-term asset, and purchases are classified as investing activities on the statement of cash flows. Movies and games in the library are amortized over periods ranging from 3 to 12 months, down to an estimated residual value of $2 to $5 per unit. Estimates surrounding the useful lives and residual values are continually evaluated.

The revenue-sharing arrangements complicate the accounting to some extent. The cost of rental product purchased pursuant to these arrangements equals the sum of the low initial cost and an estimate of the revenues to be shared with the studios. The portion of the capitalized film cost attributable to revenue sharing is not amortized, but expensed as the related revenue is earned. All other amounts in the rental film library, including the upfront cost and the price paid for any films not acquired under revenue-sharing arrangements, are amortized in the manner described above.

Required

(a) Focusing on the balance sheet and the statement of cash flows, do you agree with how Blockbuster accounts for its rental library? What logic might the company offer to defend its approach?

(b) How else might the company account for the rental library? What effects would the alternative approach have on the financial statements? Be specific.

(c) Regarding Blockbuster's cash flow performance, is Ronald right to worry, or is the company stronger than the earnings suggest?

5.2   Monahan Manufacturing: preparing and interpreting a statement of cash flows

Balance sheets for Monahan Manufacturing, Inc. appear in Exhibit 5.8. Additional information includes the following (all amounts in thousands):

Exhibit 5.8   Monahan Manufacturing, Inc.: balance sheets for December 31, 2011 and 2012 (in thousands of dollars)

	December 31	
	2011	**2012**
ASSETS		
Current Assets		
Cash	$1,790	$1,620
Accounts Receivables	4,730	5,260
Inventories	5,020	6,040
Total Current Assets	$11,540	$12,920
Noncurrent Assets		
Land	$2,970	$3,150
Buildings and Equipment	43,390	47,730
Accumulated Depreciation	19,870	21,820
Total Noncurrent Assets	$26,490	$29,060
Total Assets	$38,030	$41,980
LIABILITIES and SHAREHOLDERS' EQUITY		
Current Liablities		
Accounts Payable	$2,060	$2,790
Taxes Payable	1,370	1,450
Other Short-term Payables	2,940	3,630
Total Current Liabilities	$6,370	$7,870
Noncurrent Liabilities		
Long-term Loans	$9,920	$9,670
Shareholders' Equity		
Common Stock	$8,360	$8,520
Retained Earnings	13,380	15,920
Total Shareholders' Equity	$21,740	$24,440
Total Liabilities and Shareholders' Equity	$38,030	$41,980

- Net income for 2012 was $2840.
- Dividends declared and paid were $300.
- Depreciation expense on buildings and machinery was $2550 for the year.
- The firm sold for $125 machinery originally costing $750 and accumulated depreciation of $600.
- The firm retired bonds during the year at their book value.

Required

Prepare a statement of cash flows for Monahan Manufacturing for 2012 using the indirect method to compute cash flow from operations. Comment on the pattern of cash flows from operating, investing, and financing activities.

5.3   A tale of three companies: cash flows at Sun Microsystems, Wal-Mart, and Merck

Exhibits 5.9, 5.10, and 5.11 present five years of cash flow statements for Sun Microsystems, Wal-Mart, and Merck, respectively. Sales figures are also provided.

In the 1980s, Sun Microsystems was mainly a producer of computer workstations. By 1988 it was the industry leader, thanks largely to superior operating efficiencies and an ability to bring innovative products to market faster than its competitors. Founded in 1982, Sun went public in 1986.

Wal-Mart, a discount retail chain, was founded in 1962, becoming a publicly traded company in 1970. The company achieved its first billion-dollar sales year in 1979. Strategies in the 1980s centered on innovative practices in supply chain management and in the use of information technology, combined with aggressive price competition. The company also embarked on a massive store-building campaign.

Merck was founded in 1891 as the US subsidiary of a German chemical and pharmaceutical company, becoming independent of its parent during World War I. Over the ensuing decades, Merck became a fully integrated, multinational producer of pharmaceutical products. The company has long depended heavily on its research efforts, funded in-house and through joint ventures, to develop innovative, patent-protected drugs. Throughout the 1980s, Merck was consistently among the top three drugs companies in the world.

During the observation period, macroeconomic performance was robust, as shown by real GDP growth rates in the US:

1984	7.2%
1985	4.1%
1986	3.5%
1987	3.4%
1988	4.1%

Exhibit 5.9   Sun Microsystems statement of cash flows (amounts in millions)

	1984	1985	1986	1987	1988
Operations					
Net income	$3	$9	$12	$36	$66
Depreciation	1	4	6	25	51
Working capital provided by operations	$4	$13	$18	$61	$117
(Inc.) decr. in receivables	−9	−5	−24	−58	−117
(Inc.) decr. in inventories	−8	−8	−21	−32	−77
(Inc.) decr. in other current assets	−1	−1	−18	−31	−30
Inc. (decr.) in accounts payable – trade	4	4	21	33	58
Inc. (decr.) in other current liabilities	2	9	6	35	52
Cash flow from operations	$−8	$12	$−18	$8	$3
Investing					
Fixed assets acquired	$−5	$−15	$−36	$−76	$−117
Other investing transactions	0	−2	−2	−23	−32
Cash flow from investing	$−5	$−17	$−38	$−99	$-149
Financing					
Incr. short-term borrowing	$1	$3	$11	$21	$0
Incr. long-term borrowing	3	5	1	121	0
Issue of capital stock	11	21	47	96	63
Decr. short-term borrowing	0	0	0	0	−6
Decr. long-term borrowing	0	−1	−2	0	0
Other financing transactions	0	3	3	0	0
Cash flow from financing	$15	$31	$60	$238	$57
Change in cash	$2	$26	$4	$147	$−89
Sales (in millions of $)	NA	115	210	538	1,052

NA = not available.

Exhibit 5.10 Wal-Mart statement of cash flows (amounts in millions)

	1984	1985	1986	1987	1988
Operations					
Net income	$271	$327	$450	$628	$837
Depreciation	67	90	124	166	214
Other addbacks	9	18	7	0	1
Other subtractions	0	0	0	−1	0
Working capital provided by operations	$347	$435	$581	$793	$1,052
(Inc.) decr. in receivables	−6	−12	−33	−6	−31
(Inc.) decr. in inventories	−368	−284	−643	−575	−700
(Inc.) decr. in other current assets	−77	−12	−8	−0	−6
Inc. (decr.) in accounts payable – trade	161	287	229	127	290
Inc. (decr.) in other current liabilities	22	16	139	120	129
Cash flow from operations	$79	$430	$265	$459	$734
Investing					
Fixed assets acquired	$−322	$−513	$−675	$−757	$−797
other investing transactions	148	−160	−4	−51	9
Cash flow from investing	$−174	$−673	$−679	$−808	$−788
Financing					
Incr. short-term borrowing	$0	$0	$0	$104	$0
Incr. long-term borrowing	129	298	460	194	248
Issue of capital stock	6	5	6	7	4
Decr. short-term borrowing	0	0	0	0	−85
Decr. long-term borrowing	−16	−12	−13	−42	−21
Acquisition of capital stock	−1	−1	0	0	0
Dividends	−30	−40	−48	−68	−91
Cash flow from financing	$88	$250	$405	$195	$55
Change in cash	$−7	$7	$−9	$−154	$1
Sales (in millions of $)	6,401	8,451	11,909	15,959	20,649

Exhibit 5.11   Merck and Company statement of cash flows (amounts in millions)

	1984	1985	1986	1987	1988
Operations					
Net income	$493	$540	$676	$906	$1,207
Depreciation and amort..	162	182	194	210	205
Other addbacks..	130	86	37	0	0
Other subtractions	0	0	0	−66	−245
Working capital provided by operations	$785	$808	$907	$1,050	$1,167
(Inc.) decr. in receivables	−102	−53	−42	−170	−106
(Inc.) decr. in inventories.....................................	0	22	−35	−80	−14
(Inc.) decr. in other cash	29	−1	0	0	0
Inc. (decr.) accounts payable – trade......................	78	81	98	144	−77
Inc. (decr.) in other current liabilities	−49	152	166	379	417
Cash flow from operations.....................................	$741	$1,009	$1,094	$1,322	$1,387
Investing					
Fixed assets sold...	$0	$92	$0	$0	$0
Fixed assets acquired...	−274	−238	−211	−254	−373
Other investing transactions...............................	119	−278	−126	−206	262
Cash flow from investing......................................	$−155	$−424	$−337	$−460	$−111
Financing					
Incr. short-term borrowing.................................	$38	$0	$43	$478	$0
Incr. long-term borrowing.................................	0	0	0	0	1,997
Issue of capital stock...	2	18	25	21	30
Decr. short-term borrowing.................................	0	−79	0	0	−392
Decr. long-term borrowing.................................	−206	−8	−3	0	−1,991
Acquisition of capital stock	−164	−242	−500	−1,000	0
Dividends..	−224	−235	−278	−335	−505
Other financing trans..	0	0	0	0	31
Cash flow from financing.....................................	$−554	$−546	$−713	$−836	$−830
Change in cash	$32	$39	$44	$27	$446
Sales (in millions of $)	3,560	3,548	4,128	5,061	5,940

Required

(a) Identify five distinctive characteristics for each of the three companies, based on their cash flow statements. Compare and contrast their cash flow profiles, focusing on free cash flow and on the relationship between cash flow from operations and net income.

(b) Which of these companies is the "most successful"? How did you arrive at your conclusion?

(c) What factors might account for differences in the cash flow profiles of these three companies, apart from differences in financial performance or efficiency?

5.4 Inditex: analyzing the statement of cash flows*

Industria de Diseño Textil, SA (commonly known as "Inditex") is a global specialty retailer with eight major brands: Zara, Pull & Bear, Massimo Dutti, Bershka, Stradivarius, Oysho, Zara Home, and Uterque. Its first store opened in 1975.

Despite the recent global economic downturn, the company has recently enjoyed successful results and a rising share price. The company currently has slightly more than 100 000 employees worldwide, with stores in 77 countries, including recent expansion into Bulgaria, India, and Kazakhstan.

According to its 2010 annual report, Inditex has identified the following operating priorities:

1. Customers
2. Stores
3. Design/production
4. Logistics
5. Teams.

Required

(a) In 2009 and 2010 which individual line item consumed the most cash according to the statement of cash flows?

(b) Where did the company obtain the cash to pay for the item identified in part (a)?

(c) Why is depreciation and amortization added back to income before taxes when calculating cash from operations?

(d) Review the subsection titled changes in assets and liabilities within the statement of cash flows. Note that for the individual line items listed as increase in inventories

---

*This case was prepared by Professor Daniel Bens, INSEAD.

and increase in accounts receivable the signs of the adjustments flip from FY2009 to FY2010 (i.e., added back in 2009 but deducted in 2010). What was the firm doing differently across the two years that caused the sign of the adjustments to flip?

(e) Review management's discussion of the historical results in 2010 as well as their forecast for 2011 and focus on their discussion of new store openings.

1. Does Inditex appear to be contracting or expanding its store presence?
2. Where on the statement of cash flows can one find information about the cash needed to open new outlets?
3. Focusing just on the historical data, compare the rate of depreciation and amortization to the level of capital expenditure. Does this analysis support the level of expansion described by management in the text disclosures?

(f) Review management's discussion on dividend policy. Consider these dividend plans in light of the expansion plans from part (e). Do these two strategies appear consistent?

(g) In the disclosures that follow, management makes the following statement:

"The operating working capital position remains negative, a consequence of the business model."

Then a table appears detailing this negative working capital position. How do you interpret this disclosure? That is, what operational decisions is management making and executing as part of their "business model" that leads to this result? Is it a good or a bad outcome?

1. PERFORMANCE IN FY2010

Figures expressed in millions of Euros

Net sales reached €12 527 million in FY2010, with sales growth of 13% (10% in local currencies).

In FY2010 INDITEX **retail space** increased 10%. Total selling area at FYE reached 2 587 648 square meters:

	31 Jan 2011	**31 Jan 2010**	**Chg % 10/09**
ZARA	1,687,949	1,541,291	10%
PULL & BEAR	196,320	175,574	12%
MASSIMO DUTTI	143,023	138,001	4%
BERSHKA	262,009	232,319	13%
STRADIVARIUS	154,253	133,062	16%
OYSHO	60,474	54,930	10%
ZARA HOME	72,748	65,761	11%
UTERQÜE	10,871	7,770	40%
Total	**2,587,648**	**2,348,709**	**10%**

Net store openings in FY2010 the year amounted to 437 reaching a total of 5044 stores in 77 countries. In FY2010 INDITEX has opened stores in 45 countries:

	Net openings	Total stores	
Concept	FY2010	31 January 2011	31 January 2010
ZARA	123	1,518	1,395
ZARA KIDS	(8)	205	213
PULL & BEAR	56	682	626
MASSIMO DUTTI	33	530	497
BERSHKA	69	720	651
STRADIVARIUS	78	593	515
OYSHO	40	432	392
ZARA HOME	23	284	261
UTERQÜE	23	80	57
Total	**437**	**5,044**	**4,607**

A list of quarterly openings and stores opened as at FYE by concept and by country is included in Annexes IV and V.

Like-for-like sales increased 3% in FY2010 (5% in 1H and 2% in 2H). The like-for-like calculation includes 81% of FY2010 store sales (i.e., sales in stores opened for the whole of fiscal years 2010 and 2009).

Net sales by concept in FY2010 and FY2009 are shown in the table below:

Concept	FY2010	FY2009	% Chg. 10/09
ZARA	8,088	7,077	14%
PULL & BEAR	857	771	11%
MASSIMO DUTTI	897	790	14%
BERSHKA	1,247	1,177	6%
STRADIVARIUS	780	702	11%
OYSHO	304	280	9%
ZARA HOME	294	243	21%
UTERQÜE	59	44	36%
Total sales	**12,527**	**11,084**	**13%**

The ongoing expansion of the Group has led to a widely diversified sales platform. All the concepts have increased their sales demonstrating their global scalability.

REGION	FY2010	FY2009
EUROPE EX-SPAIN	45%	46%
SPAIN	28%	32%
ASIA	15%	12%
AMERICAS	12%	10%
Total	100%	100%

Gross profit rose to €7422 million, 17% higher than the previous year. The Gross margin has reached 59.3% of sales (57.1% in FY2009).

Operating expenses have been tightly managed over the year and have grown by 12.6%, mainly as a result of the new retail space added and include all the start-up costs for new openings and €12 million for the launch of Zara e-commerce.

In millions of euros	FY2010	FY2009	Chg% 10/09
Personnel expenses	2,009	1,792	12%
Rental expenses	1,272	1,134	12%
Other operating expenses	1,171	1,027	14%
Total	**4,452**	**3,953**	**13%**

At FYE2010 the number of employees was 100 138 (92 301 at FYE2009).

FY2010 **EBITDA** came to €2966 million, 25% higher than the previous year, and EBIT to €2290 million, 33% higher.

The breakdown of EBIT by concept is shown below:

	Ebit by concept (in millions of euros)			% sales	% total
Concept	FY2010	FY2009	CHG% 10/09	FY2010	FY2010
ZARA	1,534	1,104	39%	19.0%	67.0%
PULL & BEAR	139	101	37%	16.2%	6.1%
MASSIMO DUTTI	172	117	47%	19.2%	7.5%
BERSHKA	197	196	1%	15.8%	8.6%
STRADIVARIUS	176	149	18%	22.5%	7.7%
OYSHO	45	38	19%	14.9%	2.0%
ZARA HOME	39	25	60%	13.3%	1.7%
UTERQÜE*	−12	−2	–	–	–
Total ebit	**2,290**	**1,728**	**33%**	**18.3%**	**100%**

*includes €12 million for accelerated depreciation of assets

The following chart shows the breakdown of Financial results.

In millions of euros	FY2010	FY2009
Net finance income (losses)	18	8
Foreign exchange gains (losses)	13	(5)
Total	**31**	**4**

Net income came to €1732 million, 32% higher than the previous year.

INDITEX's Board of Directors will propose to the General Shareholders Meeting a dividend increase of 33%, composed of an ordinary dividend of €1.40 per share and a bonus dividend of €0.20 per share, equating to a total dividend of €1.60 per share. €0.80 will be payable on 2 May 2011 as interim ordinary dividend and €0.80 would be payable on 2 November 2011 as final ordinary and bonus dividend.

INDITEX continued to show a strong financial condition over Fiscal 2010:

	31 January 2011	31 January 2010
Cash & cash equivalents	3,433	2,420
Current financial debt	(3)	(35)
Non current financial debt	(4)	(5)
Net financial cash (debt)	**3,427**	**2,380**

The **operating working capital** position remains negative, a consequence of the business model:

	31 January 2011	31 January 2010
Inventories	1,215	993
Receivables	482	422
Payables	(2,672)	(2,270)
Operating working capital	**(976)**	**(856)**

Funds from operations reached €2540 million in FY2010, 23% higher than the previous year.

Capital Expenditure for the FY2010 amounted to €754 million driven by 437 store openings in the year.

Dividends paid to shareholders reached €751 million.

2. START OF FY2011

Store sales in local currencies have increased by 10% from 1 February to 14 March 2011. The Spring-Summer season is influenced by the performance over the Easter period due to its significant sales volumes.

Expected Capital Expenditure in FY2011 is approximately €800 million as a result of the store opening plan for the year. Additionally, we have incurred an extraordinary, one-off investment of €230 million for the acquisition of unique retail premises at 666 Fifth Avenue, New York, for a global flagship for Zara.

Inditex expects to open between 460 – 500 net stores in FY2011. Approximately 70% of the new contracts have been signed but in some cases openings may not take place in FY2011.

Concept	Range	
ZARA	125	130
PULL & BEAR	45	50
MASSIMO DUTTI	40	45
BERSHKA	70	75
STRADIVARIUS	80	85
OYSHO	40	45
ZARA HOME	35	40
UTERQÜE	25	30
Total	**460**	**500**

Inditex plans to open in Australia in April and will launch South Africa in Autumn-Winter 2011, demonstrating its global reach.

On the second of September 2010 Zara launched e-commerce and is now operating in 16 European markets. Zara plans to begin e-commerce sales in the United States and Japan in Autumn-Winter 2011.

Additionally, all Inditex concepts plan to be present in e-commerce in 2011 with the launch of Massimo Dutti, Bershka, Pull & Bear, Stradivarius, Oysho and Uterque e-commerce operations in selected European markets over the second half of 2011.

3. TABLES AND APPENDICES TO FOLLOW

CONSOLIDATED FINANCIAL STATEMENTS

FY2010 income statement

In millions of euros	FY2010	FY2009
Net sales	12,527	11,084
Cost of sales	(5,105)	(4,756)

(Continued)

In millions of euros	FY2010	FY2009
Gross profit	**7,422**	**6,328**
Gross margin	59.3%	57.1%
Operating expenses	(4,452)	(3,953)
Other net operating income (losses)	(4)	(1)
Operating cash flow (ebitda)	**2,966**	**2,374**
Ebitda margin	23.7%	21.4%
Amortisation and depreciation	(676)	(646)
Operating income (ebit)	**2,290**	**1,728**
Ebit margin	18.3%	15.6%
Financial results	31	4
Income before taxes	**2,322**	**1,732**
Ebt margin	18.5%	15.6%
Taxes	(580)	(410)
Net income	**1,741**	**1,322**
	13.9%	11.9%
Non-controlling interests	9	8
Net income attributable to the controlling company	**1,732**	**1,314**
Net income margin	13.8%	11.9%
Earnings per share, cents euro (*)	**278**	**211**

(*) SHARES FOR EPS CALCULATION 623.1 MILLION FOR 2010 AND 2009

Consolidated Balance Sheet as 31 January 2011

In millions of euros

Assets	31 January 2011	31 January 2010
Current assets	**5,203**	**3,944**
Cash & Cash equivalents	3,433	2,420
Receivables	482	422
Inventories	1,215	993
Other	73	109
Noncurrent assets	**4,624**	**4,392**
Property, plant and equipment	3,414	3,307
Intangible asets	687	665
Financial investments	9	15
Other	513	404

In millions of euros

Assets	31 January 2011	31 January 2010
Total assets	**9,826**	**8,335**
Total equity & Liabilities		
Current liabilities	**2,675**	**2,305**
Payables	2,672	2,270
Financial debt	3	35
Noncurrent liabilities	**728**	**660**
Financial debt	4	5
Deferred taxes	173	173
Other	551	482
Equity	**6,423**	**5,371**
Equity attributable to the group	6,386	5,329
Non-Controlling interests	37	41
Total equity & Liabilities	**9,826**	**8,335**

FY2010 Consolidated Statement of Cash Flows

In millions of euros	**FY2010**	**FY2009**
Income before taxes	**2,322**	**1,732**
Adjustments to income		
Depreciation and amortization	636	625
Foreign exchange impact	(30)	31
Other	120	63
Corporate income tax	**(508)**	**(391)**
Funds from operations	**2,540**	**2,060**
Changes in assets and liabilities		
Increase in inventories	(227)	48
Increase in accounts receivable	(120)	163
Decrease in current liabilities	363	50
Changes in working capital	**16**	**261**
Cash from operations	**2,556**	**2,321**
Investments in intangible assets	(74)	(27)

(Continued)

In millions of euros	FY2010	FY2009
Investments in property, plant and equipment	(617)	(461)
Addition to other long-term financial investments	(26)	–
Other assets investments	(37)	(13)
Other investing activities	–	(10)
Capital expenditure	**(754)**	**(510)**
Net decrease in long-term financial debt	(1)	(4)
Net decrease in other long-term debt	(33)	11
Net increase in current debt	(32)	(204)
Dividends	(751)	(662)
Other financing activities	(1)	–
Cash used in financing activities	**(819)**	**(859)**
Net increase in cash and cash equivalents	984	953
Foreign exchange impact on cash & Cash equivalents	30	1
Cash and cash equivalents at beginning of the year	2,420	1,466
Cash and cash equivalents at end of the year	**3,433**	**2,420**

Notes

1. Firms using the direct method must disclose the reconciliation between net income and cash flow from operations (as in the indirect method).
2. The T-account for common stock is not included because there was no change in the accounting balance for 2009 (i.e., the ending balance is the same as the beginning balance).
3. Discrepancies can also arise because of currency effects.
4. This example assumes that the acquired company's receivables balance did not change after we bought it until the end of the current year. If $15 million of receivables were acquired, but receivables increased by, say, $20 million, $5 million of the increase would be deemed to have resulted from operations while the other $15 million of the increase would be classified as an investing cash flow.
5. Natural resources businesses, such as coalmines and oil companies, also add back depletion expense.
6. Provisions are routinely taken for the costs of restructuring, warranties and guarantees, environmental cleanup, and litigation.
7. The following discussion on working capital is adapted from S.D. Young and S.F. O'Byrne, *EVA and Value Based Management: A Practical Guide to Implementation*, 2001, McGraw-Hill.
8. As companies become more aggressive in revenue recognition (i.e., reporting revenues that would not have been reported under similar circumstances in previous years), the likely effect is to increase receivables and net income, but not cash flow. Therefore, the ratio of CFFO to net income should decline.
9. Just prior to the sale, Blockbuster paid a special dividend of $5 per share. Most of the dividends went to Viacom.

CHAPTER 6

Financial Statement Analysis

Introduction

Corporate financial reporting serves many purposes, but perhaps its most important role is to provide useful information to investors. In this chapter we look at how to analyze financial statements in order to make better investment decisions.

Financial statement analysis unlocks the clues about a company's future from its recent past and, in so doing, makes possible intelligent forecasts of future performance. It helps investors to decide whether or not a company's shares are worth buying, or if the company is a creditworthy borrower. For the equity investor, the decision depends ultimately on perceptions of value. If the value of a company, based on forecasts of future performance, is perceived to be greater than its market price, we buy. Otherwise, we don't. In short, much of the usefulness of financial statement analysis comes down to the quality of the forecasts and company valuations it produces.

To produce forecasts and valuations that help investors determine where their capital is likely to earn its highest risk-adjusted returns, a thorough financial statement analysis must follow four sequential steps:

1. Business and industry analysis
2. Accounting analysis
3. Financial analysis
4. Valuation.

1. **Business and industry analysis** identifies the main competitive forces in the company's industry, its key business risks, and sources of competitive advantage.
2. **Accounting analysis** identifies the accounting policy choices made by management, and evaluates the appropriateness of those choices.
3. **Financial analysis** evaluates the past performance of a firm using its financial statements and related information, and seeks to determine the sustainability of that performance.
4. **Valuation** takes the inputs from the first three steps and translates them into a set of financial forecasts to produce estimates of company value.

In the sections that follow, we will be showing how to perform the first and third of these steps. Although there is also a brief discussion of accounting analysis (the second step), the topic is discussed in later chapters. Valuation is discussed in Chapter 7. Once again, we will draw on the financial documents produced by SAP Group to illustrate how to perform a comprehensive financial statement analysis.

Business and industry analysis

The goal of business and industry analysis is to learn whatever we need to know about the business, its industry, and its competitors that might affect future profitability – including prospects for growth, how firms in the industry compete, the role of technology and innovation, marketing and distribution, and the relative power of key players in the value chain, e.g., suppliers and customers. This involves both:

- industry analysis (understanding the forces that drive profitability in the industry), and
- the analysis of competitive strategies (how the company positions itself in the industry to create and sustain competitive advantage).

Industry analysis

The most popular approach to industry analysis is known as the "5-forces" or "Porter" model, as described by Michael Porter in his book *Competitive Strategy* (1998).

The Porter model provides a systematic approach to studying the economic structure of an industry by analyzing the five basic competitive forces that affect industry returns. Any of these forces, if strong enough, can reduce or even eliminate industry profits.

At the center of the model is *rivalry among existing firms*, because it may be affected by each of the other forces. The term "rivalry" is used to reflect the jockeying for market share by firms within the industry. Questions then need to be posed, including:

- How fast is the industry growing?
- Is it stagnant or declining?

- How many competitors are there?
- Do firms compete mainly on price or differentiation?
- Is there a history of cooperative pricing or is price competition more "cut-throat"?
- What are the key economic and regulatory issues faced by companies in this industry?

For example, slow growth, a large number of competitors, and intense price-based competition exert downward pressure on profit margins.

The *threat of new entrants* looks beyond existing rivalries and considers how the industry's competitive landscape might unfold in the future. Here we ask the following:

- Who are the *potential* competitors and how might their entry affect competitive rivalry?
- Are there strong barriers (such as patents, economies of scale, access to distribution channels, strong branding, legal constraints, or high capital needs) that limit the threat of new entrants?
- Does government policy protect incumbents?
- Are there first-mover advantages, such as an experience curve, that might put new entrants at a cost disadvantage and thus strongly favor existing businesses?

For example, the absence of strong barriers implies that incumbents will have to divide up market share among more sellers, leading ultimately to an erosion of profits.

The *threat of substitute products* considers whether the industry is under threat from other products. If customers perceive that substitutes may satisfy their needs, competing businesses will be drawn into price comparisons and price cutting.

In assessing the threat from substitutes, we ask the following questions:

- Are close substitutes available?
- What are the price/value characteristics of substitutes?
- How sensitive are buyers to changing prices?
- Are buyers able and willing to switch, and how costly is it to switch?

The availability of close substitutes, combined with low switching costs, exerts downward pressure on industry profits.

The *bargaining power of buyers* focuses on the ability of buyers to negotiate from a position of strength, thereby reducing industry profits. Questions to ask here include the following:

- Are buyers highly concentrated or diffuse?
- Do purchasers buy in large quantities?
- Are substitute products available?
- How costly is it for buyers to switch?

This power is likely to be greater when the number of buyers is relatively small, when the purchasing volume of individual buyers is high, when products or services are commoditized (i.e., difficult or impossible to differentiate), and the costs of switching from one seller to another are low. When any of these conditions are present, downward pressure can be exerted on prices and operating margins.

The *bargaining power of suppliers* is the flip side to buyers' bargaining power. It poses similar questions, but from the opposite end of the value chain. For example:

- How much power do suppliers have to raise price?
- How many suppliers are there, and are there available substitutes?
- How costly is switching to new suppliers?

Significant supplier power implies that sizable portions of the wealth-creating potential of a value chain may accrue to suppliers instead of companies in the target industry. For example, distributors of processors in the personal computer industry face severe downward pressure on profit margins because of the overwhelming power of Intel, their principal supplier. So even if the value chain is highly profitable, the bargaining power of Intel ensures that the portion of that profitability available to distributors is highly constrained.

The 5-forces model is an enduring and adaptable approach to understanding industry economies, a necessary starting point to understanding firm-specific profitability. However, there is one obvious drawback to the framework, at least in the form in which it is commonly presented: it assumes that all industry players – competitors, buyers, sellers, etc. – are threats to profitability. As the growing use of strategic alliances suggest, interactions among firms in an industry can be positive, as well as negative. One famous example was the cooperation of Sony and Toshiba in establishing a global standard for DVDs. Such cooperation allowed the two firms, hitherto known for their fierce rivalry, to boost industry growth and profitability. Other, more recent examples include an agreement between automakers BMW and Fiat to jointly produce components and systems for some of their vehicles, arrangements by airlines to share check-in, gate management, and other facilities, and a contract between parcel delivery companies DHL and UPS to grant each other access to spare capacity.

Complementary products can also have a positive effect on profitability. For example, manufacturers of home cinema systems have benefited from the rapid growth in the market for big-screen televisions. In effect, the complementary product (e.g., big-screen TVs) boosts demand for the industry's product offerings, with correspondingly positive effects on profit margins. Product tie-ins between Hollywood studios and McDonald's for action films and animated features are another example in which companies in two ostensibly different industries benefit from the presence of the other.

These examples teach us that a comprehensive industry analysis doesn't just assess threats to profit, but also opportunities.

Competitive strategy

The 5-forces analysis identifies the threats to profits for all firms in an industry. The analysis of competitive strategy focuses on how individual firms are likely to cope with these threats, and also any opportunities that may arise from cooperation with other players. In light of industry structure and profitability, we ask: "How does the company create a sustainable competitive advantage that might lead to abnormal profits?" Or to put it another way, "How does the firm position itself to capture at least some of the industry's profit-making potential?"

The existence of abnormal profits implies that the company generates returns greater than its cost of capital. In a competitive market, such profits are possible only if the company can do something better than its competitors. A fundamental truism of valuation states that value creation is not possible without abnormal profits, and abnormal profits are not possible without competitive advantage.

Broadly speaking, firms create a competitive advantage through cost leadership, differentiation, or some combination of the two.

Cost leadership

This may be achieved because the company delivers the same product or service offered by its competitors at a lower cost. They may have attained this position through more efficient production, design improvements, lower input costs (e.g., cheaper labor or materials), economies of scale or scope, tighter cost control, or more efficient distribution. If a firm has truly achieved such an advantage, it can earn above-normal profits while charging the same prices as its competitors. Alternatively, it can lower prices, forcing its less efficient competitors to exit the industry.

Dell's strategy of executing "good enough" technology faster and cheaper than all of its key rivals in the computer business is a prime example of a company that pursued cost leadership with success.

Differentiation

A differentiation strategy implies that the firm seeks to be "different" along some dimension that customers care about. Whether it's different or "better" in an objective sense is less important than whether it is perceived by customers to be better. Companies might try to differentiate in terms of product quality, service quality, faster or more flexible delivery, product innovation, or strong brands. If a firm has truly succeeded in differentiating itself from competitors, it should be able to command a premium price from its customers. Think of powerful brand names, such as McDonald's or Gucci, that allow their owners to charge more than competitors for ostensibly similar products.

Appendix 6.1 provides a business and industry analysis and a competitive strategy analysis of SAP Group. We will later draw on this analysis to show how such knowledge and insight about a company and its industry can be used to interpret the company's financial performance.

Accounting analysis

As you will have become aware of by now, financial statements don't always provide a complete and truthful picture of a company's performance and financial condition. The data needed to form such a picture are filtered by GAAP/IFRS and by managerial discretion, both of which can distort the quality of the reported information. The reader must therefore know how to adjust the reported numbers, when necessary, in order to overcome these distortions. The result of such adjustments is that the financial figures used for analytical purposes may differ in material ways from the numbers that appear in the official financial statements.

Financial statement analysis is a "garbage in, garbage out" system: it's only as good as the quality of the numbers that go into it. The main purpose of accounting analysis is to assess the *quality* of the financial statements, and to adjust where necessary. Ultimately, it's about whether or not the numbers can be trusted. We therefore need to judge whether the accounting methods chosen appear appropriate, the estimates reasonable, and the accounting policy consistently applied.

Issues relating to financial reporting quality were addressed in Chapter 4 (revenue recognition) and will also be discussed from Chapter 8 onward.

Financial analysis

In this phase, the performance of the firm is assessed in the context of its industry and competitive strategies. Financial statement ratios are the most common tools used for this purpose. (The ratios discussed in this section are summarized in Appendix 6.2.)

Ratio analysis focuses on the relationships between two or more financial statement numbers. How these ratios are then used depends largely on the purpose of the financial analysis. For example, trade creditors and banks offering short-term credit facilities are primarily interested in the short-term liquidity of the business, and will select a set of ratios that address this issue. Other creditors, such as bondholders and banks offering longer-term loans, are interested in long-term liquidity and capital structure and in the company's ability to generate sufficient cash flow over the term of a loan to pay interest and principal. The range of financial ratios of interest to this group include the same ratios looked at by short-term creditors, but will also include ratios that deal with broader issues related to how the company finances its assets.

Equity investors care most about long-term earnings and the cash-flow-generating power of the firm. Because shareholders are residual claimants on the firm and its resources, equity analysis must address the same issues of concern to creditors. Unless a company can repay its loans, there is no residual cash for shareholders. But equity investors must also care about the size and risk of any residual earnings or cash flows. Thus, their perspective is the most comprehensive of any investor group.

For whatever purpose they're put to, ratios should tell a story. It's the story of the company's strategy, and whether or not that strategy is working. It confirms whether or not the company has a competitive advantage – some feature of the business that allows it to beat the competition – and whether or not that advantage is sustainable. Companies with a sustainable competitive advantage should have the means to service any and all debts, and to provide competitive returns to equity investors. Ratio analysis helps us to interpret business results and determine if such advantages have been achieved.

The insights gained are then used to forecast future performance and value the firm. In deciding whether or not to invest in a particular company, investors try to estimate the returns and the riskiness of returns expected from that investment. In short, they seek to maximize expected returns for a given level of risk, or minimize risk for a given level of expected returns. The goal is to maximize risk-adjusted returns. It stands to reason, therefore, that when using financial statements to analyze and value the firm, special emphasis is given to understanding profitability (the source of returns) and risk. Ratio analysis focuses on these two issues. In the discussion below, we illustrate how to perform such an analysis drawing on the financial statements of SAP Group.

ROE and ROIC

Let's begin with profitability. To say that a company has achieved a certain level of profit is of little analytical interest unless we can also say something about the amount of capital used to generate it. We do this in two ways:

- **return on equity** (ROE), and
- **return on invested capital** (ROIC).

ROE

This measures earnings available to common shareholders as a percentage of equity capital.[1] To many analysts, this is the most important of all financial statement ratios because it measures the profitability of the firm from the owners' perspective.

$$\text{ROE} = \frac{\text{Net Income}^2}{\text{Average Shareholders' Equity}}$$

For SAP in 2009 (see Exhibit 1.1),[3]

$$\text{ROE} = \frac{1750}{7831} = 22.3\%$$

Average shareholders' equity $= (7171 + 8491) \div 2$

2009:	22.3%
2008:	27.1%
2007:	30.3%

Average shareholders' equity equals the beginning balance plus the ending balance divided by two. Because balance sheet numbers are snapshot figures (i.e., measured at a point in time) the standard practice is to calculate average figures when a balance sheet account, such as shareholders' equity, is tied to an income statement or cash flow number. An alternative approach is to use the beginning balance in the denominator.

SAP's ROE of 22.3% is high, although it has fallen sharply over the past two years. A quick review of the income statement reveals that SAP's net income has declined in the two years since 2007 (from €1908m to €1848m to €1750m). In addition, shareholders' equity has risen sharply, mainly from reinvested earnings. In other words, not only did the numerator for ROE decrease from 2007 to 2009, but the denominator increased. Taken together, these trends explain the sharp fall in ROE.

Although ROE is a popular measure of performance in the analyst community, there is a important drawback to it from an analytical point of view: ROE is a function of both operating profitability and the financing choices made by management. Therefore, if ROE increases or decreases, without further analysis we cannot say whether this change is a function of changes in the underlying profitability of the business or whether it is a function of changes in how the company finances its assets. For this reason, we believe that ROIC is a better place to start the analysis of a company's performance.

ROIC

An alternative approach to measuring profitability, return on invested capital (ROIC), looks at the firm from an "unlevered," or zero-debt, perspective. When the firm is viewed in this way, the influence of financing choice (debt vs. equity) is neutralized. ROIC is measured as follows:

$$ROIC = \frac{NOPAT}{Average\ Invested\ Capital}$$

NOPAT is net operating profit after tax. Invested capital measures assets independently of how they were financed. For this reason, ROIC is a measure of profitability from an operating and investment perspective, without regard to financing choices.

The balance sheets in Figure 6.1 clarify how invested capital is defined.[4] On the right we see a managerial, or operating, balance sheet in which short-term, noninterest-bearing liabilities

Figure 6.1   The regular vs. managerial balance sheet

are netted against short-term operating assets – inventories, receivables, and prepaid expenses. The sum from either side of this balance sheet is known as "invested capital." Other common terms for invested capital include "net operating assets" and "capital employed." Return on capital employed and return on net operating assets are simply alternative ways of expressing the same idea as ROIC and are thus conceptually equivalent.

Subtracting short-term, noninterest-bearing liabilities (NIBL) from the sum of receivables, inventories, and prepaid assets yields what is commonly known as the working capital requirement (WCR). The WCR is an integral part of invested capital.[5]

So why do we subtract noninterest-bearing current liabilities in deriving invested capital, when it might be easier to use total assets from the regular balance sheet?[6] The reason is subtle, but important to understanding what the term "invested capital" really means. Although accounts payable and other nondebt current liabilities are to some extent interest-bearing (if they weren't, suppliers extending credit in competitive markets would go bankrupt), digging out the interest component is seldom worth the effort. In addition, the entire cost of goods and services bought in from suppliers, including any interest component, is reflected in either cost of sales or selling, general, and administration (SG&A) expenses. Therefore, the company is charged, albeit indirectly, for these interest costs.

By including an item in invested capital (and thus in the denominator of ROIC), the implication is that the firm should earn a return on it for the capital provider. But in the case of short-term, noninterest-bearing liabilities, the interest component of the expense is already included in the numerator. Therefore, we exclude such items from the denominator when calculating the profitability of assets. Otherwise, the interest charges for these liabilities would be counted twice.

For SAP, NOPAT and invested capital are calculated as follows:[7]

NOPAT (2009): Operating income $(1 - T)$ + Equity income, net of tax
€2,588 $(1 - 0.281)$ + €1 = €1,861

Equity income arises from the normal course of SAP's operating and investing activities, and therefore should be included in NOPAT.

Invested capital: *Total assets – Short-term noninterest-bearing liabilities*
(end of 2008)   €13,900 – €5,824 = €8,076
(end of 2009)   €13,374 – €3,416 = €9,958
(average 2009)   (€8,076 + €9,958) ÷ 2 = €9,017

Therefore, ROIC for 2009 equals

$$\frac{1861}{9017} = 20.6\%$$

2009:   20.6%
2008:   25.3%
2007:   26.9%

ROIC has decreased since 2007, but the decrease is smaller than that of ROE. This difference can be explained by SAP's growing shareholders' equity (and reduced financial leverage). In short, SAP's operating profitability deteriorated, while the sharp decline in ROE was caused both by declining ROIC and by changes in the company's capital structure.

DuPont analysis

To study changes in ROIC over time, and to better explain differences between a company's profitability and that of its competitors, ROIC can be disaggregated using DuPont analysis.[8]

DuPont analysis progressively disaggregates, or breaks down, broad measures of profitability such as ROIC into two or more constituent elements. As we will see, much of the benefit of ratio analysis is not just in understanding individual ratio values, but also in the relationships between and among key ratios. DuPont analysis provides the framework for examining such relationships.

To illustrate, consider the following:

$$\underset{\substack{\text{NOPAT} \\ \text{Margin}}}{\frac{\text{NOPAT}}{\text{Sales}}} \times \underset{\substack{\text{Invested Capital} \\ \text{Turnover}}}{\frac{\text{Sales}}{\text{Average Invested Capital}}}$$

Notice that the "sales" terms cancel out, resulting in the same numerator and denominator as ROIC, which means that ROIC is the product of NOPAT margin and invested capital turnover. The logic of the DuPont framework is to then break down these components of profitability into even more finely granulated measures of performance, helping us to identify the sources of profit and value creation in the business.

NOPAT margin is operating profit, net of tax, as a percentage of sales. Invested capital turnover measures how much revenue was generated during the year as a function of the assets available. If either ratio increases, holding the other constant, ROIC increases.

SAP's 2009 NOPAT margin equals:

$$\frac{1861}{10\ 672} = 17.4\%$$

2009:   17.4%
2008:   16.4%
2007:   17.8%

These figures show that SAP's after-tax operating profits dipped slightly in 2008, but recovered in 2009. Every €100 of revenue produced in 2009 yielded €17.40 in NOPAT, an improvement of €1 over the previous year.

SAP's invested capital turnover for 2009 equals:

$$\frac{10\,672}{9017} = 1.18$$

2009:   1.18
2008:   1.54
2007:   1.51

Invested capital turnover is a measure of operating efficiency. Efficiency in this context refers to the company's ability to manage its operating assets. Companies acquire assets to produce and sell their products and services. However, as the balance sheet shows (remember, balance sheets must balance!), all assets have to be financed, and there is always an opportunity cost to financing. Therefore, assets should be acquired only if their incremental contribution to profit more than offsets the opportunity cost of capital. When measuring efficiency, we are gauging the company's ability to convert these costly resources into sales.

For every €100 of invested capital held by SAP in 2007, €151 in revenue was produced, decreasing to €118 by 2009. We can now explain why SAP's ROIC dropped by five percentage points from 2008 to 2009. The disaggregation of ROIC into constituent components reveals that the improvement in operating margins was overwhelmed by the decline in invested capital turnover. The sharp reduction in 2009 was caused by a large increase in capital investment that year. This result is not unusual. Often, when companies embark on major capital spending programs, the short-term effect is a decline in turnover ratios. This decline results from a lag between investment and subsequent increases in revenue.

While NOPAT margin and invested capital turnover are both components of a higher-order ratio (e.g., ROIC), they too can be disaggregated. For NOPAT margin, the most common approach is to prepare a common-size income statement, in which all components of the statement are expressed as a percentage of sales. Exhibit 6.1 shows common-size income statements for SAP Group.

A similar approach is to prepare base-year, or trend, financial statements. Instead of expressing income statement items as a percentage of sales, each item is expressed as a percentage of the value for the base year sales.[9] Exhibit 6.2 shows base-year income statements for SAP. Each item for the 2008 and 2009 statements is shown as a percentage of the value for 2007.

Invested capital turnover is dissected by calculating a set of turnover ratios. For example, PP&E turnover can be used to measure the efficiency of the company's long-term productive assets in generating sales:

$$\text{PP\&E Turnover} = \frac{\text{Sales}}{\text{Average Property, Plant \& Equipment}}$$

The expected value for this ratio is largely a function of industry, with companies in capital-intensive industries reporting the lowest. Ratio values are normally much higher in light industry, or in services. The nature of the software industry suggests that SAP's PP&E

Exhibit 6.1   SAP Group common-size income statements: 2007: in €million 2008 and 2009: as a percentage of total sales

| | Year ended December 31 | | |
	2009	**2008**	**2007**
Total sales	100.0	100.0	€10,256
Cost of sales	(33.4)	(34.8)	(3,441)
Gross profit	66.6	65.2	6,815
Marketing and admin expenses	(42.3)	(41.9)	(4,117)
Operating income	24.3	23.3	2,698
Interest expense (finance costs)	(0.9)	(1.1)	(7)
Other income	0.1	0.7	131
Income before taxes	23.5	22.9	2,822
Income taxes	(6.4)	(6.7)	(916)
Net income	17.1	16.2	€1,906

Exhibit 6.2   SAP Group base-year income statements: 2007: in €million 2008 and 2009: as a percentage of 2007

| | Year ended December 31 | | |
	2009	**2008**	**2007**
Total sales	104.1	112.9	€10,256
Cost of sales	103.6	117.1	(3,441)
Gross profit	104.3	110.7	6,815
Marketing and admin expenses	109.8	117.7	(4,117)
Operating income	95.9	100.1	2,698
Interest expense (finance costs)	1442.9	1757.1	(7)
Other income	16.0	55.7	131
Income before taxes	88.9	93.9	2,822
Income taxes	74.8	84.7	(916)
Net income	95.6	98.4	€1,906

Note: The increase in finance costs in 2008 and 2009 compared to 2007 was mainly due to the credit facility SAP Group entered into in connection with the acquisition of Business Objects in 2008.

turnover should be higher than that of most companies. SAP is a capital-intensive company, but most of that capital is in the form of know-how and IT capacity. The IT capacity is included in PP&E, but know-how is not.

Depreciation and amortization policies impact this ratio too. Companies that use accelerated depreciation methods for their financial statements tend to report higher PP&E

turnover because assets (the denominator of the ratio) are written down more quickly. In contrast, SAP uses straight-line depreciation, which further contributes to a low turnover ratio.

SAP's PP&E turnover for 2009 equals:

$$\frac{10\,672}{1388^*} = 7.69X$$

* [(1405 + 1371) ÷ 2]
2009:   7.69X
2008:   8.51X
2007:   8.13X

PP&E turnover improved in 2008, then declined in 2009. As in the case with invested capital turnover, the decline in PP&E turnover can be explained by high capital spending in 2009. One thing to look for in 2010 and beyond is whether that capital spending has led to correspondingly higher revenues. In other words, unless SAP continues its policy of aggressive capital investments, we should see an improvement in the PP&E turnover ratio in 2010.

We now turn our attention to the main components of working capital. A set of turnover ratios is calculated here too. We begin with the receivables turnover ratio:

$$\frac{\text{Net Sales on Account}}{\text{Average Accounts Receivable}}$$

For SAP,

$$\frac{10\,672}{2817.5^*} = 3.79X$$

* [(3128 + 2507) ÷ 2]
2009:   3.79X
2008:   3.84X
2007:   3.84X

When calculating the ratio, the definition of receivables should be restricted to "trade" receivables, i.e., monies owed by customers only. Other receivables (monies owed to the company as a result of returns to suppliers, loans to employees, or the overpayment of taxes) should be included with prepaid expenses as "other current assets." Otherwise, any analysis of receivables turnover, and the management of customer accounts, will be distorted. The numerator should be based on credit sales, but because such information is usually not available to external readers, total sales are used instead.

As with inventory, receivables turnover is easily converted into days. The resulting figure, the accounts receivable period, is also called the average collection period (ACP):

$$\frac{365}{\text{Average Receivable Turnover}}$$

For SAP,

$$\frac{365 \text{ days}}{3.79} = 96 \text{ days}$$

2009:	96 days
2008:	95 days
2007:	95 days

As receivable turns increase, the ACP becomes shorter. This means that the company is speeding up the collection of cash from its customers. A decrease in receivable turns has the opposite effect. Note that the ACP, or receivables period, for SAP is stable over the 3-year observation period.

A brief digression on inventory

The SAP Group is a service company, and therefore does not sell products from inventory. To demonstrate how to analyze inventory, we will briefly examine the accounts of Anheuser-Busch InBev, the world's largest brewer.

To illustrate how to calculate the key ratios, we use the following data taken from AB InBev's 2010 annual report:

(in millions)	
Revenues	$36,297
Cost of goods sold	16,151
Beginning inventories	2,354
Ending inventories	2,409
Average inventories	2,382
Average accounts receivable	4,369
Average accounts payable	6,181

First, we calculate the inventory turnover ratio:

$$\frac{\text{Cost of Goods Sold}}{\text{Average Inventory}}$$

For AB InBev,

$$\frac{16\ 151}{2382} = 6.8\text{X}$$

Cost of goods sold is used in the numerator, instead of sales, because it excludes the profit margin. Using cost, instead of sales, provides a more accurate indicator of how quickly the inventory is converted into products and then sold.

Like PP&E turnover, this ratio is industry- and product-line specific. Therefore, considerable care is required when interpreting it. Mergers, acquisitions, spin-offs, and divestitures will cause product mix to change, resulting in changes to inventory turns, without respect to whether working capital management improved, deteriorated, or stayed the same.

Most analysts think of inventory in terms of days. This figure is easily calculated by dividing the inventory turnover ratio into 365, the number of days in the year:

$$\frac{365}{\text{Inventory Turnover}}$$

For AB InBev, days of inventory equal:

$$\frac{365\ \text{days}}{6.8} = 54\ \text{days}$$

This ratio indicates that, on average, it takes AB InBev 54 days from the acquisition of raw materials to the sale of finished products to customers. The aim here is to measure the company's efficiency in managing credit and the speed with which cash is collected from its customers.

An important advantage of converting inventory and receivables turnovers into days is that we can then easily calculate the length of the company's "operating cycle":

$$\text{Operating Cycle (in days)} = \text{Days Inventory Held} + \text{Accounts Receivable Period}$$

For AB InBev, the average length of the operating cycle in 2009 equals:

$$54\ \text{days} + 44\ \text{days}^{10} = 98\ \text{days}$$

The length of the cycle is the amount of time, in days, from the acquisition of inventory (materials in the case of manufacturers, and merchandise in the case of retailers and distributors) to the collection of cash from customers. All else being equal, the shorter the cycle, the better. This qualifier is important, because technology and market competition impose limits on how short inventory and receivables periods can be. For example, once inventories drop below a certain level, efficiency might be compromised. The firm may face production bottlenecks because of shortages for key inputs. Also, low levels of finished goods inventories might lead to lost sales as frustrated customers go elsewhere. Similarly, competitive constraints may require a company to extend a certain level of credit; any efforts to reduce it may lead to lost sales.

But conditional on these competitive constraints, we prefer cycle times to be as short as possible. The shorter the cycle, the less investment, and the less cash, that a company has tied up in its operations. As the cash tied up in the cycle is reduced, the cash flow available for shareholders and other capital providers increases, thus increasing the value of the firm. In other words, more efficient working capital management creates value for shareholders.

Efficiency can further be evaluated using the cash conversion efficiency ratio, which measures a company's ability to convert sales into operating cash flow:

$$\frac{\text{Cash Conversion Efficiency Ratio}}{\text{Sales}} = \text{CFFO}$$

where CFFO is cash flow from operating activities.

SAP's cash conversion efficiency ratio for 2009 is:

$$\frac{3015}{10\,672} = 28.3\%$$

2009:	28.3%
2008:	18.6%
2007:	18.8%

This means that for every €100 of sales in 2009, SAP generated €28.3 of operating cash flow to cover capital investment and cash payments to capital providers. Two years earlier, €100 of revenue generated €9.5 less in operating cash. Given that the cash cycle has changed little from 2007 to 2009, the likely cause of this improvement is the increase in operating profitability.

ROE and the analysis of financial risk

We can now extend the DuPont framework to include the influence of capital structure on profitability. This is accomplished by multiplying the components of ROIC – profit margin and invested capital turnover – by the product of the common earnings leverage ratio and the capital structure leverage ratio.

$$
\underbrace{\frac{NOPAT}{Sales}}_{\substack{NOPAT \\ Margin}} \times \underbrace{\frac{Sales}{Average\ Invested\ Capital}}_{Invested\ Capital\ Turnover} \times \underbrace{\frac{Net\ Income}{NOPAT}}_{\substack{Common \\ Earnings \\ Leverage}} \times \underbrace{\frac{Average\ Invested\ Capital}{Average\ Shareholders'\ Equity}}_{Capital\ Structure\ Leverage}
$$

The first of these leverage ratios measures the percentage of unlevered profits that belong to the company's shareholders. For the all-equity firm (i.e., a firm that finances its net operating assets, or invested capital, entirely with equity), this ratio takes on a value of 1. In other words, if there are no debts, unlevered profit and net income must be the same. As the company levers up, levered and unlevered profits diverge and the value of the ratio declines.

The second leverage ratio is a measure of capital structure. Like common earnings leverage, it takes on a value of 1 for the unlevered firm. In such a case, invested capital must equal shareholders' equity, because invested capital is financed entirely with equity. As the company levers up, assets (and invested capital) are acquired while shareholders' equity is unchanged, resulting in an increase in the value of the ratio. In summary, for the unlevered firm, both leverage ratios equal 1, which means that ROIC and ROE are the same. As firms lever up, common earnings leverage decreases while capital structure leverage increases. The product of these two ratios is call *adjusted leverage*. Multiplying this figure by ROIC yields ROE.

Now that our analysis has been extended to include financing, we can turn our attention to financial risk. The analysis of risk is viewed from both a liquidity and capital structure perspective.

Liquidity refers to the ability of a company to raise cash from all sources, including operations, asset sales, and lines of credit from banks. Liquidity analysis tends to focus on the short term because it considers the company's ability to service current (i.e., short-term) obligations.

The capital structure perspective focuses on the mix of debt (both short- and long-term) and equity used to finance the company's assets, and asks whether or not the current level of debt, also known as *financial leverage*, is appropriate. This task is conducted by comparing various risk ratios such as debt–equity and interest coverage against industry benchmarks.

We'll begin with an analysis of SAP's liquidity. Metrics such as the current ratio and quick ratio are popular ways to measure it. The current ratio is defined as follows:

$$
\frac{Current\ Assets}{Current\ Liabilities}
$$

Remember that current assets are those assets that will be used up or converted to cash within one year (or longer, if the operating cycle is longer than a year). The intuition behind the current ratio is that a company's ability to pay off its current liabilities is based on its current assets, because these are the assets that will be converted most quickly into cash. The higher the current ratio, it is said, the safer the company – at least in the short term.

SAP's current ratio at the end of 2009 is:

$$\frac{5255}{3416} = 1.54$$

2009:   1.54
2008:   0.96
2007:   1.94

These values indicate that for every €100 of short-term liabilities at the end of 2009, SAP had €154 in cash and other short-term assets.

The current ratio has been an important indicator of financial safety for over 100 years. But despite a venerable history, its relative importance has declined in recent years. One important weakness of this ratio is that it includes all current assets in the numerator, mixing the most liquid assets such as cash and marketable securities with less liquid assets such as inventories.

The quick ratio addresses this problem by excluding all but the most highly liquid current assets from the numerator, while using the same denominator as the current ratio. The ratio is defined as follows:

$$\frac{\text{Highly Liquid Assets}}{\text{Current Liabilities}}$$

Highly liquid assets are usually defined as the sum of cash, marketable securities, and accounts receivable.

For SAP,

$$\frac{4791}{3416} = 1.40$$

2009:   1.40
2008:   0.82
2007:   1.74

The quick ratio has fluctuated noticeably since 2007, with a sharp decrease in 2008 and a rebound in 2009. A quick ratio of 1.40 means that for every €100 of short-term liabilities, SAP has €140 available in cash and other liquid assets to pay those liabilities. Compared to most companies, this figure is high.

Although the quick ratio solves one problem of the current ratio (by limiting the numerator to only the most liquid current assets), another problem with the current ratio is not solved. The numerator and denominator of both ratios come from the balance sheet, and balance sheet numbers reflect measurement at a point in time. These are static measures that do not provide a dynamic, or flow, perspective on liquidity.

Still, investors continue to use one or the other of these ratios as short-term risk measures. For example, some banks continue to use the current ratio as a statistical screen in credit-granting decisions, especially those involving small businesses.

One noteworthy fact about the current ratio is that average values have declined significantly over the past 25 years, especially among American and European companies. The main reasons for this decline are the growing awareness of the capital costs that come with carrying too much working capital, mainly in the form of receivables and inventories, and the pressure on companies to get rid of surplus cash. The result is that the sum of cash, receivables, and inventories as a percentage of current liabilities is lower today than it was in the 1980s. Today, current ratios for most large, publicly traded companies range between 1.0 and 1.5, with many healthy companies reporting ratios under 1.0. Twenty-five years ago, current ratios of 2.0 or higher were more common than they are now.

A more dynamic perspective on short-term liquidity is available from the same working capital ratios we examined earlier, and from cash flow analysis. For example, days of receivables is a liquidity measure because the shorter the period, the closer the receivables are to being realized as cash. A similar argument can be made for inventories.

Cash flow from operations (CFFO) is another important indicator of liquidity. Its CFFO of roughly €3 billion in 2009 suggests that SAP easily generates the cash it needs to service all debts, short-term and long-term. The company generates operating cash flow of roughly €12 million each working day.[11] This means that in a typical working day, SAP collects cash from its customers, pays its suppliers, employees, marketing costs, administrative expenses, and taxes, and still has €12 million in cash left over.

In contrast to short-term liquidity analysis, the capital structure perspective focuses on the extent to which the company relies on debt, short-term and long-term, to finance its assets. The more debt a company has, the greater its financial risk. By financial risk, we mean the risk of financial distress (i.e., the risk that a company will struggle to pay its debts). In its most extreme form, financial distress leads to bankruptcy. Therefore, when we evaluate the financial risk of a company, we examine the risk that debts will not be paid and the business will fail.

The analysis of financial risk focuses on two major questions:

- Does the company pursue appropriate financing strategies?
- Is there significant bankruptcy risk?

We answer these questions by focusing on the company's capital structure. Although a broad range of financing alternatives are available to corporate finance specialists, at its most basic the capital structure question centers on how much debt and how much equity a firm should use to finance its assets. This is commonly known in finance circles as "debt–equity choice." Once that decision is made, the firm can then determine which financial instruments – e.g., short-term debt, long-term debt, convertible bonds, warrants, preferred stock, common shares, etc. – are most appropriate for achieving the target capital structure. The two most important factors to consider in debt–equity choice are the tax shield from interest payments, and the costs of financial distress (or bankruptcy) that arise from too much debt.

Debt finance is cheaper than equity finance because it's less risky from the investors' perspective. Lenders are contractually entitled to interest and principal payments, while firms are under no such obligation to make payments to shareholders. Also, lenders have priority of claim over shareholders in the event that the firm is liquidated. Because their investment is riskier, equity investors require higher returns. It is commonly assumed, therefore, that a firm's cost of capital can be reduced simply by replacing equity with relatively cheaper debt. But the contributions of Nobel Economics Laureates Franco Modigliani and Merton Miller (often referred to as M&M) teach us that reality is more complicated.

They proved that in a world without taxes and bankruptcy costs, asset financing does not matter.[12] The intuition behind this insight is that as a firm increases its borrowings, and as debt thus comprises a larger portion of total financing, the equity that remains becomes riskier. To compensate shareholders for the added risk, firms must offer the expectation of correspondingly higher returns. Also, the debt itself becomes riskier because there is more of it. The result: whatever benefit the firm gets from replacing expensive equity with cheaper debt is offset by the increased cost of the debt and of the remaining equity. The cost of capital does not change and, as we will see in our discussion on valuation, neither does the value of the firm.

When asked, "Why do we borrow?," corporate managers often respond by saying, "because of leverage, and leverage has a magnifying effect on profits and ROE." But M&M proved that this benefit is illusory. The "adjusted leverage" factor observed in the DuPont disaggregation of ROE offers no value-creating advantages (or value-destroying disadvantages) for the firm. Debt finance can still be beneficial, but not because of the leverage effect.

The M&M model assumes no taxes[13] and no bankruptcy costs. Of course, in the real world there are taxes and bankruptcy costs, and this simple fact changes everything. Interest on debt is tax-deductible, but the cost of equity is not. Therein lies the principal benefit of injecting debt into a company's capital structure. It explains why highly profitable companies that can easily finance all of their investments without borrowing still choose to borrow anyway. The tax deductibility of interest offers a valuable tax shield, allowing the company to reduce its tax bill.[14] For this reason alone, it is wrong to assume that the less debt a company has, the better. However, it can be said that the less debt a company has, the lower the risk of financial distress.

But just as it is wrong to assume that less debt is better than more debt, it is equally wrong to assume the reverse. The problem with debt is that the more of it a company has, the greater the risk that the company will encounter financial distress, or even bankruptcy. Outside the artificial M&M world, financial distress is costly. These costs include the direct out-of-pocket expenses paid to lawyers, accountants, and investments bankers to reorganize a firm, renegotiate its debts, or undertake other activities to fend off bankruptcy. Perhaps even more significant are the indirect costs of financial distress, costs that cannot be directly observed but have profound value implications. For example, in companies where after-sales service and warranty protection are critical attributes of the products they sell, customers may be reluctant to buy from companies that are thought to be in financial difficulty.

The key point here is that debt carries costs as well as benefits. When we examine the capital structure and financial risk of a firm, we are judging whether we believe the firm has achieved a proper balance of debt and equity, one that allows the exploitation of valuable tax shields without putting the firm in a position where debts might become overwhelming and the business fails. In short, are the company's financing policies appropriate, or do we believe the firm to be under- or overleveraged? And if the firm is overleveraged (i.e., it has too much debt), what is the likelihood that it will experience financial distress, if it hasn't already?

One popular way of measuring financial risk is the debt–equity ratio:

$$\frac{\text{Interest-bearing Debt}}{\text{Shareholders' Equity}}$$

Interest-bearing debt includes all bank loans, whether short-term or long-term, corporate bonds, capital leases, and any other form of financing a company might obtain from the money and capital markets. Trade payables and any other liabilities that arise spontaneously from operating activities are excluded.

For SAP, the debt–equity ratio at the end of 2009 is:

$$\frac{875}{8491} = 0.10\text{X}$$

2009:   0.10X
2008:   0.36X
2007:   0.01X

This means that for every €100 of shareholders' equity at the end of 2009, SAP had €10 in debt finance, versus €36 in 2008 and €1 in 2007.

An alternative approach to measuring financial risk is known as "times interest earned," which is measured as follows:

$$\frac{\text{Operating Income}}{\text{Interest Expense}}$$

The logic of this ratio is that a company's ability to pay interest charges derives from its pretax operating profits, sometimes called "interest coverage." Because these profits come from operations, they are potentially recurring. A rule of thumb is that interest coverage should be at least 5X for cyclical companies in the up-phase of the business cycle, which means that operating profits can later decline by as much as 80%, and still be sufficient to cover interest payments. The standard for companies with more stable earnings is about 3X. This is not to say that a company with interest coverage below these figures is unsafe or poorly managed, but rather that it is unlikely to get an investment grade rating from Moody's or Standard & Poor's (S&P) for its bond issues.[15]

For SAP, interest coverage for 2009 equals:

$$\frac{2588}{101} = 25.6X$$

2009:	25.6X
2008:	22.0X
2007:	385.4X

An interest coverage of 25.6X clearly puts SAP among the ranks of safe, creditworthy companies.

Because of its utility in signaling the risk of default, the interest coverage ratio also plays a role in debt covenants. A debt covenant is a provision in a lending contract that is designed to reduce conflicts of interest between lenders and borrowers and, therefore, to reduce the likelihood that the latter will take actions that harm the former. Such covenants can take on many forms. For example, they may place limits on new borrowing, or prohibit share repurchases or dividend payments without the lender's approval. Covenants can also serve as signals of deteriorating financial performance, especially when expressed in the form of financial statement ratios. If deterioration occurs, a negotiation of the lending contract may be triggered. The practical effect of these provisions is that a firm can make all of the scheduled debt payments on time, and yet be judged to have violated the terms of the contract. For example, covenants might state a minimum value for interest coverage. If the condition is not met (i.e., the ratio value falls under the threshold), the result is "technical default." The lender can then decide whether to waive or modify the restrictions, ask for a higher interest rate to compensate for the perceived increase in risk, or terminate the relationship and demand immediate repayment.

A variant on interest coverage, EBITDA interest coverage, adds depreciation and amortization to operating income.[16] Depreciation and amortization are taken directly from the cash flow statement. The ratio is calculated as follows:

$$\frac{\text{EBITDA}}{\text{Interest Expense}}$$

For SAP, EBITDA interest coverage for 2009 is:

$$\frac{2588 + 499}{101} = 30.6X$$

2009:   30.6X
2008:   26.3X
2007:   422.9X

One criticism of interest and EBITDA coverage is that both rely on accounting earnings, whereas interest payments must be made with cash. Although EBITDA does add back depreciation and amortization, it ignores changes in working capital and is thus a flawed measure of cash flow. The cash coverage ratio was developed to address this weakness by focusing directly on operating cash. It is calculated as follows:

$$\text{Cash Coverage} = \frac{\text{Cash Flow from Operations} + \text{Interest Paid} + \text{Taxes}}{\text{Interest Paid}}$$

SAP's cash coverage for 2009 equals:

$$\frac{3015 + 101 + 685}{101} = 37.6X$$

2009:   37.6X
2008:   24.9X
2007:   407.9X

For SAP, the interest coverage, EBITDA coverage, and cash coverage ratios tell similar stories. In 2009, SAP generated over €37 in pretax operating cash flow for every €1 of interest paid. This figure, combined with ratio values for the two previous years, confirms that SAP generates ample cash flows to meet its interest payments.

An important limitation of all coverage ratios, whether based on earnings or cash flow, is that they focus exclusively on interest. Principal, too, must be repaid. An alternative approach to risk measurement relates cash flow to levels of indebtedness (i.e., the principal on out-standing debts). One example is the ratio of free operating cash flows to total debt:

$$\frac{\text{Free Operating Cash Flows}}{\text{Total Debt}}$$

Free operating cash flows (FOCF) are defined as cash flow from operating activities, net of capital expenditures. The measure is used as a proxy for the amount of cash generated from core operations. SAP had free operating cash flows in 2009 of €3015m – €180m, or €2835 million.[17]

Total debt is defined as all debts, short-term and long-term, apart from short-term operating liabilities such as accounts payable. For SAP, we include post-retirement benefits, long-term debt, deferred income taxes, and other long-term liabilities.[18] This yields total debt of €1578 million at the end of 2009. Short-term bank loans should be included too, as should the capitalized value of any off-balance-sheet debts such as operating leases.

For SAP, the ratio of FOCF to total debt for 2009 equals:

$$\frac{2835}{1578} = 179.7\%$$

2009:	179.7%
2008:	54.4%
2007:	273.0%

Although the above ratios are widely used to assess a firm's capital structure, none of these measures provides a probabilistic assessment of bankruptcy risk. We can say, for example, that a particular value for a given ratio is associated with a particular bond rating. But such insights do not provide an estimate of the likelihood that the company will default on its debts. For this reason, formal bankruptcy prediction models were developed. Altman's Z-score and Ohlson's O-score are two popular examples.[19] In contrast to the ratio-by-ratio approach discussed here, these models take a multivariate approach. Statistical techniques are used to discriminate between samples of bankrupt and nonbankrupt firms. An equation is derived from a set of financial statement ratios that are found to be the best discriminators. The coefficients for the chosen ratios and the ratio values for the subject firm are then used to produce a composite score that predicts the likelihood of future bankruptcy.

These and similar models continue to be employed, especially by banks and other credit-granting institutions, but they have fallen out of favor in recent years with the bond-rating agencies. A more sophisticated approach has evolved, drawing on option pricing theory. It's based on the idea that the equity of a firm can be viewed as a call option on the value of the firm's assets. When the value of the assets is below the face value of liabilities, the call option is left unexercised and the bankrupt firm is turned over to its bankers and bondholders. In other words, the firm becomes bankrupt. An option pricing model, such as Black–Scholes–Merton, is used to convert equity prices and their volatility into a probability estimate that this eventuality (the value of assets falling below the value of debt) will happen. The great virtue of this approach is that it incorporates the myriad of insights and knowledge embedded in corporate share prices.

Key lessons from the chapter

- A thorough financial analysis should follow four sequential steps: business and industry analysis, accounting analysis, financial analysis, and valuation.
- The final two steps should tell the story of the company's strategy and competitive landscape in numbers.

- Business and industry analysis identifies the main competitive forces in the company's industry, its key business risks, and sources of competitive advantage. This analysis is critical because financial statement numbers have little meaning and defy interpretation unless they are placed in an economic and strategic context. Business and industry analysis is a necessary first step to the analysis of financial statements.
- Even the most sophisticated financial analysis cannot overcome unreliable financial statement numbers. That's why accounting analysis is so important. It begins by identifying critical accounting issues in the subject company's industry, and the key accounting policies adopted by the company. If needed, accounts should be adjusted before ratios are calculated and analyzed.
- Financial analysis evaluates the recent performance of the firm using its financial statements and related information, and seeks to determine the sustainability of that performance.
- Valuation takes the inputs from the first three steps and translates them into a set of financial forecasts to produce estimates of company value.
- Ratio analysis works best in a DuPont setting. Much of the story behind the ratios is revealed not just in the ratios themselves but in the interaction and interrelationships among the ratios. The DuPont framework provides an integrative framework that allows for a more holistic approach to the analysis of financial statements.
- Always begin a ratio analysis from the unlevered perspective. This permits an examination of operating and investing activities without being encumbered by financing issues. Only when knowledge of operating and investing activities is exhausted do we then think about financial risk and capital structure.
- Operating cycle in days equals the days inventory is held plus the accounts receivable period. This metric is indispensable for helping analysts to assess both the operating efficiency of the company and the liquidity of its working capital components, such as inventories and receivables.

Key terms and concepts from the chapter

Business and industry analysis	Return on equity	DuPont analysis
Accounting analysis	Return on invested capital	Turnover ratios
Financial analysis	Managerial balance sheet	Leverage ratios
Porter 5-forces model		Liquidity ratios
Competitive analysis	NOPAT	Profitability ratios
		Coverage ratios

Questions

1. What is the primary purpose of "accounting analysis"?

2. Explain how and why short-term creditors, long-term creditors, and shareholders approach ratio analysis differently.

3. What is the difference between ROIC and ROE?

4. Under what conditions is ROIC equal to ROE?

5. Explain why, all else being equal, an increase in accounts payable and other operating liabilities causes ROIC to increase.

6. True or false: A decrease in SG&A expenses as a percentage of sales will increase ROE and share price.

7. Many companies state ROE targets as important corporate goals. Do you agree with this practice? Why or why not?

8. What is DuPont analysis and what purposes does it serve?

9. True or false: The shorter the operating cycle, the better.

10. Describe the limitations of the current ratio and quick ratio as indicators of liquidity. What alternatives are available for assessing the liquidity of a firm?

11. Average current ratios in Europe and North America are noticeably lower today than they were 30 years ago. What might account for this change?

12. What is the primary purpose of turnover ratios?

13. Describe the major financial risk ratios and what they are designed to reveal.

14. True or false: The greater the interest coverage, the better.

Appendix 6.1   An industry and competitive analysis of SAP Group

A 5-forces analysis of SAP Group and the enterprise software industry – as of 2010

Rivalry among existing firms

SAP Group is the largest player in the enterprise software industry – a term recently coined to encompass the related ERP (enterprise resource planning), CRM (customer relationship management), and SCM (supply chain management) software markets. SAP Group concentrates on ERP software and boasts more than 100 000 installations in more than 120 countries. The annual revenues of the group exceed €10 billion.

In the past 20 years, the industry has experienced several waves of high M&A activity. Today, the share of the world's five largest players is at least 60% in every business segment.

The rivalry among existing firms is highly intense. Oracle Corporation is SAP's largest competitor. Other major players include Sage, Microsoft, and Infor Global Solutions.

Following the global financial crisis in 2008, M&A activity in the industry slowed. However, there were signs in early 2010 that acquisition activity in the sector was beginning to pick up. Further consolidation now appears likely in the coming years as the biggest players go after highly innovative small companies.

Threat of new entrants

Although many local and regional companies have found niches in small corners of the market, the need for first-class after-sales support and high switching costs for the clients of the enterprise software installations make it virtually impossible for any of the smaller players to compete on a global scale with industry leaders.

The leading companies are also on a constant lookout for new developments and promising trends in software development and often acquire fast-growing companies before they become a major threat.

Threat of substitute products

Although there has been a discernible trend toward using open-source alternatives (e.g., Pentaho business intelligence software or Sugar Open Source CRM software) instead of buying expensive licenses from the big vendors, the absence of global presence and the lack of aggressive marketing are strong limiting factors for spreading such alternatives beyond local and regional markets.

However, a possibility exists that in the next several years the market share of the leading companies won't be so dominating and the constant development of new technologies and industry solutions in the open-source software will present a much bigger threat to the incumbents than today.

The bargaining power of buyers

Buyers have some bargaining power before their first purchase and installation of the enterprise software package. But once the purchase and the installation have been made, the power of buyers declines sharply. Switching costs are very high in the enterprise software industry. Besides, the majority of vendors use their own proprietary standards. Users become hooked to these standards and vendor upgrades and after-sales support. In addition, many public and government buyers are obliged either by their shareholders or by the existing regulations to use the enterprise software solutions developed by the biggest vendors, and therefore the bargaining power of such buyers is limited even before the first purchase and installation.

In view of the complexity of their products and the relevant nontransparency of the development and installation costs when executing customized solutions, vendors can easily hide their real costs and practice price discrimination, thus reducing considerably the bargaining power of buyers.

However, the development of open-source alternatives, the global financial crisis of 2008, and the subsequent cuts in public spending and IT budgets have given buyers more power in their negotiations with the vendors of enterprise software packages.

The bargaining power of suppliers

The suppliers for the enterprise software industry do not have a lot of bargaining power. The switching costs for the hardware products used for software development are not high, especially taking into account that the hardware becomes outdated quickly and has to be changed anyway. As for the suppliers of human resources for software development, the globalization of the human resources market and the possibility of outsourcing software development (partially or completely) using foreign companies in the countries where such human capital is much cheaper have reduced the bargaining power of these "human capital" suppliers.

On the other hand, sometimes a new client needs to transfer an already existing installation from another vendor to the new vendor's package. Or the complex maintenance of the existing installation where the old software was used is necessary. In these cases, the vendor of the enterprise software has to use highly specific skills that are sometimes hard to find and the suppliers of these skills have a great deal of leverage.

A competitive strategy analysis of SAP Group

Sources of competitive advantage

The strategies of SAP Group emphasize differentiation more than cost leadership. Differentiation is achieved mainly through (1) protecting and strengthening existing brands, such as SAP Business Suite and SAP NetWeaver, (2) creating new brands, such as SAP Business ByDesign, (3) exploiting the intellectual property and advanced technologies of acquired companies, such as Coghead or Sybase, (4) further developing the network of software solution providers, value-added resellers, distributors, technology and services partners, (5) creating SAP solutions for small businesses and midsize companies, and (6) pursuing growth opportunities in selected foreign markets.

The sustainability of SAP Group competitive advantage is enhanced by (1) the global power of its brands, especially in the ERP business segment, (2) a dominant market position, which gives it greater bargaining power than its competitors (and thus discourages new entrants), (3) continuous investments in research and development facilities, and (4) a well-balanced policy of acquisitions and organic growth.

Major business risks

Major risks include (1) competitive pressures from large players such as Oracle Corporation and Microsoft, (2) challenges from new products and technologies such as open-source alternatives or enterprise cloud computing companies (e.g., Salesforce.com), (3) hidden liabilities and synergy risks from new acquisitions, (4) existing financial weakness among key buyers, and (5) exposure to currency fluctuations due to a geographic presence in various regions.

Appendix 6.2   Summary of financial statement ratios

$$\text{Return on Equity} = \frac{\text{Net Income Available to Common Shareholders}}{\text{Average Common Shareholders' Equity}}$$

$$\text{Return on Invested Capital} = \frac{\text{NOPAT}}{\text{Average Invested Capital}}$$

$$\text{NOPAT Margin} = \frac{\text{NOPAT}}{\text{Sales}}$$

$$\text{Invested Capital Turnover} = \frac{\text{Sales}}{\text{Average Invested Capital}}$$

$$\text{PP\&E Turnover} = \frac{\text{Sales}}{\text{Average Property, Plant and Equipment}}$$

$$\text{Inventory Turnover} = \frac{\text{Cost of Goods Sold}}{\text{Average Inventory}}$$

$$\text{Days Inventory Held} = \frac{365}{\text{Inventory Turnover}}$$

$$\text{Accounts Receivable Turnover} = \frac{\text{Net Sales on Account}}{\text{Average Accounts Receivable}}$$

$$\text{Accounts Receivable Period} = \frac{365}{\text{Accounts Receivable Turnover}}$$

$$\text{Cash Conversion Efficiency Ratio} = \frac{\text{Cash Flow from Operations}}{\text{Sales}}$$

$$\text{Common Earnings Leverage} = \frac{\text{Net Income}}{\text{NOPAT}}$$

$$\text{Capital Structure Leverage} = \frac{\text{Average Invested Capital}}{\text{Average Shareholders' Equity}}$$

$$\text{Current Ratio} = \frac{\text{Current Assets}}{\text{Current Liabilities}}$$

$$\text{Quick Ratio} = \frac{\text{Highly Liquid Assets}}{\text{Current Liabilities}}$$

$$\text{Debt/Equity Ratio} = \frac{\text{Interest} - \text{bearing Debt}}{\text{Shareholders' Equity}}$$

$$\text{Times Interest Earned} = \frac{\text{Operating Income}}{\text{Interest Expense}}$$

$$\text{EBITDA Coverage} = \frac{\text{EBITDA}}{\text{Interest Expense}}$$

$$\text{Cash Coverage} = \frac{\text{Cash Flow from Operations} + \text{Interest Paid} + \text{Taxes}}{\text{Interest Expense}}$$

$$\text{Free Operating Cash Flows to Total Debt} = \frac{\text{Free Operating Cash Flows}}{\text{Total Debt}}$$

Problems

6.1 Financial statement detective exercise

Exhibit 6.3 shows common-size balance sheets and income statements for 12 companies, described below. Your job is to match each company with its financial statements.

Exhibit 6.3 Common-size financial statements

	1	2	3	4	5	6	7	8	9	10	11	12
Balance sheet (year-end)												
Cash and marketable securities	2.1%	20.0%	22.5%	37.9%	13.4%	11.7%	4.0%	30.8%	17.6%	19.9%	42.7%	14.1%
Receivables	7.5	4.8	18.0	17.8	12.5	26.0	4.2	76.8	13.6	9.0	25.7	8.9
Inventories	3.7	2.1	0.1	17.7	22.5	7.3	8.6	—	8.1	0.9	0.1	2.4
Property, plant, and equipment	301.5	182.6	94.5	51.3	67.9	79.0	34.4	26.9	47.5	6.1	24.8	76.3
Accumulated depreciation	(99.7)	(49.0)	(38.6)	(16.3)	(30.7)	(46.4)	(16.6)	(15.6)	(27.7)	(2.7)	(11.5)	(25.4)
Investments	7.0	—	15.2	8.6	8.5	28.8	3.2	2.6	7.5	8.8	1.3	5.2
Other assets	47.2	13.1	51.1	123.5	9.4	30.4	15.8	70.6	33.8	5.2	17.8	104.8
Total assets	269.3%	173.6%	162.8%	235.5%	103.5%	136.8%	53.6%	192.1%	100.4%	47.2%	100.9%	186.3%
Current liabilities	40.4%	32.8%	53.1%	50.4%	34.4%	46.2%	26.4%	118.4%	33.6%	28.7%	34.3%	21.2%
Long-term debt	76.3	26.0	39.8	13.9	14.4	28.2	13.4	30.3	12.4	1.0	0.1	73.4
Other noncurrent liabilities	81.0	5.5	7.8	41.3	13.8	8.7	2.4	16.5	8.0	4.3	5.4	24.8
Shareholders' equity	71.6	109.3	62.1	129.9	40.9	53.7	11.4	26.9	46.4	13.2	61.1	66.9
Total liabilities and shareholders' equities	269.3%	173.6%	162.8%	235.5%	103.5%	136.8%	53.6%	192.1%	100.4%	47.2%	100.9%	186.3%
Income statement												
Operating revenues	100.0%	100.0%	100.0%	100.0%	100.0%	100.0%	100.0%	100.0%	100.0%	100.0%	100.0%	100.0%
Other revenues	—	—	0.7%	—	1.4%	4.3%	—	—	—	—	—	—
Cost of goods sold (excluding depreciation) or operating expenses	58.7	75.4	74.4	11.1	86.5	73.8	74.9	98.3	45.1	80.9	31.6	33.1
Depreciation and amortization	11.4	6.6	7.8	9.7	4.3	5.6	2.9	3.2	4.7	0.7	2.8	21.2
Selling and administrative	15.9	16.2	—	32.2	—	11.3	16.2	—	36.0	8.7	25.1	31.0
Interest expense	4.6	1.3	1.1	0.7	1.4	0.1	0.7	2.5	1.3	—	0.1	7.9
Research and development	—	—	—	14.4	—	4.2	—	—	1.6	0.9	13.6	—
Income taxes	2.5	2.7	2.2	5.1	1.7	3.7	1.2	4.1	2.8	2.8	10.1	2.8
Other	(1.5)	(7.0)	11.5	5.2	(1.8)	(1.0)	1.8	0.6	0.8	(0.2)	(0.7)	(4.0)
Total expenses	91.6%	95.2%	97.0%	78.4%	92.1%	97.7%	97.7%	108.7%	92.3%	93.8%	82.6%	92.0%
Net income	8.4%	4.8%	3.7%	21.6%	9.0%	6.6%	2.3%	(8.7)%	7.7%	6.2%	17.4%	8.0%
Cash flow from operations	25.2%	17.7%	7.9%	31.1%	10.6%	13.3%	5.8%	7.1%	12.0%	10.8%	24.3%	28.2%
Free operating cash flow	10.6	(9.5)	5.9	25.6	5.5	4.7	3.1	4.8	7.6	9.7	23.1	18.5

Accor

One of the world's leading hotel operators, owning or managing almost 4000 properties throughout the world. It serves travelers in Europe through its flagship chains Mercure, Novotel, and Sofitel, and its economy chains Ibis and Formule 1. In the US, it operates budget brands Motel 6 and Red Roof Inns. Accor has embarked on a sale and leaseback strategy for its upscale properties to reduce exposure to slowdowns in the market and is working to transition many of its midscale hotel leases to variable cost arrangements.

Arcelor

Arcelor was formed by the combination of three European steel companies and is now the second largest steel manufacturer in the world. The company produces carbon steel and stainless steel for the automotive, construction, appliance, and packaging industries.

Carrefour

Carrefour is the world's second largest retailer. Based in France, it operates more than 11 000 stores under two dozen brand names, including Carrefour (hypermarkets), Champion (supermarkets), and Shopi (convenience stores). Unable to build new stores in France, until recent changes in French law, Carrefour has expanded through acquisitions, at home and abroad.

Dell

Dell is the world's #1 direct-sale computer vendor. In addition to a full line of desktop and notebook PCs (about 80% of total sales), Dell also offers workstations, storage systems, network servers, and Ethernet switches. Dell's direct-sales, built-to-order model allows for lower inventories and lower operating costs, a necessity for the PC price wars and the occasional slump in corporate IT spending.

Deutsche Telekom

The #1 telecom company in Europe. Deutsche Telekom is Germany's leading fixed-line phone operator, its T-Mobile unit serves millions of wireless phone customers, and T-Online is one of the Europe's leading internet service providers. Although privatized in the 1990s, the German government still holds a 15% stake and an additional 22% through a state-owned development bank.

The FPL Group

The FPL Group is a holding company with operations across the US. Most revenue comes from its utility subsidiary, the largest electricity provider in the state of Florida. The electricity is generated from the company's nuclear and fossil-fueled power plants.

Interpublic

Interpublic is one of the world's largest advertising and marketing services companies. Operating through offices in 130 countries, its flagship agencies include McCann Worldgroup, Lowe & Partners, and Hill, Holliday. Like all of the global players in its industry, much of Interpublic's growth has come from acquisitions.

Nestlé

Nestlé is the world's #1 food company. It is the world leader in coffee (Nescafé), and is also one of the largest bottled water (Perrier) and baby-food manufacturers. At last count, it is the owner of over 9000 branded products worldwide. Nestlé's recent purchase of Ralston-Purina has made it a top player in the pet food business. In addition to its food business, Nestlé owns nearly 27% of cosmetic giant L'Oreal.

Pfizer

Pfizer is the world's largest research-based pharmaceutical company. Its best-known products include Viagra, Zoloft, and Lipitor. In addition to prescription drugs, Pfizer also makes a broad range of popular over-the-counter remedies, including Sudafed and Benadryl.

SAP

SAP is the world's leading provider of enterprise resource planning software used to integrate corporate back-office functions such as human resources, accounting, distribution, and manufacturing. The company also offers a range of products on supply chain and customer relationship management. SAP's large customer base provides a steady stream of recurring licensing and service revenue.

Southwest Airlines

Southwest Airlines offers low-cost, no-frills air travel to 60 cities in the US. A model for low-fare upstarts the world over, the company has enjoyed over 30 straight years of profitability. Southwest's business model is simple: flights are short (most are under two hours), and the airline usually lands at small airports to avoid congestion at large hubs. Originally concentrated in the western part of the US, Southwest has expanded into key eastern markets, such as Philadelphia.

Toyota

Toyota is the world's #2 car maker (by sales) and its most profitable. In addition to long-standing core brands – Camry, Land Cruiser, Celica, Corolla, and the luxury Lexus line – Toyota has pioneered the market for hybrid-powered sedans (Prius). While most of its North American and European competitors are downsizing operations, Toyota continues to pursue an aggressive growth strategy.

6.2   Effects of transactions on selected balance sheet figures

	Total current assets	Total current liabilities	Working capital requirement	Current ratio
(a) Additional common stock is issued for cash				
(b) Merchandise is sold, above cost, for cash				
(c) A piece of equipment is sold for more than book value				
(d) Payment is made to trade creditors for previous purchases				
(e) A cash dividend is declared and paid				
(f) A stock dividend is declared and paid				
(g) Cash is obtained through long-term bank loan				
(h) A profitable firm increases the accumulated depreciation account for property, plant and equipment				
(i) Current operating expenses are paid				

(Continued)

	Total current assets	Total current liabilities	Working capital requirement	Current ratio
(j) Ten-year notes are issued to pay off accounts payable				
(k) Accounts receivable are collected				
(l) Equipment is purchased with short-term notes				
(m) Merchandise is purchased on credit				
(n) Taxes payable are increased				
(o) Marketable securities are sold below cost				

Required

Indicate the effects of the previous transactions on each of the following: total current assets, total current liabilities, working capital requirement, and current ratio. Use + to indicate an increase, − to indicate a decrease, and 0 to indicate no effect. Assume an initial current ratio is greater than 1.

6.3   Calculating and interpreting PP&E turnover ratios

Texas Instruments (TI) designs and manufactures semiconductor products for use in computers, telecommunications equipment, automobiles, and other electronics-based products. The manufacturing of semiconductors is highly capital intensive. Hewlett-Packard Corporation (HP) manufactures computer hardware and various imaging products, such as printers and fax machines. HP outsources the manufacture of a portion of the components for its products. HP acquired Compaq Computer in the middle of 2002. Exhibit 6.4 presents selected data for TI and HP for 2002, 2003, and 2004.

Required

(a) Compute the PP&E turnover for each firm for 2002, 2003, and 2004.
(b) Suggest reasons for the differences in the PP&E turnovers of TI and HP. Be specific.
(c) Suggest reasons for the changes in the PP&E turnovers of TI and HP during the three-year period. Be as specific as the data allow.

Exhibit 6.4 Selected data for Texas Instruments and Hewlett-Packard (in millions)

	2004	**2003**	**2002**
Texas Instruments			
Sales	$12,580	$9,834	$8,383
Cost of goods sold	6,902	5,728	5,313
Capital expenditures	1,298	800	802
Average PP&E	4,025	4,463	5,192
Percentage PP&E depreciated	59.1%	56.7%	49.6%
Percentage change in sales	+27.9%	+17.3%	−17.8%
Hewlett-Packard			
Sales	$79,905	$73,061	$56,588
Cost of goods sold	60,340	53,858	41,793
Capital expenditures	2,126	1,995	1,710
Average PP&E	6,894	6.703	5,661
Percentage PP&E depreciated	51.9	51.3%	44.8%
Percentage change in sales	+9.4	+29.1%	+25.1%

6.4 Financial statement detective exercise in the pharmaceutical industry

Exhibit 6.5 presents common-size income statements and balance sheets for seven firms that operate at various stages in the value chain for the pharmaceutical industry. (The companies are real, but the names have been disguised.) These common-size statements express all amounts as a percentage of sales revenue. Exhibit 6.5 also shows the cash flow from operations to capital expenditures ratio for each firm. A dash for a particular financial statement item does not necessarily mean that the amount is zero. It merely indicates that the amount is not disclosed. The seven companies and a brief description of their activities follow.

Required

Match the financial statements with the company described below. Give the reasons for your choice. Be as specific as possible in explaining why you chose a particular set of financial statements for one of the below companies.

1. Wilson Pharma: Engages in the development, manufacture, and sale of ethical drugs (i.e., drugs requiring a prescription). Ethical drug companies must obtain

approval of new drugs from government regulators, such as the US Food and Drug Administration (FDA). Patents protect such drugs from competition until either other drug companies develop more effective products or the patent expires.

2. American Biotech: Engages in the development, manufacture, and sale of drugs based on biotechnology research. The biotechnology segment is less mature than the ethical drug industry, with relatively few products having received regulatory approval.

3. Mauborgne Laboratories: Engages in the development, manufacture, and sale of generic drugs. Generics have the same chemical compositions as drugs that had previously benefited from patent protection. In recent years, generic drug companies have benefited from the patent expiration of several blockbuster ethical drugs. However, the big ethical drug companies have increasingly offered generic versions of their products to compete against generic drug companies.

4. Morris & Morris: A huge global enterprise that engages in the development, manufacture, and sale of over-the-counter health care products. Also, the company operates in consumer segments where brand recognition is important.

5. Chang Labs: Offers laboratory testing services and expedition of the drug approval process for ethical drug companies. Cost of goods sold for this company represents the salaries of personnel conducting the laboratory testing and drug approval services.

6. Crimson Health: Distributes drugs as a wholesaler to drugstores and primary care facilities, including hospitals and clinics. It also offers pharmaceutical benefit management services (PBMS) to help customers order more efficiently, contain costs, and monitor their purchases. Cost of goods sold includes the cost of drugs sold plus the salaries of personnel providing PBMS.

7. Eberhard: Operates a nationwide chain of drugstores, some of which are owned while others are leased.

Exhibit 6.5   Common-size financial statement data

	(1)	(2)	(3)	(4)	(5)	(6)	(7)
Income statement							
Sales	100.0%	100.0%	100.0%	100.0%	100.0%	100.0%	100.0%
Cost of goods sold	(47.0)	(11.0)	(24.0)	(58.4)	(28.9)	(73.3)	(92.5)
Selling and administrative	(18.8)	(24.2)	(36.7)	(31.0)	(36.3)	(21.0)	(4.2)
Research and development	(8.0)	(21.5)	(13.2)	–	(10.9)	–	–
Interest	–	(.3)	(1.0)	(2.6)	(1.6)	–	(.3)
Income taxes	(10.6)	(14.1)	(7.0)	(3.2)	(6.8)	(2.2)	(1.0)
Other	3.5	5.2	(1.5)	1.0	1.4	.1	(.2)
Net income	19.1%	34.1%	16.6%	5.8%	16.9%	3.6%	1.8%

Exhibit 6.5 Continued

	(1)	(2)	(3)	(4)	(5)	(6)	(7)
Balance sheet							
Cash	33.7%	66.3%	21.4%	34.9%	24.2%	.1%	1.9%
Receivables	27.5	12.3	19.4	26.4	14.0	3.2	5.0
Inventories	19.1	8.9	12.4	–	9.1	14.1	13.1
Other current	7.6	8.6	15.9	5.4	8.7	.4	2.3
Investments	–	–	–	–	–	–	–
Property, plant,							
and equipment, net	19.9	48.5	44.6	22.4	23.4	17.7	3.8
Other noncurrent assets	49.9	15.9	48.9	31.2	37.2	.4	4.4
Total assets	157.7%	160.5%	162.6%	120.3%	116.6%	35.9%	30.5%
Current liabilities	34.4%	25.0%	51.4%	28.5%	24.4%	12.2%	13.7%
Long-term debt	2.8	5.6	11.4	2.0	6.5	–	3.9
Other noncurrent							
liabilities	2.2	–	23.8	–	2.3	2.6	1.6
Shareholders' equity	118.3	129.9	76.0	89.8	73.4	21.1	11.3
Total equities	157.7%	160.5%	162.6%	120.3%	116.6%	35.9%	30.5%
Cash flow from operations/							
capital expenditures	2.2	3.4	2.3	1.3	2.8	.6	1.3

6.5 Comprehensive financial ratio analysis

Financial statements for Wertenbroch Company, a distributor of kitchenware, are presented below (all amounts in thousands of euro).

Statements of financial position

	2012	2011
Assets		
Land	€260	€260
Buildings and equipment (net)	360	350
Prepaid expenses	58	46
Inventories	250	270
Receivables (net)	196	160
Short-term investments	104	80
Cash	140	130
	€1,368	€1,296

Equities and liabilities

Share capital	€400	€400
Retained earnings	272	232
Long-term debt	300	300
Short-term debt	200	200
Accounts payable	96	84
Accrued liabilities	100	80
	€1,368	€1,296

Income statements

	2012	2011
Revenues	€1,700	€1,580
Cost of goods sold	1,240	1,150
Gross profit	460	430
Other operating expenses	303	283
Operating profit	157	147
Interest expense	34	23
Income before taxes	123	123
Income taxes	37	36
Net Income	€86	€88

Additional information:

- All sales were on account.
- No share transactions took place in either year.
- Total assets at the beginning of 2011 were €1260.
- Accounts payable and accrued liabilities at the beginning of 2011 totaled €146.
- Receivables (net) at the beginning of 2011 were €176.
- Inventory at the beginning of 2011 was €236.
- Shareholders' equity at the beginning of 2011 was €594.
- Cash flow from operations was €175 in 2011 and €198 in 2012.
- Capital expenditures were modest in both years.
- The tax rate is 30%.

Required

Using whatever ratios you need, analyze the liquidity, operating efficiency, and profitability of Wertenbroch Company for 2011 and 2012. Has Wertenbroch's performance improved or deteriorated over the two years? Be as specific as the data allow.

6.6 Profitability analysis for The Home Depot

The Home Depot, Inc. operates as a home improvement retailer primarily in the United States, Canada, and Mexico. It operates The Home Depot stores, which sell building materials, home improvement supplies, and lawn and garden products to do-it-yourself customers, home improvement contractors, and building maintenance professionals.

The company also operates The Home Depot and EXPO Design Center stores that offer various installation services, which include products, such as carpeting, flooring, cabinets, countertops, and water heaters primarily to business-to-business customers. In addition, the company offers credit purchase programs through third-party credit providers. Meanwhile, The Home Depot has centralized purchasing and invested more than a billion dollars in state-of-the-art technology, including self-checkout aisles and in-store Web kiosks.

Since 2002, Home Depot's return on invested capital has risen from below 16% to nearly 21% last year. This profitability increase is impressive when one considers the severe competition in the industry from other big box stores (e.g., Lowes), the well-known hardware coop Ace Hardware, lumber yards, and the host of other retailers who supply the products carried by Home Depot.

Key profitability ratios for Home Depot for the last three years are shown below:

	2004	2005	2006
ROIC	18.7%	19.7%	20.7%
NOPAT margin	6.6%	6.8%	7.2%
IC turnover	2.84X	2.88X	2.85X
A/R turnover	67.0X	66.3X	54.3X
Inventory turnover	5.3X	5.3X	5.3X
PP&E turnover	3.6X	3.6X	3.6X
COGS/sales ratio	68.2%	66.6%	66.5%
SGA/sales ratio	19.6%	20.9%	20.2%
Sales (in millions)	$64,816	$73,094	$81,511
Ending IC (in millions)	$25,392	$28,576	$32,994

Required

(a) Explain how Home Depot has achieved an increase in ROIC over the three years. Be as specific as the data allow. Give likely reasons for changes in specific ratios.
(b) Home Depot's accounts receivable turnover is very high. How does Home Depot achieve this turnover? What is the benefit of the high accounts receivable turnover in terms of profitability, liquidity, and cash flows?

6.7   Comparative analysis of receivables and inventories

The following information is taken from the annual reports of The Coca-Cola Company and PepsiCo, Inc. The two companies are fierce competitors, but they differ in important respects. Coca-Cola is more "cola-centric," which means that its core Coke and Diet Coke brands play a more dominant role in the company than Pepsi brand cola does in PepsiCo. Although Coca-Cola is the world leader in soft drinks, by a large margin, PepsiCo is the bigger company because of greater diversification. Both companies sell bottled water and other beverages (e.g., health and energy drinks), but these products feature more prominently in PepsiCo. Also, PepsiCo is the world leader in salty snacks through its Frito Lay business.

(in millions)		Coca-Cola	PepsiCo
Accounts receivable, net	31 Dec. 2010	$ 4,430	$ 6,323
	31 Dec. 2011	4,920	6,912
Inventories	31 Dec. 2010	2,650	3,372
	31 Dec. 2011	3,092	3,827
Net revenue	2010	35,119	57,838
	2011	46,542	66,504
Cost of goods sold	2010	12,693	26,575
	2011	18,216	31,593

Required

(a) For each company, calculate the receivables period, the inventory period, and the length of the operating cycle for 2011. Assume that all sales are on credit.
(b) Comment on any differences you observe between the two companies. What reasons can you give for why the companies have different operating cycles?

Case studies

6.1   Profitability analysis and WalMart's suppliers

WalMart, the world's largest retailer, is legendary for squeezing price concessions and ever greater operating efficiencies from its suppliers. To what extent do such concessions hurt financial performance?* One recent study has found that suppliers identifying WalMart as a primary customer financially underperformed compared to companies that did not identify themselves in this way. Especially revealing is the observation that among the 10 largest suppliers to WalMart in 1994, four subsequently went bankrupt and a fifth was taken private as it was failing. But should suppliers just say "no" to WalMart? Or is it simply too big to ignore?

Consider the case of Dell, the computer maker. While the overall computer market has been growing, Dell's own share of that market is falling. In a first step toward transforming its model of direct selling to consumers, the company announced in May 2007 that it would begin selling two models of its low-end Dimension line through more than 3000 WalMart stores in the US and Canada. Dell's share price fell by 1.4% on the news, partly because of analyst fears that the company might see a further deterioration of its already battered profit margins.

Still, some analysts viewed the move favorably. "They got products on the shelf of the No. 1 retailer in the world," according to one such analyst. "Dell is finally listening to its customers."

Bain & Company, the management consultants, have studied the effect of doing business with WalMart. "The fact of the matter is, the way WalMart is continuing to grow means that our clients cannot grow their business without finding a way to be successful with WalMart," according to Gib Carey, the partner in charge of the study. "We have clients out there who would like that not to be true. . . . But we think that WalMart is an essential retailer, in a way that no other retailer is."

To understand the effect of WalMart on supplier profitability, Bain staffers conducted an analysis of 38 publicly traded companies that did more than 10% of their business with WalMart. Bain also analyzed the performance of 20 companies in similar industries that were not significant WalMart suppliers, as a control group. The analysis produced a consistent pattern. For every percentage point of increased business these companies were doing with WalMart, operating margins declined to some extent. That is, the more business a company does with WalMart, the less profitable each sale is. "It may be pressure," says Carey, "or it may be that companies are intentionally letting some profit margins decline to aggressively grow their business with WalMart."

---

*This case is adapted from material found in *The Wal-Mart Effect*, by Charles Fishman, London: Penguin Books, 2006. The following article was also consulted: "Dell, in shift, will offer PCs at Wal-Mart," by Matt Richtel, *The New York Times*, 25 May 2007.

According to the Bain study, companies doing 10% or less of their business with WalMart had operating profit margins of 12.7%. Companies that became what Carey calls "captive suppliers" to WalMart – selling more than 25% of their output to WalMart – see their profit margin cut almost in half, to 7.3%. "What we've found as we've continued to work with clients," says Carey, "is that WalMart is really forcing companies to either get their act together, or get crushed."

Required

(a) If "profitability" (i.e., operating margin) is lower for companies that derive a lot of their business from WalMart, why sell to WalMart? What logical reasons can a company give for such a practice if greater sales to WalMart are associated with lower margins?

(b) How would a company know if an expected decline in profit margin was a price worth paying for WalMart's business? Be specific. What measures would need to be considered to address this issue?

6.2   LVMH and Warnaco: strategy and financial statement analysis*

LVMH was created in 1987 with the merger of Moët Hennessy and Louis Vuitton. However, the history of those merged companies goes back centuries. LVMH is diversified into a number of brands, with operations in five segments: wines and spirits; fashion and leather goods; perfumes and cosmetics; watches and jewelry; and selective retailing. The luxury brands they manage are among the world's most recognizable: Dom Pérignon champagne, Christian Dior perfume, and TAG Heuer timepieces, and several others.

Warnaco is a more focused group, with an emphasis on the design and manufacture of intimate apparel, sportswear, and swimwear. The brands that they supply products for include Calvin Klein and Speedo. While these brands are respected for their quality, they are not viewed as competing for the same high-end customers as LVMH.

The intent of this case is not to assess how the firms compete against each other. Rather, given that they likely have different operating strategies, how might an analyst detect these differences in the accounting numbers?

---

*This case was prepared by Professor Daniel Bens, INSEAD.

Required

(a) Calculate ROIC for both companies for fiscal 2011. For calculations requiring a tax rate, assume 33.3% for LVMH (the French corporate rate), and 35% for Warnaco (the US corporate rate). Based on this analysis alone, how do the companies compare in terms of their performance?

(b) Review the description of each company above and think about the strategic positioning of their products. How are the two companies similar, and how do they differ?

(c) Break down ROIC into its components, NOPAT margin and invested capital (IC) turnover.

(d) Based on your calculations in part (c), and your analysis in part (b), does the breakdown for ROIC into NOPAT margin and IC turnover align with your expectations regarding company strategy? What does this say about management's ability to deliver performance in accordance with their stated objectives?

Excerpts from LVMH's financial statements

CONSOLIDATED BALANCE SHEET

Assets (EUR millions)	Notes	2011	2010	2009
Brands and other intangible assets – net	3	11,482	9,104	8,697
Goodwill – net	4	6,957	5,027	4,270
Property, plant and equipment – net	6	8,017	6,733	6,140
Investments in associates	7	170	223	213
Noncurrent available for sale financial assets	8	5,982	3,891	540
Other noncurrent assets		478	319	750
Deferred tax		716	668	521
Noncurrent assets		**33,802**	**25,965**	**21,131**
Inventories and work in progress	9	7,510	5,991	5,644
Trade accounts receivable	10	1,878	1,565	1,455
Income taxes		121	96	217
Other current assets	11	1,455	1,255	1,213
Cash and cash equivalents	13	2,303	2,292	2,446
Current assets		**13,267**	**11,199**	**10,975**
Total assets		**47,069**	**37,164**	**32,106**

Liabilities and equity
(EUR millions)

	Notes	2011	2010	2009
Share capital		152	147	147
Share premium account		3,801	1,782	1,763
Treasury shares and LVMH-share settled derivatives		(485)	(607)	(929)
Cumulative translation adjustment		431	230	(495)
Revaluation reserves		2,689	1,244	871
Other reserves		12,798	11,370	10,684
Net profit, Group share		3,065	3,032	1,755
Equity, Group share	14	22,451	17,198	13,796
Minority interests	16	1,061	1,006	989
Total equity		**23,512**	**18,204**	**14,785**
Long term borrowings	17	4,132	3,432	4,077
Provisions	18	1,400	1,167	990
Deferred tax		3,925	3,354	3,117
Other noncurrent liabilities	19	4,506	3,947	3,089
Noncurrent liabilities		**13,963**	**11,900**	**11,273**
Short-term borrowings	17	3,134	1,834	1,708
Trade accounts payable		2,952	2,298	1,911
Income taxes		443	446	221
Provisions	18	349	339	334
Other current liabilities	20	2,716	2,143	1,874
Current liabilities		**9,594**	**7,060**	**6,048**
Total liabilities and equity		**47,069**	**37,164**	**32,106**

CONSOLIDATED INCOME STATEMENT

(EUR millions, except for earnings per share)	Notes	2011	2010	2009
Revenue	22	23,659	20,320	17,053
Cost of sales		(8,092)	(7,184)	(6,164)
Gross margin		15,567	13,136	10,889
Marketing and selling expenses		(8,360)	(7,098)	(6,051)
General and administrative expenses		(1,944)	(1,717)	(1,486)

(EUR millions, except for earnings per share)	Notes	2011	2010	2009
Profit from recurring operations	22–23	**5,263**	**4,321**	**3,352**
Other operating income and expenses	24	(109)	(152)	(191)
Operating profit		**5,154**	**4,169**	**3,161**
Cost of net financial debt		(151)	(151)	(187)
Other financial income and expenses		(91)	763	(155)
Net financial income (expense)	25	**(242)**	**612**	**(342)**
Income taxes	26	(1,453)	(1,469)	(849)
Income (loss) from investments in associates	7	6	7	3
Net profit before minority interests		**3,465**	**3,319**	**1,973**
Minority interests		(400)	(287)	(218)
Net profit, Group share		3,065	3,032	1,755
Basic Group share of net earnings per share (EUR)	27	**6.27**	**6.36**	**3.71**
Number of shares on which the calculation is based		488,769,286	476,870,920	473,597,075
Diluted Group share of net earnings per share (EUR)	27	**6.23**	**6.32**	**3.70**
Number of shares on which the calculation is based		492,207,492	479,739,697	474,838,025

Excerpts from Warnaco's financial statements

CONSOLIDATED BALANCE SHEETS

(Dollars in thousands, excluding per share data)

	December 31, 2011	January 1, 2011
Assets		
Current assets:		
Cash and cash equivalents...	$232,531	$191,227
Accounts receivable, less reserves of $94,739 and $95,639 as of December 31, 2011 and January 1, 2011, respectively	322,976	318,123
Inventories..	350,835	310,504
Assets of discontinued operations	—	125
Prepaid expenses and other current assets........................	99,686	100,389
Deferred income taxes	58,602	58,270
Total current assets	1,064,630	978,638

(Continued)

	December 31, 2011	January 1, 2011
Property, plant and equipment, net..	133,022	129,252
Other assets:		
Licenses, trademarks and other intangible assets, net.....	320,880	373,276
Deferred financing costs, net...	8,790	2,540
Deferred income taxes	21,885	11,769
Other assets...	58,695	42,519
Goodwill...	139,948	115,278
Total assets..	$1,747,850	$1,653,272
Liabilities, Redeemable Non-Controlling Interest and Stockholders' Equity		
Current liabilities:		
Short-term debt...	$47,513	$32,172
Accounts payable...	141,797	152,714
Accrued liabilities...	212,655	227,561
Liabilities of discontinued operations	6,797	18,800
Accrued income taxes payable...	41,762	37,957
Deferred income taxes	1,476	262
Total current liabilities	452,000	469,466
Long-term debt	208,477	—
Deferred income taxes	37,000	74,233
Other long-term liabilities..	137,973	136,967
Commitments and contingencies		
Redeemable non-controlling interest	15,200	—
Stockholders' equity:		
Preferred stock (See Note 13)..	—	—
Common stock: $0.01 par value, 112,500,000 shares authorized, 52,184,730 and 51,712,674 issued as of December 31, 2011 and January 1, 2011, respectively	522	517
Additional paid-in capital	721,356	674,508
Accumulated other comprehensive income	16,242	43,048
Retained earnings	625,760	501,394
Treasury stock, at cost 11,790,428 and 7,445,166 shares as of December 31, 2011 and January 1, 2011, respectively	(466,680)	(246,861)
Total stockholders' equity..	897,200	972,606
Total liabilities, redeemable non-controlling interest and stockholders' equity...	$1,747,850	$1,653,272

CONSOLIDATED STATEMENTS OF OPERATIONS

(Dollars in thousands, excluding per share amounts)

	Fiscal 2011	Fiscal 2010	Fiscal 2009
Net revenues..	$2,513,388	$2,295,751	$2,019,625
Cost of goods sold	1,412,446	1,275,788	1,155,278
Gross profit	1,100,942	1,019,963	864,347
Selling, general and administrative expenses.................	844,696	758,053	638,907
Amortization of intangible assets....................................	47,957	11,549	11,032
Pension expense	26,744	2,550	20,873
Operating income..	181,545	247,811	193,535
Other loss..	631	6,238	1,889
Interest expense...	16,274	14,483	23,897
Interest income..	(3,361)	(2,815)	(1,248)
Income from continuing operations before provision for income taxes and noncontrolling interest.................	168,001	229,905	168,997
Provision for income taxes..	36,006	82,107	64,272
Income from continuing operations before noncontrolling interest...	131,995	147,798	104,725
Loss from discontinued operations, net of taxes............	(4,802)	(9,217)	(6,227)
Net income	127,193	138,581	98,498
Less: Net income (loss) attributable to the noncontrolling interest	(257)	—	2,500
Net income attributable to Warnaco Group	$127,450	$138,581	$95,998
Amounts attributable to Warnaco Group common shareholders:			
Income from continuing operations, net of tax..........	$132,252	$147,798	$102,225
Discontinued operations, net of tax	(4,802)	(9,217)	(6,227)
Net income	$127,450	$138,581	$95,998
Basic income per common share attributable to Warnaco Group common shareholders (see Note 14):			
Income from continuing operations.........................	$3.07	$3.26	$2.22
Loss from discontinued operations	(0.11)	(0.20)	(0.13)
Net income...	$2.96	$3.06	$2.09

(Continued)

	Fiscal 2011	Fiscal 2010	Fiscal 2009
Diluted income per common share attributable to Warnaco Group common shareholders (see Note 14):			
Income from continuing operations.........................	$3.01	$3.19	$2.19
Loss from discontinued operations	(0.11)	(0.20)	(0.14)
Net income...	$2.90	$2.99	$2.05
Weighted average number of shares outstanding used in computing income per common share (see Note 14):			
Basic...	42,425,750	44,701,643	45,433,874
Diluted	43,299,849	45,755,935	46,196,397

Notes

1. If the company has preferred shares, preferred dividends are subtracted from net income. The numerator should equal the net income available to common shareholders only.
2. SAP uses the term "profit after tax" for "net income."
3. For this and the ratios to follow, values will be shown initially for 2009 and then for the years 2007–2009.
4. NIBL = non-interest-bearing liabilities; WCR = the working capital requirement.
5. The definition of invested capital used here applies at group level only. It is common practice to exclude cash when measuring invested capital at division or business unit levels. The reason for this treatment is that cash tends to be centrally managed and is therefore not the responsibility of division managers.
6. The discussion on how to calculate invested capital is adapted from S.D. Young and S.F. O'Byrne, *EVA and Value Based Management: A Practical Guide to Implementation*, McGraw-Hill, 2001.
7. SAP uses the term "operating profit" in place of "operating income." The latter term is more common.
8. Readers familiar with the "ROIC trees" popularized by strategy consultants McKinsey should recognize DuPont analysis. ROIC trees and DuPont analysis are essentially the same.
9. Although we don't show it here, similar analyses can be performed for the balance sheet.
10. The accounts receivable turnover ratio equals revenues ($36 297m) divided by average accounts receivable ($4369m), or 8.31 times. The average receivable period equals 365 divided by 8.31, or 44 days.
11. €3 billion ÷ 250 days (assuming five working days each week and 50 working weeks each year).
12. The following discussion on M&M is adapted from S.D. Young and S.F. O'Byrne, *EVA and Value Based Management: a Practical Guide to Implementation*, New York: McGraw-Hill, 2001.
13. More precisely, M&M assume that tax laws are nondiscriminatory, meaning that they don't favor one form of financing over another. Therefore, the M&M model still holds even if there are taxes, as long as tax law doesn't favor debt over equity, or vice versa.
14. The value of this tax shield varies from country to country. In the US and Germany, provisions in their tax codes designed to reduce the double taxation of dividends have the effect of reducing the relative tax advantages of debt. In countries with tax laws that are somewhat more hostile to equity investors, such as the UK, the tax advantages of debt are greater.

15. "Investment grade" is defined as a rating of BBB– or better from S&P or Baa3 (or better) from Moody's. Bonds with lower ratings are considered "speculative grade." "Junk bond" is popular slang for speculative grade debt. The distinction between the two grades is important because many institutional investors are barred, by law or policy, from buying junk bonds. This helps to explain why a company's borrowing costs tend to spike upwards when its debt falls below investment grade.

16. EBITDA is earnings before interest, tax, depreciation, and amortization. It is a popular, though flawed, proxy for cash flow. Chapter 7, Business Valuation and Financial Statement Analysis, discusses this issue in detail.

17. Credit analysts view FOCF as a better indicator of a company's ability to repay debt than free cash flow measures that subtract all forms of investment from operating cash, including the purchase of financial securities. The idea is that other investments, including corporate acquisitions, are more discretionary in nature than capital investments. Because assets wear out and must be replaced, at least some capital investment is expected, even for companies that are no longer growing. (This is why FOCF is calculated net of capital expenditures.) But companies can always choose to avoid the takeover market and focus on organic growth (i.e., growth of existing businesses) instead. Corporate treasury movements (i.e., the purchase and sale of financial instruments, usually short-term, to manage the company's liquid resources) are also considered discretionary.

18. There is some debate over whether deferred tax liabilities and provisions should be included among total debts. If there is reason to doubt that a portion of either liability will not result in a future cash payment, that portion should be excluded. What this example shows is that the definition of total debt is not entirely straightforward.

19. E. Altman, "Financial ratios: discriminant analysis and the prediction of corporate bankruptcy," *Journal of Finance*, 1968, pp. 589–609; and J. Ohlson, "Financial ratios and the probabilistic prediction of bankruptcy," *Journal of Accounting Research*, 1980, pp. 109–131.

Business Valuation and Financial Statement Analysis

The final stage of financial statement analysis converts what has already been learned from the first three steps – industry and business analysis, accounting analysis, and ratio analysis – into forecasts of future benefits. This note shows how to convert such forecasts into estimates of value.

Valuation principles

The key question to ask whenever we think of investing is how much the right to a future stream of benefits from the investment is worth to us today.[1] This value is a function of the *magnitude, timing*, and *uncertainty* of these future benefits.

By magnitude we mean that, all else being equal, the greater the benefit (whether we define it as "cash flow" or something else), the better. Timing means that we would rather have the benefit now than have to wait for it. For example, the earlier we expect to receive a cash flow, the more valuable that cash flow is to us today. Uncertainty refers to the possibility that the expected benefits might not materialize. Intuitively, the greater this uncertainty, the less valuable an expected benefit is to us now.

These insights are captured in the discounted cash flow (DCF) approach to valuation. With this approach, we project expected future cash flows (magnitude and timing), then discount them at an interest rate, or rate or return. The discount rate reflects both the time value of money (i.e., the idea that **investors would rather have cash today than** tomorrow and must therefore be paid to wait) and a risk premium that reflects the incremental return investors require to compensate them for the risk that the cash flow might not materialize (uncertainty). This approach is summarized in the formula:

$$\text{Value} = \sum_{t=1}^{t=n} \frac{\text{CF}_t}{(1+r)^t}$$

where n is the economic life of the investment (usually expressed in years);[2] CF_t is the expected cash flow in period t; and r is the discount rate that reflects the perceived riskiness, or uncertainty, of the cash flows.

This equation tells us that the value of any asset, including a business enterprise, is equal to the sum of discounted cash flows. The discount rate is the opportunity cost of capital, which measures the return that investors would expect to receive if the cash were invested elsewhere in assets or companies of similar risk.[3]

Valuation: from theory to practice

The value of the firm equals the present value of its future cash flows, or more specifically, "free cash flows," plus the value of any existing cash balances. We define free cash flow as the amount of cash generated in any given year from the company's operations, net of the investment to be made in that year.

Recalling the cash flow statement, all cash flows are the result of operating, investing, or financing activities. Think of free cash flow as operating cash flows, net of investing cash flows, thus representing the amount of operating cash left over for distribution to the firm's capital providers. It's the prospect of receiving such cash in future that motivates investors to contribute cash now.

Free cash flow is calculated as follows:

$$
\begin{array}{rl}
& \text{Operating income } (1-T) \\
+ & \text{Depreciation} \\
- & \text{Investment} \\
\hline
= & \text{Free Cash Flow}
\end{array}
$$

Operating income, sometimes known as EBIT, or Earnings before Interest and Tax, is the profit expected from the firm's normal, recurring business activities (sales − operating expenses). When operating income is multiplied by $(1-T)$, where T is the corporate tax rate, the result is net operating profit after tax, or NOPAT. Depreciation (amortization too, if there is any) is added back because it' not a cash expense. Finally, investment in working capital and in property, plant and equipment (PP&E) is subtracted.[4]

Alternatively, free cash flow can be calculated as follows:

$$\text{NOPAT} - \text{Change in Invested Capital}$$

where the change in invested capital equals investment in working capital and PP&E, minus depreciation (and amortization).

To illustrate the equivalency of these alternative definitions of free cash flow, assume that:

$$\text{Operating income} = \$1000$$
$$T = 30\%$$
$$\text{Investment} = \$600$$
$$\text{Depreciation} = \$350$$

Free cash flow equals:

$$
\begin{array}{rl}
 & \$1000\,(1-30\%) \\
+ & 350 \\
- & 600 \\
\hline
= & \$450
\end{array}
$$

Alternatively, free cash flow can be calculated by subtracting the change in net operating assets ($600 – $350) from NOPAT ($700). Here too, free cash flow is $450.

Value is simply the sum of future free cash flows, discounted at the opportunity cost of capital, as shown below:

$$\text{Value}_0 = \frac{\text{Free Cash Flow}_1}{(1+\text{OCC})} + \frac{\text{Free Cash Flow}_2}{(1+\text{OCC})^2} + \ldots$$

where OCC is the opportunity cost of capital.

One practical problem with this model is the theoretically indefinite life of the business. Obviously, annual cash flows cannot be estimated in perpetuity. This problem is usually solved by dividing the future cash flows into two separate elements, one that reflects the present value of cash flows during an explicit forecast period and the other that reflects the present value of cash flows after the forecast period. The latter value is commonly known

Exhibit 7.1 Forecasts for SAP Group: Free cash flows and economic profit (€ million)

	2010	2011	2012	2013	2014	2015	2016	2017	2018	2019	2020
Income statement											
Sales	11,098.9	11,542.8	11,542.8	11,542.8	11,542.8	11,542.8	11,542.8	11,542.8	11,542.8	11,542.8	11,542.8
NOPAT	1,942.3	2,031.5	2,124.8	2,197.3	2,272.2	2,351.7	2,434.1	2,519.3	2,607.4	2,698.7	2,779.6
Balance sheet											
Beginning IC	9,958.0	8,244.9	8,003.0	7,803.0	8,656.1	8,959.0	9,272.6	9,597.2	9,933.1	10,280.7	10,589.1
Capital charges	896.2	742.0	720.3	702.3	779.0	806.3	834.5	863.7	894.0	925.3	953.0
Economic profit	1,046.1	1,289.5	1,404.5	1,495.0	1,493.2	1,545.4	1,599.5	1,655.5	1,713.5	1,773.4	1,826.6
Free cash flow	3,655.4	2,273.4	2,324.9	1,344.2	1,969.3	2,038.2	2,109.5	2,183.4	2,259.8	2,390.3	2,462.0
Assumptions											
Sales growth	4.0%	4.0%	4.0%	4.0%	4.0%	3.5%	3.5%	3.5%	3.5%	3.5%	3.0%
NOPAT margin	17.5%	17.6%	17.7%	17.6%	17.5%	17.5%	17.5%	17.5%	17.5%	17.5%	17.5%
IC turnover	1.3	1.4	1.5	1.6	1.5	1.5	1.5	1.5	1.5	1.5	1.5
OCC	9%	9%	9%	9%	9%	9%	9%	9%	9%	9%	9%
	1,942.3	2,031.5	2,124.8	2,197.3	2,272.2	2,351.7	2,434.1	2,519.3	2,607.4	2,698.7	2,779.6

NOPAT = net operating profit after tax; IC = invested capital.

Exhibit 7.2 Valuation summary for SAP Group (€ million)

	(1) Nonoperations value	(2) Beginning invested capital	(3) Value from forecasts for 2010–19	(4) Terminal value	(5) Value of the firm
Discounted cash flow	1,884.00	N/A	14,809.60	13,046.14	29,739.74
Economic profit	1,884.00	9,958.00	9,324.57	8,573.18	29,739.74

Note: The value of the firm (column 5) equals the sum of columns 1, 3, and 4 for the DCF method, and the sum of columns 1 through 4 for the EP method.

Terminal value

Of course, SAP Group is expected to survive far beyond 2019. Therefore rather than make specific, year-by-year forecasts of performance for all future periods – a practical impossibility – we estimate a terminal value for the end of the forecast horizon. This estimate requires a forecast of future free cash flows, or EP, from 2020 onward.

There are a number of approaches to estimating this terminal value, but we believe that the best approach is one that assumes rapid convergence to a competitive equilibrium at the end of the forecast horizon. This means that value-creating investment is not likely to continue indefinitely. Instead, we expect that after the 10-year forecast horizon, any further investments made by SAP Group will be value-neutral. Investments made beyond the horizon will generate enough NOPAT to cover the opportunity cost of capital, but no value-creating returns will be earned. This means that while the return on invested capital (ROIC) might remain well above the company's OCC for a long time, the return on any newly invested capital, or RONIC, is expected to equal the OCC.

RONIC equals the incremental NOPAT in a given year (i.e., the increase in NOPAT over the previous year), divided by incremental invested capital. For example, RONIC in 2015 equals the increase in NOPAT over the previous year, €79.5 million (€8959.0 million – €8656.1 million), divided by the increase in invested capital, €302.9 million (€13 878.5 million – €13 330.5 million), or 26.2%. This level is not sustainable, however, because it is significantly greater than the company's opportunity cost of capital (9%).

Such an approach to terminal value assumes that SAP Group will sustain any competitive advantage created before the end of 2019, but no further source of competitive advantage is expected. We believe this to be the most reasonable assumption one can make about terminal value because otherwise the valuation would implicitly assume that the company can create additional sources of competitive advantage in perpetuity. Competitive forces should prevent such a thing from happening. The practical effect of this assumption is that any growth achieved beyond the forecast horizon will be value-neutral.[6]

To calculate a terminal value for SAP Group, NOPAT and free cash flow are estimated for 2020, the terminal year. We begin by estimating sales for 2020, based on the assumption that sales will grow by 3% from the previous year. The resulting sales forecast, €1883.7 million, is multiplied by the long-run NOPAT margin assumption, 17.5%, to yield NOPAT, €2779.6 million. To estimate the terminal value, NOPAT is divided by the 9% OCC:

$$\frac{€279.6 \text{ million}}{0.09} = €30\ 884.4 \text{ million}$$

This figure reflects the value at the end of the investment horizon (end of 2019) for all free cash flows from 2020 onward. We then discount the terminal value (expected 10 years hence) by the 9% OCC, resulting in €13 046.1 million (Exhibit 7.2). When added to nonoperating sources of value (the cash balance of €1884 million at the end of 2009) and the present value of the free cash flows over the 10-year forecast horizon, we get an estimated value for SAP Group of €29 739.7 million, or about €29.7 billion.[7]

It should be noted that €29.7 billion is our estimate for the value of the firm, also called "enterprise value," and not the value of SAP Group's equity. It's the present value of current cash and future cash flows for all capital providers, including lenders. Given that lenders have priority of claim over shareholders, their claims must be subtracted from the value of the firm to arrive at equity value.[8]

If we assume that the market value of debt is equal to its book value,[9] the equity value for SAP is calculated as follows:

Value of the firm:	€29 739.7 million
Debt:	1 578.0 million
Value of equity:	€28 161.7 million

This means that the shares of SAP Group are worth approximately €28.2 billion.

At the beginning of 2010, when the 2009 financial statements of SAP were issued, the market value of SAP's equity (otherwise known as its "market capitalization" or "market cap") was about €40.5 billion, roughly €12.3 billion greater than the above figure. On the basis of this estimate, we would conclude that the shares of SAP are overvalued.

A brief word on growth rates

You may have noticed in the SAP example that we assumed zero growth in NOPAT for the terminal value period. We could have made other growth assumptions, but they would have had no influence on the valuation. The reason is because our terminal value is based on the assumption that RONICs beyond the forecast horizon will equal the OCC. To borrow from the corporate finance lexicon, all investments in the terminal value period are expected to have zero *net present value* – no value is created or destroyed. This is the essence of the competitive equilibrium assumption, and the reason we assume zero growth for the terminal period.

However, there is a popular variant on the two-stage DCF model presented in this chapter in which the growth assumption beyond the explicit forecast horizon does matter. This three-stage model features two continuing value periods, instead of the single (terminal) period in the two-stage version. In the first of these continuing value periods, RONICs will exceed the OCC, which is why this stage is sometimes called the *over-performance* or *competitive-advantage* period. The fundamental assumption here is that while some source of continuing competitive advantage allows for RONICs to exceed the OCC, RONIC will gradually converge to the OCC by the end of the period. To put it another way, because RONIC exceeds the OCC, the growth in NOPAT will exceed any increased investment, causing an increase in expected free cash flow. For this reason, the growth assumption in the first continuing value period will have a significant effect on the valuation.

Relative valuation

A popular alternative to DCF and EP-based valuation is known as "relative valuation." Under this approach, the value of a company is determined in relation to how similar companies are priced in the market. The term "relative" means that value is defined relative to other, similar businesses, and not in any absolute sense (as with the DCF and EP approaches).

The idea is that the market pays for a certain attribute – earnings, sales, cash flow, or something else – that gives rise to value. Market price is then converted into a multiple of this attribute. For example, if the market is paying between €17 and €21 for every dollar of net income reported by companies in a certain industry, an estimate of value can be derived simply by taking the product of this multiple (somewhere between 17 and 21) and earnings per share (EPS). If we deemed 20 to be a proper multiple for a given firm, and EPS was €4, the value of each share of stock is estimated to be €80 (€20 × €4). If shares were selling for less than €80, we would say that they trade at a discount. If, on the other hand, the shares were selling for more than €80, we would say that they trade at a premium.

From the above example it should be obvious that this method is much easier than the DCF/ EP approaches. But as we will see below, there is a cost to this simplicity.

Performing a relative valuation

Here's how relative valuations are usually done:

1. *A list of comparable companies is created.* Usually these comparables are publicly traded (and therefore have easily observed market prices). The comparables may be industry peers, but it often pays to look beyond the industry for companies of similar size and with similar risk profiles.
2. *Market values are converted into trading multiples*, such as price–earnings (p/e), price-to-book (p/b), enterprise value-to-sales, and enterprise value-to-EBITDA ratios. The idea is to identify some attribute of a firm that gives rise to value, and to define the market price with respect to this attribute. While some attributes apply to any business – examples include earnings, EBITDA, and sales – other attributes are industry-specific. Examples of the latter type include number of rooms (hotel industry), kilowatt hours (power generation), and number of subscribers (cable television and mobile phone operators).
3. *Multiples are adjusted for differences between the comparables and the subject firm.* For example, if the comparables have an average p/e ratio of 15, but the subject company has an above-average growth rate, the p/e used for valuation purposes will probably be higher than 15.

The resulting multiples can then be used for a variety of purposes. For example, portfolio managers may use them to determine if a target company is underpriced (selling at a discount to its peers) or overpriced (selling at a premium).

One reason for the popularity of this approach is that key data – prices and multiples for comparable companies – are widely available. Reuters, Bloomberg, and other investor services provide such data via the internet, either free of charge or for a small fee.

Until recently, most relative valuations focused on p/e ratios, and this approach continues to be popular. But in some investment circles, EBITDA multiples are now the most common relative valuation approach. EBITDA is thought to offer the following advantages:

- It can be calculated for firms with net losses because most such businesses at least show a positive EBITDA. (Obviously, p/e ratios cannot be used if earnings are negative.) Even firms with negative operating cash flow may have a positive EBITDA, because the latter measure does not subtract taxes or interest.

- It controls for differences among companies in their depreciation and amortization policies.
- EBITDA is popular for leveraged (i.e., high debt) transactions, such as management buy-outs, because it is thought to represent cash generated by the firm before all discretionary expenditures, including asset replacement, and therefore represents the amount of operating cash available to support debt repayments.
- Because it ignores the costs of financial leverage, it allows for comparisons among firms with different capital structures.

Still, there are some important drawbacks and limitations to the use of EBITDA. For example, it ignores changes in working capital and thus overstates cash flow in periods of working capital growth. In profitable, fast-growing industries, EBITDA is a poor proxy for operating cash. Also, EBITDA does not consider the amount of required reinvestment, which can be a serious drawback in industries where the rate of technological change is high or in any business where assets are short-lived and must be frequently replaced.

Although EBITDA is useful in its simplicity, it is worth asking why so many analysts rely on it as a proxy for cash flow when other, more valid, measures are easily available.

Relative valuation: the verdict

Relative valuation may be easy, but it can easily go wrong. Perhaps the most serious deficiency is a direct consequence of its simplicity. One attractive aspect of multiples-based valuation is that it doesn't require the extensive range of assumptions required of a good DCF/EP model. For example, the pricing of companies using earnings or EBITDA multiples does not require explicit assumptions on reinvestment rates, returns on new invested capital, or terminal values. But contrary to popular wisdom, a multiples approach does incorporate these assumptions. The assumptions are buried in the multiple itself.

For example, any time you value a company using a p/e ratio or EBITDA multiple, you are making the same assumptions as users of sophisticated DCF models. The difference is that while they are forced to make the assumptions explicitly, your assumptions are embedded in the multiple. The problem with this approach is that you could be making wildly unrealistic assumptions regarding, say, RONIC, and not even know it. Your earnings multiple might assume a RONIC several percentage points greater than OCC, in perpetuity. Economic logic tells us that this is a practical impossibility in competitive markets. But you will never know this assumption is being made because you aren't forcing yourself to make it explicitly.

One could even argue that multiples-based valuations aren't really valuations at all, but merely ways of describing prices that have already been paid for similar assets. To our way of thinking, there is only one legitimate reason why you might resort to multiples: to communicate valuations, especially during negotiations with other investors. For example, many private equity firms value a target company using a rigorous DCF/EP model, and then translate the valuation into multiples. In effect, multiples constitute a language, a way for business people and investors to talk to each other in mutually understandable terms. But while multiples can be highly effective as communication tools, a proper valuation requires a DCF or EP approach.

Key lessons from the chapter

- The value of any firm equals the present value of its expected future cash flows plus the value of existing cash balances and any nonoperating assets.
- Free cash flows are calculated as follows: net operating profit after tax plus depreciation less investments in net operating assets. Free cash flows are the key to valuation because they equal the cash flows generated from recurring operations, net of investment, and therefore represent the amount of cash flow available in a given year for distribution to the firm's capital providers. In effect, shareholders and debt providers invest in companies because of the expectation of future free cash flows.
- An alternative approach to valuation focuses on EP, but yields results that are mathematically equivalent to the DCF model.
- EP, also known as economic value added, equals net operating profit after tax (NOPAT), net of capital charges. Capital charges equal the product of invested capital and the opportunity cost of capital.
- Relative valuation, based on multiples of price/earnings, EBIT, EBITDA and other accounting variables, are more popular approaches to valuation than DCF. However, relative valuation suffers from several flaws. First, determining the appropriate multiples for a given company is always problematic. For a company to be truly "comparable" with other companies, it must be similar on a broad range of dimensions, including expected growth, accounting policy, physical asset endowment, and a host of other factors. Second, it can be argued that relative valuation isn't really valuation at all, but merely a way to describe the price recently paid for supposedly similar assets. It therefore ignores the fundamental truth that value and price are not the same. Our aim in valuation is to identify value, not price.

Key terms and concepts from the chapter

Time value of money	Economic profit	Terminal value
Free cash flows	Forecast period	Relative valuation

Questions

1. Compare and contrast the discount cash flow (DCF) approach to valuation with the economic profit approach. Which do you prefer, and why?

2. True or false: Using the economic profit approach for valuation yields identical results to the DCF approach.

3. EVA® is a well-known version of economic profit. Contrast and compare the two measures.

4. What factors influence the length of the explicit forecast horizon in a DCF valuation model? Why 5 years, or 10?

5. How are nonoperating assets (such as excess cash and real estate no longer used in current operations) handled in DCF models?

6. Numerous approaches are used to estimate terminal values for DCF models. Which approach do you prefer, and why?

7. What accounts for the popularity of relative valuation approaches (p/e ratios, EDITDA multiples, etc.)?

8. What are the drawbacks of relative valuation?

Problems

7.1   Estimating the value of Home Depot

Note: This problem is a continuation of the Home Depot exercise found at the back of Chapter 6.

Assume that your analysis of Home Depot's competitive strategy, industry economics, and previous financial performance lead you to make the following forecasts:

*   Sales will grow 12% per year in 2007 and 2008, and 10% per year in 2009, 2010, and 2011.
*   NOPAT margins will equal 8% throughout the entire forecast horizon.

- The invested capital turnover (calculated on beginning IC) will equal 2.85 throughout the entire five-year forecast horizon except for 2007. In 2007, set beginning IC equal to Home Depot's ending IC from 2006 (a 2.77 invested capital turnover will exist in 2007).
- Terminal value will be estimated using the following approach which assumes a perpetuity:

$$\text{Terminal value} = (\text{NOPAT}_{2011} \div \text{OCC})$$

- The opportunity cost of capital (OCC) = 11%.

Required

(a) Based on the above forecasts, estimate the expected economic profit for each year in the forecast horizon (2007–2011). Refer to the Home Depot question at the back of the previous chapter for any additional information that you need.

(b) Assume that 2.124 billon shares of stock are outstanding, and the shares sell for $40 per share at the time of your investment decision. Assume that nonoperating assets are insignificant, all flows occur at the end of the period, and the market value of debt is $4 billion. Based on either an economic profit-based or discounted cash flow valuation model, is Home Depot Corporation a buy, hold, or sell?

The present value factors at 11% are as follows:

1 period	-	0.90090
2 periods	-	0.81162
3 periods	-	0.73119
4 periods	-	0.65873
5 periods	-	0.59345

7.2   Explaining differences in p/e ratios

The price/earnings ratios (from early 2012 prices and 2011 earnings) of several large companies are shown below:

Apple	23
Coca-Cola	13
Bank of China	9
Oracle	23

SABMiller	30
EDF (France)	56
Gazprom	6

Required

What factors might explain the differences in p/e ratios observed among these companies?

7.3   Explaining differences in p/e ratios

The price/earnings ratios (from early 2012 prices and 2011 earnings) of several large pharmaceutical companies are shown below:

Pfizer	20
Johnson & Johnson	12
GlaxoSmithKline	38
AstraZeneca	8
Eli Lilly	8
Bayer	37
Abbot Laboratories	17

Required

What factors might explain the differences in p/e ratios observed among these companies?

Case study

7.1   Valuation based on discounted cash flows: the case of Vardon Golf Ltd.

Vardon Golf Ltd. is a privately held maker of golf clubs. For decades it produced a full range of clubs, but recently most of its sales have come from hybrids, clubs that combine the best attributes of fairway woods and long irons. The company also produces putters that are starting to find some traction among professionals and low-handicap amateurs.

The company is profitable, but Cooper Palmer, a private equity firm based in London, believes that it has underperformed relative to its potential.

You are an analyst at Cooper Palmer and have been asked to perform a valuation of Vardon Golf. Financial data for 2012, the year just past, include the following:

Revenue	£10,000,000
Earnings before income and tax	2,000,000
Taxes on EBIT	600,000
Cash	£200,000
Working capital requirement (WCR)	1,500,000
Net fixed assets (NFA)*	7,500,000
Total invested capital	£9,200,000

*Net fixed assets = Property, plant and equipment, net of depreciation.

If the company continues under current management, the following performance parameters are expected:

Annual revenue growth*	4%
EBIT margin	20%
Tax rate	30%
Cash as a % of revenue	2%
WCR as a % of revenue	15%
NFA as a % of revenue	75%
Continuing value growth rate for NOPAT	2%

*For the years 2013 through 2017.

However, the partners at Cooper Palmer are convinced that if they ran the company, Vardon could realize growth opportunities and operating efficiencies not expected under current ownership. For example, cost savings would boost EBIT margins and improved asset utilization would reduce required investments in WCR and NFA. Based on your discussion with the partners, you reestimate the parameters as follows:

Annual revenue growth	6%
EBIT margin	22%
Tax rate	30%
Cash as a % of revenue	2%
WCR as a % of revenue	12%
NFA as a % of revenue	65%
Continuing value growth rate for NOPAT	3%

Required

(a) Assuming a 5-year explicit forecast horizon and an opportunity cost of capital of 9%, estimate the value of Vardon Golf under current ownership.

(b) Reestimate the value of Vardon Golf based on the partners' assessments of potential operating improvements. Vardon's current owners are willing to sell the company for £17.75 million. Is that an attractive price for Cooper Palmer?

Notes

1. This section has been adapted from S.D. Young and S.F. O'Byrne, *EVA and Value Based Management: A Practical Guide to Implementation*, McGraw-Hill, 2001.
2. When valuing businesses, n is usually set to ∞.
3. A common error in valuation is to discount future cash flows at the cost of financing. To see the error in this practice, consider the following example. You have an investment opportunity that is expected to yield 10%. A bank is willing to lend the capital at 6%. Should you borrow the funds and invest them at 10%? The answer seems obvious, but imagine that other investments of similar risk are expected to yield 14%. Your original investment no longer seems like a good idea, does it? The moral of this story is that the relevant benchmark is not the cost of financing, but the rate of return one can expect from similar investment. Hence, the expected future cash flows must be discounted at the opportunity cost of capital.
4. PP&E is defined here as any form of capital expenditure, not just investment in tangible fixed assets.
5. €3655.4 million × 0.91743 (the present value factor one period hence at 9%).
6. To clarify, SAP Group may grow beyond 2020, but the growth will be neither value creating nor value destroying. One practical effect of this assumption is that whatever growth rate we choose for SAP beyond 2020 will have no effect on value. Higher growth will translates into higher NOPAT, but the increase in NOPAT will be exactly offset by the required increase in capital investment. Therefore, higher growth assumptions have no effect on future free cash flows (nor, for that matter, to lower growth assumptions).
7. Including the full amount of the cash balance in the value of the firm assumes that the market values existing cash euro for euro. In effect, it assumes that cash represents a zero NPV investment..
8. Debt is defined here as the sum of short-term financial liabilities, long-term financial liabilities, tax liabilities, and long-term provisions. SAP's total debt at the end of 2009 is €1578 million.
9. The assumption that book value of debt is equal to its market value is not entirely valid, but in a relatively stable interest-rate environment, we would expect the two figures to be roughly equal, especially for blue-chip companies like SAP. Still, if we had an actual market value for the debt (i.e., what the debt claims were selling for at the time of the valuation), we would subtract that figure from the value of the firm to arrive at equity value.

CHAPTER 8

Accounting for Receivables and Bad Debts

Introduction

Receivables are amounts owed to a business by outsiders. Most receivables arise from credit sales to customers and are called "accounts receivable" or "trade receivables." In this chapter we discuss the accounting for customer-based receivables under US GAAP and IFRS. Both regimes require that accounts receivable appear in the balance sheet at **net realizable value**. In theory, this value should reflect the amount owed to the company by its customers. But not all receivables are collected (customers go bankrupt) and some merchandise might be returned. The accounting for receivables must incorporate both of these factors. The appendix to this chapter discusses the banking-industry analog to uncollectible accounts – loan loss reserves.

Estimating bad debts

Some credit sales never get collected. Most companies establish credit policies that balance the expected cost of credit sales (e.g., billing costs, collection costs, and the risk of bad debts) with the benefit of increased sales. Companies choose what they believe will be the profit-maximizing policy.

The challenge from an accounting point of view is that accounts receivable should reflect how much cash the company expects to collect from its customers, not how much cash is owed to it. Therefore, estimates of bad debts, otherwise known as "uncollectible accounts," must be made.

This estimate can be done in either of two ways:

- the sales revenue approach, or
- the gross accounts receivable approach.

The sales revenue approach

Under this approach the company estimates bad debt expense based on a percentage of sales. For example, if a company has revenues of $5 million, and a review of customer accounts, current economic conditions, and historical experience suggests that 1% of these revenues will be uncollectible, the following entry would be made:

Bad debt expense	$50,000	
Allowance for doubtful accounts		$50,000

The bad debt expense appears as an operating expense on the income statement. The allowance for doubtful accounts is a "contra-asset" (as mentioned in Chapter 2) in that it offsets the gross receivables in determining the net receivables reported on the balance sheet. If half of the $5 million in sales remained uncollected at the end of the year, net accounts receivable would be $2.45 million ($2.5 million – $50 000).

The gross accounts receivable approach

This approach affects the same accounts but arrives at the estimates by focusing on the receivables balance instead of sales revenues. For example, if historical experience and other factors suggest that 3% of receivables are uncollectible, and the balance in gross receivables is $2.5 million, the balance in the contra-account must be $75 000 ($2.5 million × 3%). The company then makes whatever entry is needed to bring the balance in the contra-account to this amount. If no previous entry has been made (i.e., the current balance is 0), the following entry is required:

Bad debt expense	$75,000	
Allowance for doubtful accounts		$75,000

If, on the other hand, the contra-asset already had a balance of $40 000, the entry would be:

Bad debt expense	$35,000	
Allowance for doubtful accounts		$35,000

Writing off accounts

Regardless of which method is chosen to estimate bad debts, accounts are written off using the following entry:

Allowance for doubtful accounts	XX	
Accounts receivable		XX

By writing off a specific account (i.e., the account of a specific customer), the company is conceding that the cash expected from the sale will never be collected. An important point to note from the above entry is that the income statement is unaffected. Writing off specific accounts, after they prove to be uncollectible, has no effect on earnings. The earnings impact is felt only when the allowance is taken (or adjusted).

The direct method: an alternative approach

Thus far, we have assumed that the company is using the "allowance method" in accounting for bad debts. This method is required under both US GAAP and IFRS. An alternative approach, sometimes allowed (or even required) for tax purposes, is called the "direct method." This method may even be used under US GAAP or IFRS, but only under those rare instances when the allowance method is not practical. Under the direct method, bad debt expense is recognized only when individual accounts are written off. No estimates of bad debts are made, and there is no allowance account. When a specific account is deemed to be uncollectible, the following entry is made:

Bad debt expense	XX	
Accounts receivable		XX

Although this method offers the virtue of simplicity, it has been rejected for financial reporting purposes because:

- Companies can easily manipulate bad debt expense by determining the precise timing that a specific account is written off. For example, if a company is having a mediocre year, it may choose to delay the recognition of a bad debt related to a specific account until the following accounting period.
- The accounts receivable balance is misleading. Instead of reflecting what the company expects to collect in cash from its credit sales, it reflects the total amount owed by customers, even those amounts that will later prove to be uncollectible.
- It violates the matching principle. Instead of matching bad debt expense against the sales related to the expense, the expense is typically recognized in a later accounting period.

What happens when written-off accounts are later collected?

Occasionally, a company will recover at least a portion of what was owed by a customer whose account was written off. The accounting treatment for such recoveries depends on whether the allowance or direct method is used. Under the allowance method, the following entry is made:

Cash	XX	
Allowance for doubtful accounts		XX

In effect, the reduction to the contra-asset that occurred when the account was written off is restored. The income statement is unaffected; the recovery is treated as a balance sheet event only.

Recoveries under the direct method are different. Because the actual write-off of the customer's account had an income statement effect, the recovery too affects the income statement:

Cash	XX	
Other income		XX

The contra-asset account is not affected because there is no contra-asset account under the direct method.

The "aging" of accounts receivable

Regardless of which approach is chosen to estimate bad debt expense under the allowance method (percentage of sales or percentage of gross receivables), the company must periodically determine whether or not the balance in the contra-asset is adequate. In other words, does the contra-asset reflect a good-faith estimate regarding the proportion of remaining receivables that will prove to be uncollectible? To make this judgment, an "aging of accounts receivable" is performed. This process is so fundamental to the accounting for receivables that even if the company does not perform the aging, you can be certain that the auditors will.

The aging is done by categorizing each receivable based on the number of days it is overdue. A bad-debt percentage is then assigned to each category, and a mathematical average is taken to determine the appropriate balance in the allowance account.

To illustrate, assume that Morris Inc. has $10 million of outstanding receivables, distributed as shown in Table 8.1. On the basis of this aging schedule, management would assume that the

Table 8.1 Distribution of Morris Inc.'s outstanding receivables

(1) Number of days overdue	(2) Amount	(3) Probability of noncollection	(2) × (3)
0	$6 million	0.3%	$ 18,000
30–90	3 million	1.2%	36,000
90–180	0.6 million	10.0%	60,000
>180	0.4 million	50.0%	200,000
			$ 314,000

allowance account requires a balance of $314 000. If the existing balance is $200 000, the following entry would be required:

Bad debt expense	114,000	
Allowance for doubtful accounts		114,000

But notice that if the balance in the allowance account was far higher, say, $450 000, the following entry would be made:

Allowance for doubtful accounts	136,000	
Other income		136,000

This example shows that if Morris Inc. had overprovisioned for bad debts in previous years, it can reverse a portion of the balance in the allowance account, and boost earnings. When companies overprovision in this way, "hidden" or "cookie-jar" reserves are created. US GAAP and IFRS prohibit this practice, but the doctrine of conservatism (which in this case means ensuring that the allowance account is never too low) gives companies some latitude in creating such reserves.

Sales returns and allowances

Sometimes the wrong goods are shipped to customers or the correct goods arrive damaged. In either case, the customer will return the item or request a discount. In such cases, accounts receivable must be reduced and a charge is made to the income statement. For example, if Morris, Inc. agrees to reduce by $15 000 the price of goods that arrived damaged at a customer, the following adjusting entry is required:

Sales returns and allowances	15,000	
Accounts receivable		15,000

The entry reflects that fact that the client owes $15 000 less than was previously billed, and that sales revenue is effectively reduced. Notice that sales revenues are not reduced directly. A contra-account (contra to sales revenues) is created instead, sales returns and allowances, which allows the company to keep a record of the frequency and amount of returns and price reductions. The sales figure reported on the income statement equals net sales (sales minus the sales returns and allowances).

In industries or sectors where product returns are common and significant in monetary terms, the company not only recognizes returns as they occur, but an estimate must also be made at the end of each accounting period for the amount of future returns and allowances arising from receivables already on the books. Otherwise, the matching principle would be violated. The following entry is made:

Sales returns and allowances	XX	
Allowances for sales returns		XX

The debit is the contra-account to sales revenues, while the credit is contra to accounts receivable. In practice, however, estimated sales returns and allowances are small enough in most industries to ignore the above entry. Consequently, no end-of-year adjustment is typically made for these items. Also, when the actual returns and allowances change little from year to year, the above entry is not required because its effect on earnings will be minor.

Although less prone to manipulation than sales revenue, accounting games can be played with returns and allowances. These games fall into two basic categories:

1. Failure to record returns, and
2. Deliberately misestimating the amount of returns for future periods.

In the former case, a company may deliberately ship the wrong product to customers near the end of the year, or ship the correct product in the wrong amount, without any adjustment. The effect is to overstate revenues and profits in the current period. In the second, a company can understate expected returns, boosting current sales and profits, or overstate expected returns, thereby creating hidden reserves that can boost profits in the following year.

Analyzing receivables

Receivables are often the flip side to revenues. As companies recognize revenues, they often recognize accounts receivable at the same time. Therefore, the analysis of receivables plays an important role in the analysis of revenue recognition. Common sense suggests that as companies become increasingly aggressive in the recognition of revenue (for example, recognizing revenue too quickly), an increase in accounts receivable should be observed. For this reason, experienced analysts examine trends in the ratio of "receivables-to-sales." If the ratio is trending upwards, it could indicate any combination of the following possibilities:

- The company has become more lenient in its credit terms, extending credit to riskier customers or extending payment terms to existing customers.
- The company is encountering collection problems from several customers, perhaps because customers are in financial difficulty or they are retaliating for poor service or quality problems.
- Revenue-recognition policies are becoming more aggressive, as the company recognizes revenue earlier in its operating cycle than in previous periods or, in the most extreme cases, recognizes revenue for bogus sales.

One of the analyst's tasks in cases where the receivables-to-sales ratio is increasing is to determine which of the above explanations is relevant. An examination of the statement of cash flows is also helpful for this purpose. If receivables are growing more quickly than sales, the impact should be observed in the working capital requirement and in cash flows from operating activities.

Key lessons from the chapter

- Receivables are amounts owed to a business by outsiders. Most receivables arise from credit sales to customers.
- Accounts receivables appear on the balance sheet at net realizable value. Net realization value should reflect the amount of cash that the company expects to receive from its customers. This amount equals gross accounts receivable, minus an allowance for doubtful accounts.
- Most companies establish credit policies that balance the expected costs of credit sales with the benefit of increased sales.
- Estimates of bad debts can be done in either of two ways: the sales revenue approach or the gross accounts receivable approach.
- The aging of accounts receivable is done by categorizing each receivable based on the number of days it is overdue. A bad-debt percentage is then assigned to each category, and a weighted average is taken to determine the appropriate balance in the allowance account.
- Analyzing receivables plays an important role in the analysis of revenue recognition. If accounts receivable grow faster than revenues, it could indicate that the company has become more aggressive in its revenue-recognition policies, or that it is encountering problems in collecting cash from customers.
- Therefore, a growing receivables-to-sales ratio is a red flag that should be analyzed and explained.

Key terms and concepts from the chapter

Accounts receivable	Gross accounts	Sales returns and
Net realizable value	receivable approach	allowances
Allowance for doubtful	Writing off receivables	Sales discounts
accounts	Aging of accounts	Receivables-to-sales
Contra-asset account	receivables	ratio
Sales revenue approach	Contra revenue account	

Questions

1. What are the major differences between the allowance method and the direct method in accounting for bad debts?

2. What are the advantages of the allowance method (relative to the direct method)?

3. Most tax authorities require use of the direct method. What reasoning would a tax official give for not permitting the allowance method?

4. Why might the allowance for doubtful accounts have a debit balance during the accounting period, but never at the end of the period?

5. Consider the following statement: "The fewer the uncollectible accounts, the better." Can you think of instances where this statement might be false?

6. What factors cause the balance in the allowance for doubtful accounts to increase or decrease from one year to the next?

7. How are recoveries of cash from previously written-off accounts treated under the allowance method? The direct method? Why is the accounting treatment for such events different under the two methods?

8. Many companies sell their receivables, either through a process known as "factoring" or through "securitization." Why do companies do this?

Appendix 8.1 Accounting for loan loss reserves

Banks and other institutions in the financial services sector do not have accounts receivable in quite the manner discussed in this chapter. Instead, they have *loans* receivable. On the surface, the accounting for loan receivables is similar to that of accounts receivable, but there are differences.

Most national banking regulators require that banks include in their financial statements a contra-asset account called allowance for loan losses (also known as reserves for loan losses). This account absorbs losses both from loans that the bank has already identified as nonperforming (i.e., bad loans) and from some apparently good loans that will later prove to be nonperforming. In other words, banks establish reserves for both performing and nonperforming loans.[1] For example, IAS 30 (the relevant IFRS standard) states that the amount of losses that are specifically identified and the potential losses *not* specifically identified should both be recognized as expenses and deducted from the carrying amount of the loans. It should be noted that while IFRS and US GAAP have specific standards dealing with bad loans, the accounting is partly influenced by regulatory imperatives unique to the banking sector.

The reserve for loan loss account is established and maintained by periodic charges against earnings. The charges (called loan loss provisions, or something similar) show up on the income statement as an expense. The loan loss provision is an expense that, when recognized, increases the contra-asset. The provision is determined after management reviews the bank's loan portfolio and determines the appropriate level of reserves.[2] The balance in the reserve account should be set by management's judgment and applied with consistency from one period to the next.

Banks make additions to the reserve account when (1) it has become apparent that a loan or group of loans is more likely to be in part or wholly uncollectible; (2) a large unanticipated charge-off has occurred for which the bank did not set aside adequate reserves; or (3) the amount of loans in the bank's portfolio has increased. According to SFAS 5, the primary standard governing the accounting for bad loans under US GAAP, the evaluation and measurement should take into account environmental factors and document the following: delinquency and impaired loan trends, charge-off and recovery trends, volume and terms of loans, changing in lending practices, experience of lending personnel, national and local economies, industry conditions, among other factors.

When loan losses are recognized, that is, when a bank decides that some portion of a loan will not be collected and therefore must be charged off or written down, the amount of the loss is deducted from both the asset (loans, gross) and the contra-asset (reserves for loan losses). Net loans will be unaffected.

To recap, the contra-asset rises by the amount of the loan loss provision and is reduced by charge-offs.[3] It is then netted against gross loans to determine net loans, which is the amount that goes into the determination of total assets on the balance sheet.

Loan loss accounting basics

To illustrate the accounting for bad loans, consider a bank with €5000 in loans on the balance sheet and €100 in the loan loss reserve account as of the end of 2011. Net loans are therefore €4900:

$$\text{Loans (5000)} - \text{Loan Loss Reserve (100)} = \text{Net Loans (4900)}$$

On 25 May 2012, a loan in the amount of 5 is judged to be uncollectible and is written off. The bank records the following journal entry:

Loan loss reserve	5	
Loans		5

The net loans remain at 4900. Note that the accounting for writing off loans largely parallels that of receivables. When receivables are written off, both the contra-asset and the receivables account are reduced, and net receivables are unchanged.

On 10 August 2012, a loan in the amount of 20 is deemed uncollectible and is written off. The journal entry will be similar to the one above:

Loan loss reserve	20	
Loans		20

The net loan value on the books is still 4900 (4975 − 75).

At the end of 2012, bank management estimates that the loan loss reserve should be 120. The contra-asset account must therefore be increased by 45 (120 − 75). The bank records the following entry:

Loan loss provision	45	
Loan loss reserve		45

Net loans are now 4855 (4975 − 120), a decrease of 45 from the beginning of 2012. The decrease results from the write-offs of (5 + 20), plus the net increase in the reserve (120 − 100, or 20).

Loan loss disclosures

In this section we report excerpts from the note dealing with bad loans appearing in 2011 annual report of HSBC, one of the world's largest banks. Comments and analysis will follow.

> Management is required to exercise judgment in making assumptions and estimates when calculating loan impairment allowances on both individually and collectively assessed loans and advances. Of the Group's total loans and advances to customers before impairment allowances of US$958bn (2010: US$978bn), US$17bn or 2% (2010: US$16bn; 2%) were individually assessed for impairment, and US$941bn or 98% (2010: US$962bn; 98%) were collectively assessed for impairment. The most significant judgmental area is the calculation of collective impairment allowances. The geographical area with most exposure subject to this judgment is North America. Collective impairment allowances in North America were US$7bn, representing 62% (2010: US$9bn; 64%) of the total collectively assessed loan impairment allowance.
>
> The methods used to calculate collective impairment allowances on homogeneous groups of loans and advances that are not considered individually significant . . . are subject to estimation uncertainty, in part because it is not practicable to identify losses on an individual loan basis because of the large number of individually insignificant loans in the portfolio.
>
> The methods involve the use of statistically assessed historical information which is supplemented with significant management judgment to assess whether current economic and credit conditions are such that the actual level of inherent losses is likely to be greater or less than that suggested by historical experience. In normal circumstances, historical experience provides the most objective and relevant information from which to assess inherent loss within each portfolio. Sometimes, however, it provides less relevant information about the inherent loss in a given portfolio at the balance sheet date, for

example, when there have been changes in economic, regulatory or behavioral conditions which result in the most recent trends in portfolio risk factors being not fully reflected in the statistical models. . . . Risk factors include loan portfolio growth, product mix, unemployment rates, bankruptcy trends, geographical concentrations, loan product features, economic conditions such as national and local trends in housing markets, the level of interest rates, portfolio seasoning, account management policies and practices, changes in laws and regulations, and other influences on customer payment patterns. Different factors are applied in different regions and countries to reflect local economic conditions, laws and regulations. The methodology and the assumptions used in calculating impairment losses are reviewed regularly in the light of differences between loss estimates and actual loss experience.

Under certain specified conditions, the Group provides loan forbearance to borrowers experiencing financial difficulties by agreeing to modify the contractual payment terms of loans in order to improve the management of customer relationships, maximize collection opportunities and, if possible, avoid default or repossession. Where forbearance activities are significant, higher levels of judgment and estimation uncertainty are involved in determining their effects on loan impairment allowances.

Source: HSBC 2011 Annual Report.

The following discussion highlights key features of the HSBC disclosure:

- At the end of 2011, HSBC reports total loans of $958 billion. About 2% of this figure, or $2 billion, were individually assessed for impairment. This means that the loans were evaluated for credit risk on a loan-by-loan basis. This treatment is normally reserved for large loans. The remaining 98% are collectively assessed for impairment, which means that estimates for the contra-asset are made on a pooled, or portfolio, basis. To do otherwise, that is, to evaluate credit risk on each loan individually, would be excessively costly. As HSBC notes, "It is not practicable to identify losses on an individual loan basis because of the large number of individually insignificant loans in the portfolio."
- Because it lacks specific credit risk data for each loan, estimating the proper amount of reserves for the 98% of loans that are collectively assessed is a highly uncertain process.
- HSBC then describes the information sources relied on to estimate the required balance in the reserve account. Because the myriad of conditions leading to loan defaults is always subject to change, the methods and assumptions used to calculate impairment losses are regularly under review and undergo frequent modifications.
- The estimate of loan impairments is further complicated by the bank's practice of sometimes granting "loan forbearance." In such cases, the original terms have been changed to facilitate repayment from a financially distressed borrower.

The overriding message from these disclosures is that estimating loan impairment, and therefore the proper balance in the reserves for loan losses account, is a highly uncertain exercise, even in the best of times. It requires complex analytical tools, combined with large doses of judgment and, let's face it, guesswork. For this reason, incorrect provisioning is common in the banking sector. Indeed, it's even to be expected. Sometimes the provisioning is too low, resulting in overstated profits and overstated net loans. Other time, the result is overprovisioning, in which hidden (or cookie-jar) reserves offer opportunities to artificially boost reported profits in future periods.

Problems

8.1 Bad debts on loans receivable

Excerpts from the 2008 Annual Report for J.P. Morgan Chase & Co. ("JPMC") are provided in Exhibit 8.1.

Note that the balance in the allowance for loan losses account at the end of JPMC's fiscal 2006 was $7279 million and the balance in their loan *asset* account was $483 127 million at the same date.

Required

(a) Calculate JPMC's allowance for loan losses as a percentage of gross loans outstanding for each of the three years for which information has been provided.
(b) What is the dollar value of JPMC's loan write-offs in 2007 and 2008?
(c) Comment upon JPMC's loan loss provisioning over the periods shown. Do they appear to have used the provision to create hidden reserves? Are they sitting on a "cookie jar" reserve or are you expecting a big hit to the income statement in future periods as a result of past underprovisioning for bad loans?

Exhibit 8.1 Consolidated balance sheets

December 31, (in millions, except share data)	2008	2007
Assets		
Cash and due from banks	$26,895	$40,144
Deposits with banks	138,139	11,466
Federal funds sold and securities purchased under resale agreements (included $20,843 and $19,131 at fair value at December 31, 2008 and 2007, respectively)	203,115	170,897
Securities borrowed (included $3,381 and zero at fair value at December 31, 2008 and 2007, respectively)	124,000	84,184
Trading assets (included assets pledged of $75,063 and $79,229 at December 31, 2008 and 2007, respectively)	509,983	491,409
Securities (included $205,909 and $85,406 at fair value at December 31, 2008 and 2007, respectively, and assets pledged of $25,942 and $3,958 at December 31, 2008 and 2007, respectively)	205,943	85,450

(Continued)

Exhibit 8.1 Continued

December 31, (in millions, except share data)	2008	2007
Loans (included $7,696 and $8,739 at fair value at December 31, 2008 and 2007, respectively)	744,898	519,374
Allowance for loan losses	(23,164)	(9,234)
Loans, net of allowance for loan losses	721,734	510,140
Accrued interest and accounts receivable	60,987	24,823
Premises and equipment	10,045	9,319
Goodwill	48,027	45,270
Other intangible assets:		
Mortgage servicing rights	9,403	8,632
Purchased credit card relationships	1,649	2,303
All other intangibles	3,932	3,796
Other assets (included $29,199 and $22,151 at fair value at December 31, 2008 and 2007, respectively)	111,200	74,314
Total assets	**$2,175,052**	**$1,562,147**

Consolidated statements of cash flows

Year ended December 31, (in millions)	2008	2007	2006
Operating activities			
Net income	$5,605	$15,365	$14,444
Adjustments to reconcile net income to net cash (used in) provided by operating activities:			
Provision for credit losses	20,979	6,864	3,270
Depreciation and amortization	3,143	2,427	2,149
Amortization of intangibles	1,263	1,394	1,428
Deferred tax (benefit) expense	(2,637)	1,307	(1,810)
Investment securities (gains) losses	(1,560)	(164)	543
Proceeds on sale of investment	(1,540)	—	—
Gains on disposition of businesses	(199)	—	(1,136)
Stock-based compensation	2,637	2,025	2,368
Originations and purchases of loans held-for-sale	(34,902)	(116,471)	(178,355)
Proceeds from sales, securitizations and paydowns of loans held-for-sale	38,036	107,350	173,448
Net change in:			
Trading assets	(12,787)	(121,240)	(61,664)
Securities borrowed	15,408	(10,496)	916
Accrued interest and accounts receivable	10,221	(1,932)	(1,170)
Other assets	(33,629)	(21,628)	(7,193)
Trading liabilities	24,061	12,681	(4,521)
Accounts payable and other liabilities	1,012	4,284	7,815
Other operating adjustments	(12,013)	7,674	(111)
Net cash provided by (used in) operating activities	**23,098**	(110,560)	(49,579)

Consolidated statements of income

Year ended December 31, (in millions, except per share data)	2008	2007	2006
Revenue			
Investment banking fees	**$5,526**	$6,635	$5,520
Principal transactions	**(10,699)**	9,015	10,778
Lending & deposit-related fees	**5,088**	3,938	3,468
Asset management, administration and commissions	**13,943**	14,356	11,855
Securities gains (losses)	**1,560**	164	(543)
Mortgage fees and related income	**3,467**	2,118	591
Credit card income	**7,419**	6,911	6,913
Other income	**2,169**	1,829	2,175
Noninterest revenue	**28,473**	44,966	40,757
Interest income	**73,018**	71,387	59,107
Interest expense	**34,239**	44,981	37,865
Net interest income	**38,779**	26,406	21,242
Total net revenue	**67,252**	71,372	61,999
Provision for credit losses	**20,979**	6,864	3,270
Noninterest expense			
Compensation expense	**22,746**	22,689	21,191
Occupancy expense	**3,038**	2,608	2,335
Technology, communications and equipment expense	**4,315**	3,779	3,653
Professional & outside services	**6,053**	5,140	4,450
Marketing	**1,913**	2,070	2,209
Other expense	**3,740**	3,814	3,272
Amortization of intangibles	**1,263**	1,394	1,428
Merger costs	**432**	209	305
Total noninterest expense	**43,500**	41,703	38,843
Income from continuing operations before income tax expense (benefit)	**2,773**	22,805	19,886
Income tax expense (benefit)	**(926)**	7,440	6,237
Income from continuing operations	**3,699**	15,365	13,649
Income from discontinued operations	**—**	—	795
Income before extraordinary gain	**3,699**	15,365	14,444
Extraordinary gain	**1,906**	—	—
Net income	**$5,605**	$15,365	$14,444
Net income applicable to common stock	**$4,931**	$15,365	$14,440

8.2   Determining bad debt expense from an aging schedule

Hilary Company's year-end accounts receivable show the following balances by age:

Age of accounts	Balance
Not due yet	€600,000
0–30 days	200,000
31–60 days	45,000
61–120 days	20,000
More than 120 days	10,000

The credit balance in the allowance for doubtful accounts is now €8600. Hilary Company's prior collection experience suggests that Hilary should use the following percentages to compute the total uncollectible amount of receivables: 0–30 days, 0.5% 31–60 days, 1.0% 61–120, 10%, and more than 120 days, 70%.

Required

Prepare the journal entry to record Hilary's bad debt expense.

8.3   Analyzing receivables and the allowance for doubtful accounts

Vermeulen Company of Ghent, a producer of custom-made furniture, was founded in 2010. Revenues in its first year were €3.5 million, all on account. The balance in the receivables account at the end of the year was €1 million. The company estimated uncollectible receivables at 2% of sales. Based on an aging schedule and other information about customer accounts, €40 000 of receivables were written off on 31 December 2010.

One year later, on 31 December 2011, the balances in selected accounts were as follows:

Sales	€4.0 million
Accounts receivable (gross)	€1.5 million
Allowance for doubtful accounts	€50,000

On 31 December 2011, Vermeulen Company estimated that its accounts receivable balance contained €55 000 of likely uncollectibles. An adjusting entry was made to the

allowance account to reflect this estimate. As in the previous year, all sales were on account.

Required

1. What was the balance in accounts receivable (gross) at the end of 2010?
2. What was the balance in the allowance for doubtful accounts account at the end of 2011?
3. What was the bad debt expense for 2011?
4. What was the amount, in euro, of the specific accounts receivable written off during 2011?
5. How much cash was collected in 2011 from customers?
6. What is the balance of accounts receivable (net) on the statement of financial position (i.e., balance sheet) dated 31 December 2011?

8.4 Provisions for credit losses

Credit Suisse is a Switzerland-based financial services company filing their financial statements under US GAAP. The balance in their allowance for loan losses at the end of 2007 was CHF 1000 million, and their net loans outstanding were CFH 221 570 million. Financial statements are shown in Exhibit 8.2.

Required

(a) Calculate Credit Suisse's allowance (i.e., reserves) for loan losses as a percentage of *gross loans* outstanding for each of the three years for which information has been provided.

(b) What is the amount of Credit Suisse's loan write-offs for 2008 and 2009? *Hint:* You might want to reconstruct the T-account for the allowance for loan losses.

(c) Comment upon Credit Suisse's loan loss provisioning over the periods shown. Do they appear to have used the provision for create hidden reserves? Are they sitting on a "cookie jar" reserve at the end of fiscal 2009 or are you expecting a hit to the income statement in future periods because of past underprovisioning for bad loans? Explain.

Exhibit 8.2 Consolidated balance sheets

	Reference to notes	end of 2009	end of 2008
Assets (CHF million)			
Cash and due from banks		51,857	90,035
Interest-bearing deposits with banks		1,177	2,012
Central bank funds sold, securities purchased under resale agreements and securities borrowing transactions	13	209,499	269,028
of which reported at fair value		128,303	164,743
Securities received as collateral, at fair value		37,516	29,454
of which encumbered		27,816	16,665
Trading assets, at fair value	14	332,238	342,778
of which encumbered		112,843	69,921
Investment securities	15	11,232	13,823
of which reported at fair value		10,793	13,019
Other investments	16	23,993	27,002
of which reported at fair value		21,126	24,866
Net loans	17	237,180	235,797
of which reported at fair value		36,246	32,314
allowance for loan losses		(1,395)	(1,639)
Premises and equipment	18	6,436	6,350
Goodwill	19	9,267	9,330
Other intangible assets	19	328	423
of which reported at fair value		30	113
Brokerage receivables		41,960	57,498
Other assets	21	68,744	85,797
of which reported at fair value		29,125	34,086
of which encumbered		975	3,329
Assets of discontinued operations held-for-sale	4	0	1,023
Total assets		**1,031,427**	**1,170,350**

Consolidated statements of operations

	Reference to notes	2009	2008	2007
Consolidated statements of operations (CHF million)				
Interest and dividend income	6	25,288	47,939	62,550
Interest expense	6	(18,397)	(39,403)	(54,108)
Net interest income	6	6,891	8,536	8,442
Commissions and fees	7	13,750	14,812	18,929
Trading revenues	29	12,151	(9,880)	6,146
Other revenues	8	502	(4,200)	5,804
Net revenues		**33,294**	**9,268**	**39,321**
Provision for credit losses	9	**506**	**813**	**240**
Compensation and benefits	10	15,013	13,254	16,098
General and administrative expenses	11	7,701	7,809	6,833
Commission expenses		1,997	2,294	2,410
Total other operating expenses		9,698	10,103	9,243
Total operating expenses		**24,711**	**23,357**	**25,341**
Income/(loss) from continuing operations before taxes		**8,077**	**(14,902)**	**13,740**
Income tax expense/(benefit)	25	1,835	(4,596)	1,248
Income/(loss) from continuing operations		**6,242**	**(10,306)**	**12,492**
Income/(loss) from discontinued operations, net of tax	4	169	(531)	6
Net income/(loss)		**6,411**	**(10,837)**	**12,498**
Less net income/(loss) attributable to noncontrolling interests		(313)	(2,619)	4,738
Net income/(loss) attributable to shareholders		**6,724**	**(8,218)**	**7,760**
of which from continuing operations		6,555	(7,687)	7,754
of which from discontinued operations		169	(531)	6

(Continued)

Exhibit 8.2 Continued

	Reference to notes	2009	2008	2007
Basic earnings per share (CHF)				
Basic earnings/(loss) per share from continuing operations	12	5.14	(7.51)	7.06
Basic earnings/(loss) per share from discontinued operations	12	0.14	(0.50)	0.01
Basic earnings/(loss) per share	12	**5.28**	**(8.01)**	**7.07**
Diluted earnings per share (CHF)				
Diluted earnings/(loss) per share from continuing operations	12	5.01	(7.51)	6.77
Diluted earnings/(loss) per share from discontinued operations	12	0.13	(0.50)	0.01
Diluted earnings/(loss) per share	12	**5.14**	**(8.01)**	**6.78**

Consolidated statements of cash flows

in	2009	2008	2007
Operating activities of continuing operations (CHF million)			
Net income/(loss)	**6,411**	**(10,837)**	**12,498**
Less net income/(loss) attributable to noncontrolling interests	(313)	(2,619)	4,738
Net income/(loss) attributable to shareholders	**6,724**	**(8,218)**	**7,760**
(Income)/loss from discontinued operations attributable to share-holders, net of tax	(169)	531	(6)
Income/(loss) from continuing operations attributable to shareholders	**6,555**	**(7,687)**	**7,754**
Adjustments to reconcile net income/(loss) to net cash provided by/(used in) operating activities of continuing operations (CHF million)			
Impairment, depreciation and amortization	1,114	1,174	893
Provision for credit losses	506	813	240
Deferred tax provision/(benefit)	875	(4,935)	(1,076)
Share of net income from equity method investments	(29)	17	(101)
Trading assets and liabilities, net	(11,471)	113,153	(65,739)
(Increase)/decrease in other assets	27,189	1,203	(64,540)

in	2009	2008	2007
Increase/(decrease) in other liabilities	(40,993)	28,217	61,191
Other, net	2,068	(2,084)	3,503
Total adjustments	(20,741)	137,558	(65,629)
Net cash provided by/(used in) operating activities of continuing operations	**(14,186)**	**129,871**	**(57,875)**

Case studies

8.1   Receivable and bad debts at Toyota

Toyota is one of the world's largest automobile manufacturers. Like all major players in the industry, the company provides credit to its customers, mainly in the form of installment sales on passenger cars and commercial vehicles. Toyota's ending balance sheet for fiscal year 2005 reveals accounts receivable (gross) of $15.05 billion.*

Accounting for bad debts

Toyota maintains an allowance for doubtful accounts representing management's estimate of the amount of asset impairment. According to the company's 2005 Annual Report:

> The allowances are determined based on a systematic, ongoing review performed as part of the credit-risk evaluation process, historical loss experience, current economic conditions, and the estimated fair value and adequacy of collateral. This evaluation is inherently judgmental and requires material estimates, including the amounts and timing of future cash flows expected to be received, which may be susceptible to significant change. Although management considers the allowance for doubtful accounts . . . to be adequate based on information currently available, additional provisions may be necessary due to (i) changes in management estimates and assumptions about asset impairments, (ii) information that indicates changes in expected future cash flows, or (iii) changes in economic and other events and conditions.
>
> *Source:* Toyota 2005 Annual Report.

---

*Toyota also has a dedicated financing arm for leasing transactions. Finance receivables (net) were $28.03 billion at the end of fiscal year 2005.

Activity in the allowance for doubtful accounts relating to accounts receivable for the years ended 31 March 2003, 2004, and 2005 is summarized as follows:

in millions of US dollars
For the years ended March 31,

	2003	2004	2005
Allowance for doubtful accounts at beginning of year..	$599	$532	**$611**
Provision for doubtful accounts......................................	60	165	**157**
Write-offs...	−60	−26	**−129**
Other..	−67	−60	**−83**
Allowance for doubtful accounts at end of year	$532	$611	**$556**

The other amount includes the impact of consolidation and deconsolidation of certain entities due to changes in ownership interest and currency translation adjustments. A portion of the allowance for doubtful accounts balance at 31 March, 2004 and 2005 totaling $322 million and $371 million, respectively, is attributed to certain noncurrent receivable balances which are reported as other assets in the consolidated balance sheets.

Required

(a) Toyota prepares its accounts using US GAAP, which requires the use of the allowance method in accounting for bad debts. Why is this approach preferred to the direct method? What are the disadvantages of the direct method? Are there any drawbacks or limitations to the allowance method?

(b) Give the summary journal entries to record the activity in the allowance for doubtful accounts for 2005. Be specific as to which accounts are affected.

(c) What factors might explain the trends, from 2003 to 2005, in the provision for doubtful accounts?

(d) Suppose Toyota writes off an account, but the customer subsequently pays. How would Toyota account for the recovery? How would recoveries be accounted for under the direct method?

8.2 Johnson Perry

Johnson Perry is a major producer of pet foods and livestock feed. The company's primary customers are supermarket chains, discount retailers, pet shops, and feed wholesalers and distributors. The balance sheet and income statement from the 2010 Annual Report are shown in Exhibit 8.3, along with a schedule on changes in the allowance for doubtful accounts found in the notes.

Required

(a) Considering the company's recent experience in estimating uncollectible accounts, project write-offs for 2011.

(b) Suppose that the company had provided an amount for doubtful accounts in 2009 using the same percentage of net sales as the 2008 provision. Describe the effect on operating income in 2009 and 2010. What factors might cause bad debt expense as a percentage of sales to change from one year to the next?

(c) Recast the relevant components of the 2010 balance sheet and income statement as if the company had been using the direct write-off method throughout its history instead of the allowance method.

Exhibit 8.3   Johnson Perry Company and subsidiaries.

consolidated balance sheet

31 December (dollars in millions)	2010	2009
Assets		
Current assets		
Cash	**$11.1**	$11.6
Marketable securities, at cost which approximates market	**116.7**	62.5
Receivables, less allowance for doubtful accounts	**255.7**	228.7
Inventories	**382.8**	412.3
Other current assets	**72.2**	60.0
Total Current assets	**838.5**	775.1
Investments and other assets	**182.1**	250.7
Property at cost		
Land	**88.8**	91.4
Buildings	**598.6**	586.2
Machinery and equipment	**1,047.3**	991.8
Construction in progress	**37.1**	42.4
	1,771.8	1711.8
Accumulated depreciation	**691.2**	623.8
	1,080.6	1,088.0
Total	**$2,101.2**	$2,113.8
Liabilities and shareholders' equity		
Current liabilities		
Current maturities of long-term debt	**$15.7**	$16.5
Notes payable	**25.2**	47.7
Accounts payable and accrued liabilities	**490.3**	428.4
Dividends payable	**20.0**	19.8

(Continued)

Exhibit 8.3 Continued

31 December (dollars in millions)	2010	2009
Income taxes	9.7	18.7
Total Current liabilities	560.9	531.1
Long-term debt	315.3	406.9
Deferred income taxes	115.0	70.6
Minority shareholders' interest in consolidated subsidiaries	5.9	5.1
Shareholders' equity		
Preferred stock, $1 par value, authorized 6,000,000 shares – none outstanding		
Common stock, $.412/3 par value, authorized 180,000,000 shares –		
Issued 112,015,371 shares in 2010 and 108,182,395 in 2009	46.7	45.1
Capital in excess of par value	144.3	87.8
Earnings invested in the business	1,251.6	1,077.9
Cumulative translation adjustment	(40.8)	(25.6)
Common stock in treasury, at cost – 16,903,420 shares in 2010 and 6,702,556 in 2009	(297.7)	(85.1)
Total Shareholders' equity	1,104.1	1,100.1
Total	**$2,101.2**	$2,113.8

consolidated statement of earnings

Year ended December 31 (Dollars in millions except per share data)	2010	2009	2008
Net sales	**$4,872.4**	$4,802.6	$5,146.4
Costs and expenses			
Cost of products sold	3,559.4	3,672.6	4,092.3
Selling, general and administrative	376.5	367.1	318.7
Advertising	438.0	384.1	343.0
Unusual or nonrecurring items		154.0	
Interest	35.2	47.5	53.9
	4,409.1	4,625.3	4,807.9
Earnings from continuing operations before income taxes	463.3	177.3	338.5
Income taxes	207.3	85.9	152.3
Earnings from continuing operations	256.0	91.4	186.2
Losses from discontinued operations		22.3	11.4
Earnings for the year	**$256.0**	$69.1	$174.8

Analysis of balance sheet changes: Allowance for doubtful accounts

	2010	2009	2008
Balance, beginning of year	$17.1	$11.8	$12.1
Provision charged to expense	4.0	8.1	2.7
Write-offs, less recoveries	(8.1)	(2.8)	(3.0)
Balance, end of year	$13.0	$17.1	$11.8

8.3   Citigroup Inc.: accounting for loan loss reserves*

Anne Yang, a buy-side[†] analyst working for a prominent asset management firm in Hong Kong, was considering whether or not to diversify her portfolio by taking a position in a financial institution such as Citigroup Inc., J.P. Morgan Chase & Co., or some other global bank.

Anne was impressed to learn that Citigroup's reported earnings for the fourth quarter of 2004 had once again surpassed the analysts' consensus estimates; this time by a penny. While she was encouraged by the earnings performance, she was confused by a comment in a recent *BusinessWeek* article which indicated that Citigroup achieved its numbers by some "cookie jar" accounting technique.[‡]

The technique discussed in the article referred to a bank's accounting for loan loss reserves. After carefully examining Citigroup's financial statements (see Exhibit 8.4) and reading the notes company's in the most recent annual report, she discovered that Citigroup reduced its loan loss reserve allowance in 2004 from $13.243 billion to $11.869 billion, and that this reduction helped boost the earnings figures. Unsure of what that meant, Anne decided to examine the issue further before making her investment decision.

Citigroup Inc.

Citigroup Inc. was formed in 1998 when Citicorp Inc. agreed to a $70 billion merger with Travelers Group Inc. At that time, Citicorp was both a consumer and commercial bank that spanned the globe, while Travelers was a large US-based financial services and insurance provider. The merged entity, Citigroup Inc., became a diversified global financial services holding company whose businesses provided a broad range of financial

---

*This case was written by Professors Jake Cohen (then at INSEAD), David Hawkins (Harvard Business School), and Gerald Lobo (University of Houston).
†Buy-side is the side of the financial industry comprising investing institutions such as the mutual funds, pension funds, and insurance firms that tend to buy securities for money-management purposes. In contrast, sell-side players offer recommendations for upgrades, downgrades, target prices, and opinions to the investing public.
‡Amey Stone, "How banks pretty up the profit picture." *BusinessWeek*, 21 February 2005.

services to consumer and corporate customers. By the end of 2004, the company had more than 200 million customer accounts and was doing business in more than 100 countries. It employed approximately 148 000 employees in the United States and roughly 146 000 employees outside the United States.

Controversy

Loan loss reserves are reserves that banks record to cover bad debt, and they represent the amount of money that management believes the bank will not be able to collect from the currently outstanding loans it has made to borrowers. The allowance (or loan loss reserves) is established through a provision for loan losses which is charged to earnings.[§] Allowance for loan losses appears on a bank's balance sheet as a contra-asset, and the amount recorded is a deduction from the outstanding loans receivables. When bad loans are eventually written off, they are charged against the loan loss reserves account.

When the economy slows down, the provision for loan losses of banks usually increases in anticipation of higher debt defaults. This results in a decrease in net income. As a result, the largest determinant of a bank's profit fluctuations is often its provision for loan losses. These higher reserves magnify the negative impact of the economic cycle on the income and capital of banks. As might be expected, the size and timing of loan loss provisions tend to improve with higher levels of economic activity.

Academic research has found that most banks around the world delayed provisioning for bad loans until it is too late – when the cyclical downturn had already set in – possibly exacerbating the negative impact of the economic cycle on the income and capital of banks.[¶]

Because loan loss provisions are based on managerial discretion, they are subject to income smoothing as management can overprovision when earnings are high and underprovision, or even release reserves, when earnings are low. Income smoothing goes against accounting regulations, as within these regulations, banks cannot shift funds around at will.

Thus, the controversy surrounding loan loss reserves revolved around whether banks with generous loan loss reserves were manipulating earnings or merely practicing conservative accounting.

Citigroup loan loss reserves footnotes

In its financial footnotes for 2004, Citigroup reported the following with regard to its loan loss reserves:

> During the past two years, the worldwide credit environment has continuously improved, as evidenced by declining cash-basis loan balances[‖] and lower delinquency rates. Accordingly, the company has reduced its Allowance for Credit Losses.

[§]Citigroup Inc. refers to loan losses as credit losses.
[¶]Luc Laeven and Giovanni Majnoni, "Loan loss provisioning and economic slowdowns: too much, too late?" *Journal of Financial Intermediation*, 12(2), (2002): pp. 178–197.

During 2004, the company released $2.004 billion of reserves, consisting of $900 million from [Global Corporate Investment Bank's (GCIB)] reserves and $1.104 billion from Global Consumer's reserves . . . At December 31, 2004, the Company's total allowance for loans, leases, and commitments was $11.869 billion.

During 2003, the Company released $508 million of reserves, consisting of $300 million in GCIB and $208 million in Global Consumer. At December 31, 2003, the Company's total allowance for loans, leases and commitments was $13.243 billion.

Management evaluates the adequacy of loan loss reserves by analyzing probable loss scenarios and economic and geopolitical factors that impact the portfolios . . .

The allowance for credit losses represents management's estimate of probable losses inherent in the lending portfolio. This evaluation process is subject to numerous estimates and judgments. The frequency of default, risk ratings, and the loss recovery rates, among other things, are considered in making this evaluation, as are the size and diversity of individual large credits. Changes in these estimates could have a direct impact on the credit costs in any quarter and could result in a change in the allowance.

At December 31, 2004 and 2003, respectively, the total allowance for credit losses, which includes reserves for unfunded lending commitments and letters of credit, totalled $3.490 billion and $4.155 billion for the Corporate loan portfolio and $8.379 billion and $9.088 billion for the Consumer loan portfolio. Attribution of the allowance is made for analytic purposes only, and the entire allowance of $11.869 billion and $13.243 billion at December 31, 2004 and 2003, respectively, is available to absorb probable credit losses inherent in the portfolio, including letters of credit and unfunded commitments . . . **

In an interview with CNBC, Citigroup CFO Todd Thomson explained how loan loss reserves were used:

We put up reserves for the bad loans we think we're going to have. If it turns out [that] we were wrong, [and] things [get] much better than we expected, then we don't need those reserves. And in fact, according to the accounting rules, we have to release those reserves . . . We have an extremely analytical process internally. We don't have that much judgment around it. We have to release the reserves as credit continues to get better.[††]

He then said:

I think credit quality is going to continue to be very good. All of our forward-looking indicators continue to tell us that on the consumer side and the corporate side we're going to have a very benign credit environment for the foreseeable future. So that's good news. What we're not going

---

**Citigroup Inc. SEC 10-K Filing, February 28, 2005, US Securities and Exchanges Commission, <www.sec. gov> (7 March 2006).

[††]"Citigroup (C) CFO Todd Thomson and Private Bank Chief Global Investment Strategist Clark Winter – Thomson and Winter report on C's earnings and discuss the banking industry and the global markets," 14 October 2004, CNBC DowJones website <www.cnbcdowjones.com.>

to see in the future is the massive improvement we've seen in credit quality, which allowed us to release these reserves. I don't anticipate that going forward we're going to be releasing reserves to this extent, unless I'm wrong and things get much better than they are today.[‡‡]

Conclusion

By now, Anne Yang felt more confident in her understanding of loan loss reserves accounting and was considering her possible investment in Citigroup. For 2004, Citigroup beat the analysts' consensus EPS estimates of $4.03 by a penny, coming in at $4.04. The company had reduced its loan loss reserves during the year citing improved credit quality. Ms Yang understood that the problem with decreasing the reserves was that as banks issued new loans, they would have to replenish the reserves. Furthermore, if credit conditions worsened, banks would have to set aside even a larger amount to cover bad debts, which would further negatively impact profits.[§§]

For Anne, it was now time to weigh whether Citigroup's accounting for loan loss was truly capturing the economic reality of the credit markets or whether it was a technique used by the bank to beat the analysts' earnings per share numbers. She wondered, was it prudent for Citigroup to reduce its allowance? After all, many people predicted that the US economy could suffer a recession in 2007 owing to falling housing prices due to Federal Reserve Bank tightening of interest rates. If that was to happen, what would be the impact on banks' performance and their loan loss reserves? Lastly, Anne was curious, had Citigroup maintained the same ratio of allowance for credit losses to loans in 2004, as it had in 2003, by how much would it have missed the consensus analysts' earnings estimates?

Required

(a) Based on the financial statements for Citibank, describe the primary differences between the financial statements of banks and those of companies not in financial services.
(b) Banks are said to be in the business of "borrowing short and lending long." What does that mean?
(c) How can banks create the "cookie jar reserves" referred to in the case?
(d) What are loan loss reserves? Using journal entries, show how the reserves are: (a) set up, (b) used, (c) written off, and (d) reversed/released.
(e) Do you agree with the following statement: "In the banking sector, conservative accounting is good accounting." Why or why not?

[‡‡]Ibid.
[§§]Amey Stone, "How banks pretty up the profit picture." *BusinessWeek*, 21 February 2005.

Exhibit 8.4   Citigroup Inc. consolidated income statement

CONSOLIDATED STATEMENT OF INCOME	*Citigroup Inc. and Subsidiaries*		
	Year ended December 31		
In millions of dollars, except per share amounts	**2004**	**2003**	**2002**
Revenues			
Loan interest, including fees	**$43,981**	$38,110	$37,903
Other interest and dividends	**22,728**	18,937	21,036
Insurance premiums	**3,993**	3,749	3,410
Commissions and fees	**16,772**	16,314	15,258
Principal transactions	**3,756**	5,120	4,513
Asset management and administration fees	**6,845**	5,665	5,146
Realized gains (losses) from sales of investments	**831**	510	(485)
Other revenue	**9,370**	6,308	5,775
Total revenues	**108,276**	94,713	92,556
Interest expense	**22,086**	17,271	21,248
Total revenues, net of interest expense	**86,190**	77,442	71,308
Benefits, claims, and credit losses			
Policyholder benefits and claims	**3,801**	3,895	3,478
Provision for credit losses	**6,233**	8,046	9,995
Total benefits, claims, and credit losses	**10,034**	11,941	13,473
Operating expenses			
Non-insurance compensation and benefits	**23,707**	21,288	18,650
Net occupancy expense	**4,847**	4,280	4,005
Technology/communications expense	**3,586**	3,414	3,139
Insurance underwriting, acquisition, and operating	**1,234**	1,063	992
Restructuring-related items	**(5)**	(46)	(15)
Other operating expenses	**18,605**	9,169	10,527
Total operating expenses	**51,974**	39,168	37,298
Income from continuing operations before income taxes, minority interest, and cumulative effect of accounting change	**24,182**	26,333	20,537
Provision for income taxes	**6,909**	8,195	6,998
Minority interest, net of income taxes	**227**	285	91
	17,046	17,853	13,448

(Continued)

Exhibit 8.4   Continued

CONSOLIDATED STATEMENT OF INCOME

In millions of dollars, except per share amounts	Citigroup Inc. and Subsidiaries Year ended December 31 2004	2003	2002
Income from continuing operations before cumulative effect of accounting change			
Discontinued operations			
Income from discontinued operations	—	—	965
Gain on sale of stock by subsidiary	—	—	1,270
Provision for income taxes	—	—	360
Income from discontinued operations, net	—	—	1,875
Cumulative effect of accounting change, net	—	—	(47)
Net income	**$17,046**	$17,853	$15,276
Basic earnings per share			
Income from continuing operations	**$3.32**	$3.49	$2.63
Income from discontinued operations, net	—	—	0.37
Cumulative effect of accounting change, net	—	—	(0.01)
Net income	**$3.32**	$3.49	$2.99
Weighted average common shares outstanding	**5,107.2**	5,093.3	5,078.0
Diluted earnings per share			
Income from continuing operations	**$3.26**	$3.42	$2.59
Income from discontinued operations, net	—	—	0.36
Cumulative effect of accounting change, net	—	—	(0.01)
Net income	**$3.26**	$3.42	$2.94
Adjusted weighted average common shares outstanding	**5,207.4**	5,193.6	5,166.2

CONSOLIDATED BALANCE SHEET

In millions of dollars	Citigroup Inc. and Subsidiaries December 31 2004	2003
Assets		
Cash and due from banks (including segregated cash and other deposits)	**$23,556**	$21,149
Deposits at interest with banks	**23,889**	19,777
Federal funds sold and securities borrowed or purchased under agreements to resell	**200,739**	172,174

CONSOLIDATED BALANCE SHEET	*Citigroup Inc. and Subsidiaries*	
	December 31	
In millions of dollars	**2004**	**2003**
Brokerage receivables	**39,273**	26,476
Trading account assets (including $102,573 and $65,352 pledged to creditors at December 31, 2004 and December 31, 2003, respectively)	**280,167**	235,319
Investments (including $15,587 and $12,066 pledged to creditors at December 31, 2004 and December 31, 2003, respectively)	**213,243**	182,892
Loans, net of unearned income		
Consumer	**435,226**	379,932
Corporate	**113,603**	98,074
Loans, net of unearned income	**548,829**	478,006
Allowance for credit losses	**(11,269)**	(12,643)
Total loans, net	**537,560**	465,363
Goodwill	**31,992**	27,581
Intangible assets	**15,271**	13,881
Reinsurance recoverable	**4,783**	4,577
Separate and variable accounts	**32,264**	27,473
Other assets	**81,364**	67,370
Total assets	**$1,484,101**	$1,264,032
Liabilities		
Non-interest-bearing deposits in U.S. offices	**$31,533**	$30,074
Interest-bearing deposits in U.S. offices	**161,113**	146,675
Non-interest-bearing deposits in offices outside the U.S.	**28,379**	22,940
Interest-bearing deposits in offices outside the U.S.	**341,056**	274,326
Total deposits	**562,081**	474,015
Federal funds purchased and securities loaned or sold under agreements to repurchase	**209,555**	181,156
Brokerage payables	**50,208**	37,330
Trading account liabilities	**135,487**	121,869
Contractholder funds and separate and variable accounts	**68,801**	58,402
Insurance policy and claims reserves	**19,177**	17,478
Investment banking and brokerage borrowings	**25,799**	22,442
Short-term borrowings	**30,968**	36,187
Long-term debt	**207,910**	162,702
Other liabilities	**64,824**	48,380

(Continued)

Exhibit 8.4   Continued

CONSOLIDATED BALANCE SHEET	*Citigroup Inc. and Subsidiaries*	
	December 31	
In millions of dollars	**2004**	**2003**
Citigroup or subsidiary-obligated mandatorily redeemable securities of subsidiary trusts holding solely junior subordinated debt securities		
of—Parent	—	5,217
—Subsidiary	—	840
Total liabilities	**1,374,810**	1,166,018
Stockholders' equity		
Preferred stock ($1.00 par value; authorized shares: 30 million), at aggregate liquidation value	**1,125**	1,125
Common stock ($.01 par value; authorized shares: 15 billion), issued shares: **2004—5,477,416,086** shares and 2003—5,477,416,254 shares	**55**	55
Additional paid-in capital	**18,851**	17,531
Retained earnings	**102,154**	93,483
Treasury stock, at cost: **2004—282,773,501 shares** and 2003—320,466,849 shares	**(10,644)**	(11,524)
Accumulated other changes in equity from nonowner sources	**(304)**	(806)
Unearned compensation	**(1,946)**	(1,850)
Total stockholders' equity	**109,291**	98,014
Total liabilities and stockholders' equity	**$1,484,101**	$1,264,032

CONSOLIDATED STATEMENT OF CASH FLOWS	*Citigroup Inc. and Subsidiaries*		
	Year ended December 31		
In millions of dollars	**2004**	**2003**	**2002**
Cash flows from operating activities of continuing operations			
Net income	**$17,046**	$17,853	$15,276
Income from discontinued operations, net of tax	—	—	717
Gain on sale of stock by subsidiary, net of tax	—	—	1,158
Cumulative effect of accounting changes	—	—	(47)
Income from continuing operations	**17,046**	17,853	13,448
Adjustments to reconcile net income to net cash (used in) provided by operating activities of continuing operations			
Amortization of deferred policy acquisition costs and present value of future profits	**687**	547	405

CONSOLIDATED STATEMENT OF CASH FLOWS	*Citigroup Inc. and Subsidiaries*		
	Year ended December 31		
In millions of dollars	**2004**	**2003**	**2002**
Additions to deferred policy acquisition costs	**(1,303)**	(976)	(865)
Depreciation and amortization	**2,060**	1,574	1,521
Deferred tax (benefit) provision	**(983)**	861	(204)
Provision for credit losses	**6,233**	8,046	9,995
Change in trading account assets	**(43,071)**	(80,111)	(10,625)
Change in trading account liabilities	**13,110**	30,443	10,883
Change in federal funds sold and securities borrowed or purchased under agreements to resell	**(28,131)**	(32,228)	(2,127)
Change in federal funds purchased and securities loaned or sold under agreements to repurchase	**22,966**	19,468	7,176
Change in brokerage receivables, net of brokerage payables	**81**	14,188	(1,070)
Change in insurance policy and claims reserves	**1,699**	1,128	3,272
Net (gains)/losses from sales of investments	**(831)**	(510)	485
Venture capital activity	**(201)**	134	577
Restructuring-related items	**(5)**	(46)	(15)
Other, net	**8,239**	4,775	(6,827)
Total adjustments	**(19,450)**	(32,707)	12,581
Net cash (used in) provided by operating activities of continuing operations	**(2,404)**	(14,854)	26,029
Cash flows from investing activities of continuing operations			
Change in deposits at interest with banks	**(2,175)**	(3,395)	2,935
Change in loans	**(68,451)**	(30,012)	(40,780)
Proceeds from sales of loans	**15,121**	18,553	17,005
Purchases of investments	**(195,903)**	(208,040)	(393,344)
Proceeds from sales of investments	**112,470**	127,277	280,234
Proceeds from maturities of investments	**63,318**	71,730	78,505
Other investments, primarily short-term, net	**(29)**	130	(531)
Capital expenditures on premises and equipment	**(3,011)**	(2,354)	(1,377)
Proceeds from sales of premises and equipment, subsidiaries and affiliates, and repossessed assets	**3,106**	1,260	2,184
Business acquisitions	**(3,677)**	(21,456)	(3,953)
Net cash used in investing activities of continuing operations	**(79,231)**	(46,307)	(59,122)

(Continued)

Exhibit 8.4 Continued

CONSOLIDATED STATEMENT OF CASH FLOWS	*Citigroup Inc. and Subsidiaries*		
	Year ended December 31		
In millions of dollars	**2004**	**2003**	**2002**
Cash flows from financing activities of continuing operations			
Dividends paid	**(8,375)**	(5,773)	(3,676)
Issuance of common stock	**912**	686	483
Issuance of mandatorily redeemable securities of parent trusts	—	1,600	—
Redemption of mandatorily redeemable securities of parent trusts	—	(700)	—
Redemption of mandatorily redeemable securities of subsidiary trusts	—	(625)	(400)
Redemption of preferred stock, net	—	(275)	(125)
Treasury stock acquired	**(779)**	(2,416)	(5,483)
Stock tendered for payment of withholding taxes	**(511)**	(499)	(475)
Issuance of long-term debt	**75,764**	67,054	39,520
Payments and redemptions of long-term debt	**(49,686)**	(45,800)	(47,169)
Change in deposits	**65,818**	42,136	30,554
Change in short-term borrowings and investment banking and brokerage borrowings	**(4,363)**	6,647	11,988
Contractholder fund deposits	**11,797**	8,346	8,548
Contractholder fund withdrawals	**(7,266)**	(5,976)	(5,815)
Net cash provided by financing activities of continuing operations	**83,311**	64,405	27,950
Effect of exchange rate changes on cash and cash equivalents	**731**	579	98
Discontinued operations			
Net cash used in discontinued operations	**—**	—	(237)
Proceeds from sale of stock by subsidiary	**—**	—	4,093
Change in cash and due from banks	**2,407**	3,823	(1,189)
Cash and due from banks at beginning of period	**21,149**	17,326	18,515
Cash and due from banks at end of period	**$23,556**	$21,149	$17,326
Supplemental disclosure of cash flow information for continuing operations			
Cash paid during the period for income taxes	**$6,808**	$6,113	$6,834
Cash paid during the period for interest	**$18,544**	$15,732	$20,226
Non-cash investing activities			
Transfers to repossessed assets	**$1,046**	$1,077	$1,180

Citigroup Inc. SEC 10-K Filing, February 28, 2005, US Securities and Exchanges Commission <www.sec.gov> (March 7, 2006).

Notes

1. "Performing" means that payments are made on time. "Nonperforming" loans are those that are, say, at least three months past due or impaired in some other way.
2. The loan loss provision might actually be negative in some years, thereby increasing pretax income. This can happen if the bank overprovisioned for loan losses in previous years.
3. More specially, "net" charge-offs. If previously written-off loans are repaid, the amounts are restored to the contra-asset. Therefore, the account is reduced by total charge-offs, net of recoveries.

CHAPTER 9

Accounting for Inventory

Introduction

Retail, distribution, and manufacturing companies purchase or produce goods and then try to sell them for a profit. These goods are referred to as "inventory" and are classified as a current asset, often the largest current asset on a company's balance sheet. Both US GAAP and International Financial Reporting Standards (IFRS) define inventories as assets that are held for sale in the ordinary course of business, in the process of production or for sale in the form of materials, or supplies to be consumed in the production process or in rendering services. Thus, inventory can take any of the following physical forms: raw materials and supplies, work-in-process, or finished goods. Most companies report an aggregate sum for all inventories on the balance sheet, with a more detailed description of the physical state of inventory provided in the notes.

By contrast, Procter & Gamble Co. (P&G), a global giant in personal care, household cleaning and pharmaceutical products, discloses each class of inventory directly on its balance sheet – see Table 9.1. We chose P&G as an example because its balance sheet allows us to see how costs flow through the inventory accounts as the operating cycle of the business turns. Here's how the process unfolds'

P&G reports raw materials and supplies of $1692 billion at the end of fiscal year 2010. As materials and supplies are purchased, the company records the following journal entry:

Raw materials and supplies	XX	
Cash or accounts payable		XX

Table 9.1   Current assets of Procter & Gamble (amounts in millions)

	June 30	
	2010	**2009**
Current assets		
Cash and cash equivalents	$2,879	$4,781
Accounts receivable	5,335	5,836
Inventories		
Materials and supplies	1,692	1,557
Work-in-process	604	672
Finished goods	4,088	4,651
Total inventories	6,384	6,880
Deferred income taxes	990	1,209
Prepaid expenses and other current assets	3,194	3,199
Total current assets	18,782	21,905

These raw materials are then moved into a work-in-process account as the manufacturing process begins:

Work in process inventory XX	
Raw materials and supplies	XX

After materials are introduced to the assembly line or shop floor, they are gradually converted into finished goods. This conversion process also requires labor and the use of other resources (e.g., maintenance, public utilities, depreciation on machines and equipment, etc.). These resources are commonly known as "manufacturing overhead." Because labor and manufacturing overhead are required for the conversion process, the costs of these factors of production are capitalized (i.e., included on the balance sheet). The capitalization occurs through the work-in-process account. The costs will stay there until the manufacturing process is complete.

P&G explains this process in the note shown in Box 9.1.

Box 9.1   P&G cost of products sold

Cost of products sold is primarily comprised of direct materials and supplies consumed in the manufacture of product, as well as manufacturing labor, depreciation expense and direct overhead expense necessary to acquire and convert the purchased materials and supplies into finished product. Cost of products sold also includes the cost to distribute products to customers, inbound freight costs, internal transfer costs, warehousing costs and other shipping and handling activity.

The entries to record these costs include:

Work-in-process inventory	XX	
Accrued labor costs or Cash		XX

To record the costs of direct and indirect manufacturing labor[1]

Work-in-process inventory	XX	
Accumulated depreciation		XX

To record the depreciation of equipment, buildings, and machines

Work-in-process inventory	XX	
Freight-in payable or Cash		XX

To record inbound freight costs

Similar entries would be required for any other conversion costs incurred by P&G. The debit is always to the work-in-process account. The balancing credit is made to cash, a short-term liability, or a contra-asset, depending on the nature of the cost.

As individual units of product are completed, the costs associated with those units are transferred out of work-in-process and into finished goods inventory:

Finished goods inventory	XX	
Work-in-process inventory		XX

The inventory then remains on the balance sheet, in the finished goods account, until it is sold. According to the P&G balance sheet, most of the company's inventory at the end of fiscal year 2010, $4088 billion, was in the form of finished goods and is awaiting sale.

When inventory is finally sold, the cost flows out of finished goods inventory and into the income statement through an expense called cost of goods sold:

Cost of goods sold	XX	
Finished goods inventory		XX

As an American company, P&G reports under US GAAP. According to US GAAP, inventory is reported on the balance sheet at the lower of cost or market value. A similar requirement exists under IFRS, although there are slight differences between the two regimes in the definition of market value. Lower of cost or market means that if a company's inventory is deemed to be worth less than its cost, the appropriate inventory account (usually materials or finished goods) must be written down to market value. The amount of the write-down is recognized as a loss on the income statement. The journal entry would look like this:

Loss on write-down of inventory	XX	
Inventory		XX

If the company suffers a significant write-down of inventory during the year, you should expect to see some disclosure of it in the financial statement notes.

Table 9.2 Procter & Gamble's income statement for 2008–2010 (amounts in millions except per share amounts)

	Years ended June 30		
	2010	**2009**	**2008**
Net sales	$78,938	$76,694	$79,257
Cost of goods sold	37,919	38,690	39,261
Selling, general and administrative expense	24,998	22,630	24,017
Operating income	16,021	15,374	15,979
Interest expense	946	1,358	1,467
Other non-operating income (expense), net	(28)	397	373
Earnings before income taxes	15,047	14,413	14,885
Provision for income taxes	4,101	3,733	3,594
Net earnings	$10,946	$10,680	$11,291

P&G's income statements for the years 2008–2010 are shown in Table 9.2. Cost of goods sold appears on the line immediately below revenues. This information reveals that in 2010 P&G earned $78.9 billion in revenues (net sales) and incurred $37.9 billion in cost of goods sold. This latter figure implies that the units of inventory sold in 2010 cost P&G $37.9 billion to produce, although several assumptions were required to calculate it. Some companies subtract cost of goods sold from revenues to show a gross profit or gross margin. P&G prefers to report operating income as the first profit figure on its income statement.

Inventory valuation: LIFO, FIFO, and the rest

As noted above, P&G reported $37.9 billion in cost of goods sold in 2010. The balance sheet, shown earlier, reported inventory of about $6.4 billion at the end of 2010. Most of this inventory, about $4.1 billion, was in the form of finished goods. The challenge for P&G, given that so many millions of units of product flow through the company's manufacturing facilities each year, is to know how much cost should be assigned to each unit of product. Without such knowledge, the company cannot determine how much of its manufacturing costs for 2010 belong in cost of goods sold (i.e., the income statement) and how much in inventory (i.e., the balance sheet).

The problem arises because the costs incurred by P&G to produce inventory change constantly over the course of the year. In other words, from one day to the next, the costs of producing the same product can change. If different units of inventory, even for the same products, have different costs, how do we know which costs relate to units sold and which relate to units still in inventory? Answering this question is the essence of the inventory accounting problem.

One possible approach is a technique known as "specific identification." Here, a specific cost is attached to each individual unit. As a unit is sold, its cost enters cost of goods sold and is removed from the inventory account.[2] This method is allowed and sometimes used, but tends to be practical only in companies that sell a small number of items with very high unit costs. For example, an automobile dealer might use it. But for most other companies, such as P&G, specific identification is slow, cumbersome, and costly. Even bar coding and other computer-tracking systems fail to address all of these practical concerns. Also, specific identification creates an avenue for profit manipulation. If a company wants to boost earnings in any given year, it can simply choose to sell those units of product with the lowest unit costs.

Consequently, the overwhelming majority of retail, distribution, and manufacturing companies throughout the world account for inventory by making a **cost-flow assumption**. These assumptions allow the company to take a large number of interchangeable units of product, and determine which unit costs will be assigned to cost of goods sold and which to inventory. These assumptions include: first-in-first-out (FIFO), last-in-first-out (LIFO), and average cost.

Before describing each of these alternatives in detail, we should first note that over the entire life of a company, cost of goods sold will be the same regardless of the cost-flow assumption employed. Over the life of a business, all the units of inventory will be sold or disposed of in some way. Consequently, all costs associated with inventory will be expensed. The choice of a cost-flow assumption affects only the allocation of inventory costs to particular accounting periods.

Simply put, the choice of inventory valuation method affects the amounts a company reports on its balance sheet for inventory and on its income statement for cost of goods sold (and, consequently, net income). Thus, in order to evaluate a company's financial position and performance, particularly in comparison with other companies, investors and creditors need to know which cost-flow assumption the company is using.

As shown in Box 9.2, P&G uses FIFO.

On a global scale, FIFO is the most common method, because it is relatively easy to implement, and it offers a certain intuitive appeal (in most companies, the first units acquired or produced, are the first units sold).

Box 9.2 P&G's note on its inventory valuation method

Inventory Valuation

Inventories are valued at the lower of cost or market value. Product-related inventories are primarily maintained on the first-in, first-out method. Minor amounts of product inventories, including certain cosmetics and commodities, are maintained on the last-in, first-out method. The cost of spare part inventories is maintained using the average cost method.

The lower of cost or market rule

After inventories have been manufactured or acquired, their market value will increase or decrease. The conservatism principle prevents the recognition of any increases until the item of inventory has been sold. However, if market value declines below acquisition cost, a common occurrence for goods that carry high obsolescence risk, the inventory is judged to be impaired and must be written down. For example, if Galeries Lafayette, a large Paris-based retailer, has inventory costing €50 000 with a market value of only €20 000, the following entry would be required:

Unrealized holding loss on inventory	30,000	
Inventory		30,000

The loss would be reported in the period's income statement. If the market value of the inventory partly recovers before sale to, say, €34 000, the company makes the following entry:

Inventory	14,000	
Unrealized holding gain on inventory		14,000

The unrealized holding gain can be recognized up to the amount of the original write-off. For example, if market value increases to €55 000, higher than the acquisition cost, the gain is limited to €30 000.[3]

The cost-flow assumptions: an example

To illustrate the differences among the three principal cost-flow assumptions, we draw on the example of Waller & Gamble, a retailer of toothpaste.

The inventory balance at the beginning of the year was $15 000 (15 000 units @ $1). Additional units were purchased during the year as shown in Table 9.3.

The inventory count at year-end indicates that 11 000 units were still on hand. Sales and expenses (excluding cost of goods sold) totaled $55 000 and $15 000, respectively. The rate of income tax is 30%.

To begin, let's consider the total costs that will eventually flow to the income statement from the purchase and sale of inventory. The cost of beginning inventory is $15 000. The cost

Table 9.3 Inventory purchases for Waller & Gamble

	Items purchased	Cost per item	Total cost
March 15	6,000	$1.30	$7,800
July 30	9,000	1.50	13,500
December 17	7,000	1.60	11,200
Total	22,000		$32,500

of goods purchased during the year equals $32 500. Therefore, the *cost of goods available for sale* equals $47 500. The number of units available for sale equals 15 000 (from beginning inventory), plus 22 000 (purchases during the year), or 37 000.

The major task before us now is to determine how much of the $47 500 will be assigned to cost of goods sold and how much will be kept in the inventory account. We will now look at the following in more detail:

- FIFO
- LIFO
- average cost.

First in first out or last in still here

The FIFO method is based on the assumption that the units sold are the oldest units on hand. Therefore, the cost of the inventory still on hand is assumed to be the units acquired or produced most recently (last in, still here, or LISH).

Under FIFO, the ending inventory for Waller & Gamble is based on the 11 000 units acquired most recently:

$$\text{Ending Inventory} = (7000 \text{ units} \times \$1.60) + (4000 \text{ units} \times \$1.50) = \$17\ 200$$

We now assume that whatever is no longer in inventory must have been sold. Thus

$$\text{Cost of Goods Sold} = \text{Cost of Goods Available for Sale} - \text{Ending Inventory}$$

which equals $47 500 – $17 200, or $30 300.

Cost of goods sold could also be calculated by focusing on the 26 000 units sold:

$$(15\ 000 \text{ units} \times \$1.00) + (6000 \text{ units} \times \$1.30) + (5000 \times \$1.50), \text{ or } \$30\ 300$$

It should be noted that this example assumes any units not found in inventory at the end of the year were sold. In other words, if 37 000 units were available for sale, and 11000 are in ending inventory, 26 000 units must have been sold. The problem with this assumption is that it assumes no "inventory shrinkage." Shrinkage occurs whenever inventory declines for reasons other than a sale. For example, inventory might be lost, broken, or stolen. Therefore, actual sales may have been less than 26 000 units. But even if some units disappeared because of inventory shrinkage, the costs of those units were incurred and must be expensed. The normal practice is to recognize these expenses through cost of goods sold. Put another way, even if there is shrinkage, when calculating cost of goods sold we can still assume that 26 000 units were sold.

Last in first out or first in still here

The LIFO method is based on the assumption that the newest units acquired or produced are the first units sold. The inventory still on hand is costed on the assumption that it was acquired in previous periods. In effect, inventory under LIFO is assumed to be first in still here, or FISH.

For Waller & Gamble, ending inventory under LIFO consists entirely of units already on hand at the beginning of the year, (11 000units × $1.00), or $11 000.

$$\text{Cost of Goods Sold} = \text{Cost of Goods Available for Sale} - \text{Ending Inventory}$$

$$= \$47\ 500 - \$11\ 000, \text{ or } \$36\ 500$$

Cost of goods sold under LIFO can also be calculated from the costs of inventory of the units acquired most recently:

$$(7000 \text{ units @ } \$1.60) + (9000 \text{ units @ } \$1.50) + (6000 \text{ units @ } \$1.30)$$

$$+(4000 \text{ units @ } \$1.00), \text{ or } \$36\ 500.$$

In the US, companies that use LIFO for tax must also use it for financial reporting. This requirement is known as the "LIFO conformity rule." Although most American companies do not use LIFO, it does offer one important advantage to those that do. At times of increasing prices, LIFO can lower a company's tax burden because it matches the most recent prices paid (which are higher than earlier prices) against revenues in calculating taxable income. A further advantage of LIFO is that because the most recent costs are subtracted from current revenues, it can result in a better matching of revenues and expenses. However, few companies choose LIFO for this reason. The use of LIFO is driven almost entirely by tax considerations.

Because LIFO does a poor job of tracking the actual physical flow of inventory in most companies,[4] and because governments are usually loath to provide a tax benefit that contributes little or nothing to productivity or job growth, LIFO is explicitly banned in most countries, including Australia, Canada, Denmark, France, Israel, Singapore, Sweden, and the UK. Also, LIFO is banned under IFRS. A few countries, apart from the US, still allow the use of LIFO for tax purposes, but the number is dwindling. A recent example is Japan, which has disallowed LIFO since 2010. Even the US is contemplating legislation to eliminate the practice – to raise revenue and in anticipation of eventual IFRS adoption in the US. But as of this writing, LIFO is still allowed, but its use is becoming rare outside the US.

For those companies that use LIFO for financial reporting purposes, a "LIFO reserve" must be disclosed in the notes to the financial statements. This reserve measures the difference between the inventory balance under LIFO and what it would be under FIFO. Therefore,

$$\text{LIFO Inventory} + \text{LIFO Reserve} = \text{FIFO Inventory}$$

This disclosure is important because it allows the financial-statement reader to convert a LIFO company's accounts into a FIFO equivalent, thus facilitating comparison between companies that use different inventory methods. Also, changes in the reserve can be used to adjust cost of goods sold. For example, if the reserve increases, the implication is that cost of goods sold in that year was higher under LIFO. Subtracting the change in the reserve can convert a LIFO-based cost of goods sold into its FIFO equivalent.

LIFO presents two fundamental problems for companies that use it:

- First, it is more complicated, and therefore more costly to administer, than other cost-flow assumptions.
- Second, LIFO gives rise to a "LIFO layer problem."

In any year in which inventory grows (i.e., the number of units acquired or produced exceeds the number sold), a layer of inventory from that year remains in the inventory account. To illustrate, imagine a company that increases its inventory for 10 consecutive years. For each of those 10 years, a LIFO layer of inventory costs is left behind. As long as inventory grows, or at least remains constant, these layers present no real problem for the company or the financial statement reader. But if inventory costs have been steadily increasing over this 10-year period, a problem emerges when the company starts to reduce inventory levels. When inventory levels are reduced, the company is forced to dig into LIFO layers from previous years. The result: current selling prices are matched with older inventory costs.

The LIFO liquidation process begins with the layer created in the previous year, then goes on to the layer created in the year before that, and so on. At some point, especially if the company undergoes a major restructuring effort and liquidates the entire inventory, it could be forced to match very old costs against current revenues. Artificially high profits then result and, unfortunately for the reporting entity, so too does a large tax bill.

The LIFO liquidation problem helps to explain why LIFO systems are more costly to administer than those of the other inventory methods. Tax authorities require companies to maintain meticulous records on each layer for every product or material accounted for under LIFO, which typically demands additional software and personnel support. This fact implies that the expected tax savings need to be substantial; otherwise LIFO is not worth the effort.

Average cost

This method calculates cost of goods sold as an average of the cost to purchase or manufacture all of the inventories available for sale during the year. The first step is to compute the average cost per unit:

$$\text{Cost per Unit} = \text{Cost of Goods Available for Sale} \div \text{Number of Units Available for Sale}$$

For Waller & Gamble, the average cost per unit equals $47 500÷37 000 units, or $1.284. Ending inventory therefore equals the number of units in ending inventory, 11 000, multiplied by the average cost of $1.284 per unit, or $14 124.

Table 9.4   Waller & Gamble's income statement and balance sheet

Income statement	FIFO	LIFO	Average
Revenues	$55,000	$55,000	$55,000
Cost of goods sold	30,300	36,500	33,376
Expenses	15,000	15,000	15,000
Earnings before taxes	9,700	3,500	6,624
Taxes @ 30%	2,910	1,050	1,987
Net income	6,790	2,450	4,637
Balance sheet	**LISH**	**FISH**	**Average**
Beginning inventory	$15,000	$15,000	$15,000
Ending inventory	17,200	11,000	14,124

> Cost of Goods Sold equals Cost of Goods Available for Sale, minus Ending Inventory,
>
> $47 500 – $14 124, or $33 376

Alternatively, COGS (cost of goods sold) can be calculated from the product of the number of units sold, 26 000, and the unit cost, $1.284, or $33 376.

Inventory cost-flow assumptions: a summary

As the above example demonstrates, the choice of inventory method can have a significant impact on the income statement and balance sheet. For Waller & Gamble, the figures are summarized as shown in Table 9.4.

Notice that net income is far higher under FIFO than under LIFO, with average cost somewhere in between. In a period of rising prices for inventory, these differences are expected. Eventually the differences between profits under FIFO and LIFO will reverse, with the liquidation of low-cost LIFO layers.

Key lessons from the chapter

- Retail, distribution, and manufacturing companies purchase or produce goods and try to sell them for a profit. These goods are referred to as "inventory" and are classified as current assets.

- For manufacturing companies, inventory goes through three stages: raw material, work-in-process, and finished goods.
- Inventory is carried on the balance sheet at the lower of cost or market value.
- The most direct approach to costing inventory is the specific identification method. However, most companies find it impractical. Instead, they make a cost-flow assumption.
- In the absence of specific identification, cost-flow assumptions allow a company to decide which unit costs will be assigned to cost of goods sold and to inventory. These assumptions include: FIFO, LIFO, and average cost.
- Any company that uses LIFO for financial reporting purposes is required to disclose a "LIFO reserve" in the notes to the financial statements. This reserve measures the difference between the inventory balance under LIFO and what it would be under FIFO.
- LIFO presents two fundamental problems for companies that use it: first, it is more complicated, and therefore more costly to administer, than other cost-flow assumptions. Second, LIFO gives rise to a "LIFO layer problem."
- Partly because of the LIFO layer problem, LIFO is not permitted under IFRS. It is permitted for tax purposes in some countries, but the number is dwindling. Soon, LIFO may become a US-only phenomenon. If the US adopts IFRS, in place of US GAAP, LIFO would probably disappear there too. In a few years, therefore, LIFO may cease to exist entirely.
- The choice of inventory method can have a significant impact on the income statement and balance sheet, especially if input prices (e.g., for raw materials) are trending up or down. When input prices are stable, the choice of cost-flow assumption has little effect on the financial statements.

Key terms and concepts from the chapter

Raw materials inventory	Lower of cost or market	Average cost method
Work-in-process	Obsolescence impairment	Specific identification
Finished goods inventory	Last in first out (LIFO)	LIFO reserve
	First in first out (FIFO)	Liquidation of LIFO layers

Questions

1. How would the inventory accounts in a retailer or distribution business differ from those in a manufacturing company?

2. Which cost-flow assumption is most common, and why?

3. Why is the LIFO cost-flow assumption not allowed under IFRS?

4. What are the advantages of LIFO accounting?

5. What are the disadvantages of LIFO accounting?

6. Can you think of why rapid economic growth and expanding industrial power in China has resulted in LIFO accounting becoming more attractive (in the few countries that allow it, of course)?

7. True or false: Inventory accounting should follow from the actual physical flow of the inventory.

8. What is the meaning of "lower of cost or market" and how does it apply to inventory accounting? What is the logic behind this rule?

9. How can a company create hidden reserves from inventory accounts?

10. What is the difference between a perpetual and a periodic inventory system? Which system would you expect a large supermarket chain or discount retailer to use, and why?

11. What is a major advantage and disadvantage of the specific identification method?

12. Do you expect the use of specific identification accounting to become more common or less common in the future? Why?

13. True or false: Inventory cost-flow assumptions don't matter much in periods of stable prices.

Problems

9.1   Calculating inventory under the FIFO and average-cost methods

Entreprise Renaud, a distributor of ski equipment, sells a snowboard known as the RemyGlide. Information relating to Renaud's purchases of RemyGlide snowboards during October is shown below. During the same month, 121 RemyGlide snowboards were sold. Renaud uses a periodic inventory system.

Date	Transaction	Units	Unit cost	Total cost
1 Oct	Inventory	52	€194	€10,088
10 Oct	Purchase	90	204	18,360
18 Oct	Purchase	40	208	8,320
25 Oct	Purchase	100	210	21,000
Totals		282		€57,768

Required

(a) Compute the ending inventory at 31 October and the cost of goods sold for the month of October using the FIFO and average cost methods.
(b) For both FIFO and average cost, calculate the sum of ending inventory and cost of goods sold. What do you notice about the answers you found for each method?

9.2   Inventories and ratio analysis

The following information is available for Romaine Corporation, a wholesaler, for 2010, 2011, and 2012:

	2010	2011	2012
Beginning inventory	€ 50,000	€150,000	€200,000
Ending inventory	150,000	200,000	240,000
Cost of goods sold	450,000	560,000	650,000
Sales	600,000	800,000	950,000

Required

Calculate inventory turnover, the inventory period, and the gross profit percentage for Romaine Corporation for each of the three years. Comment on any trends.

9.3 Correcting inventory errors

An internal audit at Parker Corporation discovered the following inventory valuation errors:

- The 2010 year-end inventory was overstated by $34 000.
- The 2011 year-end inventory was understated by $70 000.
- The 2012 year-end inventory was understated by $23 000.

The reported income before tax for Parker was:

2010	$142,000
2011	$273,000
2012	$170,000

Required

Determine what income before taxes for 2010, 2011, and 2012 should have been after correcting for the errors.

9.4 The lower of cost or market rule

Segal Company, a retailer of Nokia mobile phones, uses FIFO for costing its inventory. A physical count of inventory at the end of the year revealed the following:

Model 3720	60 units at a per unit cost of €90
Model 6700	150 units at a per unit cost of €85
Model 6303	100 units at a per unit cost of €75

The net realizable value per unit at year-end was €72, €130, and €105 for the Models 3720, 6700, and 6303, respectively.

Required

Determine the amount of ending inventory that should appear on the balance sheet.

9.5   Calculating cost of goods sold under FIFO and specific identification

It is 10 December and Fraser Home Goods has four high-end microwave ovens in stock. All are identical, and each is priced at £200. The four ovens were purchased on different dates and at different cost: Oven #1 was purchased on 15 June at a cost of £80; oven #2 on 3 August for £75; oven #3 on 5 September for £70; and oven #4 on 2 October for £65.

Required

(a) Calculate the cost of goods sold using FIFO, assuming that three of the four ovens were sold before the end of the year.
(b) If Fraser uses the specific identification method instead, how could it maximize earnings from the sale of the three ovens? How could it minimize earnings?
(c) Which of these two methods is better, and why?

Case studies

9.1   LIFO accounting at Tamar Chemicals
Purchasing policy under LIFO

Tamar Chemicals sells chemical compounds made from a material known as Rtu330. The company has used LIFO as its inventory cost-flow assumption since it was founded 25 years ago.

The inventory of Rtu330 on 31 December 2011 comprised 4000 kilograms, costing $161 200. Most of the cost comes from inventory acquired in previous years, as shown in the following table:

Year acquired	Purchase price per kilogram	2011 Year-end inventory	
		kilograms	Cost
2002	$30	2,000	$60,000
2007	46	200	9,200
2008	48	400	19,200
2011	52	1,400	72,800
		4,000	$161,200

Rtu330 cost $62 per kilogram throughout most of 2012. It is now late 2012, and prices are not expected to change before the end of the year. But Tamar's purchasing agent expects the price to fall back to $57 early in 2006. Sales for 2012 require 7000 kilograms of Rtu330. Current policy is to maintain a stock of 4000 kilograms. Because of the pending price drop, the purchasing agent suggests that the company should decrease inventory to 600 kilograms by the end of 2012 and replenish it to the desired level of 4000 kilograms early next year.

The chief accountant disagrees. If inventory falls to 600 kilograms at the end of 2012, the consumption of old, low-cost LIFO layers will cause cost of goods sold to be unusually low. As a result, the company will face a high income tax liability. The chief accountant suggests that Tamar plan 2012 purchases to maintain an end-of-year inventory of 4000 kilograms.

Required

1. Assuming that sales for 2012 require 7000 kilograms of Rtu330, calculate the cost of goods sold and the end-of-year inventory for 2012 if Tamar Chemicals follows the advice of the chief accountant.
2. Recalculate cost of goods sold and the end-of-year inventory if the company follows the purchasing agent's advice.
3. The CEO wants to know what discretion the company has to vary income in 2012 by planning its purchases of Rtu330. If the firm follows the chief accountant's policy, net income for 2012 will be $60 000. What is the range of net income that the company can report by managing purchases of Rtu330? Assume a tax rate of 30%.

9.2 Deere and CNH Global: performance effects of inventory accounting choice*

Deere and CNH Global compete against each other as manufacturers in the global market for agricultural and construction equipment. Both companies operate finance subsidiaries in order to extend credit to their dealer networks and end-customers. Deere is the larger of the two companies (1.6X greater in sales, 1.4X in assets, and 1.9X in employees). CNH is headquartered in the Netherlands, but like Deere it follows US GAAP and is traded on the New York Stock Exchange.

Despite the obvious similarities between the two companies, they have chosen different cost-flow assumptions for inventory, as revealed in the disclosures shown below.

---

*This case was prepared by Professor Daniel Bens, INSEAD.

Required

(a) What is CNH's policy regarding inventory valuation and cost-flow assumptions?
(b) What is the balance in CNH's inventory account at the end of 2010, both in dollars and as a percentage of total assets?
(c) What is Deere's policy regarding inventory valuation and cost-flow assumptions?
(d) What is the balance in Deere's inventory account at the end of 2010, both in dollars and as a percentage of total assets?
(e) What would the year-end inventory amounts be for Deere if they used the FIFO cost assumption for 100% of its inventories?
(f) Calculate inventory turnover for CNH.
(g) Calculate inventory turnover for Deere using the financial data as reported.
(h) Calculate inventory turnover for Deere, *assuming that it used FIFO on 100% of its inventories*.
(i) Review the figures above. How does Deere compare to CNH on this measure when you use the data as originally reported? How do they compare when you recast Deere's financial data on the basis of FIFO?

Excerpts from Deere's financial statements

DEERE & COMPANY

STATEMENT OF CONSOLIDATED INCOME

For the Years Ended October 31, 2010, 2009, and 2008

(In millions of dollars and shares except per share amounts)

	2010	2009	2008
Net sales and revenues			
Net sales	$23,573.2	$20,756.1	$25,803.5
Finance and interest income	1,825.3	1,842.1	2,068.4
Other income	606.1	514.2	565.7
Total	26,004.6	23,112.4	28,437.6
Costs and expenses			
Cost of sales	17,398.8	16,255.2	19,574.8
Research and development expenses	1,052.4	977.0	943.1
Selling, administrative and general expenses	2,968.7	2,780.6	2,960.2
Interest expense	811.4	1,042.4	1,137.0
Other operating expenses	748.1	718.0	697.8
Total	22,979.4	21,773.2	25,312.9
Income of consolidated group before income taxes	3,025.2	1,339.2	3,124.7
Provision for income taxes	1,161.6	460.0	1,111.2
Income of consolidated group	1,863.6	879.2	2,013.5
Equity in income (loss) of unconsolidated affiliates	10.7	(6.3)	40.2
Net income	1,874.3	872.9	2,053.7

	2010	2009	2008
Less: Net income (loss) attributable to noncontrolling interests	9.3	(.6)	.9
Net income attributable to Deere & Company	$1,865.0	$873.5	$2,052.8
Per share data			
Basic	$4.40	$2.07	$4.76
Diluted	$4.35	$2.06	$4.70
Dividends declared	$1.16	$1.12	$1.06
Average shares outstanding			
Basic	424.0	422.8	431.1
Diluted	428.6	424.4	436.3

The notes to consolidated financial statements are an integral part of this statement.

DEERE & COMPANY

CONSOLIDATED BALANCE SHEET
As of October 31, 2010 and 2009
(In millions of dollars except per share amounts)

	2010	2009
Assets		
Cash and cash equivalents	$3,790.6	$4,651.7
Marketable securities	227.9	192.0
Receivables from unconsolidated affiliates	38.8	38.4
Trade accounts and notes receivable – net	3,464.2	2,616.9
Financing receivables – net	17,682.2	15,254.7
Restricted financing receivables – net	2,238.3	3,108.4
Other receivables	925.6	864.5
Equipment on operating leases – net	1,936.2	1,733.3
Inventories	3,063.0	2,397.3
Property and equipment – net	3,790.7	4,532.2
Investments in unconsolidated affiliates	244.5	212.8
Goodwill	998.6	1,036.5
Other intangible assets – net	117.0	136.3
Retirement benefits	146.7	94.4
Deferred income taxes	2,477.1	2,804.8
Other assets	1,194.0	1,458.4
Assets held for sale	931.4	
Total assets	$43,266.8	$41,132.6

(*Continued*)

	2010	2009
Liabilities and stockholders' equity		
Liabilities		
Short-term borrowings	$7,534.5	$7,158.9
Payables to unconsolidated affiliates	203.5	55.0
Accounts payable and accrued expenses	6,481.7	5,371.4
Deferred income taxes	144.3	167.3
Long-term borrowings	16,814.5	17,391.7
Retirement benefits and other liabilities	5,784.9	6,165.5
Total liabilities	36,963.4	36,309.8
Commitments and contingencies (Note 22)		
Stockholders' equity		
Common stock, $1 par value (authorized – 1,200,000,000 shares; issued – 536,431,204 shares in 2010 and 2009), at paid-in amount	3,106.3	2,996.2
Common stock in treasury, 114,250,815 shares in 2010 and 113,188,823 shares in 2009, at cost	(5,789.5)	(5,564.7)
Retained earnings	12,353.1	10,980.5
Accumulated other comprehensive income (loss):		
Retirement benefits adjustment	(3,797.0)	(3,955.0)
Cumulative translation adjustment	436.0	400.2
Unrealized loss on derivatives	(29.2)	(44.1)
Unrealized gain on investments.	10.6	5.6
Accumulated other comprehensive income (loss)	(3,379.6)	(3,593.3)
Total Deere & Company stockholders' equity	6,290.3	4,818.7
Noncontrolling interests	13.1	4.1
Total stockholders' equity	6,303.4	4,822.8
Total liabilities and stockholders' equity	$43,266.8	$41,132.6

The notes to consolidated financial statements are an integral part of this statement.

15. Inventories

Most inventories owned by Deere & Company and its U.S. equipment subsidiaries are valued at cost, on the "last-in, first-out" (LIFO) basis. Remaining inventories are generally valued at the lower of cost, on the "first-in, first-out" (FIFO) basis, or market. The value of gross inventories on the LIFO basis represented 59% of worldwide gross inventories at FIFO value on 31 October 2010 and 2009. The pretax favorable income effect from the liquidation of LIFO inventory during 2009 was approximately $37 million. If all inventories had been valued on a FIFO basis, estimated inventories by major classification at 31 October in millions of dollars would have been as follows:

	2010	2009
Raw materials and supplies	$1,201	$940
Work-in-process	483	387
Finished goods and parts	2,777	2,437
Total FIFO value	4,461	3,764
Less adjustment to LIFO value	1,398	1,367
Inventories	$3,063	$2,397

Excerpts from CNH'S financial statements: CNH Global N.V. Consolidated statements of operations for the years ended December 31, 2010, 2009, and 2008

	Consolidated		
	2010	2009	2008
	(in millions, except per share data)		
Revenues			
Net sales	$14,474	$12,783	$17,366
Finance and interest income	1,134	977	1,110
	15,608	13,760	18,476
Costs and expenses			
Cost of goods sold	11,891	10,862	14,054
Selling, general and administrative	1,698	1,486	1,698
Research, development and engineering	451	398	422
Restructuring	16	102	39
Interest expense – Fiat subsidiaries	112	189	308
Interest expense – other	718	482	457
Other, net	306	334	342
	15,192	13,853	17,320
Income (loss) before income taxes and equity in income (loss) of unconsolidated subsidiaries and affiliates	416	(93)	1156
Income tax provision	77	92	385

(*Continued*)

	Consolidated		
	2010	2009	2008
	(in millions, except per share data)		
Equity in income (loss) of unconsolidated subsidiaries and affiliates:			
Financial services	11	9	13
Equipment operations	88	(46)	40
Net income (loss)	438	(222)	824
Net loss attributable to noncontrolling interests	(14)	(32)	(1)
Net income (loss) attributable to CNH Global N.V.	$452	$(190)	$825
Earnings (loss) per share attributable to CNH Global N.V. common shareholders			
Basic	$1.90	$(0.80)	$3.48
Diluted	$1.89	$(0.80)	$3.47

CNH Global N.V. Consolidated balance sheets as of December 31, 2010 and 2009

	Consolidated	
	2010	2009
	(in millions, except share data)	
Assets		
Current assets		
Cash and cash equivalents	$3,618	$1,263
Restricted cash	914	128
Deposits in Fiat subsidiaries' cash management pools	1,760	2,251
Accounts and notes receivable, net	8,621	5,190
Inventories, net	2,937	3,297
Deferred income taxes	633	517
Prepayments and other	822	462
Total current assets	19,305	13,108
Long-term receivables	5,407	3,236
Property, plant and equipment, net	1,786	1,764
Investments in unconsolidated subsidiaries and affiliates	490	415
Equipment on operating leases, net	622	646

	Consolidated	
	2010	**2009**
	(in millions, except share data)	
Goodwill	2,385	2,374
Other intangible assets, net	679	717
Other assets	915	948
Total	$31,589	$23,208
Liabilities and equity		
Current liabilities		
Current maturities of long-term debt – Fiat subsidiaries	$253	$836
Current maturities of long-term debt – other	3,641	1,550
Short-term debt – Fiat subsidiaries	194	537
Short-term debt – other	3,669	1,435
Accounts payable	2,367	1,915
Other accrued liabilities	3,345	2,678
Total current liabilities	13,469	8,951
Long-term debt – Fiat subsidiaries	331	1,516
Long-term debt – other	8,209	3,534
Pension, postretirement and other postemployment benefits	1,770	1,871
Other liabilities	426	526
Redeemable noncontrolling interest	4	—
Equity		
Common shares, €2.25 par value; authorized 400,000,000 shares in 2010 and 2009, issued 238,588,630 shares in 2010, 237,553,331 shares in 2009	599	595
Paid-in capital	6,198	6,188
Treasury stock, 154,813 shares in 2010 and 2009, at cost	(8)	(8)
Retained earnings	658	210
Accumulated other comprehensive loss	(142)	(267)
Noncontrolling interests	75	92
Total equity	7,380	6,810
Total	$31,589	$23,208

Inventories

Inventories are stated at the lower of cost or net realizable value. Cost is determined by the first-in, first-out method. The cost of finished goods and work-in-progress includes the cost of raw materials, other direct costs and production overheads. Net realizable value is the estimate of the selling price in the ordinary course of business, less the cost of completion and selling. Provisions are made for obsolete and slow-moving inventories.

Notes

1. For P&G, indirect labor refers to any personnel in a factory setting who are not directly involved in producing the company's products. Examples include maintenance, security, engineering, accounting, and computer services staff.
2. When a firm records the cost of goods sold each time an inventory item is sold, it uses a "perpetual" inventory system. In this chapter, however, we assume the use of a "periodic" inventory system. Here, a firm determines the cost of goods sold at the end of each period by taking a physical inventory; any units acquired that are not in ending inventory are assumed to have been sold.
3. US GAAP does not allow for any recovery from written-off inventory. If market value increases subsequent to a write-off, the company must wait until the inventory is sold before recognizing a gain.
4. An obvious exception would be a business where inventory is stored in piles, with the items on top sold first.

CHAPTER 10

Accounting for Property, Plant and Equipment

Introduction

Property, plant and equipment (PP&E) is defined as tangible assets that are held for use in the production or supply of goods or services, for rental to others, or for administrative purposes. They are expected to be used for more than one year. In this chapter we look at the accounting for PP&E by examining the financials of McDonald's Corporation. The following discussion applies to both US GAAP and International Financial Reporting Standards (IFRS), unless otherwise noted. This chapter also discusses intangible assets.

PP&E is usually reported on the balance sheet at historical cost (in the case of land) or at historical cost less accumulated depreciation (for depreciable assets such as buildings and machinery). At the end of 2009, McDonald's reported PP&E with an historical cost of $33.4 billion and $11.9 billion of accumulated depreciation – see Table 10.1. The resulting net book value, $21.5 billion, represents 71% of total assets. Such a high figure is common in capital intensive businesses like McDonald's.

The following disclosure from the company's notes provides a breakdown of PP&E, or "Net property and equipment" (see Table 10.2) as McDonald's calls it. The overwhelming majority of the company's assets are held in the form of land and buildings used for the many thousands of restaurants owned around the world. Further information on the company's assets is revealed in Tables 10.3 and Table 10.4.

In 2009, the company opened 824 traditional McDonald's restaurants and 44 satellite restaurants (small, limited-menu restaurants for which the land and building are generally leased), and closed 215 traditional restaurants and 142 satellite restaurants.

Table 10.1   McDonald's Corporation - assets (in millions, US$)

	2009/12/31	2008/12/31
Current assets		
Cash and equivalents	$1,796.0	$2,063.4
Accounts and notes receivable	1,060.4	931.2
Inventories, at cost, not in excess of market	106.2	111.5
Prepaid expenses and other current assets	453.7	411.5
Total current assets	3,416.3	3,517.6
Other assets		
Investments in and advances to affiliates	1,212.7	1,222.3
Goodwill	2,425.2	2,237.4
Miscellaneous	1,639.2	1,229.7
Total other assets	5,277.1	4,689.4
Property and equipment		
Property and equipment, at cost	33,440.5	31,152.4
Accumulated depreciation and amortization	(11,909.0)	(10,897.9)
Net property and equipment	21,531.5	20,254.5
Total assets	30,224.9	28,461.5

Table 10.2   Disclosure from McDonald's notes regarding breakdown of PP&E (in millions, US$)

	2009/12/31	2008/12/31
Land	$5,048.3	$4,689.6
Buildings and improvements on owned land	12,119.0	10,952.3
Buildings and improvements on leased land	11,347.9	10,788.6
Equipment, signs, and seating	4,422.9	4,205.1
Other	502.4	516.8
	33,440.5	31,152.4
Accumulated depreciation and amortization	(11,909.0)	(10,897.9)
Net property and equipment	$21,531.5	$20,254.5

Table 10.3   Additional information on McDonald's assets

Systemwide restaurants at year end	2009	2008
US	13,980	13,918
Europe	6,785	6,628
APMEA	8,488	8,255
Other countries and corporate	3,225	3,166
Total	32,478	31,967

Table 10.4 Capital expenditures (in millions, US$)

	2009/12/31	**2008/12/31**	**2007/12/31**
New restaurants	$ 809	$ 897	$ 687
Existing restaurants	1,070	1,152	1,158
Other properties^a	73	87	102
Total	$ 1,952	$ 2,136	$ 1,947
Total assets	$30,225	$28,462	$29,392

^aPrimarily corporate equipment and other office-related expenditures.

The capital investments made in 2009 (see Table 10.4) can be summarized as follows (in millions, US$):

PP&E	$1,952	
Cash/Liabilities		$1,952

Initial recognition of PP&E

The initial measurement of PP&E includes not just the costs directly incurred to acquire the asset (for example, the price paid to a manufacturer for a piece of equipment), but also those costs directly attributable to bringing the asset to the location and working condition necessary for it to operate in the way management intends. Examples include the costs of site preparation, initial delivery and handling, installation and assembly, and employee benefits arising from construction or acquisition of the asset. Even borrowing costs incurred during the period of acquiring, constructing, or producing the asset are sometimes included in historical cost.

Some assets, especially those with considerable environmental consequences, may lead to significant costs upon retirement of the asset. The asset cannot simply be thrown away when its useful life is over, but rather must be carefully disposed of. This means that when such assets are acquired, an asset-retirement obligation (i.e., a liability) is incurred. The fair value of this liability must be recognized when the asset is acquired if a reasonable estimate of it can be made. These costs are added to the asset's carrying amount. The journal entry would look like this:

PP&E	XX	
Liability		XX

Subsequent expenditures: repair or improvement?

The costs of maintenance and repairs incurred after the asset has been put into service are expensed as incurred. Replacement parts can be capitalized when certain criteria are met, but parts that are used for routine maintenance are usually expensed. The journal entry is:

Repair expense	XX	
Cash		XX

In contrast, major overhauls of an asset are capitalized when deemed to be an "improvement." In this case, the journal entry would be:

```
PP&E      XX
  Cash          XX
```

The line separating one type of cost from the other (i.e., routine repair and maintenance vs. improvement) is not always obvious. Often, judgment is required. However, US GAAP and IFRS do provide some guidance on how to determine the appropriate accounting treatment. To be considered an improvement, the expenditure must:

1. increase the asset's useful life,
2. increase the quality of the asset's output,
3. increase the quantity of the asset's output, or
4. reduce the cost associated with operating the asset.

If the expenditure meets one of these criteria, the expenditure should be capitalized. Otherwise, it should be expensed.

Accounting for depreciation

Apart from land, assets categorized as PP&E tend to wear out over time, and therefore must be depreciated. To depreciate an asset, the following must be determined:

1. **The depreciable basis of the asset**. For many assets, if not most, the depreciable basis and acquisition cost are the same. To illustrate, if a machine costs $100 000, the total amount to be depreciated over the asset's life is also $100 000. However, many other assets are expected to have significant residual, or salvage, values at the end of their useful lives. For example, trucks and airplanes typically have residual values substantially greater than zero. In such cases, the depreciable basis of the asset equals the acquisition cost minus the residual value. For example, if a truck costs $60 000, and is expected to be worth $10 000 at the end of its useful life for the company, only $50 000 is to be depreciated.
2. **The estimated useful life**. The estimated life is normally defined as the period of time, usually expressed in years, that the company is expected to derive economic benefits from the use of the asset. For some assets, however, useful life is expressed in units other than time. A common example is any transportation vehicle – such as automobiles, vans, or trucks. In such cases, useful life may be defined as miles or kilometers driven. Other examples where useful life is defined in terms other than calendar time include some classes of machinery, in which useful life is defined as number of units produced; oil wells, where life is usually defined as number of barrels to be extracted; and coal mines, where life is defined as numbers of tons of coal to be mined.
3. **Depreciation method**. The depreciation method is the pattern by which the depreciable basis of an asset will be allocated to the future accounting periods that will benefit from

the use of an asset. The most common method, and the one used by McDonald's (see Box 10.1), is straight-line, in which each year of the asset's use receives an identical amount of depreciation expense. However, other, more accelerated approaches may be used. Accelerated methods are popular for tax purposes because they allow companies to enjoy the tax benefits provided by depreciation charges more quickly than they would under the straight-line method. In effect, accelerating depreciation increases the present value of the tax shield, thereby reducing the effective cost of the asset.

Every depreciation method yields an identical amount of total depreciation expense over an asset's useful life. The only difference is in the pattern, that is, the amount of depreciation expense recognized in each year of the asset's life. For example, the straight-line method allocates depreciation evenly across time, while the accelerated methods, such as double-declining-balance (see below), allocate the depreciable basis more rapidly in the early years and more slowly in the later years.

To illustrate the different allocation patterns that arise from the use of different depreciation methods, let's assume that McDonald's buys a machine for $300 000. Management estimates that it will use the machine for four years. At the end of the fourth year, the machine is expected to have a salvage value of $60 000. If the company chooses the straight-line depreciation method,

$$
\begin{aligned}
\text{Depreciation per year} &= (\text{Cost} - \text{Salvage Value}) \div \text{Useful Life} \\
&= (\$300\,000 - \$60\,000) \div 4 \text{ years} = \$60\,000/\text{year}
\end{aligned}
$$

McDonald's will make the following entry each year, for the next four years:

Depreciation expense	$60,000	
Accumulated depreciation		$60,000

A common alternative to straight-line depreciation is the accelerated method known as "declining balance." Under this approach, the annual depreciation charge is based on the

---

Box 10.1   McDonald's note on depreciation method used

McDonald's – Property and equipment

Property and equipment are stated at cost, with depreciation and amortization provided using the straight-line method over the following estimated useful lives: buildings – up to 40 years; leasehold improvements – the lesser of useful lives of assets or lease terms, which generally include option periods; and equipment – three to 12 years.

Table 10.5   Double-declining-balance depreciation

Date	Depreciation factor	Depreciation expense	Cost	Accumulated depreciation	Book value
1/1/10			$300,000	$ 0	$300,000
12/31/10	50%	$150,000[a]	300,000	150,000	150,000
12/31/11	50%		300,000	225,000	75,000
12/31/12	50%	15,000[b]	300,000	240,000	60,000
12/31/13	50%	0	300,000	240,000	60,000

[a]Depreciation Expense = (Book Value at Beginning of the Period) × (Depreciation Factor).

[b]Book Value × Depreciation Factor = $75 000 × 50% = $37 500. If McDonald's depreciated $37 500 in 2012, the asset's book value would drop below salvage value. To prevent this from happening, depreciation expense for 2012 is limited to $15 000.

straight-line depreciation rate (in this case 25% per year), multiplied by a number greater than 1 but usually not greater than 2. Because the annual depreciation rate exceeds the straight-line rate, the higher rate must be applied to a declining balance, to ensure that total depreciation charges do not exceed the asset's depreciable basis.

In this example, we assume that McDonald's chooses double-declining-balance, which means that the annual depreciation charge is twice the straight line rate (i.e., 50%). See Table 10.5 for details of double-declining-balance depreciation.

Notice that the 50% depreciation rate is applied to a smaller balance each year. Notice also that the asset is fully depreciated by the end of the third year. If there had been no salvage value, and the depreciable basis of the asset was $300 000 (instead of $240 000), the company would recognize $37 500 of depreciation expense for both Years 3 and 4.

Unlike the straight-line method, salvage value is not taken in account up front. The annual depreciation rate of 50% is applied to the total cost of the asset, not the cost less salvage value. This explains why the depreciation charge for the first year, $150 000, is more than double the charge under straight-line. However, the company must ensure that accumulated depreciation does not allow net book value to fall below salvage value.

Changes in depreciation estimates or methods

Changes in depreciation policy are common. Depreciation methods can change, while changes in estimates of useful life or salvage value are even more common. McDonald's explains this in its annual report – see Box 10.2.

Changes in depreciation policy are treated on a *prospective basis*. This means that when a company changes depreciation method, or changes estimates of useful lives or residual value, no adjustments are made to financial statements from previous years.

To illustrate, assume that a $6 million asset is depreciated over six years using the straight-line method. Depreciation expense is $1 million each year over the asset's life. Now assume that after the second year, when the net book value is $4 million ($6 million – $2 million of depreciation), the company decides that the asset will last another five years, instead of four. In

---

> ### Box 10.2   McDonald's explanation of changes in depreciation methods
> #### McDonald's – Property and equipment
>
> Property and equipment are depreciated or amortized on a straight-line basis over their useful lives . . . The Company periodically reviews these lives relative to physical factors, economic factors and industry trends. If there are changes in the planned use of property and equipment, or if technological changes occur more rapidly than anticipated, the useful lives assigned to these assets may need to be shortened, resulting in the accelerated recognition of depreciation and amortization expense or write-offs in future periods.

---

other words, the company is changing the estimated useful life from six years to seven. With $4 million of depreciable cost, and five years of remaining useful life, the annual depreciation charge is $800 000, instead of $1 million, as it was in the previous two years. No correction is made to the depreciation expense recognized in the previous two years. Instead, the adjustment is made going forward. This approach is also required for changes in depreciation method too – for example, when an accelerated method is replaced with straight-line.

Asset impairment

Apart from an exception reported later in this chapter, PP&E is carried at cost less accumulated depreciation, unless the value of an asset has been "impaired." Impairment means that the fair value of the asset (i.e. usually defined as the future cash flows benefits an owner can expect if the asset is held in use; otherwise, the price a company can expect from selling the asset) is significantly and permanently below that of net book value. The disclosure shown in Box 10.3 reveals how McDonald's deals with impairments of PP&E. Loss on impairment is an income statement account, which means that impairment is a profit-reducing (or loss-increasing) event.

US GAAP and IFRS are broadly similar in how impairment is defined. Under both regimes, intangible assets with indefinite lives (e.g., trademarks, brand names, etc.) must be reviewed at least annually for impairment and more frequently if impairment indicators are present. Impairment of PP&E is not tested annually, but rather when there are indicators of impairment. Indicators that assets have been impaired, and therefore should be written down, may arise from external events such as a significant decline in market value for the asset or changes in the technological, market, economic, or legal environment. Despite these similarities, however, differences exist between the two regimes in the way in which impairment is reviewed, recognized, and measured.

According to IAS 36 (the main standard under IFRS), an asset is considered impaired to the extent that the carrying value on the balance sheet exceeds its recoverable amount. The recoverable amount is the greater of: (1) fair value less selling costs, and (2) value in use

---

Box 10.3

McDonald's – Long-lived assets impairment review

Long-lived assets (including goodwill) are reviewed for impairment annually in the fourth quarter and whenever events or changes in circumstances indicate that the carrying amount of an asset may not be recoverable. In assessing the recoverability of the Company's long-lived assets, the Company considers changes in economic conditions and makes assumptions regarding estimated future cash flows and other factors. Estimates of future cash flows are highly subjective judgments based on the Company's experience and knowledge of its operations. These estimates can be significantly impacted by many factors including changes in global and local business and economic conditions, operating costs, inflation, competition, and consumer and demographic trends. A key assumption impacting estimated future cash flows is the estimated change in comparable sales. If the Company's estimates or underlying assumptions change in the future, the Company may be required to record impairment charges.

(the present value of future cash flows in use, including disposal value). IFRS defines fair value as "the amount for which an asset could be exchanged or a liability settled between knowledgeable, willing parties in an arm's length transaction." This fair value definition is essentially market value, assuming the existence of an active market for the asset. Value in use refers to the discounted present value of cash generated by the asset in question. This concept recognizes that sometimes (indeed, most times) an asset is more valuable as used in the business (value in use) than it would be if used by others (fair value). Otherwise, why would a business retain the asset?

To illustrate, suppose a taxi company owns a vehicle with a carrying value of €12 000 (cost of €30 000 less accumulated depreciation of €18 000). The asset has a fair value of €10 000 (market price, net of selling costs) and a discounted cash flow (value in use) of €14 000. The recoverable value is €14 000 and, thus, there is no impairment. Alternatively, imagine the same facts except that the value in use is €11 000. Thus, the recoverable value is €11 000 (the higher of fair value and value in use). In this case, the carrying value (€12 000) is higher than the recoverable value and there is an impairment of €1000. The journal entry would be:

Impairment loss	€1,000	
Accumulated impairment loss		€1,000

Accumulated impairment loss is a contra-asset account and is deducted from the impaired asset account on the balance sheet.

On the other hand, the US GAAP method for impairment testing is a two-step approach that requires a recoverability test be performed first – the carrying amount of the asset is compared to the sum of future *undiscounted* cash flows generated through use and eventual disposal. If the carrying value of the asset is greater than the total undiscounted cash flows, the present (i.e., discount) value of the future cash flows must be determined. The impairment loss equals the difference between the carrying value and the discounted cash flows.

Returning to the example above, assume that the sum of the *undiscounted* cash flows from the future use of the taxi equals €13 500. Under US GAAP, no impairment would be recorded because the carrying value is €12 000. However, because the *discounted* cash flow is €11 000, an impairment loss is recorded under IFRS. If, on the other hand, the sum of the undiscounted cash flows was €11 900, the asset would be deemed "unrecoverable" (the carrying value of €12 000 is greater than €11 900) and thus subject to impairment. The impairment loss would be calculated as the difference between the €12 000 carrying value and the sum of the discounted cash flows of €11 000. The journal entry would be:

Impairment loss	€1,000	
Asset		€1,000

Note that the credit entry under IFRS was to "accumulated impairment loss," a contra-asset account, but under US GAAP the credit is made directly to the asset account. This difference stems from another difference between the two reporting regimes: if an asset's value recovers, the previous impairment loss can be reversed under IFRS, but not under US GAAP. Any future recovery in value under IFRS is recognized by reducing the balance in the contra-asset. If recovery is complete, the contra-asset is brought to zero.

Fair value vs. historical cost

The most important difference between US GAAP and IFRS in the accounting for PP&E is that the latter gives companies the option of reporting PP&E at fair value, even if fair value is greater than acquisition cost. When assets are written up, the entry looks like this:

PP&E	XX	
Revaluation surplus		XX

where revaluation surplus is a shareholders' equity account. The income statement is not affected at the moment that the asset is revalued.

However, the overwhelming majority of companies reporting under IFRS have chosen not to exercise this option. The primary reason for this reluctance is that once fair value is used, frequent updates are required, unless the company chooses to revert to historical cost. Also, the company must subject all assets of the same class to revaluation. For example, it cannot choose to revalue some of its real estate, while using historical cost for the rest. Because this process is costly, most companies reporting under IFRS use historical cost for PP&E, just like companies reporting under US GAAP. But remember that fair value must be used under both regimes in the case of impaired assets.

If an IFRS company elects to use fair value for nonimpaired assets, meaning that the carrying (balance sheet) value is increased above acquisition cost, any subsequent impairment can be offset against increases recognized in previous years. In other words, the impairment loss is offset against previous revaluations for the same asset. The income statement is unaffected. But any uncovered loss (i.e., a loss greater than previous revaluations) must be recognized as a loss on the income statement.

Divestitures and asset sales

Gains and losses resulting from the disposal of PP&E are based on the difference between the proceeds received from the disposal and the asset's book value. Therefore, one would have to know the book value of each individual property in order to be able to determine the gain or loss from selling it. Book value equals the original cost of the asset less any accumulated depreciation associated with it.

If the asset is sold for a price greater than net book value, the company records the following entry:

Cash	XX	
Accumulated depreciation	XX	
Asset (at cost)		XX
Gain on disposal of asset		XX

The gain on disposal is an income statement account. Therefore, the gain increases net income for the period. If the asset is sold for a price lower than net book value, the company records a loss (also an income statement account):

Cash	XX	
Accumulated depreciation	XX	
Loss on disposal of asset	XX	
Asset (at cost)		XX

Intangible assets

Intangible assets are nonfinancial assets that lack the physical substance of land, building, equipment, and machinery. Common examples include patents, copyrights, customer lists, and brand names. The accounting for intangible assets is roughly the same under US GAAP and IFRS. The initial recording of the acquired intangible asset is at cost.

To illustrate, in April 2012 Microsoft paid AOL $1 billion for 800 patents. Most of these patents relate to instant messaging and e-mail as well as browser and search engine technologies. The journal entry to record the acquisition of the patents would have been:

Patents	$1bn	
Cash		$1bn

with patents being classified as a long-term asset.

Finite-lived intangible assets (that is, assets that have a limited legal or economic life) are amortized using the straight-line method over their estimated useful lives and are tested for impairment annually. In the case of patents, the useful life is the legal life or the economic life (i.e., the period over which the asset is expected to provide economic benefits to the owner), whichever is less. For example, if the legal life of a patent is 20 years, but the rate of technology in the industry results in nearly all patents becoming obsolete before their legal expiration, a shorter time period is used for amortization purposes. Assuming the average useful life of the patents acquired by Microsoft is 10 years, the following journal entry would be recorded each year for the next 10 years:

Amortization expense	$100m	
Patent		$100m

Indefinite-lived intangible assets – intangibles with no legal limits on their useful lives, such as brand names and trademarks – are carried at cost with annual impairment testing.

With a few exceptions – notably costs from the development phase of R&D under IFRS and software development under both regimes – internally generated intangible assets are not recorded on the balance sheet. For example, the billions that pharmaceutical companies spend on research are typically expensed as incurred, and therefore do not result in a capitalized intangible asset. Here's how Microsoft disclosed its R&D spending in the 2011 Annual Report:

> During fiscal years 2011, 2010, and 2009, research and development expense was $9.0 billion, $8.7 billion, and $9.0 billion, respectively. These amounts represented 13%, 14%, and 15%, respectively, of revenue in each of those years. We plan to continue to make significant investments in a broad range of research and product development efforts.

The journal entries recorded in 2011 for these activities sum up to:

Research and development expense	$9bn	
Cash		$9bn

There is one important difference in the accounting for intangible assets under US GAAP and IFRS. In a practice that mirrors the accounting for tangible PP&E, intangible assets previously written down may be revalued upward under IFRS if the annual impairment test indicates an increase in fair value. Under US GAAP, once an intangible asset is written down because of impairment, it may never be written up.

On a final note, we leave the subject of goodwill, perhaps the most important of all intangible assets, to Chapter 18.

Key lessons from the chapter

- Property, plant and equipment (PP&E) is defined as tangible assets that are held for use in the production or supply of goods or services.
- PP&E is usually reported on the balance sheet at historical cost, or historical cost less accumulated depreciation.
- The initial measurement of PP&E includes all costs to get the asset ready for its intended use.
- Maintenance costs are expensed as incurred. Improvement costs are capitalized and depreciated over the useful life. The boundary that separates maintenance from improvements is not always obvious, which means that some judgment may be required in determining whether to expense or capitalize.
- The useful life is the period of time, usually (but not always) expressed in years, that the company is expected to derive economic benefit from use of the asset.
- The depreciation method is the pattern by which the depreciable basis of an asset will be allocated to the future accounting periods that will benefit from the use of an asset.
- The most common depreciation method, by far, is straight-line. However, other, more accelerated approaches may be used. These accelerated approaches are popular for tax purposes because they increase the present value of the tax shields offered by depreciation.
- Depreciation methods for given assets can change, although changes in estimates of useful life or salvage value are more common.
- PP&E should be carried at cost less accumulated depreciation, unless the fair value of an asset has been "impaired." Impairment means that the fair value of an asset is significantly and permanently below that of net book value.
- Gains and losses resulting from the disposal of PP&E are based on the difference between the proceeds received from disposal and the asset's net book value.

Key terms and concepts from the chapter

Historical cost	Accelerated method	Useful life
Depreciation	Double-declining method	Residual/salvage value
Amortization	Sum-of-the-years digits	Gain/loss of disposal
Depletion	method	Asset impairment
Net book value	Straight-line method	Intangible assets

Questions

1. Describe each of the following terms: depreciation, amortization, and depletion.

2. Why do tax laws permit accelerated depreciation methods?

3. IFRS permits the use of fair value accounting for property and plant assets. Why, then, do most companies prefer to use historical (or acquisition) cost?

4. Why are transport, installation and training costs added to the asset account, and not expensed immediately?

5. What is goodwill? What is the proper accounting treatment for it?

6. Why does the accounting treatment for repairs and maintenance differ from that of improvements?

7. Why are research costs expensed under IFRS, but development costs are capitalized? What's the difference between "research" and "development"?

8. True or false: the amortization period for an intangible asset is equal to its legal life.

9. How should a company account for an asset, such as a building or piece of equipment, that has been fully depreciated?

10. Why are brand names and trademarks not amortized?

11. True or false: most large, publicly traded companies use straight-line depreciation for book purposes but accelerated methods for tax.

12. How is a gain or loss determined on an asset sale?

Problems

10.1 Comparing the effects of depreciation choice on financial ratios

Dieter Loch AG is about to purchase two new assets – a machine for €75 000 and a state-of-the art forklift truck for €40 000. The assets would be acquired at the beginning of 2013. The company's 2012 income statement and other information are shown below:

Sales	€550,000
Cost of goods sold	310,000
Gross profit	240,000
SG&A expenses	140,000
Income before tax	100,000
Income taxes	30,000
NOPAT	€70,000

Additional information:

- Dieter Loch management expects the addition of the two assets to generate a 20% annual growth rate in sales.
- Depreciation on the new machine will be included as part of cost of goods sold. Depreciation on the new forklift will be classified under other operating expenses.
- Excluding the new machine's depreciation, cost of goods sold is expected to increase at an annual rate of 7%.
- Excluding the new forklift's depreciation, selling, general, and administrative (SG&A) expenses are expected to grow at an annual rate of 5%.
- Dieter Loch's invested capital, not counting the new machine and forklift, is expected to increase at a rate of 15% per year. Average invested capital at the end of 2012 was €500 000.

- Both the machine and the forklift have an estimated useful life of five years, and zero residual value.
- The tax rate is 30%.

Required

(a) Can you explain why depreciation charges on the two assets are classified differently – COGS for the machine and SG&A for the forklift?

(b) Prepare forecasted income statements for 2013 and 2014, assuming that Dieter Loch AG elects to use straight-line depreciation for both assets.

(c) Calculate the firm's gross profit percentage, NOPAT margin, and return on invested capital.

(d) Repeat (b), assuming that the company elects to use the double-declining balance method instead for both assets.

(e) Repeat (c). How does the choice of different depreciation methods affect the behavior of the ratios in 2013 and 2014?

10.2   Analyzing depreciation on PP&E

The following note is taken from the 2004 Annual Report of ExxonMobil Corporation:

	Dec. 31, 2004		Dec. 31, 2003	
	Historical cost	**Accumulated depreciation**	**Historical cost**	**Accumulated depreciation**
(millions of dollars)				
Upstream	$148,024	$62,013	$138,701	$58,727
Downstream	62,014	29,810	59,939	29,566
Chemical	21,777	10,049	20,623	10,115
Other	10,607	6,767	10,052	6,557
Total	$242,422	$108,639	$229,315	$104,965

In the upstream segment, depreciation is on a unit-of-production basis, so depreciable life will vary by field. In the downstream segment, investments in refinery and . . . manufacturing facilities are generally depreciated on a straight-line basis over a 25-year life and service station buildings and fixed improvements over a 20-year life. In the chemical segment, investments in process equipment are depreciated on a straight-line basis over a 20-year life. Accumulated depreciation and depletion totaled $133 783 million at the end of 2004 and $124 350 million at the end of 2003.

Required

Based on the above note, answer the following:

(a) By 2004, what percentage of the upstream segment costs have been depreciated? Assume no salvage value and assume that in 2005, no upstream acquisitions or divestitures take place. If the upstream PP&E are used to produce 10% of their capabilities, what would be the depreciation expense and net book value at the end of 2005?

(b) By 31 December 2003, assuming a 20% salvage (residual) value, on average, what is the age of the chemical PP&E?

(c) Assuming no divestiture or retirement of assets, what was the depreciation expense for all PP&E in 2004?

10.3   Calculating and analyzing amortization expense

The 2003 Annual Report for Microsoft reports the acquisition of Navision:

In fiscal 2003, Microsoft acquired all of the outstanding equity interests of Navision a/s, Rare Ltd., and Placeware, Inc. Navision, headquartered in Vedbaek, Denmark, is a provider of integrated business solutions software for small and mid-sized businesses in the European market that is part of the Microsoft Business Solutions segment. Navision, Rare, and Placeware have been consolidated into our financial statements since their respective acquisition dates. The estimated fair values of the assets acquired and liabilities assumed at the date of the acquisitions for fiscal 2003 are as follows:

(In millions)	Navision a/s at July 12, 2002	Rare Ltd. at September 24, 2002	Placeware, Inc. at April 30, 2003
Current assets	$240	$25	$30
Property, plant, and equipment	8	8	7
Intangible assets	169	75	30
Goodwill	1,197	281	180
Total assets acquired	1,614	389	247
Current liabilities	(148)	(12)	(32)
Long-term liabilities	(1)	(13)	
Total liabilities assumed	(149)	(12)	(45)
Net assets acquired	$1,465	$377	$202

The note provides supplemental information on the intangible assets acquired by Microsoft:

The components of intangible assets acquired in the acquisitions above are as follows (no significant residual value is estimated for these assets):

	Navision a/s	Weighted average life	Rare Ltd.	Weighted average life	Placeware, Inc.	Weighted average life
Contract-based	$115	6 years	$16	5 years	$1	6 years
Technology-based	48	4 years	36	5 years	4	4 years
Marketing-related	4	3 years	10	5 years	2	1 year
Customer-related					23	10 years
Research and Development	2[a]		13[a]			
Total	$169	5 years	$75	5 years	$30	8 years

[a]Amounts assigned to research and development assets were written off in accordance with FIN 4. Those write-offs were included in research and development expenses.

Required

(a) How much amortization expense would you expect Microsoft to record in 2004 for the intangible assets purchased in 2003?

(b) What impact would the amortization expense have on each of the company's three principal financial statements?

10.4 Calculating depreciation expense

On 1 January 2013, Double Happiness Delivery Company acquired a new truck for $90 000. The truck is estimated to have a useful life of five years and no residual value.

Required

Indicate the amount of the depreciation charge for each year of the asset's life under the following methods:

(a) The straight-line method.
(b) The declining balance method at twice the straight-line rate, with a switch to straight-line in 2016. Why would the company switch to straight-line after using the declining balance method for the same asset?

10.5 Effects of changes in estimates on depreciation expense

At the end of each year, Patty Chu, the chief accountant at Rex Lin Enterprises, a Singapore-based trading company, reviews long-term assets at the end of each year to determine whether changes are called for in how these assets are depreciated. In December 2011, her attention focused on two assets in particular:

	Date acquired	Cost	Accumulated depreciation end of 2011	Useful life	Residual value
Warehouse	1/1/07	$200,000	$50,000	25 years	$10,000
Building	1/1/06	1,600,000	228,000	40 years	100,000

Patty is proposing the following changes:

For the warehouse: a decrease in the useful life to 20 years, and a decrease in residual value to $6000.

For the building: an increase in the useful life to 50 years, and a decrease in the residual value to $55 000.

Before agreeing to the changes, Patty's bosses would like to know what the depreciation charges will be for each asset if the changes are adopted. All assets are depreciated using the straight-line method.

Required

Calculate the revised annual depreciation expenses for each asset in 2012, and compare them to what the expenses would be if the changes were not made.

10.6 Interpreting disclosures for property, plant and equipment

Petrobras, which operates in the energy sector, is Brazil's largest company. Its shares trade on several of the world's leading stock exchanges. A portion of Petrobras' balance sheet, its income statement, and extracts from a note on PP&E are presented in Exhibit 10.1.

Required

Based on the information provided, answer the following questions:

(a) What portion of Petrobras' "Equipment and other assets" had been "used up" by the end of fiscal 2008?
(b) How many years are left in the lives of Petrobras' "Equipment and other assets," on average? State clearly any assumptions that you make in arriving at your estimate.
(c) Suppose that Petrobras assumes a zero salvage value for their "Equipment and other assets." For each $100 in new asset investments, what is the annual amount of depreciation expense charged to the income statement?
(d) Suppose that other leading energy companies charge $12 in depreciation expense for each $100 invested in new equipment. Are Petrobras' depreciation policy assumptions materially different from those of their competitors? Support your answer.
(e) What line item on Petrobras' income statement is most affected by their depreciation policy? Explain why.
(f) Aside from comparing Petrobras' depreciation policy assumptions to those of their competitors, what other "red flags" might one look for in order to assess whether Petrobras is overly conservative or overly aggressive in taking depreciation expenses? Is there any evidence of these issues on Petrobras' financial statements?

Exhibit 10.1   Petrobras disclosures

STATEMENTS OF INCOME

December 31, 2008 and 2007

(In thousands of reais, except net income per share at paid-up capital)

STATEMENTS OF INCOME	NOTE	CONSOLIDATED 2008	2007
Gross operating revenues			
Selling expenses			
Products		266,217,208	218,050,202
Services, mainly freight		276,872	203,972
		266,494,080	**218,254,174**
Sales charges		(51,375,544)	(47,676,449)
Net operating revenues		**215,118,536**	**170,577,725**
Cost of products and services sold		(141,623,359)	(104,398,043)
Gross profit		**73,495,177**	**66,179,682**
Operating income (expenses)			
Selling expenses		(7,162,264)	(6,059,734)
Financial			
Expenses	18	(4,193,135)	(3,292,002)
Revenues	18	3,494,430	2,417,659
Exchange and monetary variations, net	18	3,827,489	(3,146,547)
Administrative and general expenses			
Management and board of directors remuneration		(35,792)	(29,259)
Administrative		(7,211,566)	(6,398,633)
Taxes		(862,766)	(1,255,511)
Cost of research and technological development		(1,705,572)	(1,712,338)
Loss of recovery of assets		(933,088)	(446,129)
Exploratory costs for the extraction of crude oil and gas		(3,494,258)	(2,569,724)
Healthcare and pension plans	21	(1,427,395)	(2,494,510)
Other operating income and expenses, net	18	(4,712,243)	(5,188,393)
		(24,416,160)	**(30,175,121)**
Equity in income of subsidiaries and associated companies			
Equity in earnings (losses) of investments	13	(874,218)	(465,274)
Income from operations before income and social contribution taxes, employee and management profit sharing and minority interest		48,204,799	35,539,287
Social contribution	20,5	(4,169,529)	(2,876,775)
Income tax	20,5	(11,792,449)	(8,395,983)
Income before employees' and directors' profit-sharing and minority interest		32,242,821	24,266,529
Employees' and directors' profit-sharing	22	(1,344,526)	(1,011,914)
Income before minority interest		30,898,295	23,254,615
Minority interest		2,089,497	(1,742,826)
Net income for the year		32,987,792	21,511,789
Net income per share at the end of the year - R$		3,76	4,90

See the accompanying notes to the financial statements.

BALANCE SHEETS
December 31, 2008 and 2007
(In thousands of reais)

		CONSOLIDATED	
ASSETS	NOTE	2008	2007
Current assets			
Cash and cash equivalents	5	15,888,596	13,070,849
Marketable securities	10	288,751	589,788
Trade accounts receivable, net	6	14,903,732	11,328,967
Dividends receivable	7.1	20,101	80,596
Inventories	8	19,977,171	17,599,001
Taxes and contributions	20.1	9,641,247	7,781,536
Prepaid expenses		1,393,879	1,429,829
Other current assets		1,461,801	1,493,200
		63,575,278	**53,373,766**
Non-current assets			
Long-term receivables			
Trade accounts receivable, net	6	1,326,522	2,901,902
Petroleum and alcohol account – STN	9	809,673	797,851
Marketable securities	10	4,066,280	3,922,370
Project financing	11.2		
Deposits in court	12	1,853,092	1,693,495
Prepaid expenses		1,400,072	1,514,301
Advance for pension plan	21		1,296,810
Deferred income and social contribution taxes	20.3	10,238,308	8,333,490
Inventories	8	303,929	236,753
Other long-term receivables		1,256,96	1,325,865
		21,254,843	**22,022,837**
Investments	13	5,106,495	7,822,074
Property, plant and equipment	14	190,754,167	139,940,726
Intangible assets	15	8,003,213	5,532,053
Deferred charges		3,469,846	2,536,344
		228,588,564	**177,854,034**
		292,163,842	**231,227,800**

See the accompanying notes to the financial statements.

**PROPERTY, PLANT AND EQUIPMENT
BY TYPE OF ASSET**

		CONSOLIDATED			
		2008			2007
	ESTIMATED USEFUL LIFE IN YEARS	COST	ACCUMULATED DEPRECIATION	NET	NET
Buildings and improvements	25 to 40	9,382,619	(3,115,564)	6,267,055	3,800,350
Equipment and other assets	3 to 30	119,999,208	(55,854,051)	64,145,157	49,414,524
Land		1,138,720		1,138,720	854,848
Material		6,034,143		6,034,143	4,247,098
Advances to suppliers		5,189,735		5,189,735	2,624,093
Expansion projects		59,238,898		59,238,898	39,964,366
Oil and gas exploration and production development costs (E&P)		83,883,258	(35,142,799)	48,740,459	39,035,447
		284,866,581	**(94,112,414)**	**190,754,167**	**139,940,726**

10.7 Capitalizing or expensing costs

Air France, a subsidiary of the Air France-KLM Group, is one of the world's largest airlines. It operates a mixed fleet of Airbus and Boeing wide-bodied jets on long-haul routes and relies mainly on the Airbus A320 family of aircraft for shorter flights. Assume that Air France made the following expenditures related to these aircraft in the current year:

(a) Routine maintenance and repairs on various aircraft costing €1.1 billion.
(b) The jet engines on several of the airline's A321s received a major overhaul at a cost of €18 million. The intent of the overhaul was to improve fuel efficiency and reduce carbon emissions.
(c) The avionics were replaced on the fleet of Boeing 747s. This is expected to extend the useful life of the planes by 3 years.
(d) Noise abatement kits were installed on some of the older A320s in accordance with EU regulations on maximum allowable noise levels on takeoff. The equipment and installation cost €14 million.
(e) The airline painted several of its aircraft as part of a campaign to promote new routes to Asia. The painting cost €1.2 million.

(f) The existing seats on several A320s were replaced with more comfortable seats costing €3.5 million.
(g) New jet engines were installed on several A318s. The total cost was €42 million.

Required

Which of the above expenditures should be capitalized and which should be expensed? Explain your answers.

10.8   Journal entries for depreciation and amortization expense

Prepare journal entries for each of the following transactions or events for Liu Cybersystems:

(a) Acquired computers costing $800 000 and software costing $80 000 on 1 January 2011. Liu expects the computers to have a service life of 10 years and $80 000 residual value. The software is expected to have a service life of four years and zero residual value.
(b) Paid $40 000 to install the computers at Liu's office. Paid $20 000 to test the software.
(c) Liu records depreciation and amortization expense for the computers and the computer software using the straight-line method for 2011 and 2012.
(d) On 1 January 2013, new software on the market makes the software acquired in 2011 obsolete.
(e) On 2 January 2013, Liu revised the depreciable life of the computers to a total of 14 years and the salvage value to $112 000. Give the entry to record depreciation expense for 2013.
(f) On 31 December 2014, Liu sells the computers for $520 000. Give the required journal entries for 2014.

CHAPTER 11

Leases and Off-Balance-Sheet Debt

Introduction

In this chapter we address the accounting treatment for leases and off-balance-sheet debt. The discussion on leases is limited to the lessee's perspective. Leasing is a critically important topic for the financial statement reader because in many industries it has become the most common form of asset financing. The economic rationale for such a large industry is complex, and beyond the scope of this book, but accounting practice has certainly played an important role in the pervasive use of leasing.

Capital vs. operating leases

A lease is an agreement between two parties for the rent of an asset. The lessor is the legal owner of the asset who rents out the asset to the lessee. At the end of the lease period the asset is usually returned to the lessor. The lessee pays a periodic (monthly, quarterly, yearly) rental fee to the lessor in return for use of the asset. The accounting treatment for the lease depends on the nature of the lease.

US GAAP and IFRS distinguish between two types of leases: capital and operating. In the case of the former, future lease payments are capitalized at an appropriate borrowing rate, with the present value appearing as both an asset and a liability on the balance sheet. Operating

| Depreciation expense | 7,985.40 | |
| Accumulated depreciation | | 7,985.40 |

Record depreciation for 2014.

Lease liability	9,260.00	
Interest expense	740.00	
Cash		10,000

Lease payment for 2014.

In the first year of the lease, 2010, classifying the contract as an operating lease leads to both higher net income and a lower debt/equity ratio. Ignoring tax effects, net income is reduced by $10 000 each year because of the rent expense. On the other hand, if the lease is capitalized, total expenses in 2010 would be $11 179.56 (interest expense of $3194.16 + depreciation expense of $7985.40). But notice that by 2014, the operating lease treatment leads to lower net income. By the final year of the lease's term, most of the principal has been paid, meaning that the interest portion of the annual lease payment is small ($740.00). When added to the annual depreciation expense, the total comes to just $8725.40. Therefore, operating lease treatment results in lower total expenses and higher net income in the early years of the lease, while the reverse is true in the latter years of the lease term. The total (pretax) expense over the five years is the same under either approach, in this case, $50 000. However, the timing of the expense is different, as well as the effect on the Bankers Group balance sheet.

Note also that as long as a portion of the loan principal has not been paid, capital lease treatment will always result in higher reported debt. Debt/equity ratios will also be higher, not just because of the higher debt, but because the lower net income reported in the early years under capital lease treatment leads to lower retained earnings (and, therefore, lower shareholders' equity).

Interpreting lease disclosures

All companies reporting under US GAAP and IFRS are required to provide supplemental disclosures on lease commitments in the notes to their financial statements. These disclosures should include the minimum, noncancelable payments required under both capital and operating leases for each of the ensuing five years, and a total amount for all years thereafter. To illustrate, we use the example of AMR, Inc., the holding company for American Airlines. The note in Box 11.1 comes from AMR's 2009 Annual Report.

This note reveals that the present value of lease payments under capital leases is $689 million at the end of 2009. This means that the AMR balance sheet dated 31 December 2009 included $689 million of liabilities related to those leases. The total minimum payments required by AMR are $1152 million, of which $463 million represents the interest component. One way to interpret these figures is that AMR has future mortgage payments of

Box 11.1 AMR's note on leases from their 2009 Annual Report

AMR's Footnote No. 5 – Leases

AMR's subsidiaries lease various types of equipment and property, primarily aircraft and airport facilities. The future minimum lease payments required under capital leases, together with the present value of such payments, and future minimum lease payments required under operating leases that have initial or remaining noncancelable lease terms in excess of one year as of December 31, 2009, were (in millions):

Year Ending December 31,	Capital Leases	Operating Leases
2010	$181	$1,057
2011	184	1,032
2012	134	848
2013	119	755
2014	98	614
2015 and thereafter	436	5,021
	1,152	$9,327
Less amount representing interest	463	
Present value of net minimum lease payments	$689	

At December 31, 2009, the Company was operating 181 jet aircraft and 39 turboprop aircraft under operating leases and 80 jet aircraft under capital leases. The aircraft leases can generally be renewed at rates based on fair market value at the end of the lease term for one to five years. Some aircraft leases have purchase options at or near the end of the lease term at fair market value.

$1152 million on 80 jet aircraft (see description in the note), of which $689 million is the principal amount of the loan.

The note also reveals the minimum payments required under operating leases. Assuming no additional leases, AMR can be expected to report rent expense of $1057 million in 2010 for the 181 jet aircraft and 39 turboprop aircraft accounted for as operating leases. The total amount of $9327 million is not a present value, but is rather the total nominal payments AMR is expected to make under these leases.

Many analysts would attempt to convert this stream of future cash flows into a present value, and include the resulting amount as part of the company's debt. One approach is to take the payments from 2015 and thereafter, $5021 million, and divide by the minimum payments from the previous year, $614 million. This amount, slightly greater than eight, implies that AMR can expect minimum annual payments of $614 million for about eight years beyond

2015. Based on an implied borrowing rate, the analyst can then convert the assumed cash-flow stream, plus the minimum payments from the first five years, into a present value. This figure would then reflect the value of the debt represented by the operating leases.

Off-balance-sheet debt

The operating lease is a prototypical example of what has come to be known as *off-balance-sheet (OBS)* debt. More generally, OBS debt describes the acquisition of cash, goods, or services without the borrowing arrangements being formally acknowledged as a liability on the balance sheet. Operating leases fall into a broader category of OBS debt known as executory contracts. Here, firms sign contracts promising to pay specified amounts in the future in exchange for future benefits. These benefits can take on many forms, such as the take-or-pay contracts signed by petroleum refiners to ensure access to adequate supplies of petroleum. What all such contracts have in common is that they give the company access to a vitally needed resource without having to formally acquire it or to acknowledge the corresponding obligation in the accounts. The financial statements are usually unaffected by such arrangements until cash payments are made, although some form of disclosure should appear in the notes if the amounts are material. The payments will either be accumulated in inventory accounts, as in the case of petroleum refiners, or sent directly to cost of goods sold.

Another type of OBS finance, introduced in Chapter 5, is the securitization of receivables.[2] Here, a firm transfers its receivables to a separate legal entity, which then packages the receivables as securities and sells them to investors. The cash paid by investors is then passed back to the company. In effect, it constitutes a form of borrowing in which the receivables act as collateral. However, if the transfer occurs in a certain way, the company may be able to "derecognize" the receivables and remove them, and any corresponding debt, from the balance sheet.

Why companies engage in OBS debt is a complicated subject, and beyond the scope of this book. But we will say that there are positive aspects to the practice (that is, actions that are potentially value enhancing for the firm) and negative aspects (actions that are value destroying). For example, OBS financing arrangements may allow a company to avoid violating debt covenants that restrict the amount of debt that appear in the financial statements. In such case, OBS financing allows the company to avoid costly loan renegotiations with its bankers. The problem, however, is that for such practices to work bankers and other lenders have to be strikingly naïve. From our experience, the lenders who survive over the long term are anything but naïve and will build protections against OBS debt into their lending contracts.

It is also worth noting that the trend under US GAAP and IFRS is to force companies to bring many financing arrangements that traditionally have been OBS into the balance sheet. So while the controversy continues, an ever smaller range of transactions qualifies for OBS treatment. Operating leases may soon be next. Like several controversial areas of financial reporting, lease accounting will undergo major changes in the near- to medium-term future as a consequence of the US GAAP–IFRS convergence project. As of this writing, a Discussion

Memorandum issued jointly by the FASB and the IASB proposes the elimination of operating leases. In short, all leases will have to be capitalized. In the US alone, this change could mean that upwards of $1 trillion dollars' worth of operating leases will appear on corporate balance sheets for the first time. It remains to be seen just what economic effects this proposal will have if and when it is implemented.

Key lessons from the chapter

- A lease is an agreement between two parties for the rental of an asset.
- Accounting rules distinguish between two types of leases: capital and operating.
- Operating leases are treated as rental contracts, with periodic lease payments recorded as an operating expense. Operating leases are the most common form of off-balance-sheet financing.
- Capital leases are viewed as a purchase agreement. This implies that the company has, in substance, acquired an asset and that the lease is simply a note payable for the acquisition of the asset.
- Under US GAAP four "bright line" rules are used for determining whether a lease is classified as a capital lease. If a company meets at least one of the rules, the lease is classified as a capital lease. Otherwise, it is classified as an operating lease.
- IFRS tends to be more principles-oriented in drawing the capital/operating lease distinction. The idea is that the accountants preparing the financial statements, and their auditors, should rely more on professional judgment than on detailed rules.
- All companies reporting under US GAAP and IFRS are required to provide supplemental disclosures on lease commitments in the notes to their financial statement.
- Many analysts attempt to convert the minimum lease payments required under operating leases into a present value, and include the resulting total as part of the company's assets and debt for the purpose of calculating financial statement ratios.
- The FASB and the IASB have produced a joint proposal that would effectively end operating leases. If this standard takes effect, huge amounts of debt will have to be brought into corporate balance sheets.

Key terms and concepts from the chapter

Capital or finance lease	Off-balance-sheet	The criteria for capital-
Operating lease	financing	izing leases

Questions

1. This issue wasn't discussed in the chapter, but why do you think so many assets are leased instead of bought? What are the advantages of leasing relative to buying?

2. Why are managers so often averse to capitalizing leases?

3. True or false: Leasing reduces a firm's lending capacity.

4. True or false: All else being equal, a profitable company is more likely to rely on leasing to finance its assets than an unprofitable company.

5. In what ways is the economic substance of a lessee's capital lease similar to, and different from, that of purchasing the asset using proceeds from a secured (i.e., collateralized) loan?

6. How is cash flow from operations affected by the capitalization of a lease that had previously been recognized as an operating lease?

7. Lease accounting is likely to undergo important changes in the near future. What are these changes likely to be, and do you agree with them?

Problem

11.1   The financial reporting effects of selling receivables

The following note appears in Daimler's 2011 Annual Report:

> Based on market conditions and liquidity needs, Daimler may sell portfolios of retail and wholesale receivables to third parties. At the time of the sale, Daimler determines whether the legally transferred receivables meet the criteria for derecognition in conformity with the appropriate provisions. If the criteria are not met, the receivables continue to be recognized in the Group's statement of financial position.

As of 31 December 2011, the carrying amount of receivables from financial services sold but not derecognized for accounting purposes amounted to €3496 million (2010: €1254 million). The associated risk and rewards are similar to those with respect to receivables from financial services that have not been transferred.

Required

(a) Why does Daimler sell receivables from its financial services arm?
(b) What does Daimler mean by "derecognition" from the sale of receivables? What entry does the company make to record the sale of receivables when the sales are derecognized?
(c) What is meant by receivables "sold but not derecognized"? What entry is made in this case?

Case studies

11.1 Lease accounting at Metro AG

Metro AG is one of the world's largest discount retailers. Headquartered in Germany, its activities are segmented as follows:

- Cash and carry (47%): Food and nonfood products at wholesale prices, primarily to business customers, under the Metro and Makro store brands.
- Hypermarkets and supermarkets (21%): Food products under the Extra store brand and, in hypermarkets, food and nonfood products under the Real store brand.
- Specialty stores (25%): Two chains in this group, Media Markt and Saturn, offer electronic products, and the other, Praktiker, specializes in the home improvement market.
- Department stores (7%): A variety of household and clothing products in more upscale shopping environments under the Kauflof store brand.

Metro generates about 53% of its sales within Germany, 45% from the rest of Europe, and 2% from elsewhere. Revenues were €53.5 billion in 2004.

Most of its nearly 4000 stores worldwide are leased. Some of these leases are capitalized (i.e., the present value of future lease payments appear on the balance sheet), but most are not.

Metro's 2004 annual report reveals the following information:

- Capital leases at the end of 2004 had a present value of €2090 million. Minimum payments required in 2005 are €280 million. The weighted-average interest rate for these leases was 6.1%.

- As of the end of 2004, minimum payments required under operating leases were €1182 million for 2005, €4234 million in total payments over the next four years (2006–2009), and €5548 million in total payments for 2010 and beyond.
- Shareholders' equity at the end of 2004 was €4739 million, debt was €9506 million, and invested capital was €14 245 million.

Metro reported the following results in 2005:

- Revenues were €55.7 billion.
- Net operating profit after tax (NOPAT) was €1368 million, based on a tax rate of 30%.
- Net income was €649 million.
- Cash flow from operations was €2.2 billion in 2005, down from €2.9 billion in 2004 and €3.1 billion in 2003.

Required

Note: Round all euro amounts to the nearest million.

(a) What reasons can you give for why Metro relies so extensively on leasing?
(b) Prepare the journal entry to record cash payments under capital leases for 2005.
(c) Prepare the journal entry to record cash payments under operating leases for 2005.
(d) Using the year-end 2004 figure for invested capital, estimate ROIC for 2005.
(e) Calculate the present value of Metro's operating leases as of the end of 2004. For your calculations, assume that (1) the lease payments are made at the end of each year, (2) the implicit weighted-average interest rate for the leases is 6%, (3) payments for 2006 through 2009 are made evenly throughout the period (i.e., lease payments are the same in each year), and (4) payments in 2010 and beyond are made evenly over the next 10 years.
(f) Give the journal entries to convert the operating leases into capital leases as of the end of 2004, and account for them as capital leases in 2005. Assume an amortization period of 15 years.
(g) Reestimate NOPAT for 2005 after accounting for the operating leases as capital leases.
(h) Reestimate ROIC, after accounting for the operating leases as capital leases.
(i) What effect will capitalization of the operating leases have on cash flow from operations?

11.2 Pennzoil-Quaker State and the sale of receivables

Pennzoil-Quaker State (PQS) is one of the world's leading producers of motor oil. The company sells some of its receivables through a special purpose entity. The receivables sold under this facility totaled $153 million at the end of Year 9 and $115 million at the end of Year 8. None of these receivables, or the related financing, appears on PQS's balance sheet.

Additional information (all amounts in millions of $)

Sales (Year 9)	$2,951
Receivables (end of Year 9)	312
Receivables (end of Year 8)	546
Total debt (end of Year 9)	1,096
Shareholders' equity (end of Year 9)	950
Cash flow from operations (Year 9)	58

Required

(a) Calculate PQS's days of receivables based on (1) end-of-year receivables, and (2) average receivables for the year.
(b) Calculate PQS's debt–equity ratio.
(c) Recalculate your answers to (a) after restoring the receivables that were removed from the balance sheet. Do the same for (b). Restate cash flow from operations, if necessary. What insights can you draw from these adjustments?

11.3 Executory contracts

Alcoa is one of the world's leading producers of aluminum and related products. According to the company's Year 6 Annual Report, Alcoa's Australian subsidiary is party to a number of natural gas and electricity contracts that expire at various times over the next 20 years.

Under these take-or-pay contracts, Alcoa of Australia is obligated to pay for a minimum amount of natural gas or electricity even if these commodities are not required for operations. Commitments related to these contracts total (in millions):

Year 7	$176
Year 8	180
Year 9	185
Year 10	178
Year 11	154
Thereafter	2,243

Required

(a) Using a discount rate of 6%, calculate the present value of Alcoa's take-or-pay contracts. Assume payments are made at the beginning of each year. Make whatever assumptions you think are appropriate regarding the $2243 million of commitments after Year 11. Assume that your analysis takes place early in Year 7.

(b) Alcoa reports the following data in its Year 6 Annual Report:

Total debt	$6,633 million
Shareholders' equity	$10,614 million

Calculate Alcoa's debt-to-equity ratio. Recalculate the ratio after adjusting for the take-or-pay contracts. Comment on the results.

(c) Should Alcoa's take-or-pay contracts appear on its balance sheet? Why or why not?

Notes

1. Although for reasons discussed later in the chapter, anticipated changes in accounting principles will likely spell the end of the operating lease as OBS vehicles in the not too distant future.

2. The theme of the discussion in Chapter 5 is when securitization is used to remove receivables from the balance sheet, it can be used to artificially boost cash flow from operations.

CHAPTER **12**

Accounting for Bonds

Introduction

To finance the purchase of assets, corporations can raise investment capital in one of two ways: debt or equity. If a company's management decides to raise debt capital they can borrow from either a financial institution, such as HSBC or Citigroup, or by issuing bonds through the capital markets.

Bonds (sometimes called "notes") are normally sold to the public through a third party ("underwriter"), e.g., an investment bank. Bonds are interest-bearing notes that involve contractual commitments requiring the issuing company to make cash interest payments to the bondholder and a principal payment when the bond matures. The maturity date is usually between 1 and 30 years from the date of the issuance. After issuance, bonds are freely negotiable; that is, they can be purchased and sold in the open market.

In this chapter, we focus on corporate bonds, drawing on the example of SAP AG (the parent company of the SAP Group) and a fictional competitor, BriteSoft Ltd. (The topic of convertible bonds – bonds that are convertible into shares of common stock – will be covered in the chapter on shareholders' equity.)

In 2010, SAP issued bonds in the capital markets. To accomplish this sale it hired a consortium of investment banks, and produced a prospectus which describes the terms of the notes. The prospectus reveals the underwriters involved, and the fees charged to SAP (see Box 12.1).

In addition, a pricing notice (Table 12.1) was published, dated 31 March 2010.

The notice reveals that SAP issued bonds with a face value (or "par value") of €500 million. The offering comprised 500 000 separate notes, each with a face value of €1000. The bonds were sold at a discount to par, 99.755% of par value to be exact, meaning that the initial selling

---

Box 12.1   SAP disclosure on the issuance of notes

General

SAP AG has agreed to sell Notes to BNP Paribas, Deutsche Bank AG, ING Bank NV and J.P. Morgan Securities Ltd. (together, the "Joint Lead Managers"), and the Joint Lead Managers have agreed, subject to certain customary closing conditions, to purchase the Notes. Proceeds to the Issuer will be net of commissions of up to 0.35 per cent of the principal amount of the Notes payable to the Joint Lead Managers. The Issuer has furthermore agreed to reimburse the Joint Lead Managers for certain expenses incurred in connection with the issue of the Notes.

Table 12.1   SAP AG (A stock corporation incorporated under the laws of the Federal Republic of Germany, having its corporate seat in Walldorf, Federal Republic of Germany): EUR 500 000 000 2.50% notes due 2014

Characteristics of the 2014 notes	
Aggregate principal amount:	EUR 500 000 000
Number of notes:	500 000 notes with a nominal value of EUR 1000 each
Issue price:	99.755% of the aggregate principal amount
Interest rate:	2.50% per annum
Interest amount on first interest payment date:	EUR 12 568 493.15
Net proceeds before deduction of total expenses:	EUR 497 212 500
Underwriting commission:	0.3125% of the aggregate principal amount
Yield:	2.565% per annum

price was €997.55 per note. In other words, while the bonds had a par value of €500 million, the amount of cash raised by SAP was slightly less (€498.775 million).

Accounting for bond issuance

The price at which a firm issues bonds depends on two factors: the future cash payments that the bond contract requires the firm to make; and the rate of return demanded by investors. The required return is driven by the perceived the risk of the borrower, the general level of interest rates, and potential other factors. The issuing price equals the required cash flows, discounted at the appropriate market interest rate.[1]

When bonds are sold in the market they can sell at face (par) value, at a premium to par, or at a discount to par. To understand when each scenario will play out we need to compare the stated coupon interest rate that the bond promises to pay with the interest rate required by the market:

Coupon Rate	=	Market-required rate	Bonds will sell at face (par) value
Coupon Rate	>	Market-required rate	Bonds will sell at premium to face value
Coupon Rate	<	Market-required rate	Bonds will sell at discount to face value

The following equation can be used to determine the value of a bond that makes coupon payments annually, where C represents the coupon payment, F the face value or principal, and r the market-required interest rate:

$$B_0 = C\left[\frac{1 - (1+r)^{-t}}{r}\right] + \frac{F}{(1+r)^t}$$

Most bonds make interest payments semiannually. The equation to determine the value of such bonds is shown below. Note that the coupon payment and market-required interest rate are divided by two and the number of payments is multiplied by two.

$$B_0 = \frac{C}{2}\left[\frac{1 - (1+r/2)^{-2t}}{r/2}\right] + \frac{F}{(1+r/2)^{2t}}$$

Accounting for bonds sold at par

Let's assume that a five-year bond is issued by BriteSoft Ltd., with a coupon of 9% paying interest semiannually and a market interest rate of 9%. Because the coupon rate and market interest rate are the same, the bond is issued at face value.

The accounting entry to record the issue of a €100 000 bond would be:

| Cash | 100,000 | |
| Bonds payable | | 100,000 |

The company will later record the semiannual coupon payments as follows:

| Interest expense | 4,500 | |
| Cash or accrued interest | | 4,500 |

When bonds are redeemed at the maturity date, BriteSoft would simply pay cash to the bondholders in the amount of the face value and remove the bonds payable from the balance sheet. The journal entry will be:

| Bonds payable | 100,000 | |
| Cash | | 100,000 |

Table 12.2 summarizes the transactions that would occur over the life of the bond.

Table 12.2 The transactions and accounting for a bond sold at par.

Issue date:	1 January 2011		
Maturity face:	€100,000		
Coupon rate:	9%	Market interest rate: 9%	
Coupon payment:	Semiannually		

Semiannual interest date	Coupon payment	Interest expense	Bond carrying amount
1 January 2011			€100,000
1 July	€4,500	€4,500	100,000
1 January 2012	4,500	4,500	100,000
1 July	4,500	4,500	100,000
1 January 2013	4,500	4,500	100,000
1 July	4,500	4,500	100,000
1 January 2014	4,500	4,500	100,000
1 July	4,500	4,500	100,000
1 January 2015	4,500	4,500	100,000
1 July	4,500	4,500	100,000
1 January 2016	4,500	4,500	100,000

Accounting for bonds sold at a premium

If the coupon rate exceeds the market interest rate, the bonds will sell at a premium to face value. This result occurs because, if the bonds were sold at par, the rate of return would exceed that demanded by investors. The bonds can sell at a premium and still offer a competitive return to investors.

To illustrate, if BriteSoft issues a bond with a 9% coupon when the market interest rate is only 8%, the issuance price is €104 100. This figure is determined by discounting the expected future cash flows (€4500 every six months and €100 000 when the bond matures). The entry would be:

Cash	104,100	
Bonds payable		100,000
Bond premium		4,100

The carrying value on the balance sheet equals the credit to bonds payable, plus the bond premium, or in this case, €104 100.

As for the income statement, the premium needs to be offset against future interest expense, a process called bond premium amortization. Two methods of amortization are possible: *effective interest* and *straight line*.

Effective interest method

Under the effective interest method, the periodic interest expense is determined by multiplying the amount to be amortized (book value at the beginning of each period), by the "effective" (market) interest rate at the time the bonds were issued (8% in our example). As the issuing entity pays the coupon (€4500), which is higher than the effective interest expense (4% × €104 100, or €4164, for the first six months in year 1), the "excess" interest paid partly amortizes the premium. Put another way, the premium amortization for each (interest) period is the difference between the interest calculated at the stated coupon rate (9%) and the interest calculated at the effective rate (8%).

The virtue of this approach is that interest expense equals a fixed interest rate (the rate that prevailed in the market when the bonds were issued), multiplied by the balance in the bonds payable account at the beginning of each period. In other words, interest expense will be 8% of the outstanding balance in the bonds payable account in every period throughout the bond's life.

The journal entry on the date of the first payment will be:

Interest expense	4,164	
Amortization of bond premium	336	
Cash or accrued interest		4,500

The balance sheet total for bonds will equal €104 100, the proceeds from the bond issue, minus the amortization of the bond premium of €336, or €103 764.

The journal entry on the date of the second payment will be the following:

Interest expense	4,151	
Amortization of bond premium	349	
Cash or accrued interest		4,500

where interest expense equals the carrying value of the bond at the beginning of the period (€103 764), times the semiannual interest rate of 4%:

$$103\ 764 \times 4\% = 4151$$

The carrying value on the balance sheet will now equal €103 764, minus the amortized portion of the bond premium for the second six months (€349), or €103 415. Over time, the carrying value will converge to the par value of €100 000, reaching this value just as the bond is about to mature.

Straight-line method

Here, interest expense is a constant amount each payment period. The bond premium of €4100 is divided by 10 (the number of six-month periods over the bond's life), or €410. The interest expense in each of those 10 periods is therefore €4500, minus €410, or €4090. The resulting journal entry is:

Interest expense	4,090	
Amortization of bond premium	410	
Cash or accrued interest		4,500

Because the carrying value of the bonds decreases after each interest payment, while the interest expense is the same in each period, interest expense will gradually increase as a percentage of the carrying value.

The effective interest method is preferred because interest expense is a constant percentage of the carrying value, and that percentage is exactly equal to the market interest rate that prevailed when the bonds were issued. For this reason, the method is required under both US GAAP and IFRS. For tax purposes, however, many countries permit the straight-line approach.

In either case, by the time BriteSoft's bonds reach maturity, any premium on the bonds will have been completely amortized.

The journal entry for the payment of the principal (i.e., maturity value) will be:

Bonds payable	100,000	
Cash		100,000

The above example, for both the effective interest and straight-line methods, is summarized in Table 12.3.

Bond redemption before maturity

Corporate bonds often come with a provision that gives the issuing company the option to retire all or part of the bond issue before maturity. In effect, the bond grants a call option to the issuer, granting it the right to buy back the bonds at a stipulated price. The bonds are therefore said to be "callable." Normally, the call provision does not kick in right away. The company will have to wait some period of time, say, two to five years, before it can buy them back.

The call feature tends to be exercised in periods of declining interest rates. As interest rates fall, the value of the bond may rise above the call price, giving the company a strong incentive to repurchase the bonds. Such provisions give rise to reinvestment risk for the bondholders because, if the call is exercised, the cash proceeds will be reinvested in other financial instruments at presumably lower rates of interest. For this reason, investors demand a higher return on bonds having call features.

To illustrate the accounting, imagine bonds with a €100 000 face value and a €3000 unamortized premium are redeemed for €102 000. The following journal entry is recorded:

Bonds payable	100,000	
Premium on bonds payable	3,000	
Cash		102,000
Gain on redemption		1,000

Table 12.3   Bond issued at a premium: effective interest and straight-line methods (in box) amortization

Issue date:	1 January 2011	
Maturity face:	€100,000	
Coupon rate:	9%	Market interest rate: **8%**
Coupon payment:	Semiannually	

Semiannual interest date	Coupon payment	Interest expense	Premium amortization	Premium balance	Bond carrying amount
1 January 2011				−€4,100	€104,100
1 July	€4,500	€4,164	−€336	−3,764	103,764
1 January 2012	4,500	4,151	−349	−3,415	103,415
1 July	4,500	4,137	−363	−3,051	103,051
1 January 2013	4,500	4,122	−378	−2,673	102,673
1 July	4,500	4,107	−393	−2,280	102,280
1 January 2014	4,500	4,091	−409	−1,871	101,871
1 July	4,500	4,075	−425	−1,446	101,446
1 January 2015	4,500	4,058	−442	−1,004	101,004
1 July	4,500	4,040	−460	−544	100,544
1 January 2016	4,500	3,956	−544	0	100,000

Semiannual interest date	Coupon payment	Interest expense	Premium amortization	Premium balance	Bond carrying amount
1 January 2011				−€4,100	€104,100
1 July	€4,500	€4,090	−€410	−3,690	103,690
1 January 2012	4,500	4,090	−410	−3,280	103,280
1 July	4,500	4,090	−410	−2,870	102,870
1 January 2013	4,500	4,090	−410	−2,460	102,460
1 July	4,500	4,090	−410	−2,050	102,050
1 January 2014	4,500	4,090	−410	−1,640	101,640
1 July	4,500	4,090	−410	−1,230	101,230
1 January 2015	4,500	4,090	−410	−820	100,820
1 July	4,500	4,090	−410	−410	100,410
1 January 2016	4,500	4,090	−410	0	100,000

When a firm retires a bond for cash, it reports the cash paid in the financing section of the cash flow statement. In most cases, the amount of cash needed to retire the liability differs from the book value of the liability at the time of retirement. The retirement therefore generates a gain (when the book value exceeds cash paid), as in the above example, or a loss (when the cash paid exceeds book value). In calculating cash flow from operations under the indirect method, gains are subtracted from net income, while losses are added back.

Accounting for bonds issued at a discount

If the market-required rate exceeds the coupon rate, the bonds will sell for at a discount to par. Investors are unwilling to pay the par value for a bond that offers a coupon rate lower than the prevailing interest rate for bonds in that class.

As you may recall, in the case in the SAP offering, the price of the bond was 99.755% of par. The discount arose because the coupon rate offered on these bonds was 2.5% but the market interest rate at the time of the offering was 2.565%. The expected capital gain for investors (the difference between par and the issuance price) compensates them for the discrepancy between the cash return promised by the bond and the market interest rate.

Returning to our example for BriteSoft Ltd., if the market rate is 10% and the coupon rate remains at 9%, the €100 000 bonds will be issued at a discount, selling at a price of €96, 149. The proceeds are based on 10 payments of €4500 and the maturity value of €100 000, discounted at 10%. The journal entry would be:

Cash	96,149	
Bond discount	3,851	
Bonds payable		100,000

Although the bond's maturity value is €100 000, the carrying value on the balance sheet on the date of issuance is €96 149. Just like the bond premium example, the discount (€3851) will have to be amortized over the life of the bond. The amortization process will gradually cause the bond's balance sheet value to converge to the maturity value, such that the carrying value will be exactly €100 000 just as the bond is ready to mature.

Below, we show the entries for the first six-month period under both the effective interest and straight-line methods. The payments and interest expense under both methods are summarized in Table 12.4.

Effective interest method

Interest expense for the first six months is set equal to the semiannual market interest rate (5%), times the carrying of the debt at the moment of issuance (€96 149), or €4807. The semiannual coupon payment is €4500, as it was in the bond premium example. The resulting journal entry on the day of the first payment (6 months after the bond is issued) will be:

Interest expense	4,807	
Amortization of bond discount		307
Cash or accrued interest		4,500

Straight-line method

Under this method, an equal portion of the bond's discount is amortized for each six-month period over the bond's five-year life. This means that every six months, the bond will be

Table 12.4 Bond issued at a discount: effective interest and straight-line methods (in box) amortization

Issue date: 1 January 2011
Maturity face: €100,000
Coupon rate: 9%   Market interest rate: **10%**
Coupon payment: Semiannually

Semiannual interest date	Coupon payment	Interest expense	Premium amortization	Premium balance	Bond carrying amount
1 January 2011				€3,851	€96,149
1 July	€4,500	€4,807	€307	3,544	96,456
1 January 2012	4,500	4,823	323	3,221	96,779
1 July	4,500	4,839	339	2,882	97,118
1 January 2013	4,500	4,856	356	2,526	97,474
1 July	4,500	4,874	374	2,152	97,848
1 January 2014	4,500	4,892	392	1,760	98,240
1 July	4,500	4,912	412	1,348	98,652
1 January 2015	4,500	4,933	433	915	99,085
1 July	4,500	4,954	454	461	99,539
1 January 2016	4,500	4,961	461	0	100,000

Semiannual interest date	Coupon payment	Interest expense	Premium amortization	Premium balance	Bond carrying amount
1 January 2011				€3,851	€96,149
1 July	€4,500	€4,885	€385	3,466	96,534
1 January 2012	4,500	4,885	385	3,081	96,919
1 July	4,500	4,885	385	2,696	97,304
1 January 2013	4,500	4,885	385	2,311	97,689
1 July	4,500	4,885	385	1,926	98,075
1 January 2014	4,500	4,885	385	1,540	98,460
1 July	4,500	4,885	385	1,155	98,845
1 January 2015	4,500	4,885	385	770	99,230
1 July	4,500	4,885	385	385	99,615
1 January 2016	4,500	4,885	385	0	100,000

amortized by €3851 (the total discount), divided by 10 (the number of six-month periods over the bond's life), or $385:

Interest expense	4,885	
Amortization of bond discount		385
Cash or accrued interest		4,500

Zero-coupon bonds

A special class of long-term debt, known as "zero-coupon bonds," does not offer regular interest payments. Instead, the investor receives all the interest in one lump sum when the bond matures. The bond is therefore sold at a deep discount and redeemed a full face (i.e., par) value when it matures. The difference between face value and the issuance price is the interest that accumulates over the bond's life.

The issuing price is based on the present value of the principal amount to be received by the bondholder at maturity, with the discount rate equal to the market interest rate on date of issuance. It is calculated using the equation for the present value of a single sum:

$$PV = \frac{CF_t}{(1+r)^t}$$

Assuming BriteSoft Ltd. issues a five-year €100 000 par value zero-coupon bond when the market interest rate is 10%, the selling price would be €62 092 [€100 000 ÷ (1 + 10%)^5]. The transaction would be recorded as follows:

Cash	62,092	
Bond discount	37,908	
Bonds payable		100,000

As with coupon-paying bonds, the discount is amortized using either the effective interest method or the straight-line method. Just as in the previous examples, the bond's carrying value, which begins at €62 092, will gradually increase over the bond's life, reaching €100 000 just prior to maturity.

Below, we show the entries for the first six-month period under both methods. The figures are summarized in Table 12.5.

Effective interest method

The journal entry to record interest expense is:

Interest expense	3,105	
Amortization of bond discount		3,105

where interest expense equals the bond's carrying value at the beginning of the period (€62 092), times the semiannual interest rate of 5%. Notice that because there is no coupon payment, the full amount of the interest expense is used to amortize the bond discount.

The balance sheet value at the end of the first six-month period would equal the beginning amount (€62 092), plus the accumulated bond discount (€3105), or €65 197.

Because the bond is issued at a steep discount, and the carrying value rises over the bond's life, the interest expense noticeably increases over time.

Table 12.5 Zero-coupon bonds: effective interest and straight-line methods (in box) amortization

Issue date:	1 January 2011				
Maturity face:	€100,000				
Coupon rate:	0%		Market interest rate:	**10%**	
Coupon payment:	Semiannually				

Semiannual interest date	Coupon payment	Interest expense	Premium amortization	Premium balance	Bond carrying amount
1 January 2011				€37,908	€62,092
1 July	€0	€3,105	€3,105	34,803	65,197
1 January 2012	0	3,260	3,260	31,544	68,456
1 July	0	3,423	3,423	28,121	71,879
1 January 2013	0	3,594	3,594	24,527	75,473
1 July	0	3,774	3,774	20,753	79,247
1 January 2014	0	3,962	3,962	16,791	83,209
1 July	0	4,160	4,160	12,630	87,370
1 January 2015	0	4,368	4,368	8,262	91,738
1 July	0	4,587	4,587	3,675	96,325
1 January 2016	0	3,675	3,675	0	100,000

Semiannual interest date	Coupon payment	Interest expense	Premium amortization	Premium balance	Bond carrying amount
1 January 2011	€0			€37,908.0	€62,092.0
1 July	0	€3,790.8	€3,790.8	34,112.2	65,882.8
1 January 2012	0	3,790.8	3,790.8	30,326.4	69,673.6
1 July	0	3,790.8	3,790.8	26,535.6	73,464.4
1 January 2013	0	3,790.8	3,790.8	22,744.8	77,255.2
1 July	0	3,790.8	3,790.8	18,954.0	81,046.0
1 January 2014	0	3,790.8	3,790.8	15,163.2	84,836.8
1 July	0	3,790.8	3,790.8	11,372.4	88,627.6
1 January 2015	0	3,790.8	3,790.8	7,581.6	92,418.4
1 July	0	3,790.8	3,790.8	3,790.8	96,209.2
1 January 2016	0	3,790.8	3,790.8	0	100,000.0

Straight-line method

Here, the interest expense is a constant amount in each period, resulting in the following entry for each of the 10 periods over the bond's life:

| Interest expense | 3,790.8 | |
| Amortization of bond discount | | 3,790.80 |

where the amount of the bond discount to be amortized, and therefore the interest expense, is equal to the total discount (€37 908), divided by 10, or €3790.8.

Key lessons from the chapter

- Bonds are normally sold to the public through a third party (called an underwriter).
- Bonds are interest-bearing notes that involve contractual commitments requiring the issuing company to make cash interest payments to the bondholder and a principal payment when the bond matures.
- The price at which a firm issues bonds in the capital market depends on two factors: the future cash payments that the bond contract requires the firm to make; and the discount rate that the market deems appropriate given the risk of the borrower, the general level of interest rates in the economy.
- If the coupon rate equals the market rate, the bond will sell at par. If the coupon rate is higher than the market rate, the bond will sell at a premium. If the coupon rate is less than the market rate, the bond will sell at a discount. If the coupon rate is zero (a so-called "zero-coupon" bond), the bond will sell at a deep discount to face value.
- Under US GAAP and IFRS bond premiums and discounts are amortized using the effective interest rate method. In some countries, the straight-line approach is used for tax purposes. The former method is preferred because interest expense will be a constant percentage of the bond's carrying value throughout the life of the bond. The percentage will equal the market interest rate that prevailed when the bonds were issued. (US GAAP does allow the straight-line method, but only if it yields results similar to those under the effective rate method.)
- In most cases, the amount of cash used to retire a bond differs from the book value of the bond at the time of retirement. Thus, the retirement generates a gain (when the book value exceeds the cash payment) or a loss (when the cash payment exceeds book value).

Key terms and concepts from the chapter

Callable bonds	Market rate	Zero-coupon bond
Maturity	Sell at par	Effective interest
Face value	Sell at discount	method
Coupon rate	Sell at premium	Straight-line method

Questions

1. What are the advantages to companies of issuing bonds instead of borrowing from commercial banks?

2. Describe the relationship between interest rates and bond prices.

3. True or false: The yield on a bond is independent of the coupon rate.

4. What happens to the carrying (i.e., balance-sheet) value of a bond after issuance, both for bonds issued at a premium and those issued at a discount?

5. What are the relative advantages and disadvantages of the effective interest method and straight-line amortization for bond discounts and premiums?

6. True or false: The effective interest method gives a constant amount of interest expense on bonds each period.

7. Firm A issues €10 million face value, 8% semiannual coupon bonds at a price to yield 7% compounded semiannually. Firm B issues €10 million face value, 6% semiannual coupon bonds at a price to yield 7%. Will these firms receive the same initial issue price for these bonds? Explain.

Problems

12.1   Journal entries and balance sheet presentation for bonds

On 1 May 2012, Société LePoint issued €2 400 000, 9%, five-year bonds at face value. The bonds pay interest semiannually on 1 May and 1 November. Financial statements are prepared each year on 31 December.

Required

(a) Prepare the journal entry to record the issuance of the bonds.
(b) Prepare the adjusting entry to record the accrual of interest on 31 December 2012.
(c) Show the balance sheet presentation for bonds on 31 December 2012.
(d) Prepare the journal entry to record the payment of interest on 1 May 2013.
(e) Prepare the journal entry to record the payment of interest on 1 November 2013.
(f) Assume that on 1 November 2013, LePoint calls the bonds (i.e., buys them back) at 102. Record the redemption of the bonds.

12.2 Amortization of bond discount and premium

Carmon Trading and Distribution Company issued $30 million, 10% coupon bonds on 1 January 2002, due on 31 December 2006. The market interest rate on the issuance date was 12%, and the bonds pay interest on 30 June and 31 December of each year.

On January 1, 2003, Carmon issues another tranche of $30 million, 10% coupon bonds, due on 31 December 2007. However, the market interest rate had declined to 8% on the date of issuance. The bonds pay interest on 30 June and 31 December of each year.

At the end of 2004, the carrying value for the first tranche of bonds was $28 960 650 and $31 572 150 for the second tranche. At the end of 2005, the carrying value for the first tranche was $29 450 100 and $31 088 850 for the second tranche.

Required

(a) How much interest expense did Carmon record in 2005 for the first tranche?
(b) How much interest expense did Carmon record in 2005 for the second tranche?

12.3 Journal entries for bond issuance and subsequent interest payments

On 1 July 2012, Rosenhurst Corporation issued £6 million face value, 10%, 10-year bonds for £6 815 439. The proceeds resulted in an effective interest rate of 8%. Rosenhurst uses the effective-interest method to amortize a bond discount or premium. The bonds pay interest semiannually on 1 July and 1 January.

Required

(a) Prepare the journal entry to record the issuance of the bonds on 1 July 2012.
(b) Prepare an amortization table through 31 December 2013.
(c) Prepare the journal entry to record the accrual of interest and the amortization of the premium on 31 December 2012.
(d) Prepare the journal entry to record the payment of interest and amortization of the premium on 1 July 2013.
(e) Prepare the journal entry to record the accrual of interest and the amortization of the premium on 31 December 2013.

Note

1. Although the accounting for bonds is broadly the same under US GAAP and IFRS, one difference is worth noting. Under the former, fees paid to underwriters, investment bankers, lawyers, and accountants involved in the bond issue are recorded separately as an asset and amortized over the life of the bond. The carrying value of the bond is therefore unaffected by the fees. Under IFRS, however, the fees are treated as a reduction in the proceeds from issuance. Because the contractual obligations of the bond are the same in either case, but the recorded debt is lower under IFRS, the effective interest rate is higher than it would be under US GAAP.

CHAPTER 13

Provisions and Contingencies

Introduction

The purpose of this chapter is to address the accounting treatment for provisions and contingencies. The chapter draws on the examples of L'Oréal and Merck to illustrate the key concepts. Sources of provisioning include corporate restructuring, warranties, environmental clean-up, litigation, and onerous contracts.[1] Contingencies can arise for several reasons, but litigation-related costs are the most common.

To begin, let's imagine a vacuum-cleaner manufacturer offering a two-year warranty for its products. If something goes wrong within the warranty period, the company either repairs the machine or replaces it. This means that every time a vacuum cleaner is sold, a potential liability is assumed. For accounting purposes, the company could, in theory, report a warranty-related expense only when resources are paid out to service a warranty (as, for example, when a faulty machine is brought in by a customer for repair). But this approach would violate both the matching principle and conservatism. The matching principle says that any costs incurred to generate revenue must be "matched" against the revenue in the period in which the revenue is recognized, even if cash payments will not be made until a future period, and the amount is not known with certainty. Conservatism says that companies should not understate liabilities or expenses. If we have reason to believe that the company has incurred obligations as a result of past transactions (e.g., the sale of vacuum cleaners), the related liability and the warranty expense that go with it should be recognized immediately.

Simply put, both matching and conservatism require the recognition of the liability and expense in the period of sale, even if cash payments will not happen until later. Of course, this requirement gives rise to a problem: how do we know what the warranty cost is likely to be? In fact, we cannot know (at least not with precision), but estimates must be made anyway.

Because all provisions are estimates, and estimates are a function of a set of assumptions made by management, companies have some latitude in the figures they report in the financial statements. In short, they can underprovision or overprovision. The effect of the former is to understate expenses or losses in the current period, thereby boosting profits. Of course, under-provisioning must eventually be corrected, as actual expenditures related to the provision will, at some point, exceed the recognized provision. This means that future accounting periods will be burdened with higher expenses or losses, and thus lower profits. Overprovisioning has the opposite effect, overstating expenses in the current period (and understating profits), while understating expenses in future periods. Overprovisioning is especially important for the financial statement reader to understand because of the tendency of some companies to use it as a means of creating "hidden" or "cookie-jar" reserves. The risk of overprovisioning is highest when companies enjoy highly profitable years or, conversely, when they take huge write-offs to acknowledge underperforming assets bought in previous years. The temptation in such cases is to deliberately overstate the amount of the write-off, allowing reversals (and higher profits) in future years. This practice is widely known as "big bath accounting."

Defining provisions

IFRS has one specific standard that deals generally with how companies should account for provisions, while US GAAP has several standards addressing specific types of provisions – for example, environmental liabilities or restructuring costs.[2]

According to IFRS, a company should recognize a provision only when:

- the entity has a present obligation to transfer economic benefits as a result of past events; and
- it is probable that such a transfer will be required to settle the obligation; and
- a reliable estimate of the amount of the obligation can be made.

A present obligation arises from an obligating event and may take the form of either a legal obligation or a constructive obligation. A legal obligation may arise, for example, from minimum payments a company must make to laid-off employees. A constructive obligation may arise from the same event if the company has a practice of paying workers above the legal minimum. Even if the company is not legally obligated to make supplemental payments, but corporate history and policy suggest that they will, a constructive obligation exists. The key point is that without some obligation on the company's part, whether legal or constructive, a provision cannot be recognized. Also, if the company can avoid the expenditure by its future actions, it has no present obligation, and a provision is not recognized.

To illustrate, consider the case of restructuring events. According to IFRS, a present obligation exists only when the entity is "demonstrably committed" to the restructuring. This criterion is met when there is a binding agreement to sell or dispose of assets (legal obligation), or when the company has a detailed plan for the restructuring and is unable to withdraw because implementation has already started or the main features have been announced to those affected by the plan (constructive obligation).

The term "past events" implies that provisions cannot be taken for events that might happen in the future. In other words, a company is not permitted to recognize a provision as a sort of contingency in case some loss is incurred.

Under IFRS, "probable" means "more likely than not" (i.e., any probability greater than 50%). The meaning of probable under US GAAP normally conveys a higher probability threshold, perhaps as high as 80%.[3]

Finally, a provision should not be recognized unless a reliable estimate can be made of it. In cases where the other criteria are met but this one is not, disclosure is made in the form of a note.

Measuring the provision

According to IFRS, the amount recognized as a provision must be the best estimate of the minimum expenditure required to settle the present obligation at the balance sheet date. The entity must discount the anticipated cash flows using a discount rate that reflects current market assessments of the time value of money and those risks specific to the liability. If a range of estimates is predicted and no amount in the range is more likely than any other, the "midpoint" of the range must be used to measure the liability.

US GAAP is similar to IFRS, however, if a range of estimates is present and no amount in the range is more likely than any other amount in the range, the "minimum" (rather than the midpoint) must be used. Also, a provision is discounted only when the timing of the cash flows is fixed.

Disclosure of provisions: interpreting the notes

This section focuses on how to interpret corporate disclosures of provisions. The material in Box 13.1 comes from the 2005 annual report of L'Oréal, the Paris-based cosmetics giant.

The first panel in the note (part (a)) reports total provisions of €446.3 million as of the end of 2005 (2004 = €474.6 million), of which €289.3 million are current (i.e., payment of the liability is expected within 12 months) and €157.0 million are noncurrent. Nearly all of these provisions relate to tax risks (including, for example, disputes with fiscal authorities over the amount of tax owed), litigation, and a variety of commercial risks such as potential losses from breaches of contract and product returns. Restructuring costs contribute modestly to the totals (€32.2 million current and €2.8 million noncurrent).

The second panel (part (b)) reports on variations in provisions from the end of the previous year. In effect, it tells us the debits and credits made by L'Oréal in 2005 to the provisions account, and why those entries were made. For example, "charges" indicates the additional provisions taken by the company during the year. Although numerous entries were probably made as a result of the charges, they can be summarized as follows:

Expenses and losses   115.1
   Provisions   115.1

For tax risks, litigation, breaches of contract, product returns, and restructuring.

Box 13.1   Example of corporate disclosures of powers
Note 19 – Provision for Liabilities and Charges

a   Balances at closing date

€ millions	12.31.2005	12.31.2004
Other noncurrent provisions for liabilities and charges	**157.0**	**188.0**
Provisions for restructuring	2.8	3.7
Other non-current provision[1]	154.2	184.3
Current provisions for liabilities and charges[2]	**289.3**	**286.6**
Provisions for restructuring	32.2	44.0
Other current provision[1]	257.1	242.6
Total	**446.3**	**474.6**

[1] This item includes provisions facing tax risks and litigation, industrial and commercial risks relating to operations (breach of contract, product returns), and personnel costs.
[2] Recorded on balance sheet as *Other Current Liabilities*.

b   Variations in provisions for restructuring and other provisions for liabilities and charges during the year

€ millions	12.31.2004	Charges	Reversals (used)	Reversals (not used)	Other[1]	12.31.2005
Other provisions for liabilities and charges	426.9	109.8	−95.1	−60.2	29.9	411.3
Provisions for restructuring	47.7	5.3	−15.2	−3.5	0.7	35.0
Total	**474.6**	**115.1**	**−110.3**	**− 63.7**	**30.6**	**446.3**

[1] Mainly resulting from translating differences.

Charges and reversals may be analyzed as follows:

€ millions	Charges	Reversals (used)	Reversals (not used)
Other income and expenses	5.3	−15.2	−3.5
Operating profit	106.0	−87.2	−41.4
Income tax	3.0	−7.9	−18.8

"Reversals" indicate the reductions taken to the provisions account during the year. These reductions, recorded as debits to provisions, occur for either of two reasons:

1. The company pays off at least a portion of the liabilities incorporated in the account (e.g., redundancy payments are actually made to laid-off employees), or
2. The company is correcting an overestimation of provisions from previous years.

In L'Oréal's case, €110.3 of reversals were "used," which implies that they fall into the former category. Assuming that all of the payments were made in cash, the summary entry looks like this:

Provisions	110.3	
Cash		110.3

The reversals "not used" have a very different interpretation. In effect, L'Oréal is telling us that €63.7 million of provisions recognized in previous years will not have to be paid and, therefore, should be reversed. Put another way, provisions taken before 2005 were overstated by €63.7 million. Based on the final section of panel (b), the summary entry to record the unused provisions would be:

Provisions	63.7	
Other income and expenses		3.5
Operating profit		41.4
Income tax expense		18.8

Readers of financial statements should be especially wary of such reversals because their effect is to boost earnings. Note that all three credits are to income statement accounts, which means that the reversal allowed L'Oréal to increase reported pretax income by €63.7 million. And none of that increase in profit had anything to do with L'Oréal's activities in 2005. It simply reflected accounting adjustments. In effect, pre-2005 overprovisioning created a "hidden reserve" of profits that L'Oréal could draw on in 2005 to report higher profits. Judging whether the overprovisioning was deliberate or a good-faith reflection of conservative accounting policy is beyond the scope of this book.

Contingent liabilities

IFRS defines a contingent liability as a possible obligation whose outcome will be confirmed only on the occurrence or nonoccurrence of uncertain future events outside the entity's control. It can also be a present obligation that is not recognized because it is not probable that an outflow of economic benefits (e.g., cash) is required, or the amount of the outflow cannot be reliably measured. Contingent liabilities are disclosed in the notes unless the probability of outflows is remote (in which case no disclosure is required). The most common type of contingent liability arises from litigation, where payment by the entity will depend on a future verdict or settlement.

When a contingency is both probable and the amount can be reasonably estimated, the contingency is accounted for in the same manner as a provision. Accounting for contingencies under US GAAP and IFRS is roughly the same, with the exception (noted earlier) that the bar for determining whether or not a liability is probable is set higher under US GAAP. To illustrate how contingencies work, and to contrast contingencies with provisions, we draw on the example of Merck, the US-based pharmaceutical company. The following example focuses on Merck's problems with Vioxx, an anti-inflammatory pain medication that had to be withdrawn after the drug was linked in scientific studies to heart disease.

Three basic issues arise. How does Merck account for (1) the drug's withdrawal, (2) current and future litigation costs (mainly the fees paid to legal counsel), and (3) any losses Merck suffers because of adverse court decisions or out-of-court settlements?

The note in Box 13.2 addresses the first issue.[4]

Ignoring tax effects, the summary entries to record these estimates include:

Sales	491.6	
Payables		491.6

To record the return of Vioxx after the recall.

If the customer had not yet paid for the product, the balancing credit is to accounts receivable. If the customer had already paid, the balancing credit is to a payable (i.e., a current liability).

Materials and production expense	93.2	
Inventories		93.2

To record the write-off of Vioxx inventory.

Marketing and admin expense	141.4	
Provision		141.4

To record the provision for the costs of the withdrawal.

Box 13.2 Merck's note on the accounting for the withdrawal of Vioxx

On September 30, 2004, the Company announced a voluntary worldwide withdrawal of *Vioxx*, its arthritis and acute pain medication. . . . In connection with the withdrawal, in 2004 the Company recorded an unfavorable adjustment to net income of $552.6 million. . . . The adjustment to pre-tax income was $726.2 million. Of this amount, $491.6 million related to estimated customer returns of product previously sold and was recorded as a reduction of Sales, $93.2 million related to write-offs of inventory held by the Company and was recorded in Materials and production expense, and $141.4 million related to estimated costs to undertake the withdrawal of the product and was recorded in Marketing and administrative expense. The tax benefit of this adjustment was $173.6 million. . . . The adjustment did not include charges for future legal defense costs.

Box 13.3   Merck's note on legal costs

Legal defense costs . . . are accrued when probable and reasonably estimable. As of December 31, 2004, the Company had established a reserve of $675 million solely for its future legal defense costs related to the *Vioxx* Litigation. During 2005, the Company spent $285 million in the aggregate in legal defense costs worldwide related to *Vioxx*. . . . In the fourth quarter, the Company recorded a charge of $295 million to increase the reserve . . . to $685 million at December 21, 2005. This reserve is based on certain assumptions and is the best estimate of the amount that the Company believes, at this time, it can reasonably estimate will be spent through 2007. . . . Events such as scheduled trials, that are expected to occur throughout 2006 and 2007, and the inherent inability to predict the ultimate outcomes of such trials, limit the Company's ability to reasonably estimate its legal costs beyond the end of 2007.

This provision covers all of the costs of the product recall, apart from the write-off of inventories.

As for legal costs, those expected to be incurred before the end of 2007 were accrued, but later costs were not, as the note shown in Box 13.3 explains.

In 2004, the following entry was made:

Litigation expense	675.0	
Provisions		675.0

To record the establishment of the provision for litigation costs.

During 2005, the company disbursed $285 million to cover litigation needs:

Provisions	285.0	
Cash		285.0

To record litigation-related expenditures.

At the end of 2005, Merck management estimated that additional litigation costs, through the end of 2007, are expected to be $685 million. To bring the liability account up to the required amount, the following entry was needed:

Litigation expense	295.0	
Provisions		295.0

To record the increase in provisions.

Note that because no reliable estimate can be made for litigation costs beyond 2007, no liability is recognized.

Finally, the excerpt shown in Box 13.4 explains why the actual losses from adverse court decisions have not yet been accrued.

Box 13.4   Merck's explanation of their treatment of losses from adverse court decisions

. . . on August 19, 2005, in a trial in state court in Texas, the jury in Ernst vs. Merck reached a verdict in favor of the plaintiff and purported to award her a total of $253 million in compensatory and punitive damages. Under Texas law, the maximum amount that could be awarded to the plaintiff is capped at approximately $26 million. The Company intends to appeal this verdict after the completion of post-trial proceedings in the trial court. The Company believes that it has strong points to raise on appeal and is hopeful that the appeals process will correct the verdict. Since the Company believes that the potential for an unfavorable outcome is not probable, it has not established a reserve with respect to the verdict.

Although an analyst would rightly assume that Merck is likely to incur significant liabilities related to the thousands of cases pursued against it (losses may eventually run in the many billions of dollars), no reliable estimate of the amount could be made by the time the 2005 annual report was published. In addition, Merck could claim that losses from specific lawsuits, like the one cited above, might not result in any losses at all. As a result, no potential losses from court judgments of settlements had been acknowledged as of the end of 2005. As Merck's losses come into sharper focus, provisioning for those losses can be expected.

Contingent assets

A contingent asset is a possible asset arising from past events whose existence will only be confirmed by future events not wholly within the entity's control. Possible cash receipts from the favorable settlement of a lawsuit is one common example. Contingent assets may require disclosure but should not be recognized in the accounts. In practice, the recognition of contingent assets is rare. However, such contingencies should be disclosed in the notes if an inflow of economic benefits is probable. When the realization of benefits is virtually certain, the related asset is no longer a contingency. At this point the asset should be recognized on the balance sheet. The asymmetric treatment of contingent liabilities (which often are recognized) and contingent assets (which almost never are) is a consequence of conservatism.

The future

It should be noted that this chapter discusses the accounting for provisions and contingencies as of 2012. For reasons that won't be discussed here, efforts to achieve convergence between IFRS and US GAAP will likely lead to ever greater uses of fair value accounting for liabilities and assets. One important implication of this trend is that contingent liabilities and contingent assets might have to be recognized at fair value as of the balance sheet date. If so, the accounting practices discussed here will undergo profound changes.

Key lessons from the chapter

- Contingencies can arise for several reasons, but litigation-related costs are the most common source. Contingent liabilities are accrued (i.e., lead to an accounting entry affecting the income statement and balance sheet) only if the likelihood of the liability is greater than 50% and it can be reasonably estimated. Otherwise, the contingency is disclosed in the notes (assuming it is material).
- Contingent assets are almost never recognized, unless the receipt of economic benefits is virtually certain. The asymmetric treatment between contingent liabilities and contingent assets is driven by the conservatism doctrine.
- Because all provisions are estimates, and estimates are a function of a set of assumptions made by management, companies have some latitude in the figures they report in the financial statements.
- Analysts should recognize that companies often create "cookie jar" (or "hidden") reserves in good years and reverse them in bad years. The effect is to smooth the time series of earnings.
- The creation of hidden reserves ranks among the most common forms of financial statement manipulation.
- A company should recognize a provision only when the entity has a present obligation to transfer economic benefits as a result of a past event, it is probable that such a transfer will be required, and a reliable estimate of the amount can be made.
- The amount recognized as a provision must be the best estimate of the minimum expenditure required to settle the present obligation as of the balance sheet date.

Key terms and concepts from the chapter

Legal obligation	Contingent liabilities
Constructive obligation	Contingent assets

Questions

1. Why are contingent liabilities often recognized on the balance sheet, but contingent assets are not?

2. What requirements must be met before a provision can be recognized?

3. How are provisions used to "smooth" earnings?

4. Companies should neither over- nor underprovision for losses and routine expenses such as bad debts. And yet both forms of misstatement are common. Why?

5. True or false: The widespread adoption of IFRS has led to an increase in reported provisions.

6. What criteria determine whether a contingent liability should be accrued?

7. What is meant by the term "provisions reversal," and what effect does it have on the balance sheet and income statement?

8. True or false: When companies recognize a provision, for whatever purpose, it is highly unlikely that they will be able to deduct the loss or expense on their tax returns.

Problems

13.1 Accounting for warranties

The following note comes from a recent annual report for Sony Corporation:

> Sony provides for the estimated cost of product warranties at the time revenue is recognized by either product category group or individual product. The product warranty is calculated based upon product sales, estimated probability of failure and estimated cost per claim. The variables used in the calculation of the provision are reviewed on a periodic basis.
> Certain subsidiaries in the Electronics business offer extended warranty programs. The consideration received through extended warranty service is deferred and amortized on a straight-line basis over the term of the extended warranty.

Required

Based on this note, answer the following:

(a) How does Sony account for the product warranties? What would be the impact of the estimated cost of product warranties on each of the three principal financial statements?
(b) If Sony underestimates product warranties expense, how would it correct the error?
(c) How does Sony treat the extended warranty program at (a) time of sale, and (b) in subsequent periods? How would the accounting affect each of the three principal financial statements?

13.2 Analyzing and interpreting disclosures on the provision for warranties

Creative Technology, Ltd., a Singapore-based consumer electronics company, disclosed the following information regarding warranty provisions in its 2011 Annual Report.

The warranty period for the bulk of the products typically ranges between 1 to 2 years. The product warranty provision reflects management's best estimate of probable liability under its product warranties. Management determines the warranty provision based on known product failures (if any), historical experience, and other currently available evidence. Movements in provision for warranty are as follows:

	2011	**2010**
($000)		
Beginning of financial year	2,784	2,899
Provision (written back) made	(606)	1,915
Provision utilized	(711)	(2,030)
End of financial year	1,467	2,784

Required

(a) Make the necessary journal entries to record the movements in the provisions for warranties account for 2010 and 2011.
(b) What is meant by "provision made" and "provision written back."
(c) What does "provision utilized" mean?
(d) Describe what happened in 2011 regarding Creative's provisions.

Case studies

13.1 Accounting for contingent assets: the case of Cardinal Health

In a complaint dated 26 July 2007, and after a four-year investigation, the US Securities and Exchange Commission (SEC) accused Cardinal Health, the world's second largest distributor of pharmaceutical products, of violating generally accepted accounting principles (GAAP) by prematurely recognizing gains from a provisional settlement of a lawsuit filed against several vitamin manufacturers. Weeks earlier, the company agreed to pay $600 million to settle a lawsuit filed by shareholders who bought stock between

2000 and 2004, accusing Cardinal of accounting irregularities and inflated earnings.* The recovery from the vitamin companies should have been an unqualified positive for Cardinal Health. What happened?

Background

The story begins in 1999 when Cardinal Health joined a class action to recover over-charges from vitamin manufacturers. The vitamin makers had just pled guilty to charges of price-fixing from 1988 to 1998. In March 2000, the defendants in that action reached a provisional settlement with the plaintiffs under which Cardinal could have received $22 million. But Cardinal opted out of the settlement, choosing instead to file its own claims in the hopes of getting a bigger payout.

The accounting troubles started in October 2000 when senior managers at Cardinal began to consider recording a portion of the expected proceeds from a future settlement as a litigation gain. The purpose was to close a gap in Cardinal's budgeted earnings for the second quarter of FY 2001, which ended 31 December 2000. According to the SEC, in a November 2000 e-mail a senior executive at Cardinal Health explained why Cardinal should use the vitamin gain, rather than other earnings initiatives, to report the desired level of earnings: "We do not need much to get over the hump, although the preference would be the vitamin case so that we do not steal from Q3."

On 31 December 2000, the last day of the second quarter of FY 2001, Cardinal recorded a $10 million contingent vitamin litigation gain as a reduction to cost of sales. In its complaint, the SEC alleged that Cardinal's classification of the gain as a reduction to cost of sales violated GAAP. It is worth noting that had the gain not been recognized, Cardinal would have missed analysts' average consensus EPS estimate for the quarter by $.02.

Later in FY 2001, Cardinal considered recording a similar gain, but its auditor at the time, PricewaterhouseCoopers (hereafter PwC), was opposed to the idea. Accordingly, no litigation gains were recorded in the third or fourth quarters of FY 2001. Moreover, PwC advised Cardinal that the $10 million recognized in the second quarter of FY 2001 as a reduction to cost of sales should be reclassified "below the line" as nonoperating income. Cardinal management ignored the auditor's advice, and the $10 million gain was not reclassified.

The urge to report an additional gain resurfaced during the first quarter of FY 2002, and for the same reason as in the prior year: to cover an expected shortfall in earnings. On 30 September 2001, the last day of the first quarter of FY 2002, Cardinal recorded a $12 million gain, bringing the total gains from litigation to $22 million. As in the previous year, Cardinal classified the gain as a reduction to cost of sales, allowing the company to boost operating earnings. However, PwC disagreed with Cardinal's classification. The

---

*"Cardinal Health Settles Shareholders' Suit," The Associated Press, 1 June 2007.

auditor advised Cardinal that the amount should have been recorded as nonoperating income on the grounds that the estimated vitamin recovery arose from litigation, was nonrecurring, and stemmed from claims against third parties that originated nearly 13 years earlier.

By May 2002, PwC had been replaced as Cardinal's auditor by Arthur Andersen.[†] Andersen was responsible for auditing Cardinal's financial statements for the whole of FY 2002, ended 30 June 2002, and thus, it reviewed Cardinal's classification of the $12 million vitamin gain. The Andersen auditors agreed with PwC that Cardinal had misclassified the gain. After Cardinal's persistent refusal to reclassify the gains, Andersen advised the company that it disagreed but would treat the $12 million as a "passed adjustment" and include the issue in its Summary of Audit Differences.[‡]

In spring 2002 Cardinal Health reached a $35.3 million settlement with several vitamin manufacturers. The $13.3 million not yet recognized was recorded as a gain in the final quarter of FY 2002. But while management thought its accounting policies had been vindicated by the settlement, the issue wouldn't go away.

On 2 April 2003, an article in the "Heard on the Street" column in *The Wall Street Journal* sharply criticized Cardinal Health for its handling of the litigation gains.[§] "It's a CARDINAL rule of accounting:" the article begins, pun intended. "Don't count your chickens before they hatch. Yet new disclosures in Cardinal Health Inc.'s latest annual report suggests that is what the drug wholesaler has done not just once, but twice." Nevertheless, management continued to defend its accounting practices, partly on the grounds that the amounts later received from the vitamin companies exceeded the amount of the contingent gains recognized in FY 2001 and FY 2002. Moreover, after the initial settlement, Cardinal Health received an additional $92.8 million in vitamin-related litigation settlements, bringing the total proceeds to over $128 million.

The outcome

Cardinal management finally succumbed to reality in the following year, and in the Form 10-K (annual report) filed with the SEC for FY 2004, Cardinal restated its financial results to reverse both gains, restating operating income from the two affected quarters. But the damage had already been done. The article in *The Wall Street Journal* triggered the SEC investigation alluded to earlier. A broad range of issues, going far beyond the treatment of the litigation gains, were brought under the agency's scrutiny, culminating

---

[†]Arthur Andersen ceased operating months later in the aftermath of the Enron scandal. The Cardinal Health audit was then taken over by Ernst & Young.

[‡]A Summary of Audit Differences is a nonpublic document that lists the errors and adjustments identified by the auditor. It serves as the basis for the audit opinion. If the net effect of the errors exceeds the materiality threshold established for the client, the auditor will require an adjustment to the financial statements. "Passed adjustment" means that the error in question was waived; that is, no adjustment was demanded by the auditor.

[§]"Cardinal Health's Accounting Raises Some Questions," by Jonathan Weil, *The Wall Street Journal*, 2 April 2003, p. C1.

in the SEC complaint. Two weeks after the complaint was filed, Cardinal Health settled with the SEC, agreeing to pay a $35 million fine.

Required

(a) What justification could be given for deducting the expected litigation gain from cost of goods sold? Why did Cardinal Health choose this alternative instead of reporting it as a nonoperating item?

(b) What did the senior Cardinal executive mean when he said, "We do not need much to get over the hump, although the preference would be the vitamin case so that we do not steal from Q3"? And more specifically, what is meant by the phrase, "not steal from Q3"?

(c) What specifically did Cardinal Health do wrong that got it into trouble with the SEC?

(d) What might Cardinal Health's senior managers say in their own defense? How might they justify the timing of the $10 million and the $12 million gains?

(e) Cardinal Health ended up receiving a lot more than $22 million from the litigation settlement. Were their actions so wrong as to justify the actions of the SEC? On a scale of 1 to 10, with 1 being "relatively harmless" and 10 being "downright fraudulent," where would you classify Cardinal's behavior, and why?

13.2   Firestone Tire and Rubber Company (A)

Throughout most of the twentieth century, Firestone Tire and Rubber Company was one of the world's leading manufacturers of tires for passenger cars and trucks. In 1978 the company was forced to recall some of its radial tires for alleged defects. The following pages provide excerpts from Firestone's 1979 annual report, detailing the provisions and contingencies involved in the tire recall and related issues. The report of the company's auditors is also provided.

Required

(a) Reconstruct summary journal entries for all of the activity in the "accrued liability for tire recall" account since it was established in 1978 (see Note 15). Assume that settlements with customers take the form of both cash refunds and tire replacements. Ignore tax effects.

(b) Explain why the company has provided for potential losses on the tire recall, but not for the lawsuits relating to the defective tires.

(c) What key messages are the auditors trying to convey with the auditors' report?

15. Provision for tire recall and related costs

In October 1978, a provision for tire recall of $234.0 million ($147.4 million after income taxes) was charged against income. The provision represented management's estimate of the cost of fulfilling the company's obligations under the agreement with the National Highway Traffic Safety Administration and the Company's program of cash refunds to those customers who had received an adjustment on tires that would otherwise have been subject to recall and free replacement.

In October 1979, based on experience to date and anticipated future charges, the 1978 provision was reduced. Management also determined that the provision should be broadened to include $30.8 million of other related costs which were not considered for inclusion in the original provision. The net effect of the above was to reduce the provision by $46.9 million, for which no provision for income taxes was required because of the use of 1978 foreign tax credits of $20.8 million.

It should be recognized that the number of tires still to be returned and the other costs yet to be incurred may vary from management's estimates. Any additional adjustments required by such variance will be reflected in income in the future.

The activity in the accrued liability for tire recall and related costs for 1979 and 1978 follows:

	1979	1978
Accrued liability at beginning of year	$227.2	$ —
Amount accrued (reversed) during the year	(46.9)	234.0
Amounts charged thereto	(123.9)	(6.8)
Accrued liability at end of year	$ 56.4	$227.2

16. Contingent liabilities

Twelve purported consumer commercial class actions (one of which consolidates five previous actions) are presently pending against the Company in various state and federal courts . . . In the purported class actions, the named plaintiffs are requesting . . . various forms of monetary relief, including punitive damages, as a result of the Company's having manufactured and sold allegedly defective Steel Belted Radial 500 and other steel belted radial passenger tires.

. . . In addition to the class actions, there are several thousand individual claims pending against the Company for damages allegedly connected with steel belted radial passenger tires . . .

. . . The Company is a defendant in a purported class action which seeks, among other things, recovery for losses by stockholders who purchased the Company's common stock between December 1975 and July 1978 by reason of the decline in market price for such stock alleged to result from the Company's alleged failure to make proper disclosure of, among other things, the steel belted radial passenger tire situation.

In March 1979, the United States brought an action seeking recovery against the Company in the amount of approximately $62 million by reason of alleged illegal gold trading activity in Switzerland.

Following a federal grand jury investigation into the Company's incomes taxes, the Company entered into a plea agreement in July 1979 under which the Company pleaded guilty to two counts charging the inclusion in its taxable income for 1972 and 1973 amounts that had been generated in prior years: the courts imposed a total fine of ten thousand dollars on the Company by reason of its plea. A civil tax audit by the Internal Revenue Service is currently in progress covering some of the same matters investigated by the grand jury as well as other matters. The government may assess substantial tax, interest and penalties in connection with the matters under investigation.

The Securities and Exchange Commission is conducting an investigation of the adequacy of the Company's disclosures in earlier years concerning the Steel Belted Radial 500 tire . . .

. . . The Company has various other contingent liabilities, some of which are for substantial amounts, arising out of suits, investigations and claims related to other aspects of the conduct of its business . . .

. . . Increased uncertainties have developed during the past year with regard to some of the contingencies identified in this note. Because of the existing uncertainties, the eventual outcome of these contingencies cannot be predicted, and the ultimate liability with respect to them cannot be reasonably estimated. Since the minimum potential liability for a substantial portion of the claims and suits described in this note cannot be reasonably estimated, no liability for them has been recorded in the financial statements. Management believes, however, that the disposition of these contingencies could well be very costly. Although the Company's management, including its General Counsel, believes it is unlikely that the ultimate outcome of these contingencies will have a material adverse effect on the Company's consolidated financial position, such a consequence is possible if substantial punitive or other damages are awarded in one or more of the cases involved.

Report of independent certified public accountants

To the Stockholders and Board of Directors,
The Firestone Tire & Rubber Company:

We have examined the balance sheets of The Firestone Tire & Rubber Company and consolidated subsidiaries at October 31, 1979 and 1978, and the related statements of income, stockholders' equity, and changes in financial position for the years then ended. Our examinations were made in accordance with generally accepted auditing standards and, accordingly, included such tests of the accounting records and such other auditing procedures as we considered necessary in the circumstances.

As set forth in Note 16 to the financial statements, the Company is a party to various legal and other actions. These actions claim substantial amounts as a result of alleged tire defects and other matters. The ultimate liability resulting from these matters cannot be reasonably estimated. In our report dated December 18, 1978, our opinion on the financial statements for the year ended October 31, 1978, was unqualified. However, due to the increased uncertainties that developed during the year ended October 31, 1979, with respect to these matters, our present opinion on the financial

When the cash contributions are then made to the pension fund:

Pension liability   XX
  Cash   XX

As long as the company has made all required contributions, there are no further financial statement effects.

Defined benefit plans

In a defined benefit plan, the employer specifies the benefit that employees will receive during retirement.[1] Employers must therefore ensure that cash contributions and subsequent returns on pension fund assets are sufficient to cover the promises made to their employees. The risk of pension fund performance therefore falls entirely on the employer.

Typically, the amount of periodic benefit received in retirement is based on the employee's length of service and level of pay. This guaranteed benefit is difficult to estimate and manage given that there are so many uncertainties that can affect it, including employee life expectancy, future salaries, the possibility of early retirement, and turnover rates. To gain an appreciation for the difficulties of managing these plans we first need to distinguish between funded and unfunded plans.

According to IAS 19 (the IFRS standard that deals with pensions), the amount recognized in the balance sheet should be the present value of the defined benefit obligation (that is, the present value of expected future payments required to settle the obligation resulting from employee service in the current and prior periods), adjusted for unrecognized actuarial gains and losses and unrecognized past service cost, and reduced by the fair value of plan assets at the balance sheet date. (We will define these terms shortly.)

Similarly, but not exactly, SFAS 158 (the US GAAP equivalent to IAS 19) requires an employer to recognize the overfunded or underfunded status of a defined benefit postretirement plan as an asset or liability in its balance sheet and to recognize, through comprehensive income, changes in that funded status in the year in which the changes occur.

Unfunded defined benefit plans

Accounting for unfunded plans requires fewer estimates than a funded plan. In accordance with the matching principle, pension expense and the associated liability are accrued each period as employees earn their right to future benefits. The journal entry is:

Pension expense   XX
  Pension liability   XX

This entry is recorded for every period during the employee's working life. The primary complication stems from the need to estimate the number of years an employee will survive postretirement. That is, for how long will the company have to pay the retirement benefits? The actual pension cost cannot be known for certain until the employee's death as well as the death of any survivors who might also be covered under the pension plan and are therefore entitled to benefits. Other variables such as employee turnover rates, and future salary and wage rates, also have an impact on this calculation.

Once the employee retires and the company starts to make payments, the following journal entry is recorded:

Pension liability	XX	
Cash		XX

This entry is recorded every time a pension payment is made to the employee from the time of retirement until death.

Funded defined benefit plans

In a funded or partially funded defined benefit plan, the company makes regular contributions to a separate legal entity. The contributions are then invested with the hope of earning positive returns and growing the total asset pool. Thus, the pension fund assets are the sum of the company contributions and the returns earned through investments. The journal entry to record the contributions made by the employer to the pension fund is:

Pension expense	XX	
Cash		XX

However, it is unusual for the pension expense and the cash contributions to equal in any given year, meaning that an overfunding or underfunding situation will exist.

When the cash contributions in a given year are greater than the pension expense, the residual amount is recorded as a debit either increasing the net *over*funded situation or decreasing net *under*funding:

Pension plan expense	XX	
Pension asset or liability	XX	
Cash		XX

When the cash contributions are smaller than the pension expense, the difference is recorded as a credit either decreasing the net overfunded situation or increasing the net underfunding:

Pension plan expense	XX	
Cash		XX
Pension asset/liability		XX

Determining the pension expense for the period is somewhat more complicated. The pension plan expense is calculated by aggregating several components:

(a) service cost, which is the present value of benefits earned by employees during the accounting period. The discount rate is usually the current market interest rate for high-quality, fixed-income investments.

(b) interest costs, which is the increase in present value from benefits earned in previous years. It arises because as each year passes, earned pension benefits are one year closer to being paid, and therefore the present value of those benefits has increased.

(c) plan asset returns, which includes the interest, dividends, and other revenue derived from the plan assets, together with realized and unrealized gains or losses on the assets, less any costs of administering the plan. This component *reduces* the pension expense by the assumed investment income from the plan assets based on assumed rates of return. Technically, this is an actuarial calculation and is not based on the plan's actual returns. The expected return on plan assets is determined based on the expected long-term rate of return on plan assets and the market-related value of the plan assets, and is used to reduce the volatility which would come about from using actual returns.

(d) amortization of unrecognized gains or losses. Actual returns on plan assets in excess of or less than assumed returns above are treated as gains or losses. These gains or losses are then amortized over a period equal to the average remaining service time of employees (the average number of years to retirement). However, for the sake of simplicity we will lump both assumed returns and the gain or loss together as one component called "plan asset returns." Similarly, gains and losses will be recognized from changes in actuarial assumptions. For example, if an actuarial investigation concludes that covered employees will live longer than previously expected, a loss must be recognized for the increase in the present value of future benefits caused by the increase in longevity. Other examples of potential gains and looses include changes in expected salary growth and employee turnover. As with the differences between assumed returns and actual returns on plan assets, the gains and losses on actuarial changes are amortized over the average remaining service life of employees.

(e) prior service costs, which is the term used to describe the change in the obligation for employee service in prior periods, arising from changes to plan arrangements in the current period. Past service cost may be either positive (where benefits are introduced or improved) or negative (where existing benefits are reduced). Past service cost should be recognized immediately to the extent that it relates to former employees or to active employees already vested. Otherwise, it should be amortized on a straight-line basis over the average period until the amended benefits become vested.

(f) the effect of any plan curtailments or settlements. Gains or losses resulting from the curtailment or settlement of a plan are recognized when the event curtailments are reductions in either the scope of employees covered or in benefits.

In general, the amount that an employer reports on its balance sheet is the net of the pension benefit obligations and the pension plan assets on the balance sheet date.

> **Net Pension Asset (or Liability)**
> Pension Plan Assets (at Market Value)
> − Projected Benefit Obligation (PBO)
> = Funded Status

If the pension plan assets are greater than the pension plan obligations, the plan is said to be overfunded. Pension plans tend to become overfunded as a result of a stock market boom (provided the pension plan is invested in stocks, as many are). In such cases, a pension fund asset appears on the balance sheet. For most companies, however, pension plan assets are less than the pension plan obligations and, thus, the pension plan is underfunded. The amount of the underfunding appears on the balance sheet as a liability.

Under US GAAP and IFRS, a firm having multiple plans for different groups of employees, with some of the plans underfunded while others are overfunded, must show both a liability (for the former) and an asset (for the latter). The company is not permitted to net underfunded plans against overfunded plans, or vice versa, and report the net amount on the balance sheet.

Pension Plan Assets

Pension Plan Assets, Beginning Balance

+   Actual Returns on Investments (Interest, Dividends, Gains, and Losses)

+   Company Contributions to Pension Plan

−   Benefits Paid to Retirees

=   Pension Plan Assets, Ending Balance

Pension Obligation

Projected Benefit Obligation, Beginning Balance

+   Service Cost

+   Interest Cost

+/−   Actuarial Losses (Gains)

−   Benefits Paid to Retirees

=   Projected Benefit Obligation, Ending Balance

To better understand the accounting for defined benefit plans, we turn now to a simple case study. Europa Inc. begins operations with one employee we will call Hector. Management offers Hector a suitable compensation plan, including a defined benefit pension package. The firm estimates that Hector will work for five years, retire, and then live another five years (see Figure 14.1). Projections like this have to be made so that the company can estimate how much it will owe Hector for the promised pension.

For each year of work Hector will receive $1800 at the end of each year during retirement. Further, Europa estimates an interest rate on pension obligations of 5% and that it can earn 8% on its pension assets. The funding policy of Europa is to contribute $2500 at the end of each year that Hector works for the company.

The service cost is the cost to the employer incurred as the result of the employee's working for the firm and earning pension benefits upon retirement. In the case of Europa, for each year

Box 14.1   American Airlines: defined benefit plan disclosure

Pension obligation on at January 1, 2011	$12,968
Service cost	386
Interest cost	757
Actuarial loss (gain)	1,237
Benefit payments	(780)
Obligation at December 31, 2011	$14,568
Fair value of plan assets at January 1, 2011	$7,773
Actual return on plan assets	614
Employer contributions	525
Benefit payments	(780)
Fair value of plan assets at December 31, 2011	$8,132
Funded status at December 31, 2011	$(6,436)

Box 14.2   Pension expense relating to defined contribution plans

Components of net periodic benefit cost

Defined benefit plans:	
Service cost	$386
Interest cost	757
Expected return on assets	(657)
Amortization of:	
Prior service cost	13
Unrecognized net loss	154
Net periodic benefit cost for defined benefit plans	653
Defined contribution plans	179
Total	$832

Pension expense	XX	
Cash		XX

If the employer did not make the cash contribution at the end of the period in which service was provided, the company would record the following journal entry:

Pension expense	XX	
Pension payable		XX

Thereafter, once payment is made, the next journal entry would be recorded:

Pension payable   XX
   Cash   XX

If contributions to a defined contribution plan do not fall due within 12 months after the end of the period in which the employee renders the service, they should be discounted to their present value.

For illustration purposes, let's revisit Europa Inc. and Hector, except this time, imagine that management offers Hector €100 000 in compensation plus a defined contribution pension scheme equal to 5% of salary (see Table 14.2). As before, the firm estimates that Hector will work for five years, retire, and then live another five years. Assume that Hector's annual salary is expected to grow at 3% per year. We will make an assumption that the return on Hector's individual pension account is 8% per year and that he will withdraw the balance in the account at retirement over the five years in equal amounts in addition to taking the returns earned every year. Europa would record the following journal entries over the five years of Hector's employment:

End of $t - 5$:   Pension expense   €5,000
                    Cash   €5,000

End of $t - 4$:   Pension expense   €5,150
                    Cash   €5,150

End of $t - 3$:   Pension expense   €5,305
                    Cash   €5,305

End of $t - 2$:   Pension expense   €5,464
                    Cash   €5,464

End of $t - 1$:   Pension expense   €5,628
                    Cash   €5,628

Assumptions:

- annual salary growth of 3% per year;
- 5% of annual compensation contributed;
- 8% return on total assets;
- annual withdrawal (total assets at time of retirement/assumed retirement period) + annual return.

Table 14.2 Basic defined contribution pension example

	$t-5$	$t-4$	$t-3$	$t-2$	$t-1$	t	$t+1$	$t+2$	$t+3$	$t+4$	$t+5$
Salary	€100,000	€103,000	€106,090	€109,273	€112,551		0	0	0	0	0
Contribution	5,000	5,150	5,305	5,464	5,628		0	0	0	0	0
Return (8%)	—	400	844	1,336	1,880		2,481	1,984	1,488	992	496
Total assets	5,000	10,550	16,699	23,499	31,007		24,805	18,604	12,403	6,201	0
Withdrawals	0	0	0	0	0		8,682	8,186	7,690	7,194	6,697

Key lessons from the chapter

- A pension is a contractual benefit promised by an employer to provide an employee with a source of income during his or her retirement years.
- There are two primary types of retirement schemes: *defined benefit plans* and *defined contribution plans*.
- Defined contribution plans specify amounts to be invested for the employee during the employee's career. The employee's retirement benefits will be based on the value of these investments at retirement. Therefore, the risk of pension plan investment performance falls entirely on the employee.
- The accounting for defined contribution plans is straightforward.
- Defined benefit plans specify amounts to be received during retirement. The effect is to place the risk of future investment performance on the employer.
- The accounting for defined benefit plans is highly complex, influenced not only by investment returns (which have no effect on the accounting for defined contribution plans), but also by interest rates, employee longevity, turnover, and future salary increases.
- Pension expense for defined benefit pension plans consists of service cost, interest cost, expected return on plan assets, and amortization of past service costs and changes in actuarial assumptions.
- Overfunded defined benefit plans are reported as assets on the employer's balance sheet. Underfunded plans are reported as liabilities.
- There has been a pronounced trend in recent years towards the adoption of defined contribution plans.

Key terms and concepts from the chapter

Defined benefit plan	Service cost	Prior service costs
Defined contribution plan	Interest cost	Vesting
	Plan asset returns	
Underfunded/ overfunded plan	Amortization of unrecognized gain or loss	

Questions

1. Describe the differences between defined benefit and defined contribution plans.

2. Many companies are closing down their defined benefit plans and replacing them with defined contribution plans. Why?

3. Interest rates have sharply declined in most economies over the past 10 years. What effects would you expect this trend to have had on pension liabilities and pension expenses?

4. As a prospective employee, which type of plan (defined benefit or defined contribution) do you prefer, and why?

5. Define "underfunded" and "overfunded."

6. What is the difference between "service cost" and "interest cost?"

7. Describe the effects on pension expense of changing expected returns on pension plan investments. What happens if we increase the expected returns? What happens if we decrease them?

Case study

14.1   Comprehensive pension review problem: Cathay Pacific

Headquartered in Hong Kong, Cathay Pacific is one of the world's leading airlines. The disclosures shown below are taken from Note 19 in the Company's 2010 annual report.

Required

(a) Describe what is meant by service cost and interest cost.
(b) How much pension expense does Cathay Pacific report in 2009 and 2010 for its defined benefit plans?
(c) Cathay Pacific reports a HK$518 million expected return on plan assets as an offset to 2010 pension expense. How was this amount determined? What is the actual gain or loss realized on its 2010 plan assets? What is the purpose of using this estimated amount instead of the actual gain or loss?
(d) What factors affected Cathay Pacific's 2010 pension liability? What factors affected its 2010 plan assets?
(e) What does the term "funded status" mean? What is the funded status of the pension plans over the previous five years, from 2006 until 2010?
(f) The company reduced its discount rate from 4.8% in 2009 to 4.4% in 2010. What effect(s) did this change have on the balance sheet and the income statement?

(g) Assume that Cathay Pacific decreased its estimate of expected annual wage increases used to determine its defined benefit obligations in 2010. What effect(s) does this decrease have on its financial statements? In general, how does such a decrease affect income?

(h) What journal entry was needed to record pension plan expense in 2010 for Cathay's defined contribution plans?

Retirement benefits

The Group operates various defined benefit and defined contribution retirement schemes for its employees in Hong Kong and in certain overseas locations. The assets of these schemes are held in funds administered by independent trustees. The retirement schemes in Hong Kong are registered under and comply with the Occupational Retirement Schemes Ordinance and the Mandatory Provident Fund Schemes Ordinance ("MPFSO"). Most of the employees engaged outside Hong Kong are covered by appropriate local arrangements.

The Group operates the following principal schemes:

(a) Defined benefit retirement schemes

The Swire Group Retirement Benefit Scheme ("SGRBS") in Hong Kong, in which the Company and Cathay Pacific Catering Services (H.K.) Limited ("CPCS") are participating employers, provides resignation and retirement benefits to its members, which include the Company's cabin attendants who joined before September 1996 and other locally engaged employees who joined before June 1997, upon their cessation of service. The Company and CPCS meet the full cost of all benefits due by SGRBS to their employee members who are not required to contribute to the scheme.

Staff employed by the Company in Hong Kong on expatriate terms before April 1993 were eligible to join another scheme, the Cathay Pacific Airways Limited Retirement Scheme ("CPALRS"). Both members and the Company contribute to CPALRS.

The latest actuarial valuation of CPALRS and the portion of SGRBS funds specifically designated for the Company's employees were completed by a qualified actuary, Watson Wyatt Hong Kong Limited, as at 31st December 2009 using the projected unit credit method. The figures for SGRBS and CPALRS disclosed as at 31st December 2010 were provided by Cannon Trustees Limited, the administration manager.

	2010		2009	
	SGRBS	**CPALS**	**SGRBS**	**CPALS**
The principal actuarial assumptions are:				
Discount rate used	**4.40%**	**4.40%**	4.80%	4.80%
Expected return on plan assets	**8.00%**	**6.50%**	8.00%	6.50%
Future salary increases	**2–5%**	**1–5%**	2–5%	1–5%

The Group's obligations are 106% (2009: 97%) covered by the plan assets held by the trustees as at 31st December 2010.

	2010 HK$M	2009 HK$M
Net expenses recognized in the Group profit and loss:		
Current service cost	324	316
Interest on obligations	311	342
Expected return on plan assets	(518)	(371)
Actuarial loss recognized	1	30
Total included in staff costs	118	317
Actual return on plan assets	820	1,578

	Group	
	2010 HK$M	2009 HK$M
Net (asset)/liability recognized in the statement of financial position:		
Present value of funded obligations	7,615	7,460
Fair value of plan assets	(8,077)	(7,217)
	(462)	243

	Group	
	2010 HK$M	2009 HK$M
Movements in present value of funded obligations comprise:		
At 1st January	7,460	7,108
Movements for the year		
– current service cost	324	316
– interest cost	311	342
– employee contributions	12	14
– benefits paid	(524)	(681)
– actuarial losses	32	361
At 31st December	7,615	7,460

	Group	
	2010 HK$M	**2009 HK$M**
Movements in fair value of plan assets comprise:		
At 1st January	**7,217**	5,924
Movements for the year		
– expected return on plan assets	**518**	371
– employee contributions	**12**	14
– employer contributions	**552**	382
– benefits paid	**(524)**	(681)
– actuarial gain	**302**	1,207
At 31st December	**8,077**	7,217

	Group	
	2010 HK$M	**2009 HK$M**
Fair value of plan assets comprises:		
Equities	**5,318**	4,297
Debt instruments	**1,919**	1,725
Deposits and cash	**840**	526
Others	**—**	669
	8,077	7,217

The overall expected rate of return on plan assets is determined based on the average rate of return of major categories of assets that constitute the total plan assets.

	Group				
	2010 HK$M	**2009 HK$M**	**2008 HK$M**	**2007 HK$M**	**2006 HK$M**
Present value of funded obligations	**7,615**	7,460	7,108	8,223	7,844
Fair value of plan assets	**(8,077)**	(7,217)	(5,924)	(9,131)	(8,065)
(Surplus)/deficit	**(462)**	243	1,184	(908)	(221)

The difference between the fair value of the schemes' assets and the present value of the accrued past services liabilities at the date of an actuarial valuation is taken into consideration when determining future funding levels in order to ensure that the schemes will be able to meet liabilities as they become due. The contributions are calculated based upon funding recommendations arising from actuarial valuations. The Group expects to make contributions of HK$378 million to the schemes in 2011.

(b) Defined contribution retirement schemes

Staff employed by the company in Hong Kong are eligible to join a defined contribution retirement scheme, the CPA Provident Fund.

Under the terms of the schemes, other than the Company contribution, staff may elect to contribute from 0% to 10% of their monthly salary. During the year, the benefits forfeited in accordance with the schemes' rules amounted to HK$18 million (2009: HK$ 19 million) which have been applied toward the contributions payable by the Company.

A mandatory provident fund ("MPF") scheme was established under the MPFSO in December 2000. Where staff elect to join the MPF scheme, the Company and staff are required to contribute 5% of the employee's relevant income (capped at HK$20 000). Staff may elect to contribute more than the minimum as a voluntary contribution.

Contributions to defined contribution retirement schemes charged to the Group profit and loss are HK$756 million (2009: HK$677 million).

Note

1. In some countries, such as the UK, defined benefit plans are often described as "final salary plans," because benefits are driven, in part, by salaries in the final years of an employee's career.

CHAPTER 15

Accounting for Income Tax

Introduction

In this chapter we explore how companies account for income tax under US GAAP and IFRS. Key concepts are illustrated using the financial statements and notes of Intel Corporation.

The single most important fact to know about the accounting for income tax is that the rules for calculating profits under GAAP or IFRS – known as "book income" – do not correspond to the rules for calculating profits under tax law ("tax income"). This divergence is seen in every rich country, and, increasingly, in the developing world. While some people may be disturbed by the idea that a company can report one profit number to its shareholders and a very different (often smaller) number on its tax returns, the practice is a logical outcome of the different objectives underlying book and tax accounting.

Financial accounting exists, first and foremost, to provide relevant financial information to lenders and equity investors. To advance this aim, GAAP and IFRS rely on the matching principle and accrual accounting. For example, if a company sells products under warranty, a provision is taken in the year of sale even if the cash costs of the warranty are not incurred until future periods. But while financial accounting principles require the recognition of such expenses, tax authorities will demand that cash actually be spent to service the warranty before a tax deduction is allowed. The result is a timing difference between the recognition of warranty expense in the calculation of book and tax income.

In addition, tax law is designed to serve purposes separate and apart from the goal of promoting efficient capital allocation. Governments use taxes not just to collect revenues from businesses, but to do so in ways that advance public policy priorities. One such priority may be the promotion of capital investment. For this reason, tax law offers companies the right to accelerate depreciation charges. This practice can dramatically increase the value of the resulting tax shield, and the more valuable the tax shield, the lower the net cost of an asset to the investing firm. But actual usage or industry practice may suggest the straight-line method for book purposes. As a result, the company uses two depreciation methods – an accelerated approach for tax income and straight-line for book income.

Or consider the fines that companies pay for violating environmental or worker-safety regulations. While GAAP/IFRS recognizes these payments as expenses, the public interest demands that such expenses are not recognized for tax purposes. As a result, a permanent difference arises between expenses for book income and expenses for tax income.

As we will show in the next section, differences between book and tax income can arise in a broad range of accounting issues. Much of tax accounting deals with how companies reconcile these differences.

Temporary and permanent differences

As the above discussion suggests, the differences between the determination of tax income and book income fall into two broad categories:

- temporary differences
- permanent differences.

Temporary differences

Temporary differences result when a revenue, gain, expense, or loss enters in the calculation of book income in one period but affects tax income in a different (earlier or later) period. In the previous section, the warranty and depreciation examples fall into this category. Such differences are considered temporary because they eventually reverse. For example, if an asset is purchased for $1 million, the total amount to be depreciated over the asset's life must be $1 million (assuming no residual value). This is true under GAAP/IFRS and under tax law. In other words, net book value must be 0 in either case by the end of the asset's life. Therefore, if tax law permits accelerated depreciation (i.e., higher expense than under the straight-line method in the early years of the asset's life), charges must be lower in later years. As the end of the asset's life approaches, total book depreciation converges to total tax depreciation.

A similar argument applies to warranty expense. The only difference is that the expense for tax purposes lags the book expense instead of leading it, as it does for depreciation.

Other common sources of temporary differences include:

- **Deferred revenue**. When customers make advanced payments for goods or services, GAAP/IFRS requires the payment to be treated as a liability. Revenue is recognized later when it is deemed to have been earned. Many tax jurisdictions require such payments to be taxed when received.
- **Long-term contracts**. Book income is usually calculated using "percentage-of-completion." However, some tax authorities permit other methods.

- **Bad debts expense**. For book purposes, firms estimate uncollectible accounts in the year of sale using the allowance method. However, in most countries, bad debt expense cannot be recognized for tax purposes until a specific customer account is deemed to be uncollectible.
- **Prepaid expenses**. Under GAAP/IFRS, prepayments for rent and insurance are reported as current assets. Expenses are recognized gradually over time as the benefits from the related contracts are consumed. Tax law, on the other hand, may permit companies to deduct the full amount when the payments are made.
- **Equity income**. The equity method requires firms to recognize their proportionate share of any profits or losses reported by affiliates (investments with 20–50% ownership). Most tax codes, on the other hand, require recognition of income only when dividends are received.
- **Installment sales**. Under GAAP/IFRS, sales are generally recognized for book purposes when goods are delivered to the customer regardless of when the payments are made. If customers make payments over an extended period, tax rules may allow revenues to be recognized only as cash is received.

Temporary differences that cause tax income to be *higher* than book income in future periods, as in the case of depreciation, give rise to a "deferred tax liability." Differences that cause tax income to be *lower* in future periods, e.g., the treatment of warranties expense, give rise to a "deferred tax asset." In all cases, deferred tax accounts are reported on an undiscounted basis.

Under IFRS, deferred tax assets and liabilities are classified as noncurrent on the balance sheet, with supplemental disclosures in the notes for (a) the components of the temporary differences, and (b) amounts expected to be recovered within 12 months and beyond 12 months of the balance sheet date. US GAAP also requires a detailed breakdown of deferred tax components, but the classification rules are different. Deferred tax assets and liabilities can appear as current or noncurrent, depending on the classification of the related asset or liability responsible for the temporary difference. For example, a deferred tax liability resulting from the excess of tax depreciation over book depreciation is reported as a noncurrent liability, because the temporary difference relates to noncurrent assets. A deferred tax asset resulting from prepaid expenses might be classified as current, given that prepaid expenses are current assets.

Permanent differences

Permanent differences between tax and book income are caused by either of the following:

- An item that affects book income but which will never affect tax income. The nondeductible fine cited in the previous section is one such example. Bribes and excessively lavish entertainment expenses are others. Any income source that is exempt from income tax also falls in this category. For example, interest income on municipal bonds in the US is exempt from federal income tax. If such income is earned, it is recognized for book purposes, not for tax purposes.
- An item that affects taxable income but which will never affect book income. For example, many tax jurisdictions allow companies to deduct a portion of the dividends received from another company. Only taxable income is affected by such laws. Book income is not.

What both categories have in common is that the differences between book and tax income do not reverse. That is, any such differences are not offset by corresponding differences in subsequent periods. Therefore, they do not give rise to deferred tax liabilities or assets.

Deferred taxes and the balance sheet approach

US GAAP and IFRS require a balance sheet approach in calculating the impact of timing differences between book and tax accounting.[1] The process begins by calculating the book basis and the tax basis for each balance sheet item with a timing difference. The difference between these two values is then multiplied by the relevant tax rate to determine the deferred tax asset/liability. This balance is compared with the prior year's deferred tax balance. The process can be summarized as follows:

$$\text{Temporary Differences} = \text{GAAP/IFRS Basis of Assets or Liabilities}$$
$$- \text{Tax Basis of Assets or Liabilities}$$
$$\text{Deferred Tax Liabilities or Assets} = \text{Temporary Differences} \times \text{Tax Rate}$$

The tax rate used here is the rate expected to apply to the period when the asset is realized or the liability is settled. Therefore, if tax rates are expected to change, the balances in the deferred tax accounts will change too.

Also, as we discuss later, deferred tax assets can arise from unused tax losses that are carried forward. The deferred tax asset equals the unused tax losses, multiplied by the relevant tax rate.

Changes in any of these deferred tax accounts will then impact the income tax expense reported on the income statement:

$$\text{Tax Expense} = \text{Taxes Paid} \pm \text{Changes in Deferred Tax Assets and Liabilities}$$

The balance sheet approach: an example

Assume that on 30 June 2010 a company pays \$100 000 for a new machine. At the time of purchase, the book basis and tax basis are both \$100 000. For book purposes, the machine is depreciated over a three-year period using the straight-line method. For tax purposes, the company selects the double-declining-balance method. No residual value is expected, which means that both book and tax depreciation must equal \$100 000 over the three-year life of the asset.

For book purposes, 2010 depreciation is \$16 667, equal to \$100 000 divided by 3 (three-year expected life), divided by 2 (because the asset was put in service on 1 July 2010, the middle of the year). Tax depreciation is \$33 333, or double the amount under straight-line. Assuming no other expenses, a tax rate of 40%, and revenues of $100 000, the income statements under both book and tax accounting look like Table 15.1. The net book value under both methods is shown in Table 15.2.

The balance sheet perspective measures the asset basis under the two methods. Calculating the change in the deferred tax liability account begins with the excess of the asset's book basis over the tax basis, multiplied by the tax rate: ($83 333 − $66 667) × 40%, or $6666. This figure is then subtracted from any existing deferred tax liability already recorded for the asset. Given that this is the first year of the asset's life, there is no previous liability. Therefore, the deferred tax liability is the entire $6666 and the journal entry is reported as follows:

Tax expense	33,333	
Tax payable		26,667
Deferred tax liability		6,666

The $33 333 figure represents the expense on the income statement; the company owes $26 667 in tax to the government for that year.

Consistent with the equation shown above:

$$\text{Tax Expense} = \text{Taxes Paid} \pm \text{Changes in Deferred Tax Assets and Liabilities}$$
$$\$33\,333 = \$26\,667 + \$6\,666$$

In 2011, the company recognizes a full year of straight-line depreciation ($33 333 = $100 000/ 3 years) for book purposes and $44 444 using double-declining balance (net book value of

Table 15.1 Income statements under book and tax accounting

Tax year 2010	Book reporting		Tax reporting
Revenues	$100,000	Revenues	$100,000
Depreciation expense	16,667	Depreciation deduction	33,333
Income before tax	83,333	Taxable income	66,667
Tax expense @ 40%	**33,333**	**Tax payable @ 40%**	**26,667**
Net income	50,000		

Table 15.2 Measuring the asset basis

Asset basis	Book reporting	Tax reporting
Beginning 30 June 2010	$100,000	$100,000
Less: 2010 depreciation	16,667	33,333
Ending 31 December 2010	**$83,333**	**$66,667**

$66 667 at the beginning of 2011, divided by 3 years and multiplied by 2, to reflect double the straight-line rate). The results are summarized in Table 15.3.

The deferred tax liability at the end of 2011 equals the excess of the book basis over the tax basis, multiplied by the tax rate of 40%: ($50 000 − $22 223) × 40%, or $11 111. This means that the liability account needs to be increased by $4445, the difference between the required ending balance of $11 111 and the beginning balance of $6666. Tax expense therefore equals the taxes payable of $22 223 plus the change in the deferred tax liability of $4445. The required journal entry is:

Tax expense	26,667	
Tax payable		22,222
Deferred tax liability		4,445

In 2012 the company recognizes another full year of straight-line depreciation for book purposes, $33 333 (the same as in 2011), while depreciation expense for tax purposes is $14 815 (beginning net book value of $22 223, divided by 3 years and multiplied by 2) – see Table 15.4.

The ending balance for the deferred tax liability equals ($16 667 − $7408) × 40%, or $3704. Because the beginning balance is $11 111, the following journal entry is required:

Tax expense	26,667	
Deferred tax liability	7,407	
Tax payable		34,074

Table 15.3   Measuring the asset basis through 2011

Asset basis	Book reporting	Tax reporting
Beginning 30 June 2010	$100,000	$100,000
Less: 2010 depreciation	16,667	33,333
Ending 31 December 2010	83,333	66,667
Less: 2011 depreciation	33,333	44,444
Ending: 31 December 2011	**$50,000**	**$22,223**

Table 15.4   Measuring the asset basis through 2012

Asset basis	Book reporting	Tax reporting
Beginning 30 June 2010	$100,000	$100,000
Less: 2010 depreciation	16,667	33,333
Ending 31 December 2010	83,333	66,667
Less: 2011 depreciation	33,333	44,444
Ending: 31 December 2011	50,000	22,223
Less: 2012 depreciation	33,333	14,815
Ending: 31 December 2012	**$16,667**	**$7,408**

Table 15.5   Measuring the asset basis through 2013

Asset basis	Book reporting	Tax reporting
Beginning 30 June 2010	$100,000	$100,000
Less: 2010 depreciation	16,667	33,333
Ending 31 December 2010	83,333	66,667
Less: 2011 depreciation	33,333	44,444
Ending: 31 December 2011	50,000	22,223
Less: 2012 depreciation	33,333	14,815
Ending: 31 December 2012	16,667	7,408
Less: 2013 depreciation	16,667	7,408
Ending: 31 December 2013	**0**	**0**

where $7407 is the difference between the beginning balance and the required ending balance for the deferred tax liability. Because the required balance has declined, the account is debited.

Finally, for 2010, see Table 15.5.

By the end of 2013, the asset has been fully depreciated for both book and tax purposes, meaning that the asset basis is 0 under both measurement systems. Any remaining balance in the deferred tax liability account must therefore be reversed:

Tax expense	33,333	
Deferred tax liability	3,704	
Tax payable		37,037

Note that a similar approach is taken for any items that give rise to temporary differences between book and tax income, including differences that lead to deferred tax *assets*. In principle, deferred tax assets are recognized in the same way as deferred tax liabilities. However, as with all assets, the question of recoverability arises. Deferred tax assets are regarded as recoverable if, on the basis of available evidence, it is more likely than not that there will be enough taxable profit from which the future reversal of the underlying timing differences can be deducted. We discuss this issue in more detail in the following section.

Interpreting income tax disclosures: the case of Intel Corporation

In this section we examine the income tax disclosures of Intel based on its 2006 Annual Report. We begin with the income statement, as shown in Table 15.6. Intel reports income before taxes for 2006 of $7.068 billion. The "provision for taxes," or the "income tax expense," is $2.024 billion. The tax expense is based on the tax owed under tax law for that year, plus or minus changes in deferred tax assets and liabilities.

Table 15.6 Intel Corporation income statement

	2006	2005	2004
Net revenue	$35,382	$38,826	$34,209
Cost of sales	17,164	15,777	14,463
Gross margin	18,218	23,049	19,746
Research and development	5,873	5,145	4,778
Marketing, general and administrative	6,096	5,688	4,659
Restructuring and asset impairment charges	555	–	–
Amortization of acquisition-related intangibles and costs	42	126	179
Operating expenses	12,566	10,959	9,616
Operating income	$5,652	$12,090	$10,130
Gains (losses) on equity securities, net	214	(45)	(2)
Interest and other, net	1,202	565	289
Income before taxes	**7,068**	**12,610**	**10,417**
Provision for taxes	**2,024**	**3,946**	**2901**
Net income	$5,044	$8,664	$7,516
Basic earnings per common share	$0.87	$1.42	$1.17
Diluted earnings per common share	$0.86	$1.40	$1.16
Common shares outstanding	5,797	6,106	6,400

Tax rates

By comparing income tax expense with income before taxes, we can calculate Intel's effective tax rate. For 2006, this rate equals $2.024 \div $7.068, or 28.6%. However, the statutory tax rate in the US (that is, the rate set by law) is 35%. Whenever a company's effective and statutory tax rates differ, and they nearly always do for large publicly traded companies like Intel, reconciliation must be provided in the notes. Intel's appears in Table 15.7.

What Table 15.7 reveals is that the single biggest source for the difference is foreign taxation. Because so much of Intel's business is outside the US, the company can take advantage of preferential tax regimes in other countries. For example, Intel can use transfer pricing policies to ensure that when one of its business units sells to another, the costs are high (or the revenues low) in the high-tax jurisdiction. Such practices shift profits to countries with relatively low tax rates. As a result, the effective tax rate is significantly lower than the statutory rate.

The second biggest effect on the difference between the two tax rates in 2006 (and the largest for the two previous years) comes from the "export sales benefit." Governments in many countries grant such benefits to encourage exports. When combined with non-US tax rates and various other adjustments, Intel can reconcile the two rates (35% and 28.6%).

Deferred vs. current taxes

Table 15.8 disaggregates the provision for taxes (i.e., the income tax expense) into its current and deferred components:

spring 2011 Sony was compelled to write off ¥360 billion ($4.5 billion) of deferred tax assets. The company had incurred large operating losses as a result of the earthquake and tsunami that hit Japan in March of that year. The company admitted that the disruptions to its supply chain and the devastating effect of the natural disasters on Japan's economy meant that Sony would be unable to earn enough taxable profits in Japan in the foreseeable future to take advantage of its operating losses.[4]

Indeed, anytime a company's auditors have reason to doubt its future profitability, a large valuation allowance appears or write-offs are required. The key point here is that the firm is signaling to the financial statement reader that future cash savings on income tax will be lower than previously expected. In addition, the reader can take the reduction in deferred tax assets as a signal that future profitability will be impaired.

Key lessons from the chapter

- The rules for calculating profit under financial accounting principles, known as book income, are not the same as the rules used under tax law.
- Governments use taxes not just to collect revenues from businesses, but also to promote public policy priorities. The result is that tax law creates financial statements that are highly unlikely to be "true and fair." This problem explains why different rules are needed for investors.
- The differences between the determination of tax income and book income can be temporary or permanent.
- Temporary differences result when a revenue, gain, expense, or loss enters in the calculation of book income in one period but affects tax income in a different period.
- Common sources of temporary differences include: depreciation methods, deferred revenue, long-term contracts, bad debt expense, prepaid expenses, equity income, and installment sales.
- Permanent differences between tax and book income are caused by items that affect book income but will never affect tax income, or vice versa.
- Accounting principles require a balance sheet approach in calculating the impact of timing differences between book and tax accounting.
- Temporary differences result in either a deferred tax asset or a deferred tax liability.
- When the future realization of a deferred tax asset is uncertain – because there might not be enough taxable income for the deduction to be offset against when the reversal occurs, or tax losses might expire unused – the company must establish a deferred tax valuation allowance. This allowance serves as a contra-account to the deferred tax asset.
- The analysis of deferred taxes can often yield interesting and important insights. For example, a high deferred tax liability (compared to industry competitors) may indicate a tendency to overstate book income.

Key terms and concepts from the chapter

Deferred tax asset	Temporary differences	The balance sheet
Valuation allowance	Permanent differences	approach
Deferred tax liability		

Questions

1. What are deferred income taxes and why do they exist?

2. Define temporary differences. Give some examples.

3. Define permanent differences. Give some examples.

4. What is the difference between a deferred tax asset and a deferred tax liability?

5. What is the biggest source of deferred tax liabilities?

6. What is the biggest source of deferred tax assets?

7. What purpose is served by the deferred tax valuation allowance?

8. Why might a company have to write down a deferred tax asset?

9. True or false: The larger the gap between book income (i.e., income under GAAP or IFRS) and taxable income, the more confidence we have in the quality of the accounting numbers.

10. True or false: Analysts tend to be more concerned about deferred tax *assets* than deferred tax *liabilities*.

Problems

15.1 Calculating temporary and permanent differences

Hernan Company reports the following information for the year:

Book income before income taxes	€636,000
Income tax expense	€312,000
Income taxes payable for the year	€96,000
Income tax rate on taxable income	40%

The company has both permanent and temporary differences between book income and taxable income.

Required

(a) What is the amount of temporary differences for the year? Indicate whether the effect is to make book income larger or smaller than taxable income.
(b) What is the amount of permanent differences for the year? Indicate whether the effect is to make book income larger or smaller than taxable income.

15.2 Interpreting income tax disclosures

The following note was taken from the 2011 Annual Report of Tesco, a global UK-based grocery and discount retailing chain.

Required

(a) Based on this disclosure, which figure do you think was higher: taxable income reported under tax law, or pretax income reported under IFRS? How would you know? Does the magnitude and direction of this difference imply "conservative" accounting or "aggressive" accounting on the part of Tesco?
(b) What is meant by the term "origination and reversal of temporary differences?" What effect did the change in the UK corporate tax rate have on deferred income tax, and why?
(c) What would you expect to be the largest source of Tesco's deferred income tax liability?

Recognized in the Group income statement

	2011 £m	2010 £m
Current tax expense		
UK corporation tax	694	566
Foreign tax	181	128
Adjustments in respect of prior years	(114)	(91)
	761	603
Deferred income tax		
Origination and reversal of temporary differences	148	110
Adjustments in respect of prior years	12	124
Change in tax rate	(57)	3
	103	237
Total income tax expense	864	840

A number of changes to the UK corporation tax system were announced in the June 2010 Budget Statement. The Finance (No.2) Act 2010 included legislation to reduce the main rate of corporation tax from 28 to 27% from 1 April 2011. The proposed reduction from 28 to 27% was substantively enacted at the balance sheet date and has therefore been reflected in these Group financial statements.

In addition to the changes in rates of corporation tax disclosed above, a number of further changes to the UK corporation tax system were announced in the March 2011 UK Budget Statement. A resolution passed by Parliament on March 29, 2011 reduced the main rate of corporation tax to 26% from April 1, 2011. Legislation to reduce the main rate of corporation tax from 26 to 25% from April 1, 2012 is expected to be included in the Finance Act 2011. Further reductions to the main rate are proposed to reduce the rate by 1% per annum to 23% by April 1, 2014. None of these expected rate reductions had been substantively enacted at the balance sheet date and, therefore, are not reflected in these Group financial statements.

The effect of the changes enacted by Parliament on March 29, 2011 to reduce the corporation tax rate to 26%, with effect from April 1, 2011, is to reduce the deferred tax liability provided at the balance sheet date by £32m (£46m increase in profit and £14m decrease in the Group Statement of Comprehensive Income).

The effect of the changes expected to be enacted in the Finance Act 2011 to reduce the corporation tax rate from 26 to 25%, with effect from April 1, 2012, would be to reduce the deferred tax liability provided at the balance sheet date by a further £32m (£46m increase in profit and £14m decrease in the Group Statement of Comprehensive Income).

The proposed reductions of the main rate of corporation tax by 1% per year to 23% by April 1, 2014 are expected to be enacted separately each year. The overall effect of the further changes from 25 to 23%, if these applied to the deferred tax balance at the balance sheet date, would be to reduce the deferred tax liability by £66m (being £33m recognized in 2013 and £33m recognized in 2014).

15.3 Deferred income taxes and the statement of cash flows

The operating activities section from recent statements of cash flows for Group Air France-KLM is shown below. A note from the Group's fiscal year 2011 Annual Report is also provided.

Required

(a) Deferred taxes are a negative adjustment to net income in both years. What do these adjustments signify?
(b) What events or circumstances gave rise to the adjustments?

in € million, period from April 1 to March 31	2011	2010
Net income for the period – Equity holders for Air France-KLM	613	(1 559)
Noncontrolling interests	(1)	(1)
Amortization, depreciation, and operating provisions	1,676	1,675
Financial provisions	(3)	7
Gain on disposals of tangible and intangible assets	(11)	61
Loss/(gain) on disposals of subsidiaries and associates	(13)	—
Gain on WAM (ex Amadeus) operation	(1,030)	—
Derivatives – nonmonetary result	(25)	(8)
Unrealized foreign exchange gains and losses, net	33	13
Share of (profits)/losses of associates	21	17
Deferred taxes	(215)	(591)
Other nonmonetary items	(209)	143
Subtotal	**836**	**(243)**
(Increase)/decrease in inventories	(10)	(28)
(Increase)/decrease in trade receivables	171	(89)
Increase/(decrease) in trade payables	245	126
Change in other receivables and payables	108	(564)
Net cash flow from operating activities	**1,350**	**(798)**

12.5 Deferred tax recorded on the balance sheet

(in € millions)	April 1, 2010	Amounts recorded in income	Amounts recorded in equity	Currency translation adjustment	Reclassi- fication	March 31, 2011
Flight equipment	(1,039)	(78)	—	—	26	(1,091)
Pension assets	(683)	(50)	—	—	1	(732)
Financial debt	453	36	(236)	—	(3)	486
Other liabilities	387	(31)	—	—	(109)	11
Deferred revenue on ticket sales	206	—	(80)	—	(1)	205

(*Continued*)

(in € millions)	April 1, 2010	Amounts recorded in income	Amounts recorded in equity	Currency translation adjustment	Reclassi- fication	March 31, 2011
Others	(252)	(41)	—	—	90	(283)
Deferred tax corresponding to fiscal losses	1,452	379	—	—	(5)	1,826
Deferred tax asset/(liability)	524	215	(316)	—	(1)	422

(in € millions)	April 1, 2009	Amounts recorded in income	Amounts recorded in equity	Currency translation adjustment	Reclassi- fication	March 31, 2010
Flight equipment	(812)	(174)	(1)	1	(53)	(1,039)
Pension assets	(623)	(59)	—	(1)	—	(683)
Financial debt	442	47	(36)	—	—	453
Other liabilities	911	24	(579)	(2)	33	387
Deferred revenue on ticket sales	209	(3)	—	—	—	206
Others	(254)	(70)	62	—	10	(252)
Deferred tax corresponding to fiscal losses	599	826	—	1	26	1,452
Deferred tax asset/(liability)	472	591	(554)	(1)	16	524

Case study

15.1   Deferred tax assets and the valuation allowance: the case of Ford Motor Company

Exhibit 15.1 provides the income statements and balance sheets from Ford's 2011 Annual Report. Excerpts from the note on deferred income taxes are provided in Exhibit 15.2. The statements of cash flow for Ford reveal cash flows provided by operations of $9.784 billion, $11.477 billion, and $15.477 billion in 2011, 2010, and 2009, respectively. In 2011, Ford reported its highest net income ever (over $20 billion), an improvement of nearly $14 billion from the previous year. But did Ford's profitability really improve that much?

Exhibit 15.1 Ford Motor Company and subsidiaries: income statements for the years ended December 31, 2011, 2010, and 2009 (in millions, except per share amounts)

	2011	2010	2009
AUTOMOTIVE			
Revenues	$128,168	$119,280	$103,868
Costs and expenses			
Cost of sales	113,345	104,451	98,866
Selling, administrative and other expenses	9,060	9,040	8,354
Total costs and expenses	122,405	113,491	107,220
Operating income/(loss)	5,763	5,789	(3,352)
Interest expense	817	1,807	1,477
Interest income and other nonoperating income/ (expense), net (Note 19)	825	(362)	5,284
Equity in net income/(loss) of affiliated companies	479	526	330
Income/(Loss) before income taxes – Automotive	6,250	4,146	785
FINANCIAL SERVICES			
Revenues	8,096	9,674	12,415
Costs and expenses			
Interest expense	3,614	4,345	5,313
Depreciation	1,843	2,024	3,937
Operating and other expenses	675	845	738
Provision for credit and insurance losses	(33)	(216)	1,030
Total costs and expenses	6,099	6,998	11,018
Other income/(loss), net (Note 19)	413	315	552
Equity in net income/(loss) of affiliated companies	21	12	(135)
Income/(Loss) before income taxes – Financial Services	2,431	3,003	1,814
TOTAL COMPANY			
Income/(Loss) before income taxes	8,681	7,149	2,599
Provision for/(Benefit from) income taxes (Note 22)	(11,541)	592	(113)
Income/(Loss) from continuing operations	20,222	6,557	2,712
Income/(Loss) from discontinued operations	—	—	5
Net income/(loss)	20,222	6,557	2,717
Less: Income/(Loss) attributable to noncontrolling interests	9	(4)	—
Net income/(loss) attributable to Ford Motor Company	$20,213	$6,561	$2,717
NET INCOME/(LOSS) ATTRIBUTABLE TO FORD MOTOR COMPANY			
Income/(Loss) from continuing operations	$20,213	$6,561	$2,712
Income/(Loss) from discontinued operations	—	—	5
Net income/(loss) attributable to Ford Motor Company	$20,213	$6,561	$2,717

Exhibit 15.1   Continued

Balance sheets (in millions)

	December 31, 2011	December 31, 2010
ASSETS		
Cash and cash equivalents	$17,148	S14,805
Marketable securities (Note 6)	18,618	20,765
Finance receivables, net (Note 7)	69,976	70,070
Other receivables, net	8,565	8,381
Net investment in operating leases (Note 8)	12,838	11,675
Inventories (Note 10)	5,901	5,917
Equity in net assets of affiliated companies (Note 11)	2,936	2,569
Net property (Note 14)	22,371	23,179
Deferred income taxes (Note 22)	15,125	2,003
Net intangible assets (Note 15)	100	102
Other assets	4,770	5,221
Total assets	$178,348	$164,687
LIABILITIES		
Payables	$17,724	$16,362
Accrued liabilities and deferred revenue (Note 16)	45,369	43,844
Debt (Note 18)	99,488	103,988
Deferred income taxes (Note 22)	696	1,135
Total liabilities	163,277	165,329
EQUITY		
Capital stock (Note 24)		
Common stock, par value $.01 per share (3745 million shares issued)	37	37
Class B stock, par value $.01 per share (71 million shares issued)	1	1
Capital in excess of par value of stock	20,905	20,803
Retained earnings/(Accumulated deficit)	12,985	(7,038)
Accumulated other comprehensive income/(loss)	(18,734)	(14,313)
Treasury stock	(166)	(163)
Total equity/(deficit) attributable to Ford Motor Company	15,028	(673)
Equity/(Deficit) attributable to noncontrolling interests	43	31
Total equity/(deficit)	15,071	(642)
Total liabilities and equity	$178,348	$164,687

Exhibit 15.2 Ford Motor Company and Subsidiaries

Excerpts from Note 22
2011 Annual Report

Valuation of deferred tax assets and liabilities

Deferred tax assets and liabilities are recognized based on the future tax consequences attributable to temporary differences that exist between the financial statement carrying value of assets and liabilities and their respective tax bases, and operating loss and tax credit carryforwards on a taxing jurisdiction basis. We measure deferred tax assets and liabilities using enacted tax rates that will apply in the years in which we expect the temporary differences to be recovered or paid.

Our accounting for deferred tax consequences represents our best estimate of the likely future tax consequences of events that have been recognized in our financial statements or tax returns and their future probability. In assessing the need for a valuation allowance, we consider both positive and negative evidence related to the likelihood of realization of the deferred tax assets. If, based on the weight of available evidence, it is more likely than not that the deferred tax assets will not be realized, we record a valuation allowance.

	2011	2010	2009
Reconciliation of effective tax rate			
US statutory rate	35.0%	35.0%	35.0%
Non-US tax rates under US rates	(1.5)	(0.1)	(0.6)
State and local income taxes	1.1	1.5	(1.9)
General business credits	(1.9)	(1.8)	(6.2)
Dispositions and restructurings	6.8	(9.5)	(4.3)
US tax on non-US earnings	(0.8)	0.1	0.6
Prior year settlements and claims	(0.2)	(10.0)	10.4
Tax-related interest	(0.9)	(0.7)	(1.5)
Tax-exempt income	(3.9)	(4.7)	(10.4)
Other	(2.5)	0.2	0.2
Valuation allowances	(172.3)	(1.0)	(26.0)
Effective rate	(141.1)%	9.0%	(4.7)%

At the end of 2011, our US operations had returned to a position of cumulative profits for the most recent three-year period. We concluded that this record of cumulative profitability in recent years, our 10 consecutive quarters of pretax operating profits, our successful completion of labor negotiations with the UAW, and our business plan showing continued profitability, provide assurance that our future tax benefits more likely than not will be realized. Accordingly, at year-end 2011, we released almost all of our valuation allowance against net deferred tax assets for entities in the United States, Canada, and Spain.

At December 31, 2011, we have retained a valuation allowance against approximately $500 million in North America related to various state and local operating loss carryforwards that are subject to restrictive rules for future utilization, and a valuation allowance totaling $1 billion primarily against deferred tax assets for our South American operations.

Components of deferred tax assets and liabilities

The components of deferred tax assets and liabilities at 31 December were as follows (in millions):

	2011	2010
Deferred tax assets		
Employee benefit plans	$8,189	$6,332
Net operating loss carryforwards	3,163	4,124
Tax credit carryforwards	4,534	4,546
Research expenditures	2,297	2,336
Dealer and customer allowances and claims	1,731	1,428
Other foreign deferred tax assets	694	1,513
Allowance for credit losses	194	252
All other	1,483	2,839
Total gross deferred tax assets	22,285	23,370
Less: valuation allowances	(1,545)	(15,664)
Total net deferred tax assets	20,740	7,706
Deferred tax liabilities		
Leasing transactions	932	928
Deferred income	2,098	2,101
Depreciation and amortization (excluding leasing transactions)	1,659	1,146
Finance receivables	551	716
Other foreign deferred tax liabilities	360	334
All other	711	1,613
Total deferred tax liabilities	6,311	6,838
Net deferred tax assets/(liabilities)	$14,429	$868

Operating loss carryforwards for tax purposes were $8.5 billion at 31 December 2011, resulting in a deferred tax asset of $3.2 billion. A substantial portion of these losses begin to expire in 2029; the remaining losses will begin to expire in 2018. Tax credits available to offset future tax liabilities are $4.5 billion. A substantial portion of these credits have a remaining carryforward period of 10 years or more. Tax benefits of operating loss and tax credit carryforwards are evaluated on an ongoing basis, including a review of historical and projected future operating results, the eligible carryforward period, and other circumstances.

Required

(a) What are "net operating loss carryforwards," and why did they give rise to deferred tax assets? Answer the same question for "tax credit carryforwards."

(b) Why do depreciation and amortization give rise to deferred tax liabilities?

(c) What are the "valuation allowances" referred to in the financial statements and the notes?

(d) What happened to the valuation allowances in 2011? Give the appropriate summary journal entry. What was the effect on earnings for the year?

(e) What would Ford have reported as net income for 2011 if there had been no change in the valuation allowance?

(f) Describe, in detail, what happened in 2011 to allow Ford Motor Company to sharply reduce the allowance account.

Notes

1. There is also an income statement approach to determine deferred taxes, but we do not discuss it here because the method is no longer allowed.

2. While nearly all countries allow carryforwards, some do not allow carrybacks. Examples include Australia, Italy, Spain, and Switzerland. The US policy of allowing tax loss carryforwards for up to 20 years is unique. Other major market-based economies use either shorter periods or allow tax losses to be carried forward indefinitely. For example, France, Japan, and Korea allow only five years, while Australia, Germany, Ireland, the Netherlands, and the UK impose no time limits.

3. "Align the Books," by Tim Reason, *CFO Magazine*, November 2002.

4. "Full-year loss of Y260bn forces preliminary filing from Sony," by Jonathan Soble, *The Financial Times*, 24 May 2011.

CHAPTER 16

Accounting for Shareholders' Equity

Introduction

This chapter examines the financial reporting consequences of the most common transactions and events that impact shareholders' equity, including:

- the issuance of common and preferred shares
- the declaration and payment of cash dividends
- share repurchases
- stock dividends and stock splits
- convertible securities.

Relevant concepts and practices will be illustrated using the balance sheets and statements of shareholders' equity for The Coca-Cola Company (see Exhibits 16.1 and 16.2). Unless otherwise noted, the following discussion applies equally to financial statements prepared under US GAAP or IFRS.

Shareholders' equity: an introduction

Shareholders' equity consists of two parts:

- contributed capital, and
- earned capital.

Exhibit 16.1 The Coca-Cola Company and subsidiaries consolidated balance sheets

December 31, (in millions except par value)	2009	2008
ASSETS		
CURRENT ASSETS		
Cash, cash equivalents and short-term investments	$9,151	$4,701
Marketable securities	62	278
Trade accounts receivable, less allowances of $55 and $51, respectively	3,758	3,090
Inventories	2,354	2,187
Prepaid expenses and other assets	2,226	1,920
TOTAL CURRENT ASSETS	17,551	12,176
INVESTMENTS		
Equity method investments	6,217	5,316
Other investments, principally bottling companies	538	463
OTHER ASSETS	1,976	1,733
PROPERTY, PLANT AND EQUIPMENT – NET	9,561	8,326
TRADEMARKS WITH INDEFINITE LIVES	6,183	6,059
GOODWILL	4,224	4,029
OTHER INTANGIBLE ASSETS	2,421	2,417
TOTAL ASSETS	$48,671	$40,519
LIABILITIES AND SHAREOWNERS' EQUITY		
CURRENT LIABILITIES		
Accounts payable and accrued expenses	$6,657	$6,205
Loans and notes payable	6,749	6,066
Current maturities of long-term debt	51	465
Accrued income taxes	264	252
TOTAL CURRENT LIABILITIES	13,721	12,988
LONG-TERM DEBT	5,059	2,781
OTHER LIABILITIES	2,965	3,011
DEFERRED INCOME TAXES	1,580	877
THE COCA-COLA COMPANY SHAREOWNERS' EQUITY		
Common stock, $0.25 par value; Authorized – 5,600 shares;		
Issued – 3,520 and 3,519 shares, respectively	880	880
Capital surplus	8,537	7,966
Reinvested earnings	41,537	38,513
Accumulated other comprehensive income (loss)	(757)	(2,674)
Treasury stock, at cost – 1,217 and 1,207 shares, respectively	(25,398)	(24,213)
EQUITY ATTRIBUTABLE TO SHAREOWNERS OF THE COCA-COLA COMPANY	24,799	20,472
EQUITY ATTRIBUTABLE TO NONCONTROLLING INTERESTS	547	390
TOTAL EQUITY	$25,346	$20,862
TOTAL LIABILITIES AND EQUITY	$48,671	$40,519

Exhibit 16.2   The Coca-Cola Company and subsidiaries consolidated statements of shareowners' equity

December 31, (in millions except per share data)	2009	2008	2007
EQUITY ATTRIBUTABLE TO SHAREOWNERS OF THE COCA-COLA COMPANY			
NUMBER OF COMMON SHARES OUTSTANDING			
Balance at beginning of year	$2,312	$2,318	$2,318
Stock issued to employees exercising stock options	—	—	8
Purchases of treasury stock	(26)	(18)	(35)
Treasury stock issued to employees exercising stock options	17	12	23
Treasury stock issued to former shareholders of glaceau	—	—	4
Balance at end of year	2,303	2,312	2,318
COMMON STOCK			
Balance at beginning of year	$880	$880	$878
Stock issued to employees related to stock compensation plans	—	—	2
Balance at end of year	880	880	880
CAPITAL SURPLUS			
Balance at beginning of year	7,966	7,378	5,983
Stock issued to employees related to stock compensation plans	339	324	1,001
Tax (charge) benefit from employees' stock option and restricted stock plans	(6)	(1)	(28)
Stock-based compensation	238	265	309
Stock purchased by former shareholders of glaceau	—	—	113
Balance at end of year	8,537	7,966	7,378
REINVESTED EARNINGS			
Balance at beginning of year	38,513	36,235	33,468
Cumulative effect of the adoption of new accounting guidance	—	(8)	(65)
Net income attributable to shareowners of The Coca-Cola Company	6,824	5,807	5,981
Dividends (per share $1.64, $1.52 and $1.36 in 2009, 2008 and 2007, respectively)	(3,800)	(3,521)	(3,149)
Balance at end of year	41,537	38,513	36,235
ACCUMULATED OTHER COMPREHENSIVE INCOME (LOSS)			
Balance at beginning of year	(2,674)	626	(1,291)
Net foreign currency translation adjustment	1,824	(2,285)	1,575
Net gain (loss) on derivatives	34	1	(64)
Net change in unrealized gain on available-for-sale securities	(52)	(44)	14
Net change in pension liability	111	(972)	392
Net other comprehensive income (loss)	1,917	(3,300)	1,917
Balance at end of year	(757)	(2,674)	626

Exhibit 16.2 Continued

December 31, (in millions except per share data)	2009	2008	2007
TREASURY STOCK			
Balance at beginning of year	(24,213)	(23,375)	(22,118)
Stock issued to employees related to stock compensation plans	333	243	428
Stock purchased by former shareholders of glaceau	—	—	66
Purchases of treasury stock	(1,518)	(1,081)	(1,751)
Balance at end of year	(25,398)	(24,213)	(23,375)
TOTAL EQUITY ATTRIBUTABLE TO SHAREOWNERS **OF THE COCA-COLA COMPANY**	$24,799	$20,472	$21,744
EQUITY ATTRIBUTABLE TO **NONCONTROLLING INTERESTS**			
Balance at beginning of year	$390	$342	$333
Net income attributable to noncontrolling interests	82	67	46
Net foreign currency translation adjustment	49	(25)	1
Dividends paid to noncontrolling interests	(14)	(20)	(23)
Contributions by noncontrolling interests	40	31	41
Disposal of subsidiaries	—	(5)	(56)
TOTAL EQUITY ATTRIBUTABLE **TO NONCONTROLLING INTERESTS**	$547	$390	$342
COMPREHENSIVE INCOME			
Consolidated net income	6,906	5,874	6,027
Consolidated net other comprehensive income (loss)	1,966	(3,325)	1,918
CONSOLIDATED COMPREHENSIVE INCOME	$8,872	$2,549	$7,945

Contributed capital (sometimes called "paid-in" or "share" capital) represents the cumulative cash inflow that a company has received from the sale of various classes of stock, less the cash paid out to repurchase stock. For Coca-Cola, contributed capital equals

$$\text{Common Stock} + \text{Capital Surplus} - \text{Treasury Stock}$$

Common stock is the par value of issued shares, capital surplus is the additional capital raised above par value from the issuance of those shares, and treasury stock is the price paid for shares that were repurchased and still held in corporate treasury (i.e., have not yet been reissued or cancelled). Each of these accounts will be examined in more detail below.

    As presented on Coca-Cola's balance sheet (Exhibit 16.1), at the end of 2009, contributed capital was $880 million + $8537 million − $25398 million, or −$15981 million. The negative figure resulted from Coca-Cola paying more for the shares it bought back than what the company received when the shares were issued.

However, Coca-Cola's total shareholders' equity is strongly positive because of its earned capital. Earned capital represents the cumulative profit that has been retained by the company. For Coca-Cola, earned capital equals

$$\text{Reinvested Earnings} + \text{Accumulated Other Comprehensive Loss}$$

Reinvested earnings, also known as retained earnings, are the cumulative profits of the company that have been retained in the business (i.e., not paid out as dividends). Accumulated other comprehensive loss includes gains and losses that have not yet found their way onto the income statement. Earned capital is increased by profits and decreased by losses and dividend payments.

According to the end-of-2009 balance sheet, Coca-Cola's earned capital was $41 537 million–$757 million, or $40 780 million. Combining this figure with the contributed capital of –$15 981 million yields total equity attributable to shareowners of The Coca-Cola Company of $24 799 million.

One way to view shareholders' equity is that it represents the investment made in the firm by its shareholders. That investment is both direct (contributed capital) and indirect (earned capital). Indirect capital arises from the company earning profits that are not distributed as dividends, and are therefore reinvested in the firm on the shareholders' behalf.

Alternatively, shareholders' equity is known as book value. The term "value" is potentially misleading because the book value of equity is different than its market value. The market value of shares, otherwise known as "market capitalization," is computed by multiplying the number of common shares outstanding by the share price. In the case of Coca-Cola, the difference between its market capitalization and book value is enormous. While book value was $24 799 million at the end of 2009, the market capitalization of the company's shares was $132 billion.

Although the notion of book value might seem to be of no practical use to the financial statement reader, when combined with market value (i.e., stock price) it can offer a profitable stock-picking tool. The idea is that stocks selling for high price-to-book ratios, relative to competitors and other firms, are pricey, and therefore likely to underperform relative to stock market benchmarks in the future. Companies with low ratios, according to this practice, are relative bargains and should therefore outperform market averages. Academic evidence supports this idea. Large portfolios that comprise low price-to-book stocks tend to beat the market, while those that comprise high price-to-book tend to underperform. Coca-Cola's price-to-book ratio was 5X at the end of 2009, well above the market average. The high ratio value can be accounted for mainly by the absence of the company's powerful brands from book value.

More on contributed capital

Companies issue two types of stock: preferred and common. The difference between the two lies in the legal rights and claims conferred upon each class.

Preferred stock

As the term implies, preferred stock has some preference, or priority, over common shares. Specifically, preferred shareholders have priority over common shareholders in the receipt of dividends, and are entitled to receive payment in full if the company liquidates before common shareholders are entitled to any payout. Preferred shares are less risky to the investor than common shares, and therefore carry lower expected returns.

One common feature of preferred stock is a fixed dividend rate. For example, "6% preferred stock, par value $10 per share" pays an annual dividend equal to 6% of par, or $0.60 per share. The fixed dividend is attractive to those who seek stable income from their investments.

"Cumulative dividend preference," another common feature, requires that any dividends on preferred stock not paid in full accumulate over time. In other words, any unpaid dividends accumulated from previous years must be paid in full before any common dividends are paid.

Also, many issues of preferred stock are "convertible." This feature gives the stockholder the right to convert their stock into common shares at a predetermined exchange ratio. The benefit to investors is that they can participate in common-stock price appreciation. If the share price increase is high enough, preferred shareholders profit by converting their preferred shares into common shares.[1]

Common stock

Common shares are the basic voting stock issued by a corporation. Because they carry the company's voting power, it's the common shareholders who we think of when we use the term "owners." Common shareholders are the residual claimants on the firm, a term which means that, in the event of liquidation, all other claimants on the firm must be paid in full (i.e., creditors and preferred shareholders) before common shareholders are entitled to any payment. In fact, one way to define ownership is that it represents a residual claim on the firm's assets.

When discussing share ownership, confusion sometimes arises in distinguishing among authorized, issued, and outstanding shares.

Authorized shares

These are the maximum number of shares in any given class, common or preferred, that a company can issue. This amount is specified in the corporate charter, and is usually shown on the balance sheet. For Coca-Cola, 5.6 billion shares of common stock have been authorized. (The company does not have any preferred stock.) The corporate charter can be amended to increase the authorized share amount; however, shareholder approval is required.

Issued shares

These represent the total number of shares of stock that have been sold or distributed, and not yet retired. As shown on the balance sheet Exhibit 16.1, 3.5 billion of shares of Coca-Cola common stock were issued as of the end of 2009. This figure means that another 2.1 billion shares of common stock could be issued without amending the corporate charter.

Outstanding shares

These refer to the total number of shares owned by shareholders on any particular date. It equals the number of shares issued, less the number of shares in treasury. Treasury shares are those shares that were issued, later purchased by the company, and retained in corporate treasury.[2] (In countries that do not allow for treasury stock, outstanding shares will always equal the number of issued shares.) Coca-Cola discloses on its income statement that the average number of shares outstanding for 2009 was 2.314 billion shares. This figure is important because earnings per share calculations are based on it. The number of shares outstanding at the end of 2009 is shown directly on the balance sheet: 3.520 billion shares issued, less 1.217 billion shares in treasury, or 2.303 billion.

Accounting for stock transactions

In this section we cover the accounting for stock transactions, including stock issuances and stock repurchases.

Issuing stock

The issuance of stock increases both assets and shareholders' equity. But to understand which accounts are affected, the concept of "par value" must be addressed.

Par value is the nominal, or stated, value per share of stock. This amount is specified in the corporate charter, but has little economic meaning. Think of it as a legal figure that appears on a stock certificate, but has no bearing on what the shares are worth, even at the moment of issuance.

The par value of Coca Cola shares, according to the 2009 balance sheet, was $0.25. We'll have more to say about this figure later in the chapter.

Contributed capital also consists of capital surplus. A more common term for this account is "additional paid-in capital (APIC)." APIC is the difference between the price paid by investors when the shares were issued and the par value. For example, if Coca-Cola issues a share of stock for $50, the journal entry would be:

Cash	50.00	
Common stock (par value)		0.25
Additional paid-in capital		49.75

A standard practice in many countries is to combine common stock and additional paid-in capital into a single account, known variously as "share capital," "contributed capital," or "paid-in capital." In such cases, the above example leads to the following entry:

Cash	50.00	
Share capital		50.00

Share repurchases

Companies repurchase their own shares for many reasons. Perhaps the company has surplus cash that cannot be profitably invested. The cash could be returned to investors as dividends, but dividends are often subject to high marginal tax rates. Returning cash to shareholders through buybacks may be more tax efficient.

Another common reason for buybacks is that the repurchased shares can be used for an employee bonus or stock ownership plan. Using share buybacks instead of issuing new shares allows the company to control dilution. If new shares are issued instead, the percentage ownership held by existing owners declines. Shareholders with large blocks might resist such an approach because over time their influence or control over the business may decline. Microsoft is one such example. As employees exercised stock options throughout the 1980s and 1990s, the dilution effect was reduced by granting shares bought in the open market and kept as treasury stock. Although some dilution occurred anyway, this practice has allowed Bill Gates, Steve Ballmer, and other large shareholders to maintain control over the company.

Share buybacks can also be used to adjust a company's capital structure. Because buybacks reduce shareholders' equity, debt/equity ratios increase. In other words, buybacks allow companies to increase their financial leverage without additional borrowing. This approach may be attractive to companies that have surplus cash, but are viewed as underlevered, thus benefiting from a higher debt/equity ratio.

Under US GAAP, when shares are acquired with the intent of retiring or cancelling the shares, the following options are available:

- charge the excess of the cost of treasury stock over its par value entirely to retained earnings;
- allocate the excess between retained earnings and additional paid-in capital (APIC); or
- charge the excess entirely to APIC.

The last of these alternatives is the most common, and is broadly in line with practice under IFRS.

When treasury stock is acquired for purposes other than retirement (i.e., the intent is to hold the shares for an unspecified period), the cost of the acquired stock may be shown separately as a deduction from equity (i.e., as the contra-equity account, treasury stock) or it may be treated in exactly the same way as the retirement of stock (a reduction in par value and APIC). IFRS requires the first of these approaches. The journal entry looks like this:

Treasury stock	XX	
Cash		XX

In effect, a share repurchase has the opposite financial statement effects from a share issuance. Cash is reduced by the price paid for the shares, and shareholders' equity is reduced by the same amount.

Reissuing treasury stock

By keeping repurchased shares in treasury, the company is signaling its intent to reissue the shares in the future. Otherwise, the shares would be retired. When repurchased shares are subsequently reissued, no gain or loss is recognized. Instead, the difference between the proceeds received from the sale and the purchase price of the treasury stock is shown as an increase or decrease to additional paid-in capital.

To illustrate, assume that Coca-Cola repurchases 10 000 shares of its stock at $40 per share. It then reissues the shares on the open market for $45 per share. The journal entry would be:

Cash	450,000	
Treasury stock		400,000
APIC		50,000

Notice that no profit is acknowledged from the transaction, despite reissuance at a price exceeding the cost of the treasury shares. The logic of this treatment is that because profit or gain effectively belongs to shareholders, no profit should be recognized from a company trading stock with its own shareholders. In addition, if gains or losses could be recognized from a company trading in its own shares, managers would possess a powerful tool for profit manipulation. Prohibiting any income statement effects from such transactions removes this avenue for earnings management.

Notice also that the increase in shareholders' equity that arises from the resale of the treasury stock depends entirely on the price paid for the reissued shares. For example, if treasury stock had cost Coca-Cola only $300 000, shareholders' equity would still increase by $450 000. To make up the difference, APIC is now credited for $150 000.

Similarly, if the shares are resold at a price below the cost of the treasury stock, no loss is recognized. Again, the balancing entry is made to APIC. For example, if the shares are resold for $325 000, the journal entry becomes:

Cash	325,000	
APIC	75,000	
Treasury stock		400,000

Earned capital

We now examine the earned capital portion of shareholders' equity. Earned capital represents the cumulative profit that has been retained by the company. For Coca-Cola, it equals the sum of reinvested earnings and accumulated other comprehensive loss. Earned capital is therefore a function of any transaction or circumstance that affects either of those accounts, including:

- net income or loss
- cash dividends
- stock dividends
- any gains or losses that bypass the income statement.

Reinvested earnings, or more commonly "retained earnings," encompasses the first three items on the above list; the final item is captured by accumulated other comprehensive income (or loss).

Retained earnings

Retained earnings are the link between the income statement and the balance sheet. As seen in Table 16.1, the ending retained earnings balance equals the beginning balance, plus the current year's net income (or minus net loss), minus dividends. Coca-Cola pays only cash dividends, but if stock dividends were paid, these too would have to be deducted in order to arrive at the ending balance.

Dividends on common stock

Investors purchase common stock on the expectation of a competitive return. This return can come in two forms: stock price appreciation and dividends.

Some investors prefer to buy stocks that pay little or no dividends because companies that reinvest the majority of their earnings tend to increase their future earnings potential, along with their stock price. Wealthy investors in high tax brackets prefer to receive their return in the form of higher stock prices because capital gains may be taxed at a lower rate than dividend income. Other investors, such as retirees who need a steady income, prefer to receive their return in the form of dividends. Such investors tend to seek out stocks that pay high dividends, such as public utilities (electricity companies, etc.).

One way to determine a company's dividend policy – i.e. is it a "high" or "low" dividend stock? – is to observe its "dividend yield." This ratio measures annual dividend payments as a percentage of the share price:

$$= \frac{\text{Annual Dividends per Share}}{\text{Price per Share}}$$

Coca-Cola's dividend yield, based on 2009 dividends and the end-of-year share price, is 2.88%.

Table 16.1 Retained earnings equation

Beginning retained earnings	**Coca-Cola Company reinvested earnings, 2009**	
+ Earnings (net income)	In millions	
− Distributed earnings (dividends)	Beginning balance	$38,513
= Ending retained earnings	Net income	6,824
	Dividends	(3,800)
	Ending balance	41,537

Another way to describe dividend policy is the dividend payout ratio. This measure expresses dividends as a percentage of net income. 1 – (the dividend payout ratio) measures the portion of net income retained in the business. Another way to look at this ratio is that is shows how well dividend payments are supported by earnings. The higher the payout ratio, the greater the risk that a downturn in profits might force the company to cut its dividend. The ratio is calculated as follows:

$$= \frac{\text{Yearly Dividend per Share}}{\text{Earnings per Share}}$$

or equivalently:

$$= \frac{\text{Dividends}}{\text{Net Income}}$$

Coca-Cola's dividend payout ratio was 55.7% in 2009.

In some countries, such as the US, dividends are usually paid on a quarterly basis. In other countries, semiannual payments are more common. In either case, the common stock investor needs to be aware of three distinct dates: The declaration date, the record date, and the payment date. To illustrate, we will refer to the final quarterly dividend payment made by Coca-Cola in 2009.

Declaration date: 22 October 2009. This is the date on which the board of directors officially approves the dividend. Because the declaration commits the company to transfer assets, a liability (dividends payable) is recognized. Therefore, the following entry is made:

Retained earnings   XX
   Dividends payable   XX

Because dividends represent a distribution of earnings, the retained earnings account is charged when the dividends are declared.

Record date: 1 December 2009. This is the date on which the corporation prepares the list of current stockholders as shown on its records; dividends can be paid only to the shareholders who own stock on that date. No journal entry is required.

Payment date: 15 December 2009. The payment date is the date on which a cash dividend is paid to the shareholders of record. The journal entry is:

Dividends payable   XX
   Cash   XX

Why companies pay dividends is something of a mystery to financial economists, especially when there may be more tax-efficient ways of returning cash to shareholders, such as share buybacks. One popular argument is that dividend policy can be used by managers, in possession of superior information about their businesses, to signal their beliefs about the company's underlying profitability to the investing community.

Also, some companies face "clientele effects" among their shareholders. For example, because public utilities (such as electricity providers and water companies) have steady cash flows and pay high dividends, they tend to attract investors who seek high dividends. Such investors include tax-exempt institutions (which can avoid the high marginal tax rates associated with dividend income) and retirees who rely on dividends to supplement their income.

On the other hand, companies in high-growth industries are less likely to pay dividends and, when they do, the dividend yields are likely to be far lower than those of public utilities. The primary reason for this difference is that high-growth industries, by their nature, yield an abundance of value-creating investment opportunities. Companies will therefore use whatever cash they generate from the business for capital investment, leaving little or no cash available for shareholders. Paying high dividends in high-growth industries may be interpreted by the capital markets as a signal that the company expects growth to significantly decline in the future.

Stock dividends and stock splits

Not all dividends are paid in cash. Some companies pay dividends in the form of additional shares of stock. Additional shares can be distributed in either of two ways: stock dividends and stock splits.

Stock dividends

Stock dividends are treated as a reduction in retained earnings and an increase in contributed capital. The amount by which the relevant accounts are affected depends on the proportion of shares distributed to the total outstanding shares on the issue date. If the proportion is less than 20–25%, the distribution is deemed to be a small stock dividend. Retained earnings are reduced by the market value of the shares distributed, common stock is increased by the number of shares × par value per share, and APIC is increased for the balance. For example, if a company issues a 10% stock dividend when its share price is $30 and 50 million shares of stock are outstanding (par value = $5), the following entry is made:

Retained earnings	150 million	
Common stock		25 million
APIC		125 million

Retained earnings are charged for the market value of the distributed shares (5 million shares, or 10% of the total, × $30); common stock is credited for the par value of the shares (5 million × $5); and APIC is credited for the balance. In effect, the stock dividend gives each shareholder 1 additional share for every 10 shares already owned. Proportional ownership is unchanged.

As the above journal entry shows, one important difference between a stock dividend and a cash dividend is that the former never reduces assets. The balancing entries for the reduction of retained earnings are always other shareholders' equity accounts. For this reason, declaration of a stock dividend does not give rise to a liability. To put it another way, stock dividends merely shift amounts among different shareholders' equity accounts. Assets and liabilities are unaffected.

For large stock dividends, where the proportion of shares distributed is greater than 20–25%, retained earnings are decreased by the par value of the distributed shares. Common stock is increased by the same amount. Because the reduction in retained earnings is based on par value, no entry to APIC is needed. Returning to the above example, if the dividend was 30%, the entry becomes:

Retained earnings	75 million	
Common stock		75 million

The amount is based on the distribution of 15 million shares (30% × 50 million) × the par value of $5.

For both small and large stock dividends, companies are required to adjust shares outstanding for all prior periods for which earnings per share (EPS) are reported in the financial statements. The reasoning is that a stock dividend has no effect on the ownership percentage of each shareholder. To show a dilution, or reduction, in EPS would wrongly suggest a decline in profitability when the decline in EPS is due entirely to an increase in shares outstanding.

In any case, because the aggregate value of outstanding shares does not change, but the number of shares increases, a stock dividend should, in theory, result in a lower share price proportionate to the size of the dividend.

Stock splits

Stock splits are proportionate distributions of shares and, therefore, similar in substance to stock dividends. But unlike stock dividends, there are no financial statement effects. Retained earnings and contributed capital accounts, such as common stock and APIC, are unaffected. Confusion arises, however, because most stock splits can be viewed as large stock dividends. The distinction that separates a large stock dividend and a stock split is a subtle one, depending largely on local corporate law for the precise treatment.

The most common stock split is 2-for-1, meaning that the number of shares held by every shareholder is automatically and instantaneously doubled. For example, if a shareholder held 100 shares before the split, that investor now holds 200 shares.

Although stock splits are not considered monetary transactions, and therefore no accounting entries are expected, some jurisdictions require a proportionate adjustment to par value. For example, if par value is $5 before a 2-for-1 split, par value becomes $2.50 after the split. This rule explains why Coca-Cola's par value is only $0.25. Many years ago, its par value was far higher. But a series of stock splits over the course of many years has gradually reduced par value. For example, in the early 1990s, par value was $1, but since then Coca-Cola has had two 2-for-1 stock splits. The first of these splits reduced par value to $0.50, the second to $0.25.

Just as companies can use stock splits to reduce their share price, a reverse stock split can be used to increase it. For example, instead of, say, a 2-for-1 stock split, a company might implement a 1-for-2 reserve split. In this case, the number of shares is halved. Share price should increase proportionately, although it may not because reverse splits are often stigmatized. For example, many investors, including large mutual funds, have rules against purchasing a stock whose price is below some minimum, perhaps $5. If a company's stock is selling for $3 per share, a 1-for-2 split should lift the price above the minimum. In extreme cases, a company's share price may have dropped so low that it is in danger of being delisted from its stock exchange. This fate befell many dot-com start-ups after the boom of the late 1990s. In short, reverse stocks splits should have the short-term effect of boosting share price, but investors are rarely fooled by the gesture, especially when undertaken as an act of desperation.

However, a reverse stock split can be useful as a tactic to reduce the number of shareholders. For example, in a 1-for-100 reverse split any investor holding fewer than 100 shares receives a cash payment and no shares of stock. These investors are no longer shareholders of record. Why would a company be interested in reducing the number of shareholders on its rolls? In most jurisdictions, if the resulting number of shareholders drops below a specific threshold, the company is placed into a different, less costly, regulatory category.

Accumulated other comprehensive income

Comprehensive income is a measure of profit, but more inclusive than that of net income. It includes all changes in shareholders' equity that occur during a period except those resulting from contributions by, and distributions to, owners. Comprehensive income includes net income, but also gains and losses that net income excludes, such as:

Unrealized gains and losses on available-for-sale (AFS) securities;
Changes in fair value for certain derivative instruments;
Foreign currency translation adjustments.

Notice that the above items result from changes in market prices and foreign currency exchange rates, factors normally viewed as beyond the control of management. For this reason, some analysts consider net income to be a measure of management's performance, while comprehensive income is a measure of company performance.

"Other comprehensive income" is the term given to the above gains and losses; that is, the elements of comprehensive income that bypass net income and are therefore not included in retained earnings. The term "accumulated" implies that these gains and losses are carried forward from one year to the next, until they are realized (and thus become part of net income and ultimately, retained earnings).

For 2009, Coca-Cola reported net other comprehensive income of $1917 million. The consolidated statements of shareowners' equity (Exhibit 16.2) provides a detailed breakdown for this figure:

- a beginning balance of −$2674 million (which means that Coca-Cola had an accumulated other comprehensive *loss*);

- $1824 million of net gains from foreign currency translation (converting financial statements of foreign subsidiaries into the US dollar);
- $34 million of net gains from derivatives (options, futures, swaps, etc., used to hedge commodity price, interest rate, and foreign exchange risk);
- −$52 million from a net change (loss) in unrealized gain on available-for-sale securities (changes in fair value on certain stocks and bonds); and
- $111 million from a net change in pension liability (a US GAAP item that will soon disappear as a result of a recent change in accounting rules).

Convertible bonds

Convertible bonds allow their owner either to hold the security as a bond or to convert the security into shares of common stock. Under IFRS "split accounting" is used, whereby the proceeds of issuing debt are allocated between the two components:

- the equity conversion rights (recognized in equity); and
- the liability, recognized at fair value calculated by discounting at a market rate for non-convertible debt (recognized in liabilities).

On the other hand, under US GAAP, most forms of convertible debt are treated as a single unit and recorded as a liability; no recognition is given to the equity component. However, complex convertibles may require the recognition of the equity component as a derivative.

To illustrate the accounting for convertible bonds, assume that a company plans to issue $100 000 in bonds (in increments of $1000), paying a coupon rate of 10% (5% paid semiannually) over a 10-year period. The prevailing interest rate for bonds of that risk is 14%. Assume that the company wants to issue the bonds at par (i.e., $100 000), but without having to pay more than a 10% coupon rate. To lower the coupon rate and still satisfy the investor seeking an expected return of 14%, the firm can issue convertible bonds. Assume that each bond ($1000 par value) grants the holder the right to convert the bond into 50 shares of the company's common stock. (Holders in aggregate can convert the entire bond issue into 5000 shares.) Assuming a par value of $0.25, US GAAP accounting requires the following entry:

Cash	100,000	
Bonds payable		100,000

This entry effectively treats convertible bonds just like ordinary, nonconvertible bonds, ignoring the value of the conversion feature.

In contrast, IFRS allocates a portion of the issue price to the conversion feature. Assume that 10%, 10-year semiannual nonconvertible coupon bonds are sold for 79% of par when the market borrowing rate is 14%. Thus, if the firm can issue 10% convertible bonds at par, the conversion feature must be worth 21% of par. In effect, investors have paid 21% of the proceeds from the bond issue as a capital contribution, that is, for the right to acquire common stock later. The entry would be as follows:

Cash	100,000	
Bonds payable		79,000
Additional paid-in capital		21,000

The above entry requires a credible estimate of the proceeds of an issue of nonconvertible bonds with other features similar to the convertible bonds. Because auditors often believe that they are unable to estimate this information with reasonable objectivity, US GAAP does not allow it.

The usual entry to record the conversion of bonds into shares ignores current market prices in the interest of simplicity and merely shows the swap of shares for bonds at their book value. For example, assume that the common stock of the above company increases to $30 a share, so that the holder of one $1000 bond, convertible into 50 shares, can convert it into shares with a market value of $1500. If holders convert the entire bond issue into common shares at this time, the following journal entry is made:

Convertible bonds payable	100,000	
Common shares ($0.25 par)		1,250
Additional paid-in capital		98,750

An allowable alternative treatment recognizes that market prices provide information useful in quantifying the value of the shares issued. Under this alternative, with a $30 per share market price and $150 000 of fair value for the 5000 shares issued on conversion, the journal entry would be:

Convertible bonds payable	100,000	
Loss on conversion of bonds	50,000	
Common shares ($0.25 par)		1,250
Additional paid-in capital		148,750

The loss on conversion is an income statement account. However, despite the loss, the alternative approach results in the same total shareholders' equity as the previous approach. Lower retained earnings from the loss on conversion are offset by higher contributed capital.

The statement of shareholders' equity

All changes to equity accounts are summarized in the consolidated statements of shareholders' equity (Exhibit 16.2). Officially, this statement is given the same status as the other principal financial statements: the balance sheet, the income statement, and the statement of cash flows. However, most analysts view it more like a supporting schedule that helps the reader to understand the changes that have occurred in equity accounts over the past three years.

A review of Coca-Cola's statements of shareowners' equity reveals the following for 2009:

- Shareholders' equity increased by $6 million from the tax benefits earned when the employee stock options were exercised. Many countries, the US among them, grant companies a deduction equal to the difference between the market price of the stock on the exercise date and the strike price of the options. In other words, the extent to which the options are "in-the-money" when exercised is considered a tax-deductible compensation expense. But treating the tax benefit as a reduction in tax expense increases net income. Such treatment would violate the principle that companies should not recognize gains or losses from trading (i.e., issuing or buying back) their own shares. Therefore, the tax benefits are added to contributed capital instead (usually additional paid-in capital).
- Stock-based compensation, mainly in the form of additional option grants, increased shareholders' equity by $238 million. When companies issue options to employees, the fair value of those options is recognized as an expense as the options vest.[3] The balancing entry is to an equity account (usually additional paid-in capital, as it was in Coca-Cola's case).
- Net income increased shareholders' equity by $6824 million.
- Dividend payments decreased shareholders' equity by $3800 million.
- Other comprehensive loss (gains and losses not included in net income) increased shareholders' equity by $1917 million.
- Purchases of treasury stock decreased shareholders' equity by $1518 million.

When these (and a few other minor) changes are aggregated, the beginning and ending balances in shareholders' equity ($20 472 million and $24 799 million, respectively) are reconciled.

IFRS companies have the option of providing an alternative to the statement of shareholders' equity. Called the "statement of recognized gains and losses," it includes many of the same items, but excludes transactions with owners (such as new share issues and share buybacks). Any items excluded from the statement must be described in the notes to the financial statements.

Key lessons from the chapter

- The shareholders' equity section of the balance sheet consists of two parts: contributed capital and retained earnings.
- Contributed capital represents the cumulative investment that a company has received from the sale of various classes of shares, less the cash paid for share buybacks.
- Retained earnings are the cumulative profits of the company that have been retained in the business rather than paid out in dividends.
- Shareholders' equity is also called the "book value of equity."
- Companies issue two broad classes of shares: preferred and common. The difference between the two lies in the legal rights and claims conferred upon each class.

- Common shareholders are the residual claimants of the firm, which means that, in the event of liquidation, all other claimants on the firm must be paid in full before common shareholders are entitled to any payment.
- Common stock investors need to be aware of three distinct dividend dates: the declaration date, the record date, and the payment date.
- Comprehensive income includes net income, but also items excluded from net income but which affect shareholders' equity, such as unrealized gains and losses on available-for-sale securities, changes in the fair value of certain derivative instruments, and some foreign currency translation adjustments. The concept emerged, in part, to highlight gains and losses that, for whatever reason, bypass the income statement and therefore are not included in net income.
- Convertible bonds allow their owners to either hold the security as a bond or convert the security into shares of common stock. Under IFRS "split accounting" is used, whereby the proceeds from the issuance of convertible debt are allocated between the equity conversion rights (recognized in equity) and the liability.

Key terms and concepts from the chapter

Contributed capital	Accumulated other	Date of declaration
Earned capital	comprehensive	Date of record
Preferred stock	income	Date of payment
Common stock	Authorized shares	Dividend yield ratio
Treasury stock	Issued shares	Dividend payout ratio
	Outstanding shares	Stock splits

Questions

1. What is a convertible bond?

2. What are the advantages of a convertible bond from the standpoint of the bondholders and the issuing corporation?

3. Describe the accounting for share buybacks.

4. How is the reissuance of repurchased shares accounted for? What if the price paid for repurchased shares exceeds their cost. What if the price paid is below cost?

5. What is a stock split, and what motive might a company have for doing it?

6. What effect does a stock split have on the balance sheet?

7. What is a stock dividend and what effect does it have on the balance sheet and income statement?

8. A company issues equity for $15 a share. The stated, or par, value of those shares is $1. Give the required journal entry for a typical American company and for a typical European company.

Problems

16.1   Effect of selected transactions on net income and shareholders' equity

	Net Income	Retained earnings	Total shareholders' equity
a. A stock dividend is declared and paid			
b. Merchandise is purchased on credit			
c. Marketable securities are sold above cost			
d. Accounts receivable are collected			
e. A cash dividend is declared and paid			
f. Treasury stock is purchased and recorded at cost			
g. Treasury stock is sold above cost			
h. Common stock is sold			
i. A machine is sold for less than book value			
j. Bonds are converted into common stock			

Required

Indicate the effects of the above transactions on net income, retained earnings, and total shareholders' equity. Use + to indicate an increase and – to indicate a decrease, and 0 to indicate no effect.

16.2   Share buybacks

The following note comes from the 2007 annual report for The Walt Disney Company:

> As of the filing date of this report, the Board of Directors had not yet declared a dividend related to fiscal 2007. The Company paid a $637 million dividend ($0.31 per share) during the second quarter of fiscal 2007 related to fiscal 2006.
>
> During fiscal 2007, the Company repurchased 202 million shares of Disney common stock for $6.9 billion. During fiscal 2006, the Company repurchased 243 million shares of Disney common stock for $6.9 billion. On May 1, 2007, the Board of Directors of the Company increased the share repurchase authorization to a total of 400 million shares. As of September 29, 2007, the Company had remaining authorization in place to repurchase approximately 323 million additional shares. The repurchase program does not have an expiration date.
>
> The par value of the Company's outstanding common stock totaled approximately $26 million.

Required

(a) What reasons can you give for why Disney bought back so many of its shares (a total of nearly $14 billion in 2006 and 2007 combined)?
(b) Disney's normal policy regarding buybacks is to retain the shares in treasury (instead of cancelling them). Why is treasury stock a contra-equity account and not an asset?
(c) Based on the above note, what do you think must have happened to Disney's share price from 2006 to 2007? Did it go up, go down, or stay the same?

16.3   The financial statement effects of dividend payments and buybacks

The following note is taken from The Walt Disney Company's 2004 Annual Report:

> The Company declared an annual dividend of $0.24 per share on December 1, 2004 related to fiscal 2004. The dividend is payable on January 6, 2005 to shareholders of record on December 10, 2004. The Company paid a $430 million dividend ($0.21 per share) during the first quarter of fiscal 2004.
>
> During the fourth quarter of fiscal 2004, the Company repurchased 14.9 million shares of Disney common stock for approximately $335 million. As of September 30, 2004, the Company had authorization in place to repurchase approximately 315 million additional shares.

Based on the above note, answer the following:

(a) Explain what would be recorded on each of the dates relating to the $0.24/share dividend (i.e., provide the necessary journal entries).

(b) How would the $430 million dividend payment affect each of the three principal financial statements?

(c) How would the $335 million repurchase of Disney common stock affect each of the three principal financial statements?

16.4 The accounting and economic consequences of stock splits and stock dividends

The following note is taken from the 2005 Annual Report of eBay:

> In January 2005, our Board of Directors approved a two-for-one split of our shares of common stock to be issued in the form of a stock dividend. As a result of the stock split, our stockholders received one additional share of our common stock for each share of common stock held of record on January 31, 2005. The additional shares of our common stock were distributed on February 16, 2005. All share and per share amounts in these consolidated financial statements and related notes have been retroactively adjusted to reflect this and all prior stock splits for all periods presented.

Required

(a) What was the impact of the stock split on each of the three principal financial statements?

(b) What reasons can you give for eBay to split its stock?

(c) The note says that the stock split was issued in the form of a stock dividend. The implication is that stock splits and stock dividends are equivalent. Is this true?

Case studies

16.1 Stock options, stock dividends, and stock splits

Diodes Inc. is a manufacturer and supplier of semiconductor products, primarily to the communications, computing, industrial, consumer electronics, and automotive markets. The company is headquartered in southern California, but most of its production facilities are in Asia (China, Taiwan, and Hong Kong). Revenues and net income in 2004 were $185.7 million and $25.6 million, respectively.

In 2004, employees exercised stock options on 1 135 982 shares, with a par value of 66⅔ cents per share. The average exercise price was $5. In addition, Diodes received a tax benefit from the exercise of the stock options of $8 514 000. The tax benefit resulted from a US tax law that gives companies a tax deduction equal to the difference between the market price of their stock and the exercise price of the stock options on the date the options are exercised. The tax benefit reflects this difference, multiplied by the company's marginal tax rate. Diodes' accounting policy, in accordance with US GAAP, is to lump together the tax benefit and the cash proceeds received from the employees who exercise their options.

In November 2005, Diodes declared a 50% stock dividend, payable on 30 November 2005, to stockholders of record on 18 November 2005. Under the terms of the stock dividend, Diodes' stockholders received one additional share for every two shares held on the record date. The company expected the number of outstanding shares of common stock after the dividend to increase from 16.8 million to 25.2 million shares. The par value of the company's stock was not affected by the dividend and remained at 66⅔ cents per share. At the end of November 2005, Diodes' share price was $38.40.

Required

(a) Why do companies issue stock options to employees? What are the potential drawbacks? Why not just issue shares of stock instead of stock options?

(b) Why is the average exercise price of the stock options so low relative to the current share price?

(c) Give the summary journal entry to record the exercise of stock options in 2004.

(d) What's the difference between a stock dividend and a stock split? Why do companies issue stock dividends? What motive might they have for a stock split?

(e) Given the journal entry to record Diodes' stock dividends, how would the accounting change if the transaction was considered a stock split?

16.2 Share buybacks: economic rationale and financial reporting effects

Groupe Danone is the world's #1 producer of fresh dairy products. The company is also among the world leaders in bottled water and several other food and beverage categories. Based in France, its net revenues in 2004 were €13.7 billion.

In 2004, the following transactions affecting shareholders' equity took place:

- Dividends of €308 million were declared and paid.
- 2.6 million shares of common stock were bought back at an average price of €60.40. The shares were cancelled immediately after purchase.
- 750 000 shares of common stock (par value = €0.50) were reissued from corporate treasury at an average price of €51. The average price paid by Danone for the reissued shares was €74.67.

Required

1. Why do companies buy back their own shares?
2. Why does Danone keep some of the repurchased shares in corporate treasury, and not cancel them?
3. Give the summary journal entries to record all of the above events.

16.3 The accounting for convertible bonds

Milacron Inc. is a leading supplier of plastics-processing technologies and industrial fluids. Headquartered in Cincinnati, Ohio, the company employs 3500 people and operates major manufacturing facilities in North America, Europe, and Asia. Milacron's financial performance has been poor in recent years, including net losses of $191.1 million in 2003 (on sales of $740 million).

In March 2004, Milacron announced the issuance of bonds to Glencore Finance AG and Mizuho International. The proceeds were used to repay outstanding notes that were about to come due. Glencore and Mizuho purchased $100 million of debt in total, $30 million of which would be convertible into Milacron common stock (par value = $1) at the option of the holders.

Required

1. Why would Milacron use a "hybrid" instrument like convertible bonds, instead of issuing debt and equity securities separately?
2. Milacron raised $30 million from the issuance of the convertible bonds. Assume that a similar straight bond (a nonconvertible bond with the same coupon payments and maturity value) would have raised $26 million. Prepare the journal entry to record the issuance of the convertible bonds in accordance with IFRS.
3. Assume that early in 2005, Glencore and Mizuho exercised their option and converted the bonds into 9 million shares of Milacron common stock. The stock price on the date of the conversion was $3.75, and the net book value of bonds payable was $24 million. Prepare the journal entry to record the conversion of Milacron bonds into common stock, assuming that no gain or loss is recognized on the transaction.

16.4 Why do companies buy back their own shares?
The case of the Scomi Group

The Scomi Group is an investment holding company, based in Malaysia, with three principal subsidiaries involved in oil and natural gas support services. The group's products and services include:

- drilling fluids and related engineering services for drilling operations;
- drilling waste management equipment;
- production and industrial chemicals;
- marine vessel transportation;
- machine shops; and
- distribution.

Revenues and net income for 2004 were RM 590 million and RM 69 million, respectively.* The group's shares are traded on the Kuala Lumpur stock exchange (KLSE).

In May 2005, the Board of Directors proposed a share buyback program to the group's shareholders. The board sought permission to repurchase shares representing up to 10% of the Scomi Group's issued and paid-up capital from the open market. At the discretion of the board, any repurchased shares would either be cancelled or retained in treasury for later distribution.

In the formal proposal submitted to shareholders, the board cited the following reasons for the share buyback program:

1. It would enable the company to utilize surplus financial resources to purchase Scomi shares at prices which are viewed as favorable as well as help stabilize the supply and demand of Scomi shares traded on the KLSE, thereby supporting its fundamental value.
2. If the purchased shares are held in corporate treasury, the shares may potentially be resold on the KLSE at a higher price, enabling Scomi to realize a potential gain without affecting its total share capital.
3. Purchased shares retained in treasury may also be distributed to shareholders as dividends, which would serve to reward the shareholders of Scomi.
4. Shareholders may enjoy an increase in the value of their investment in Scomi due to the increase in net earnings per share resulting from the reduction in the number of outstanding shares.

Required

Which of the rationales offered in the proposal are sensible (i.e., value-enhancing) reasons for repurchasing shares and which are not? Defend your answers.

---

*RM = Malaysian ringgit; RM 3.80 = 1 US$.

Notes

1. In some cases, the issuing company can force conversion.
2. Some countries do not allow firms to hold repurchased shares in treasury. Instead, the shares must be cancelled.
3. The term "vested" refers to full ownership rights. Once the options are vested, the employee has the right to exercise the option. In many companies, if employees leave before the end of the vesting period, all rights to the options are lost.

CHAPTER 17

Marketable Securities and Investments

Companies often purchase the shares of other companies. In this chapter we discuss the accounting for these investments. Unless otherwise stated, the discussion applies equally to US GAAP and International Financial Reporting Standards (IFRS). Also, we focus on equity investments, although brief mention is made of debt instruments. To illustrate the concepts, we draw on the financial statements of Microsoft, the US-based software giant.

Introduction

When companies own shares in other businesses, the accounting follows one of three methods, depending on the degree of influence or control that the investor exerts over the other company. Three levels of influence/control are possible:

- **Passive**. In this case, the investor is assumed to exert no influence over the investee company. Generally, passive investment is assumed when the investor owns less than 20% of the outstanding voting shares of the investee. All such investments are accounted for using either the "market method" or the "cost method."
- **Significant influence**. Here, the investor is assumed to own enough of the investee (usually called an "affiliate" or "associate" company) to exert significant influence over operating

activities and dividend policy. Generally, such influence is assumed when the investor owns between 20 and 50% of the affiliate's outstanding voting shares. In such cases, the "equity method" of accounting must be used.

- **Control**. Control is presumed if the investor owns more than 50% of the outstanding voting shares of the investee. If control is established, the proper accounting treatment is "consolidation." In other words, the accounts of the investee (or, in this case, the subsidiary) are consolidated or combined with those of the parent company and other subsidiaries to produce the group accounts.

In this chapter we deal primarily with passive and equity-method investments, although consolidation is addressed in a brief section at the end. As we will see below, there are two basic issues that determine the accounting for equity investments: (1) how investment income is recognized, and (2) the carrying value of the investment on the balance sheet.

Investments and marketable securities at Microsoft

Before introducing the market, cost, and equity methods, consider the asset section of Microsoft's balance sheet from fiscal years 2009 and 2010 shown in Table 17.1.

Investments are shown in several accounts: cash and equivalents, short-term investments, and equity and other investments. Cash and equivalents comprise mainly demand deposits

Table 17.1   Microsoft's assets from fiscal years 2009 and 2010 (in millions, US$)

	2009/06/30	2010/06/30
Assets		
Current assets		
Cash and equivalents	$6,076	$5,505
Short-term investments	**25,371**	**31,283**
Total cash and short-term investments	**31,447**	**36,788**
Accounts receivable, net	11,192	13,014
Inventories	717	740
Deferred income taxes	2,213	2,184
Other	3,711	2,950
Total current assets	49,280	55,676
Property and equipment, net	7,535	7,630
Equity and other investments	**4,933**	**7,754**
Goodwill	12,503	12,394
Intangible assets, net	1,759	1,158
Deferred income taxes	279	0
Other long-term assets	1,599	1,501
Total assets	$77,888	$86,113

(i.e., checking accounts and the like) and low-risk, highly liquid financial instruments such as short-term government bonds. Short-term investments (sometimes called "marketable securities") contain mostly fixed-income securities, including longer-term government bonds. Notice that in Microsoft's case, the amounts are huge ($25.371 billion for 2009 and $31.283 billion for 2010).

Equity and other investments ($4.933 billion for 2009 and $7.754 billion for 2010) comprise long-term investments, both in the shares of other companies and in debt instruments that are not classified as current. The term "equity" implies that a significant portion of the total covers investments that are accounted for under the equity method, meaning that Microsoft has a large minority stake.

Investments in subsidiaries (i.e., those companies that Microsoft controls) are consolidated across all accounts, and are therefore reflected in the consolidated amounts appearing on the above balance sheet. For example, the accounts receivable balance of each subsidiary is added to that of the parent to produce the consolidated balance (after eliminating any transactions among the subsidiaries and the parent). Likewise for inventories, property and equipment, and any other balance sheet account.

The market and cost methods

The market and cost methods are used to account for passive investments. The term "passive" implies no influence or control over the affairs of the investee. The market method is used for passive investments that have an active market with published prices. In such cases, the investment is reported on the balance sheet at market (or fair) value as of the balance sheet date.

In contrast, *non*marketable equity investments are accounted for under the cost method.[1] The primary difference between the cost and market methods is that under the former historical cost is used as the balance sheet value, not market value, unless the investment is significantly and permanently impaired (in which case an impairment loss is recognized and the investment account is written down).

Debt securities, such as corporate and government bonds, are also reported under the cost method as long as management intends to hold the securities to maturity. Even though market prices for such instruments might be observable, changes in market value are ignored. The logic for this treatment is that because of management's intent, the full face value of the instrument will be received. Therefore, short-term fluctuations in market price are not relevant.[2] The official term for such instruments is "held-to-maturity" investments. Because equity investments do not mature, they are never eligible for this treatment.

Despite the difference in balance sheet accounting, the market and cost methods treat dividend payments in the same manner. For all passive investments, dividend payments are reported as "dividend income" on the income statement. (Similarly, any interest received on debt securities, whether accounted for under the cost or market method, is reported in current income.)

For cost-method investments, no other income statement effects are possible except in the case of impairment (see above) or if the shares are sold or otherwise disposed of. In the latter case, the difference between the proceeds from the sale and the book value of the investment is treated as a realized gain or loss. For example, if Microsoft pays $50 million for the shares of another company, a subsequent sale of those shares for $60 million results in the following journal entry:

Cash	$60 million	
Investments		$50 million
Gain on sale		$10 million

where "gain on sale" is an income statement account.

However, if an investment is marked-to-market at the end of each period (i.e., the shares are accounted for under the market method), other income statement effects are possible, even while the shares are still owned. Returning to the above example, assume that the shares acquired by Microsoft are publicly traded. If the value of the shares on the balance sheet date is $60 million, Microsoft reports that amount on the balance sheet. How Microsoft treats the $10 million unrealized (i.e., unsold) holding gain depends on whether the investment is designated as:

- *available-for-sale* (AFS), or as
- a *trading* security.

AFS securities are marked-to-market investments that management intends to hold for dividend income and capital gains, although the shares might be sold if the price was attractive enough or the company was strapped for cash. Trading securities are those that management intends to actively buy and sell for short-term trading profit. Frequent buying and selling usually indicate a trading security.

For most companies AFS securities are far more common than trading investments. In fact, many businesses, even large ones, do not have trading securities. There are two major reasons for this:

- First, short-term trading in securities is not considered a core competency outside the financial services sector and, therefore, is an activity largely avoided by other businesses.
- Second, AFS is a default category. Any investment that cannot be classified as either trading or held-to-maturity must, by default, be classified as AFS.

The distinction between AFS and trading is an important one because it determines how the unrealized holding gain or loss is treated. In the case of the former, any changes in market value recognized at the end of the accounting period are reported directly in the balance sheet through "other comprehensive income" (OCI), a shareholders' equity account. Gains and losses in market value are recognized in the income statement only when securities are sold. In other words, realized gains and losses appear on the income statement, but unrealized gains and losses do not.

In contrast, changes in market value for trading securities are reported in the income statement. This difference in treatment implies that the classification of passive equity investments as trading securities can have a sizable impact on the volatility of earnings. Any change in market value is shown in the income statement, even if the gain or loss is unrealized. In general, the greater the proportion of investments classified as trading, the greater the volatility of earnings.

In the above example, if shares costing $50 million have a market value of $60 million on the balance sheet date, the following entry would be required if the investment is classified as AFS:

Investments	$10 million	
OCI		$10 million

where OCI is a shareholders' equity account.

Although we ignored taxes in this example, the increase to OCI is made net of expected tax effects. As the investment is sold, impaired, or otherwise disposed of, the amount in OCI is transferred to the income statement.

If the investment is classified as a trading security, the journal entry would be:

Investments	$10 million	
Unrealized gain		$10 million

where unrealized gain is reported on the income statement.

Under both the market method and the cost method, transaction costs are considered part of the acquisition cost of the investment. For example, if a firm acquires shares in another company for $150 000, incurring $5000 in brokers' commissions, the acquisition cost of the investment is the total cost, $155 000.

We now address the issue of how to determine fair values. Although our discussion focuses on marketable securities, the principles apply equally to any assets or liabilities that are reported at fair value, including property, plant, and equipment.

The fair value hierarchy

Under US GAAP (FAS 157), fair value is defined as "the price that would be received to sell an asset or paid to transfer a liability in an orderly transaction between market participants at the measurement date." Fair value is defined similarly under IFRS as the amount for which an asset could be exchanged, or a liability settled, between knowledgeable, willing parties, in an arm's length transaction. The problem, of course, is determining price, especially when easily observable data are not available.[3] For this reason, US GAAP and IFRS rely on a three-level fair value hierarchy. The nature of the hierarchy, in which the first two levels result in "mark-to-market" accounting, is that it prioritizes observable inputs over unobservable inputs.

A Level 1 fair value is one where an active market exists for identical assets. For example, an equity investment in a company traded on the New York Stock Exchange would fall into this category, as would US treasuries or UK gilts. If such inputs are available, they must be used. If

Level 1 data are unavailable the next step is to seek out Level 2 inputs. Here, the asset in question may be traded, and therefore prices are observable, but the market is inactive with only sporadic quotes. Or, similar assets are traded in an active market, but the assets are not identical to the ones being valued. Many real estate assets would fall into this category. An active and liquid market may exist, especially in large commercial centers, but each parcel of real estate is unique.

If Level 2 inputs are unavailable, the entity must resort to the bottom tier, Level 3. At this point, the process of determining fair value is no longer considered "mark to market," because there is no market, and therefore no observable market prices. Because Level 3 inputs are unobservable, this approach is often referred to as "mark to model" in the sense that a valuation model of some sort is required. The model can be based on discounted cash flows, multiples (e.g., price/earnings or price/sales ratios), replacement cost, or any other approach acceptable to the firm's auditors. Simply put, Level 3 fair values are based not on a market price but rather a prediction of what the market price would be if a market existed. Understandably, much of the controversy and debate in fair value accounting centers on this issue.[4]

To assist the financial statement reader in the analysis and interpretation of fair value assessments, the FASB and the IASB recently issued joint guidelines on fair value disclosures. These requirements include the following:

- Companies must disclose the amounts of, and reasons for, significant transfers between Level 1 and Level 2, as well as those into and out of Level 3. Transfers into a level must be disclosed separately from transfers out of the level.
- For Level 2 and Level 3 measurements, a company must disclose information about inputs and valuation techniques used in both recurring and nonrecurring fair value measurements. If a valuation technique changes, the company must disclose the change and the reason for it.
- Activity in Level 3 fair value measurements must be reconciled from the beginning of the period to the end. Information should be presented separately for significant purchases, sales, issuances, and settlements on a gross basis. This means that the changes that took place during the year cannot be lumped together in one number.
- Fair value measurement disclosures must be presented by class of assets and liabilities, including their classification in the fair value hierarchy. The practical implication of this requirement is that the financial statement reader should expect to see a detailed breakdown of all fair value assets and liabilities according to whether their measurements were determined using Level 1, Level 2, or Level 3 inputs.

Equity method

Investments with significant influence must be accounted for using the equity method. Significant influence is assumed when the investor holds 20% or more of the voting power (directly or through subsidiaries).

However, use of the equity method is possible in cases where the holding is less than 20% if significant influence can be clearly demonstrated. The existence of significant influence by an investor is usually evidenced in one or more of the following ways:

- representation on the board of directors of the investee;
- participation in the policy-making process;
- material transactions between the investor and the investee;
- exchanges of key managerial personnel; or
- the provision of essential technical information.

The main features of the equity method are as follows:

- Investments are initially recorded at acquisition cost.
- Dividends are not treated as income, as they are under the cost and market methods. Instead, dividends are treated as a recovery of the investment and, therefore, reduce the balance in the investment account.
- The investor reports income or loss equal to its percentage ownership share of the affiliate. For example, if the affiliate reports net income of $20 million, and the investor owns 25% of the affiliate's shares, it reports $5 million of equity income on its own income statement. A loss of $20 million by the affiliate results in a $5 million equity loss on the income statement of the investor.
- The investment is not marked to market as it would be under the market method.

The equity method came into existence mainly to counter a potential form of manipulation under the cost method.[5] The concern is that a company with significant influence can use it to affect the affiliate's dividend policy. For example, if the investor needs a boost in current earnings to achieve profit growth targets, it could simply impose higher dividend payouts on the affiliate. Because dividends are treated as income under the cost (and market) methods, the investor would report higher earnings. The equity method removes this potential for earnings management by making the recognition of income independent of dividend policy. The amount of income reported by the investor is based entirely on the percentage of total equity owned and by the amount of net income or loss. Dividend policy has no influence on income because dividends are treated as returns, or recoveries, of the investor's stake in the affiliate.

Of course, as so often happens in financial reporting, where one loophole is closed, another is opened. Investors have sometimes manipulated their ownership percentages in other companies depending on whether the affiliates are reporting profits or losses. For example, in the early 1990s, when the UK was in the midst of a recession, several British companies brought the ownership interests in their investee companies just below the 20% threshold to avoid having to report their share of losses being reported by these companies. The lesson for analysts is clear: year-on-year changes in ownership interests, and their effects on the financial statements, should be closely monitored. It should also be noted that manipulation can occur at the other end of the ownership spectrum. For example, companies can choose to consolidate an affiliate's financial statements, or not, depending on whether the ownership interest is just above or just below the 50% threshold. To illustrate, Douglas Ivester, then the chief financial officer and later the CEO of Coca-Cola, created Coca-Cola Enterprises (CCE), a bottling giant, by consolidating several smaller, independent bottlers. By ensuring ownership was below 50%, or what Ivester called "the 49% solution," Coca-Cola did not have to consolidate the billions in debt held by the bottler. But while the parent did not consolidate, it certainly exercised the prerogatives of a full owner, at least in CCE's early days. Ivester had himself appointed chairman, while several other Coca-Cola veterans served on the board. There was little doubt as to who was really in charge.[6]

To illustrate how the equity method works, assume that Microsoft purchases a 30% interest in a supplier, ABC Software, paying $50 million in cash.[7] Microsoft records the purchase as follows:

Equity investments	$50 million	
Cash		$50 million

At the end of the year, ABC Software reports $20 million in net income and pays $10 million in cash dividends. To report its share of net income, Microsoft makes the following entry:

Equity investments	$6 million	
Equity income		$6 million

This entry records Microsoft's 30% share in the profits of ABC Software. The equity income account appears on the current period's income statement and will therefore boost Microsoft's earnings.

Microsoft also receives a dividend of $3 million, equal to 30% of the total dividends paid by ABC Software. The journal entry is:

Cash	$3 million	
Equity investments		$3 million

Notice that the dividend reduces the carrying value of the investment on Microsoft's balance sheet. Notice, too, that the dividend itself has no bearing on Microsoft's earnings for the year.

At the end of the first year, the balance sheet total for the investment in ABC Software equals the acquisition cost ($50 million), plus equity income ($6 million), minus dividends ($3 million), for a total of $53 million. This figure is not marked to market unless there is evidence of a significant and permanent impairment. In that case, the carrying value of the investment would be written down to fair value.

In the above example, ABC Software reported net income. What if the affiliate reported net losses instead? Microsoft would then have to recognize its proportionate share of the losses on its own income statement under the account title, equity loss. If Microsoft's share of ABC's losses equals or exceeds its interest in ABC (i.e., the balance in the investment account is brought to 0 because of the equity losses), Microsoft would stop recognizing its share of further losses. However, if Microsoft has incurred any legal or constructive obligations on behalf of ABC, a provision (liability) would have to be recognized.

A further look at Microsoft's investments

The disclosure from Microsoft's 2010 Annual Report shown in Table 17.2 provides a detailed breakdown of its investments. The total for the final three columns corresponds to the amounts reported on the balance sheet shown in Table 17.1.

Let's consider the cash and equivalents balance, $5505 million. Table 17.2 shows that this account consists mainly of cash, mutual funds, commercial paper, and certificates of deposit. Small amounts of corporate notes and municipal (i.e., city and state government) securities are included too. Notice that the holding gains and losses for this category of investment are modest. This result is expected. First, some items, including cash and certificates of deposit, are not marked to market. Obviously, if the company has $1661 million in cash, the market value of that cash is the same amount. Even those instruments that are marked to market, such as mutual funds and commercial paper, show only small changes in value. Given that all instruments in this account are highly short-term in nature (with nearly all expiring within 90 days), their market values are not highly sensitive to changes in interest rates. And given that changes in interest rates are the only factors that lead to changes in value for fixed-income instruments, any unrealized holding gains or losses should be modest.

Notice also that some mutual funds and certificates of deposit are included in the short-term investments account. The main distinction between the two classifications, cash and

Table 17.2   Detailed breakdown of Microsoft's investments (In millions), June 30, 2010

	Cost basis	Unrealized gains	Unrealized losses	Recorded basis	Cash and equivalents	Short-term investments	Equity and other investments
Cash and securities							
Cash	$1,661	$—	$—	$1,661	$1,661	$—	$—
Mutual funds	1,120	—	—	1,120	1,120	—	—
Commercial paper	188	—	—	188	13	175	—
Certificates of deposit	348	—	—	348	68	280	—
US government and agency securities	21,036	167	(1)	21,202	1,822	19,380	—
Foreign government bonds	518	13	—	531	—	531	—
Mortgage-backed securities	3,137	135	(7)	3,265	—	3,265	—
Corporate notes and bonds	7,450	289	(18)	7,721	701	7,020	—
Municipal securities	726	22	(1)	747	120	627	—
Common and preferred stock	6,640	1,030	(418)	7,252	—	—	7,252
Other investments	507	—	—	507	—	5	502
Total	$43,331	$1,656	$(445)	$44,542	$5,505	$31,283	$7,754

equivalents vs. short-term investments, is one of maturity. Mutual funds, mainly in the form of money-market funds, are classified as cash or cash equivalents if they function as demand deposits (i.e., checking accounts). Otherwise, they are classified as short-term investments.

As for short-term investments, $31 283 million, all of the components are in the form of fixed-income instruments, with US government bonds, foreign (non-US) government bonds, corporate bonds, and municipal securities representing the primary components. This breakdown is expected, given that managing short-term equity portfolios is not part of Microsoft's business model. For this reason, none of its equity investments are classified as short-term. Note also that because all of the instruments in short-term investments are due to mature within the next few months, their values are not heavily influenced by changes in interest rates. As a result, holding gains and losses are small. Also, it is highly likely that many of these bonds are classified by Microsoft as "held-to-maturity" securities, which means that they are not marked to market.

Equity and other investments, $7754 million, are mainly in the form of common shares. However, Microsoft does not disclose the portion of the total that comprises common shares accounted for under the equity method and the portion accounted for as passive investments. One conclusion we may draw, however, is that some investments have been made in publicly traded companies accounted for under the market method. This is clear from the unrealized holding loss of $418 million. The recognition of this loss implies that some of Microsoft's equity investments were marked to market. Given that equity investments are not marked to market (except in cases of impairment), the investments in question are reported under the market method (and are, therefore, passive).

Finally, given that Microsoft does not have any securities classified as "trading," all unrealized gains and losses for 2010, $1656 million and $445 million respectively, are included in other comprehensive income. None of those gains or losses is included in 2010 net income.

Further information on Microsoft's investing activities can be learned from the investing activities section of the cash flow statement shown in Table 17.3.

The cash flow statement reveals that $245 million was spent on acquiring other companies. Also, $30 168 million was spent on investments. But notice that $7453 million of cash was raised from the maturity of investments (i.e., bonds or notes coming to the end of their contractual lives) and $15 125 million from the sale of investments.

Table 17.3   The investing activities section of Microsoft's cash flow statement

Investing activities	2008	2009	2010
Additions to PP&E	(3,182)	(3,119)	(1,977)
Acquisitions of companies, net of cash acquired	(8,053)	(868)	(245)
Purchase of investments	(20,954)	(36,850)	(30,168)
Maturities of investments	2,597	6,191	7,453
Sales of investments	25,132	19,806	15,125
Securities lending payable	(127)	(930)	(1,502)
Net cash from investing	(4,587)	(15,770)	(11,314)

Finally, a note from Microsoft's Annual Report (see Table 17.4) shows the income statement effects of investing activities. Focusing on 2010, we see that Microsoft reported $843 million in dividends and interest.[8] Net gains on investments were $348 million. These net gains relate only to securities sold in fiscal year 2010.

Remember that because Microsoft does not have "trading" securities, no *un*realized gains or losses from investments are included in income. These gains and losses are reported directly in other comprehensive income, which Microsoft reports as shown in Table 17.5.

Consolidation

When one company owns more than 50% of the voting shares of another company, the investor (or parent) is assumed to control the other (i.e., the subsidiary). US GAAP and IFRS require that the parent combine the financial statements of all majority-owned companies with its own, in consolidated financial statements. It should be noted that recent changes have resulted in a new, and more expansive, definition of control. The practical effect of these changes is that consolidation may be required from large minority holdings where other shareholdings are widely dispersed, and the investor holds significantly more voting rights than any other shareholder. For example, if the investor owns 40% of the outstanding shares, and ownership of the remaining shares is dispersed among thousands of shareholders, none of whom have a

Table 17.4 The income statement effects from Microsoft's investing activities (in millions)

Year ended June 30	2008	2009	2010
Dividends and interest income	$994	$744	$843
Interest expense	(106)	(38)	(151)
Net recognized gains (losses) on investments	346	(125)	348
Net gains (losses) on derivatives	226	(558)	(140)
Net gains (losses) on foreign currency remeasurements	226	(509)	1
Other	$(143)	$(56)	$14

Table 17.5 Components of Microsoft's accumulated other comprehensive income (in millions)

	2009	2010
Net unrealized gains on derivatives	$302	$27
Net unrealized gains (losses) on investments	(233)	265
Translation adjustments and other	(240)	(206)
Accumulated other comprehensive income	$(171)	$(86)

significant holding, the 40% stake may be enough to ensure control. From 2013 onward, such investments will be consolidated in the same manner as fully owned subsidiaries.

Consolidated, or group, financial statements exist because of the "substance over form" rule. Technically, a shareholder in the parent is investing in just a single company. But because the parent controls other companies, the shareholder is indirectly investing in those too. For the financial statements to be useful in guiding capital allocation decisions by investors, they should be based on the underlying economic reality of the business. Even though the parent and each subsidiary are separate legal entities, they operate as one centrally controlled economic entity. This is the economic reality that needs to be captured by the financial reporting process.

We do not intend to discuss the detailed mechanics of consolidation in this chapter. The process is highly technical and complicated. However, any reader of the financial statements needs to understand three fundamental concepts behind the consolidation process:

1. Consolidated financial statements are not simply a matter of adding together the accounts of the parent and its subsidiaries. The major complicating factor is the presence of intercompany transactions. Parents sometimes lend money to subsidiaries, or vice versa. Also, one legal entity within the corporate group may sell products or services to another. The guiding principle is that consolidated financial statements reflect the results that the group would report if it were a single company. The consolidated accounts should therefore reflect only those transactions between the consolidated group of entities and others outside the entity. Any intercompany transactions – including loans, receivables, payables, and sales – must be eliminated. For example, if a parent reports sales of $100 million, its subsidiary reports sales of $30 million, and $10 million of the parent's sales were to the subsidiary, the consolidated income statement would show sales of $120 million. The $10 million of intercompany sales are eliminated during the consolidation process.

2. Parents often do not own 100% of their subsidiaries. The consolidation process must therefore acknowledge the ownership interest held by external minority shareholders. For example, assume that a subsidiary reports net income of $10 million and the parent owns 70% of the entity. Because the parent has operational control over the entire entity, 100% of all balance sheet and income statement accounts are consolidated with those of the parent (after controlling for intercompany transactions). Therefore, the parent recognizes the full $10 million of net income on its own income statement. However, it must also acknowledge that external parties have claims on 30% of the entity and are thus entitled to 30% (or $3 million) of the profits. This claim is shown on the income statement as "noncontrolling interest." If the parent reports total net income of $50 million, the income statement might look something like this:

Consolidated net income	$50 million
Less net income – noncontrolling interest	3 million
Net income attributable to parent company	$47 million

Noncontrolling interest, sometimes called "minority interest," is also recognized on the balance sheet. In this context, noncontrolling interest represents external interests in the shareholders' equity of subsidiaries. In the past, it was found between the liability section and the shareholders' equity section. Recent changes in accounting rules now require that it be classified as shareholders' equity. In any case, most analysts consider noncontrolling interest to be a form of equity.

3. The process by which one company acquires another nearly always gives rise to "goodwill." Consider the following example. Microsoft acquires ABC Software for $100 million. For the sake of simplicity, we assume that the acquisition is for 100% of ABC's shares (i.e., no minority interest). The purchase price is first allocated to tangible and financial assets (e.g., inventories, receivables, PP&E, etc.) at fair value as of the acquisition date. The same is done with liabilities. In this example, we assume that the fair value of the tangible assets is $80 million and the fair value of liabilities is $25 million. The resulting net of $55 million is $45 million less than the total purchase price. By default, $45 million must be allocated to intangible assets. This is done by identifying all "identifiable" intangibles – such as trademarks, brand names, patents, copyrights, customer lists, Internet domain names, franchise and royalty agreements, software, databases, and trade secrets. Each intangible is measured at its fair value.[9] If identifiable intangibles are valued at $31 million, that still leaves us $14 million short of the purchase price. That difference is allocated to goodwill, which is simply the popular term for unidentifiable intangibles.

Until a few years ago, goodwill was amortized like other assets, but no longer. Instead, companies test the goodwill for impairment at least once a year. As long as the goodwill is deemed to be unimpaired, no goodwill charge is made. But if the goodwill is deemed to be impaired, an estimate of the magnitude of the impairment is required. Goodwill is then written down to this amount, and an impairment loss is recognized on the income statement.

Key lessons from the chapter

- When companies own shares in other businesses, the accounting depends on the degree of influence or control that the investor exerts over the other company.
- Passive investors are assumed to exert no influence over the investee company. Generally, passive investment is assumed when the investor owns less than 20% of the outstanding voting shares of the investee.
- When investors own between 20 and 50% of voting shares, they are presumed to exert significant influence over operating activities and dividend policy of the investee. In such cases, the equity method of accounting is required.
- Control is presumed if the investor owns more than 50% of the outstanding voting shares of the investee.
- When one company owns more than 50% of the voting shares of another company, the parent must combine the financial statements of all majority-owned companies with its own, in consolidated financial statements.

- Passive investments fall into three basic categories: debt securities held to maturity, trading securities, and available-for-sale securities. The last of these is the default category.
- The market and cost methods are used to account for passive investments.
- For trading and available-for-sale securities, investments must be marked to market at the end of the year. The difference between the two methods lies in the treatment of the resulting unrealized holding gains and losses. In the case of the former, the gains and losses appear in that period's income statement. For the latter, the gains and losses are included in other comprehensive income.
- For most companies, available-for-sale securities are far more common than trading investments. Trading securities are rarely found outside of financial services.

Key terms and concepts from the chapter

Marketable securities	Available-for-sale	Fair value hierarchy
Passive investment	securities	Mark to market
Significant influence	Trading securities	Mark to model
Control	Held-to-maturity	
	securities	

Questions

1. What is the difference between available-for-sale securities and trading securities? How do the accounting treatments differ?

2. True or false: Debt securities can be classified as available-for-sale or for trading purposes.

3. In the aftermath of the banking and economic crisis of 2008 and 2009, several banks reclassified investments from available-for-sale or trading securities to held-to-maturity securities. What motive might they have had for doing this?

4. For equity investments, which classification is more common for industrial firms, available-for-sale or trading, and why?

5. Describe the fair value hierarchy required under US GAAP and IFRS.

6. Why are unrealized holding gains and losses on trading securities included in net income while unrealized holding gains and losses on available-for-sale securities are included in accumulated other comprehensive income?

7. What determines whether investments are classified as current or noncurrent?

8. Why was the equity method created? What purpose does it serve?

9. Can you think of an example where a company owns more than 20% of the outstanding equity of another company but does not use the equity method?

10. How is use of the equity method subject to manipulation? How might a financial statement reader detect such behavior?

Problems

17.1   Classification of long-term investments

The following note was taken from the fiscal year 2011 Annual Report of Group Air France-KLM. (Note that the Group's fiscal year runs from 1 April to 31 March.) It refers to the initial public offering (IPO) of Amadeus IT, a Spanish travel-reservations technology company. At the time of its IPO, the company was majority-owned by WAM Acquisition, whose shareholders included two London-based private equity firms, and the carriers Iberia, Deutsche Lufthansa, and Air France.

Required

(a) The note reports that as a result of the two actions undertaken by the Group, the Group's holdings in WAM decreased from 22 to 15%. In addition, "the governance of WAM was changed." What exactly does the Group mean by these statements and what were the financial reporting ramifications of these changes?

(b) What entry did Group AirFrance-KLM make to record the holding gain from its investment in WAM?

(c) The note says, "After this operation, the . . . shares . . . were reclassified as 'assets available for sale.'" What does this mean, and what effect did this change have on the financial statements?

On April 29, 2010, the company WAM (Amadeus) was the subject of an Initial Public Offering (IPO) on the Madrid stock exchange. This operation was executed in two stages:

1. A capital increase reserved to the market, to which the Group did not subscribe;
2. The concomitant sale of a portion of the shares held by the Group.

After the operation, the Group's holding decreased from 22% to 15%. At the same time, the governance of WAM was changed. These two items involved the loss of significant influence for the Group as well as a change in the valuation method of the remaining shareholding.

As a consequence, consistent with IFRS, since the April 29, 2010 IPO, the shares held by the Group have been valued at their market value (market price).

The overall profit recorded in the income statement amounting to €1030 million breaks down as follows:

- gain on disposal of shares: €280 million, including €193 million of cash received;
- valuation at the market price of the remaining shares held by the Group: €750 million.

After this operation, the WAM (Amadeus) shares held by the Group were reclassified as "assets available for sale" (in "other financial assets noncurrent"). The value of the shares is updated at each closing period as a function of the share price. The counterpart of this revaluation is recorded in other comprehensive income.

17.2 The effect of transaction cost on marketable securities and investments

Early in 2012, Yoon Industries purchased marketable equity securities for $5 million. These securities are classified as "available for sale." To acquire the securities, the company incurred transaction costs of $30 000 in addition to the $5 million. The securities had a fair value on 31 December 2012 of $4.6 million. None of these shares were sold during 2012.

Required

(a) What amount would appear in the asset account when the securities are bought?
(b) Make the journal required at the end of 2012 to reflect the fair value of the securities.

17.3   Journal entries and analysis under the equity method

At 31 December 2005, Abbott Laboratories, Inc. owns 50% of TAP Pharmaceutical Products Inc. under a joint venture agreement with Takeda Pharmaceutical Company, Limited of Japan. TAP develops and markets pharmaceutical products for the US and Canada, and is an important strategic investee for Abbott Labs. Abbott appropriately accounts for the investment in TAP using the equity method.

The Investment in affiliate account is reported by Abbott Labs in its 31 December 2005 balance sheet at $167 million. Abbott received $343, $638, and $606 million dividends from TAP in 2005, 2004, and 2003, respectively. TAP declared income of $883, $1290, and $1303 million in 2005, 2004, and 2003 respectively. At 31 December 2005, TAP's balance sheet reports assets of $1470 million, liabilities of $1136 million, and shareholders' equity of $334 million.

Required

(a) Reconstruct the journal entries made by Abbott Labs to account for its investment in TAP in 2005 using the equity method.
(b) Assuming that Abbott acquired the investment in TAP at the beginning of 2003, how much did Abbott pay for the investment?
(c) In a risk analysis of Abbott Labs, most analysts will calculate Abbott's debt-to-equity ratio. In this case, the debt-to-equity ratio may not capture an important element of Abbott's risk. What is that risk, and why doesn't Abbott's balance sheet capture it?
(d) Assume that the $167 million investment in TAP represents only a 10% (passive) interest, Abbott classifies the investment as available-for-sale, the $343 million dividends received by Abbott are a result of having a 10% interest, shares of TAP are actively traded, and TAP's *total* market capitalization at 31 December 2005 is $2000 million. Compute the effects of this investment on Abbott's 2005 income.

17.4   Review problem

For each item listed below, indicate the effect of the transaction or accounting change on current period net operating profit after tax (NOPAT), end of the current period invested capital (ending IC), and current period cash flow from operations (CFFO). Set up your answer in the following format:

Item #	Effect on NOPAT	Effect on IC	Effect on CFFO
(a)			
(b)			
(c)			
(d)			
(e)			
(f)			
(g)			
(h)			
(i)			
(j)			

Write "Increase," "Decrease," or "No effect" in each column. When you are done, you should have 30 total answers.

Items to analyze

(a) The company recorded the increases in market value of their passive investments in available-for-sale securities.

(b) Estimates of expected salvage (or residual) values used in straight-line depreciation methods for delivery vans were decreased.

(c) A large amount of production machinery was sold for cash at more than book value.

(d) The company sold equipment inventory on credit to a regular customer in the normal course of business.

(e) Cash dividends were declared and paid.

(f) A 50% stock dividend was declared and distributed.

(g) Land was revalued upward as permitted by IFRS rules. No prior write-ups or write-downs had occurred.

(h) On the last day of the year, interest-bearing convertible bonds were converted to shares of common stock.

(i) The company delayed payments to factory workers, normally due on the last day of the year, by several days.

(j) In prior years, new lease signings were treated as capital leases. Similar new leases signed at the beginning of this year are treated as operating leases.

17.5   Mark-to-market accounting for trading securities

At the end of 2012, Huber Company had investments in trading securities as follows (amounts in thousands of euro):

	Cost	Market value
Renaud Company	1,000	1,300
Helsing, Ltd	900	1,100
Neilsen Financial	1,100	900
	3,000	3,300

The shares for each company were acquired during 2012. The market values shown above are based on market prices as of the close of trading on 31 December 2012.

Required

(a) Record whatever journal entries are required to implement mark-to-market accounting for Huber Company at the end of 2012.
(b) Based on the above information, what type of business would you expect Huber Company to engage in, and why? Industrial? Trading and distribution? Retailing? Finance?

17.6   The equity method and the statement of cash flows

The statements of cash flows for the SAP Group are shown below.

Required

Based on these statements, answer the following questions:

(a) What were the entity's two major sources of cash in each year?
(b) What were the entity's two major uses of cash in each year?
(c) How much was the company's bad debt expense in fiscal 2009?
(d) Did accounts receivable increase or decrease in 2009? Explain.
(e) Did the company report gains or losses from equity method investees in fiscal 2009? Your response here should be "gains" or "losses," not "yes" or "no." Briefly support your answer, indicating why these are added or subtracted on the cash flow statement.
(f) Does the company appear to be in growth or contraction mode during the period covered by their cash flow statement? Support your answer.

Consolidated Statements of Cash Flows of SAP Group as at December 31,

€ millions	2009	2008	2007
Profit after tax	**1,750**	**1,848**	**1,908**
Adjustments to reconcile profit after tax to net cash provided by operating activities:			
Depreciation and amortization	499	539	262
Gains/losses on disposals of non-current assets	−11	11	1
Gains/losses on disposals of financial assets	−2	−16	−1
Impairment loss on financial assets recognized in profit	10	15	8
Decrease/increase in sales and bad debt allowances on trade receivables	64	76	0
Other adjustments for non-cash items	14	52	45
Deferred income taxes	−39	−91	8
Decrease/increase in trade receivables	593	−48	−521
Decrease/increase in other assets	205	−12	−277
Decrease/increase in trade payables, provisions and other liabilities	−116	−277	375
Decrease/increase in deferred income	48	61	124
Net cash flows from operating activities	**3,015**	**2,158**	**1,932**
Purchase of non-controlling interests	0	0	−48
Business combinations, net of cash and cash equivalents acquired	−73	−3,773	−672
Repayment of acquirees' debt in business combinations	0	−450	0
Purchase of intangible assets and property, plant, and equipment	−225	−339	−400
Proceeds from sales of intangible assets or property, plant, and equipment	45	44	27
Cash transferred to restricted cash	0	−448	−550
Use of restricted cash	0	1,001	0
Purchase of equity or debt instruments of other entities	−1,073	−396	−788
Proceeds from sales of equity or debt instruments of other entities	1,027	595	1,040
Net cash flows from investing activities	**− 299**	**− 3,766**	**− 1,391**
Dividends paid	−594	−594	−556
Purchase of treasury shares	0	−487	−1,005
Proceeds from reissuance of treasury shares	24	85	156
Proceeds from issuing shares (share-based compensation)	6	20	44
Proceeds from borrowings	697	3,859	47
Repayments of borrowings	−2,303	−1,571	−48
Purchase of equity-based derivative instruments (hedge for cash-settled share-based payment plans)	0	−55	0
Proceeds from the exercise of equity-based derivative financial instruments	4	24	75
Net cash flows from financing activities	**− 2,166**	**1,281**	**− 1,287**

€ millions	2009	2008	2007
Effect of foreign exchange rates on cash and cash equivalents	54	−1	−45
Net increase (decrease) in cash and cash equivalents	604	−328	−791
Cash and cash equivalents at the beginning of the period	1,280	1,608	2,399
Cash and cash equivalents at the end of the period	1,884	1,280	1,608

Interest paid in 2009, 2008, and 2007 amounted to €69 million, €105 million, and €6 million, respectively, and interest received in 2009, 2008, and 2007 amounted to €22 million, €72 million and €142 million, respectively. Income taxes paid in 2009, 2008, and 2007, net of refunds, were €722 million, €882 million, and €811 million, respectively. The accompanying Notes are an integral part of these Consolidated Financial Statements.

Case studies

17.1   Stora Enso: accounting for investments

Stora Enso is an integrated paper, packaging, and forest products company producing publication and fine papers, packaging boards and wood products. Sales were €12.4 billion in 2004. Headquartered in Helsinki, the group has about 45 000 employees in more than 40 countries. Customers are large and small publishers, printing houses and merchants, as well as packaging, joinery, and construction companies. The company's shares are listed in Helsinki, Stockholm, and New York, and its accounts are prepared in accordance with International Financial Reporting Standards (IFRS).

Investments at Stora Enso

Apart from affiliates, which are accounted for under the equity method, all of Stora Enso's investments are classified as long-term and "available-for-sale." Most of these investments are in other forestry firms or in suppliers of Stora Enso.

The carrying value of investments on the end-of-2003 balance sheet was €368.5 million. The acquisition cost of the investments was €288.0 million. The difference, €80.5 million, was classified as other comprehensive income in the shareholders' equity section of Stora Enso's balance sheet.

During 2004, the following transactions took place:

- The company made additional investments costing €13.2 million.
- Securities with an acquisition cost of €31.3 million were sold for €32.8 million.

Stora Enso's holdings were marked to market at the end of 2004 and estimated to have a fair value of €352.9 million.

Required

(a) Specify the journal entries to record the transactions that occurred in Stora Enso's investment account in 2004

(b) What journal entry should be made to mark Stora Enso's investments to market at the end of 2004?

(c) Suppose Stora Enso reclassified the investments as "trading securities." How would the accounting change as a result of the reclassification? Specify the journal entries required for 2004.

17.2   Coca-Cola and Coca-Cola Enterprises: the equity method in practice

Coca-Cola Enterprises (CCE), the world's largest bottler of Coke, was formed in 1986 from the consolidation of several bottling companies. At inception, Coca-Cola, Inc. owned 49% of CCE, allowing it to exert significant influence over operations without having to include CCE's large debts in its own balance sheet. Coca-Cola's investment in CCE has gradually declined, reaching about 36% by 2003. The investment has always been accounted for under the equity method.

On its end-of-2003 balance sheet, Coca-Cola reported the carrying value (i.e., book value) of its investment in CCE at $1260 million.

During 2004,

- CCE reported net income of $596 million and paid $76 million in dividends to its shareholders.
- Through a variety of cooperative agreements, Coca-Cola increased its net investment in CCE by $121 million. Because of capital increases in CCE, these investments did not materially affect Coca-Cola's percentage ownership.

CCE is traded on the New York Stock Exchange. At the end of 2004, Coca-Cola's stake in CCE had a market value of about $3.5 billion (based on the market capitalization of CCE's shares).

Required

(a) Make whatever journal entries are required to implement the equity method for Coca-Cola's investment in CCE for 2004.

(b) What should be the carrying value for the CCE investment on Coca-Cola's end-of-2004 balance sheet?

Notes

1. Such investments, by their nature, tend to be far less liquid than "marketable" (i.e., publicly traded) securities. Therefore, the company might not be able to dispose of the investment when desired. Because too much uncertainty exists as to whether or not the investor can actually dispose of the investment within the time limits imposed for a current asset (usually 12 months), the shares are almost certain to be classified as long-term. To put it another way, securities without readily observable market prices are nearly always classified as long-term, while nearly any investment classified as short-term is likely to be "marketable." Marketable securities are classified as short-term or long-term, depending entirely on management intent. If the intent is to hold on to the shares for the long term the investment is classified as long-term; otherwise, it is classified as short-term.
2. However, a write-down is required if a decline in value is judged to be permanent.
3. The standard on fair value applies equally to liabilities, but the focus in this chapter is on assets.
4. Another important controversy centers on the role that mark-to-market accounting may or may not have played in the recent global financial crisis. The charge is that accounting rules forcing banks and other financial institutions to write down assets led to catastrophic contagion effects – massive sell-offs led to plummeting prices, forcing banks to sell more assets to meet capital requirements, causing asset prices to fall still further, and so on. We believe that the contribution of accounting to the crisis has been seriously overstated, but the subject is beyond the scope of this book.
5. Mark-to-market accounting had not yet come into existence when the equity method was established.
6. By 2010, Coca-Cola's ownership stake in CCE had declined to 33%. It then bought out CCE's North American bottling assets and redeemed its remaining shares. CCE, therefore, has a far greater degree of operating independence than it had in Ivester's day.
7. This example assumes that there is no goodwill associated with the investment.
8. This book ignores the accounting for derivatives (i.e., options, futures, swaps, etc.). Therefore, we do not discuss the net losses on derivatives.
9. This difficult and controversial process is beyond the scope of this book.

CHAPTER 18

Accounting for Mergers and Acquisitions

Introduction

Mergers and acquisitions (M&A), or "business combinations," bring together separate companies or businesses into one reporting entity. In this chapter we focus on the financial reporting issues that arise in such transactions. Since 2005, IFRS and US GAAP have mandated that all business combinations be accounted for as acquisitions, a transaction where one of the combining entities obtains control over the other. Simply put, all corporate control transactions are assumed to be acquisitions; mergers are not recognized for financial reporting purposes.

To illustrate the accounting for acquisitions, we refer to Procter & Gamble's (P&G) acquisition of The Gillette Company. In January 2005, P&G announced that it had signed a deal to acquire 100% of Gillette, a global leader in blades and razors, oral care, and batteries.

Both IFRS and US GAAP require the "purchase method" of accounting. This method allocates the purchase price of the acquisition to all identifiable assets and liabilities on the basis of fair value. The remainder, i.e., nonidentifiable intangible assets, is captured in "goodwill." The following sections focus on the key features of the purchase method.

Purchase price/cost of acquisition

The first step in accounting for M&A is to determine the acquisition cost. This exercise is fairly straightforward when the acquisition is a cash transaction. The cost of acquisition equals the amount of cash or cash equivalents paid. Determining the acquisition cost is more complex when the consideration involves an exchange of shares.

Under IFRS, shares issued by the acquirer as consideration are recorded at fair value at the date of the exchange – the date on which the acquirer obtains control over the acquired company's net assets and operations. When the acquisition occurs in stages, the fair value of the shares issued is determined at each exchange date. In an active market, the published price of a share at the date of exchange is the best evidence of fair value. The determination of fair value in the absence of an active market (as is the case for privately held companies) is more complicated.

Under US GAAP, shares issued as consideration are measured at their market price over a reasonable period of time (i.e., a few days) before and after the parties reach an agreement on the purchase price and the proposed transaction is announced.

In filings with the Securities and Exchange Commission (SEC), P&G reported what is shown in Box 18.1 about the Gillette acquisition cost.

Contingent consideration

To ensure the success of the transaction, and to protect the acquirer from paying too much, business combinations are sometimes structured with a subsequent earn-out payment that will be made to the seller if certain measures are achieved.

If part of the purchase consideration is contingent on a future event, such as achieving specified profit levels, IFRS requires an estimate of the amount to be included as part of the cost at the date of the acquisition where it is probable that it will be paid and it can be reliably measured. Any revision to the estimate is subsequently adjusted against goodwill.

Under US GAAP, contingent consideration is generally excluded from the initial purchase price. The additional cost is not recognized until the contingency is resolved or the amount is determinable. But like IFRS, any revision to the estimate is recognized as an adjustment to goodwill.

Box 18.1   Report by P&G about Gillette acquisition cost

On October 1, 2005, we completed our acquisition of The Gillette Company. Pursuant to the acquisition agreement, which provided for the exchange of 0.975 shares of The Procter & Gamble Company common stock, on a tax-free basis, for each share of The Gillette Company, we issued 962 million shares of The Procter & Gamble Company common stock, net of shares exchanged for retained Gillette treasury shares. The value of these shares was determined using the average Company stock prices beginning two days before and ending two days after January 28, 2005, the date the acquisition was announced. We also issued 79 million stock options in exchange for Gillette's outstanding stock options. Under the purchase method of accounting, the total consideration was approximately $53.43 billion including common stock, the fair value of vested stock options and acquisition costs.

Recognition and measurement of identifiable assets

Once the purchase price is determined, it is then allocated to the target's identifiable assets and liabilities.

Current assets, liabilities, and PP&E

Exhibit 18.1 shows Gillette's balance sheet just prior to P&G's acquisition of the company. As we would expect, the assets are reported using a variety of measurement approaches, including

Exhibit 18.1 The Gillette Co. balance sheet, preacquisition (millions, except per share amount)

At December 31,	2004	2003
Assets		
Current assets		
Cash and cash equivalents	$219	$243
Short-term investments	847	438
Trade receivables, less allowances	835	920
Other receivables	376	351
Inventories	1,291	1,094
Deferred income taxes	303	344
Other current assets	197	282
Total current assets	4,068	3,672
Property, plant and equipment, net	3,747	3,644
Goodwill	1,052	1,023
Intangible assets, net	557	494
Deferred income taxes	36	38
Other assets	1,271	1,170
Total assets	$10,731	$10,041
Liabilities and stockholders' equity		
Current liabilities		
Loans payable	533	117
Current portion of long-term debt	711	742
Accounts payable and accrued liabilities	2,645	2,532
Income taxes	289	293
Deferred income taxes	25	22
Total current liabilities	4,203	3,706
Long-term debt	2,142	2,453
Deferred income taxes	723	664
Other long-term liabilities	754	929
Minority interest	73	65

Exhibit 18.1   Continued

At December 31,	2004	2003
Stockholders' equity		
Common stock, par value $1 per share		
Authorized: 2320 shares, Issued 2004 – 1382 shares	1,382	1,374
Additional paid-in capital	1,521	1,273
Earnings reinvested in the business	8,376	7,333
Accumulated other comprehensive loss	(760)	(1,088)
Treasury stock, at cost: 2004 – 392 shares; 2003 – 367 shares	(7,683)	(6,665)
Deferred stock-based compensation	–	(3)
Total stockholders' equity	2836	2,224
Total liabilities and stockholders' equity	$10,731	$10,041

Source: The Gillette Company 10-K SEC filing for year ended December 31, 2004.

historical cost, net realizable value, lower-of-cost-or-market, and cost less depreciation. However, regardless of how these items were measured in the past, all assets (and liabilities) must be recognized on the acquirer's balance sheet at fair value as of the date of acquisition.

Intangible assets

In general, intangible assets developed internally are not recognized as assets on a company's balance sheet. However, at the time of acquisition, the acquirer is expected to value any intangibles acquired and record them as assets. An intangible asset is recognized separately from goodwill if it represents contractual or legal rights, or is capable of being separated or divided and sold, transferred, licensed, rented, or exchanged. P&G reported what is shown in Box 18.2 regarding Gillette's intangibles.

In-process research & development (IPR&D)

At the time of acquisition, the acquired company may have ongoing (i.e., in-process) R&D projects. Acquired IPR&D is recognized as a separate intangible asset if it meets the definition of an intangible asset and its fair value can be measured reliably. In transactions involving research-intensive, hi-tech companies, IPR&D is often the largest asset acquired.

Restructuring provisions

At the time of the announced combination, management will often announce a postmerger restructuring plan to assist with the integration of the parent and target companies. IFRS states that the acquirer may recognize restructuring provisions as part of the acquired liabilities only

---

Box 18.2   P&G's reporting on Gillette's intangibles

The preliminary purchase price allocation to the identifiable intangible assets included in these financial statements is as follows:

	FMV	Weighted Average Life
Intangible assets with determinable lives		
Brands	$1,607	20
Patents and technology	2,716	17
Customer relationships	1,445	27
Brands with indefinite lives	23,968	Indefinite
Total intangible assets	$29,736	

The majority of the intangible asset valuation relates to brands. Our preliminary assessment as to brands that have an indefinite life and those that have a determinable life was based on a number of factors, including the competitive environment, market share, brand history, product life cycles, operating plan and macroeconomic environment of the countries in which the brands are sold. The indefinite-lived brands include Gillette, Venus, Duracell, Oral-B and Braun. The determinable-lived brands include certain brand sub-names, such as MACH3 and Sensor in the Blades and Razors business, and other regional or local brands. The determinable-lived brands have asset lives ranging from 10 to 40 years. The patents and technology intangibles are concentrated in the Blades and Razors and Oral Care businesses and have asset lives ranging from 5 to 20 years. The estimated customer relationship intangible asset useful lives ranging from 20 to 30 years reflect the very low historical and projected customer attrition rates among Gillette's major retailer and distributor customers.

when the target company has an existing liability for restructuring as of the acquisition date. US GAAP, on the other hand, does allow the acquiring company to recognize provisions beyond those already recognized by the target. However, several conditions are imposed, including the need to produce detailed restructuring plans.

Procter & Gamble's related disclosure is shown in Box 18.3.

Contingent liabilities

The most common contingent liabilities are lawsuits and environmental liabilities. An acquirer must recognize separately the target's contingent liabilities at the acquisition date as part of allocating the cost, provided fair values can be measured reliably.

> ### Box 18.3   Procter & Gamble footnote
>
> We are in the process of completing our analysis of integration plans, pursuant to which we will incur costs primarily related to the elimination of selling, general and administrative overlap between the two companies in areas like Global Business Services, corporate staff and go-to-market support, as well as redundant manufacturing capacity. Our preliminary estimate of Gillette exit costs that have been recognized as an assumed liability as of the acquisition date is $1.14 billion, including $819 million in separations related to approximately 5,600 people, $57 million in employee relocation costs and $264 million in other exit costs. We expect such activities to be substantially complete by June 30, 2008.

Goodwill

Goodwill arises as the difference between the cost of the acquisition and the fair value of identifiable assets and liabilities (including contingencies). Goodwill can result from name recognition, superior management, employee and customer loyalty, or any other attribute that makes net assets more valuable taken as a whole. In other words, because of potential synergies with P&G, Gillette may be worth more than the sum of its individual parts. Additionally, combining the two companies' assets may provide economies of scale, thereby making Gillette's assets more valuable to P&G than their individual fair values.

The accounting treatment for purchased goodwill is to capitalize it as an intangible asset. Goodwill is nonamortizable, but must be reviewed for impairment at least annually.

In Box 18.4, P&G reports the allocation of the acquisition purchase price for Gillette. The journal entry recorded by P&G for the Gillette acquisition is shown below (in millions):

Current assets	$ 5,553	
PP&E	3,673	
Intangible assets	29,736	
Other noncurrent assets	771	
Goodwill	34,943	
Current liabilities		$ 5,009
Noncurrent liabilities		16,241
P&G equity		53,426

Of course, the actual journal entry recorded by P&G included a more detailed listing of assets and liabilities. For example, current assets would have been broken down into cash, marketable securities, accounts receivable, inventory, and prepaid assets.

Negative goodwill (bargain purchase)

Goodwill arises whenever the purchase price of the acquisition exceeds the fair value of identifiable net assets (assets – liabilities). When the opposite situation occurs, "negative goodwill"

Box 18.4   P&G's report of the allocation of the acquisition purchase price for Gillette

Purchase price		$53,426
Fair market value of identifiable assets		
Current assets	$5,553	
Property, plant & equipment	3,673	
Intangible assets	29,736	
Other noncurrent assets	771	
Fair market value of identifiable liabilities		
Current liabilities	(5,009)	
Noncurrent liabilities	(16,241)	
Less: fair market value of net identifiable assets		18,483
Goodwill		$34,943

The Gillette acquisition resulted in $34.94 billion in goodwill, preliminarily allocated primarily to the segments comprising the Gillette businesses (Blades and Razors, Duracell and Braun, Health Care and Beauty).

(also known as a "bargain purchase") is the result. According to IFRS, if there is any excess of fair value over purchase price, the acquirer should reassess the identification and measurement of the acquired company's identifiable assets and liabilities. If negative goodwill remains after the reassessment, the excess is recognized immediately as profit on the income statement. This means that the term "negative goodwill" should never be seen on a corporate balance sheet.

Similarly, US GAAP defines a bargain purchase as the excess of fair value of acquired net assets over purchase cost and results in a gain recognized in the period in which the acquisition occurs. Also, like IFRS, US GAAP requires the acquiring entity to double-check its calculations before concluding that a bargain purchase exists. If the same conclusion is reached, any further excess is recognized as a gain in the income statement. The gain is calculated as the excess of the fair value of the net assets acquired over the sum of (1) the fair value of the consideration transferred, (2) the fair value of any previously held equity interests, and (3) the fair value of any noncontrolling interests.

While not expected to be common, a bargain purchase may occur if, for example, the acquired entity is purchased in a forced liquidation or distress sale.

Subsequent adjustments to acquired assets and liabilities

IFRS permits adjustments against goodwill to the provisional fair values recognized at acquisition provided those adjustments are made within 12 months of the acquisition date.

> **Box 18.5   P&G's comments on subsequent adjustments for its acquisition of Gillette**
>
> We are in the process of finalizing the allocation of the purchase price to the individual assets acquired and liabilities assumed. The preliminary allocation of the purchase price included in the current period balance sheet is based on the best estimates of management. To assist management in the allocation, we engaged valuation specialists to prepare independent appraisals. The completion of the purchase price allocation may result in adjustments to the carrying value of Gillette's recorded assets and liabilities, revisions of the useful lives of intangible assets and the determination of any residual-amount that will be allocated to goodwill. The related depreciation and amortization expense from the acquired assets is also subject to revision based on the final allocation.

Adjustments after the 12-month period must be recognized in the income statement as gains or losses. US GAAP is broadly similar to IFRS on this issue.

Box 18.5 shows what P&G had to say regarding subsequent adjustments for its acquisition of Gillette.

Goodwill impairment

Both IFRS and US GAAP require periodic reassessments of goodwill, although there are some differences in the approaches required by each accounting regime. IFRS requires a one-step impairment test. The recoverable amount of the business unit in question (i.e., the higher of its net selling price and its value in use) is compared with its carrying amount on the balance sheet. An impairment loss is recognized if the carrying value exceeds the recoverable amount.

Under US GAAP, a two-step impairment test is required:

1. The fair value and the carrying amount of the reporting unit, including goodwill, should be compared. If the fair value of the reporting unit is less than the book value, goodwill is considered impaired; then
2. The goodwill impairment should be measured as the excess of the carrying amount of goodwill over its implied fair value. The implied fair value of goodwill should be determined by allocating fair value to the various assets and liabilities included in the reporting unit in the same manner as goodwill is determined in a business combination. The impairment charge should be included in operating income.

In either case, goodwill impairment is recognized as follows:

Loss from goodwill impairment	XX	
Goodwill		XX

"Loss from goodwill impairment" is an income statement account. Until recently, goodwill was amortized like other intangibles, such as patents or copyrights. Goodwill charges would therefore reach the income statement in a stable, predictable way. But now that goodwill amortization is banned, goodwill reaches the income statement in a far less predictable fashion. Goodwill affects earnings but only when it is written off. For the typical company, expenses related to goodwill are zero in most years, but high (and in some cases, enormous) in years when write-offs are made.

Noncontrolling interest

In the previous chapter, we introduced the concept of "noncontrolling interest" (NCI). NCI, also known as "minority interest," is the portion of equity in a subsidiary not owned, directly or indirectly, by the parent. NCI is calculated as follows:

$$NCI = \text{Fair Value of Acquired Subsidiary}$$
$$\times \text{Percentage of Subsidiary Equity Not Owned by Parent}$$

To illustrate how this works, let's return to P&G's acquisition of Gillette, but now assume that P&G acquires only 80% of the outstanding stock for a price $42 740 million. Because P&G owns more than 50% of Gillette, P&G consolidates Gillette's financial results with its own. The 20% of Gillette's equity that P&G does not own is recorded at fair value on P&G's balance sheet. The fair value of the NCI is calculated as follows:

$$[(\text{Parent Purchase Price} \div \text{Parent's Controlling Interest}) \times NCI]$$
$$= [(\$42\,740 \div 80\%) \times 20\%] = \$10\,685$$

The journal entry that would be recorded at the time of Gillette's acquisition is:

Current assets	$ 5,553	
PP&E	3,676	
Intangible assets	29,736	
Other noncurrent assets	771	
Goodwill	34,943	
Current liabilities		$ 5,009
Noncurrent liabilities		16,241
P&G equity		42,740
Noncontrolling interest		10,685

NCI is recorded in the shareholders' equity section of the parent's balance sheet, separate from the parent's equity. The amounts of consolidated net income attributable to the parent and to the noncontrolling interest must be clearly identified and presented on the consolidated income statement.

Key lessons from the chapter

- The first step in accounting for M&A is to determine the acquisition cost.
- To ensure the success of a transaction, and to protect the acquirer from paying too much, business combinations are sometimes structured with a subsequent earn-out payment made to the seller if certain performance measures are achieved. The presence of an earn-out clause complicates the determination of the acquisition cost.
- Once the purchase price is determined, it is allocated to the target's identifiable assets and liabilities, including: current assets and liabilities, PP&E, intangible assets, in-process research and development, restructuring provisions, and contingent liabilities.
- Goodwill is the difference between the cost of the acquisition and the fair value of identifiable assets and liabilities.
- Goodwill can result from name recognition, superior management, employee and customer loyalty, and any other attribute that makes net assets more valuable taken as a whole.
- Negative goodwill arises when the purchase price of the acquisition is less than the fair market value of the net identifiable assets.
- All business combinations must be accounted for using the purchase method. In other words, it is assumed that one company is acquiring another company. Merger accounting no longer exists.
- When less than 100% of a controlling interest is acquired, a noncontrolling (or minority) interest must be acknowledged. This interest appears in the shareholders' equity section of the balance sheet apart from the parent's equity. The portion of net income belonging to the noncontrolling interest must be identified on the consolidated income statement.

Key terms and concepts from the chapter

Purchase price	In-process research and	Negative goodwill
Contingent	development	(bargain purchase)
consideration	Goodwill	Minority interest
Identifiable assets		

Questions

1. What is goodwill?

2. How is goodwill determined?

3. What happens to goodwill after it has been recognized?

4. True or false: "Mergers" are not recognized under current financial reporting practice.

5. When one firm acquires another firm, the former records the assets of the latter at fair value on the acquisition date, not the target's historical cost. Why?

6. What is "negative" goodwill, and how is it recognized?

7. Can you think of specific instances in which negative goodwill, or a bargain purchase, might occur?

Problems

18.1   Journal entry for an acquisition

Tan Trading Company purchased all of the outstanding shares of Lau Chemicals on 31 December 2012. Just before the purchase, the condensed balance sheets of the two companies appeared as follows:

	Tan Trading	Lau Chemicals
(amounts in $000)		
Current assets	1,480	435.5
Property, plant, and equipment, net	2,100	676
	3,580	1,111.5
Current liabilities	578	92.5
Share capital – common shares	1,950	525
Retained earnings	1,052	494
	3,580	1,111.5

The fair value of Lau Chemical's assets and liabilities is approximately the same as book value.

Tan Trading paid $1225 in cash to acquire the shares of Lau Chemicals. For the excess of the purchase price over the fair value of Lau Chemicals' net assets, $86 is attributed to PP&E, and the remainder to goodwill.

Required

Prepare the entry for Tan Trading's acquisition of Lau Chemicals.

18.2   Analysis of an acquisition

The 2003 Annual Report for Microsoft Corp. includes the following note:

> In fiscal 2003, Microsoft acquired all of the outstanding equity interests of Navision a/s, Rare Ltd., and Placeware, Inc. Navision, headquartered in Vedbaek, Denmark, is a provider of integrated business solutions software for small and mid-sized businesses in the European market that is part of the Microsoft Business Solutions segment. Navision, Rare, and Placeware have been consolidated into our financial statements since their respective acquisition dates. The estimated fair values of the assets acquired and liabilities assumed at the date of the acquisitions for fiscal 2003 are as follows:

	Navision **July 12, 2002**	**Rare Ltd.** **September 24, 2002**	**Placeware** **April 30, 2003**
(in millions)			
Current assets	$240	$25	$30
Property, plant, and equipment	8	8	7
Intangible assets	169	75	30
Goodwill	1,197	281	180
Total assets acquired	1,614	389	247
Current liabilities	(148)	(12)	(32)
Long-term liabilities	(1)		(13)
Total liabilities assumed	(149)	(12)	(45)
Net assets acquired	$1,465	$377	$202

Required

(a) How much did Microsoft pay for Navision A/S?
(b) What percentage of the Navision deal was for goodwill? What exactly is goodwill? How should Microsoft account for goodwill, at the time of acquisition and in subsequent periods?
(c) How did the acquisition of Navision affect Microsoft's statement of cash flows?

18.3 Accounting for an acquisition: Carrefour and BLC (China)

In the notes to its 2010 Annual Report, retail giant Carrefour disclosed the following acquisition:

> On July 15, 2010, Carrefour entered into an agreement to acquire 51% of Baolongcang (BLC), a chain of 11 hypermarkets located in the Chinese province of Hebei (with two subsequently sold, as was initially planned), for a value of 35 million euros. At the end of 2009, Baolongcang held 9.4% market share in Shijiazhuang, the provincial capital. Baolongcang's founders retained a 49% interest in the joint venture. The transaction closed at the end of August 2010, and the approval of the local authorities was obtained in September 2010. Goodwill in the amount of 33 million euros was recorded as of December 31, 2010. Baolongcang is fully consolidated.

Supplemental information from the acquisition is provided below (all amounts are in millions of euro):

	Book value	Market value
Fixed assets	9	8
Inventories	4	1
Trade payables	(2)	(2)
Other liabilities	(2)	(3)
Net assets	9	4
Price paid		35
Fair value of net assets acquired*		2
Goodwill		33

*(51%).

For this acquisition, Carrefour did not value noncontrolling interests at fair value.

Required

(a) Prepare the journal entry for the acquisition of Baolongcang.
(b) Carrefour made the acquisition of Baolongcang shortly after the IFRS standard on minority interest was changed. During the transition period (between adoption of the standard and the date when the standard becomes mandatory), the company chose to use the old method, in which minority interest (noncontrolling interest) is reported at book value, while the majority investor's holdings are recorded at fair value. What entry would Carrefour have made if it elected to use the new approach?

18.4   Business combinations at Tesco

On 18 June 2010 the Group acquired certain assets and liabilities of 2 Sisters Food Group, Inc. for consideration of £52m. On 19 July 2010 the Group acquired 100% of the ordinary share capital of Wild Rocket Foods, LLC for consideration of £64m. The table below sets out the provisional analysis of the net assets acquired and the fair value to the Group regarding these two acquisitions.

	Preacquisition carrying values £m	Fair value adjustment £m	Provisional fair values on acquisition £m
Noncurrent assets	45	7	52
Current assets	9	(1)	8
Current liabilities	(6)	(1)	(7)
Noncurrent liabilities	(8)	(11)	(19)
Net assets acquired	40	(6)	34
Goodwill arising on acquisitions			82
			116
Consideration:			
Cash			45
Noncash			76
Total consideration			116

The goodwill represents the benefit of supply chain efficiencies, production economies, the ability to develop new and innovative products, and further third-party revenue potential.

Required

(a) How were the two transactions financed? What impact would the financing have on the three principal financial statements?
(b) Explain the potential reasons for the adjustment in the values of net assets acquired.
(c) What is goodwill and what percentage of the transactions does it constitute?

Tables for Present Value and Future Value Factors

Future value factors for €1 compounded at i% for N periods

N	1%	2%	3%	4%	5%	6%	7%	8%	9%	10%	11%	12%	13%	14%	15%	20%
1	1.010	1.020	1.030	1.040	1.050	1.060	1.070	1.080	1.090	1.100	1.110	1.120	1.130	1.140	1.150	1.200
2	1.020	1.040	1.061	1.082	1.103	1.124	1.145	1.166	1.188	1.210	1.232	1.254	1.277	1.300	1.323	1.440
3	1.030	1.061	1.093	1.125	1.158	1.191	1.225	1.260	1.295	1.331	1.368	1.405	1.443	1.482	1.521	1.728
4	1.041	1.082	1.126	1.170	1.216	1.262	1.311	1.360	1.412	1.464	1.518	1.574	1.630	1.689	1.749	2.074
5	1.051	1.104	1.159	1.217	1.276	1.338	1.403	1.469	1.539	1.611	1.685	1.762	1.842	1.925	2.011	2.488
6	1.062	1.126	1.194	1.265	1.340	1.419	1.501	1.587	1.677	1.772	1.870	1.974	2.082	2.195	2.313	2.986
7	1.072	1.149	1.230	1.316	1.407	1.504	1.606	1.714	1.828	1.949	2.076	2.211	2.353	2.502	2.660	3.583
8	1.083	1.172	1.267	1.369	1.477	1.594	1.718	1.851	1.993	2.144	2.305	2.476	2.658	2.853	3.059	4.300
9	1.094	1.195	1.305	1.423	1.551	1.689	1.838	1.999	2.172	2.358	2.558	2.773	3.004	3.252	3.518	5.160
10	1.105	1.219	1.344	1.480	1.629	1.791	1.967	2.159	2.367	2.594	2.839	3.106	3.395	3.707	4.046	6.192
11	1.116	1.243	1.384	1.539	1.710	1.898	2.105	2.332	2.580	2.853	3.152	3.479	3.836	4.226	4.652	7.430
12	1.127	1.268	1.426	1.601	1.796	2.012	2.252	2.518	2.813	3.138	3.498	3.896	4.335	4.818	5.350	8.916
13	1.138	1.294	1.469	1.665	1.886	2.133	2.410	2.720	3.066	3.452	3.883	4.363	4.898	5.492	6.153	10.699
14	1.149	1.319	1.513	1.732	1.980	2.261	2.579	2.937	3.342	3.797	4.310	4.887	5.535	6.261	7.076	12.839
15	1.161	1.346	1.558	1.801	2.079	2.397	2.759	3.172	3.642	4.177	4.785	5.474	6.254	7.138	8.137	15.407
16	1.173	1.373	1.605	1.873	2.183	2.540	2.952	3.426	3.970	4.595	5.311	6.130	7.067	8.137	9.358	18.488
17	1.184	1.400	1.653	1.948	2.292	2.693	3.159	3.700	4.328	5.054	5.895	6.866	7.986	9.276	10.761	22.186
18	1.196	1.428	1.702	2.026	2.407	2.854	3.380	3.996	4.717	5.560	6.544	7.690	9.024	10.575	12.375	26.623
19	1.208	1.457	1.754	2.107	2.527	3.026	3.617	4.316	5.142	6.116	7.263	8.613	10.197	12.056	14.232	31.948
20	1.220	1.486	1.806	2.191	2.653	3.207	3.870	4.661	5.604	6.727	8.062	9.646	11.523	13.743	16.367	38.338
21	1.232	1.516	1.860	2.279	2.786	3.400	4.141	5.034	6.109	7.400	8.949	10.804	13.021	15.668	18.822	46.005
22	1.245	1.546	1.916	2.370	2.925	3.604	4.430	5.437	6.659	8.140	9.934	12.100	14.714	17.861	21.645	55.206
23	1.257	1.577	1.974	2.465	3.072	3.820	4.741	5.871	7.258	8.954	11.026	13.552	16.627	20.362	24.891	66.247
24	1.270	1.608	2.033	2.563	3.225	4.049	5.072	6.341	7.911	9.850	12.239	15.179	18.788	23.212	28.625	79.497
25	1.282	1.641	2.094	2.666	3.386	4.292	5.427	6.848	8.623	10.835	13.585	17.000	21.231	26.462	32.919	95.396
26	1.295	1.673	2.157	2.772	3.556	4.549	5.807	7.396	9.399	11.918	15.080	19.040	23.991	30.167	37.857	114.475
27	1.308	1.707	2.221	2.883	3.733	4.822	6.214	7.988	10.245	13.110	16.739	21.325	27.109	34.390	43.535	137.371
28	1.321	1.741	2.288	2.999	3.920	5.112	6.649	8.627	11.167	14.421	18.580	23.884	30.633	39.204	50.066	164.845
29	1.335	1.776	2.357	3.119	4.116	5.418	7.114	9.317	12.172	15.863	20.624	26.750	34.616	44.693	57.575	197.814
30	1.348	1.811	2.427	3.243	4.322	5.743	7.612	10.063	13.268	17.449	22.892	29.960	39.116	50.950	66.212	237.376
31	1.361	1.848	2.500	3.373	4.538	6.088	8.145	10.868	14.462	19.194	25.410	33.555	44.201	58.083	76.144	284.852
32	1.375	1.885	2.575	3.508	4.765	6.453	8.715	11.737	15.763	21.114	28.206	37.582	49.947	66.215	87.565	341.822
33	1.389	1.922	2.652	3.648	5.003	6.841	9.325	12.676	17.182	23.225	31.308	42.092	56.440	75.485	100.700	410.186
34	1.403	1.961	2.732	3.794	5.253	7.251	9.978	13.690	18.728	25.548	34.752	47.143	63.777	86.053	115.805	492.224
35	1.417	2.000	2.814	3.946	5.516	7.686	10.677	14.785	20.414	28.102	38.575	52.800	72.069	98.100	133.176	590.668
36	1.431	2.040	2.898	4.104	5.792	8.147	11.424	15.968	22.251	30.913	42.818	59.136	81.437	111.834	153.152	708.802
37	1.445	2.081	2.985	4.268	6.081	8.636	12.224	17.246	24.254	34.004	47.528	66.232	92.024	127.491	176.125	850.562
38	1.460	2.122	3.075	4.439	6.385	9.154	13.079	18.625	26.437	37.404	52.756	74.180	103.987	145.340	202.543	1020.675
39	1.474	2.165	3.167	4.616	6.705	9.704	13.995	20.115	28.816	41.145	58.559	83.081	117.506	165.687	232.925	1224.810
40	1.489	2.208	3.262	4.801	7.040	10.286	14.974	21.725	31.409	45.259	65.001	93.051	132.782	188.884	267.864	1469.772
45	1.565	2.438	3.782	5.841	8.985	13.765	21.002	31.920	48.327	72.890	109.530	163.988	244.641	363.679	538.769	3657.262
50	1.645	2.692	4.384	7.107	11.467	18.420	29.457	46.902	74.358	117.391	184.565	289.002	450.736	700.233	1083.657	9100.438

Present Value factors (at i%) for €1 received at the end of N periods

N	1%	2%	3%	4%	5%	6%	7%	8%	9%	10%	11%	12%	13%	14%	15%	20%
1	0.990	0.980	0.971	0.962	0.952	0.943	0.935	0.926	0.917	0.909	0.901	0.893	0.885	0.877	0.870	0.833
2	0.980	0.961	0.943	0.925	0.907	0.890	0.873	0.857	0.842	0.826	0.812	0.797	0.783	0.769	0.756	0.694
3	0.971	0.942	0.915	0.889	0.864	0.840	0.816	0.794	0.772	0.751	0.731	0.712	0.693	0.675	0.658	0.579
4	0.961	0.924	0.888	0.855	0.823	0.792	0.763	0.735	0.708	0.683	0.659	0.636	0.613	0.592	0.572	0.482
5	0.951	0.906	0.863	0.822	0.784	0.747	0.713	0.681	0.650	0.621	0.593	0.567	0.543	0.519	0.497	0.402
6	0.942	0.888	0.837	0.790	0.746	0.705	0.666	0.630	0.596	0.564	0.535	0.507	0.480	0.456	0.432	0.335
7	0.933	0.871	0.813	0.760	0.711	0.665	0.623	0.583	0.547	0.513	0.482	0.452	0.425	0.400	0.376	0.279
8	0.923	0.853	0.789	0.731	0.677	0.627	0.582	0.540	0.502	0.467	0.434	0.404	0.376	0.351	0.327	0.233
9	0.914	0.837	0.766	0.703	0.645	0.592	0.544	0.500	0.460	0.424	0.391	0.361	0.333	0.308	0.284	0.194
10	0.905	0.820	0.744	0.676	0.614	0.558	0.508	0.463	0.422	0.386	0.352	0.322	0.295	0.270	0.247	0.162
11	0.896	0.804	0.722	0.650	0.585	0.527	0.475	0.429	0.388	0.350	0.317	0.287	0.261	0.237	0.215	0.135
12	0.887	0.788	0.701	0.625	0.557	0.497	0.444	0.397	0.356	0.319	0.286	0.257	0.231	0.208	0.187	0.112
13	0.879	0.773	0.681	0.601	0.530	0.469	0.415	0.368	0.326	0.290	0.258	0.229	0.204	0.182	0.163	0.093
14	0.870	0.758	0.661	0.577	0.505	0.442	0.388	0.340	0.299	0.263	0.232	0.205	0.181	0.160	0.141	0.078
15	0.861	0.743	0.642	0.555	0.481	0.417	0.362	0.315	0.275	0.239	0.209	0.183	0.160	0.140	0.123	0.065
16	0.853	0.728	0.623	0.534	0.458	0.394	0.339	0.292	0.252	0.218	0.188	0.163	0.141	0.123	0.107	0.054
17	0.844	0.714	0.605	0.513	0.436	0.371	0.317	0.270	0.231	0.198	0.170	0.146	0.125	0.108	0.093	0.045
18	0.836	0.700	0.587	0.494	0.416	0.350	0.296	0.250	0.212	0.180	0.153	0.130	0.111	0.095	0.081	0.038
19	0.828	0.686	0.570	0.475	0.396	0.331	0.277	0.232	0.194	0.164	0.138	0.116	0.098	0.083	0.070	0.031
20	0.820	0.673	0.554	0.456	0.377	0.312	0.258	0.215	0.178	0.149	0.124	0.104	0.087	0.073	0.061	0.026
21	0.811	0.660	0.538	0.439	0.359	0.294	0.242	0.199	0.164	0.135	0.112	0.093	0.077	0.064	0.053	0.022
22	0.803	0.647	0.522	0.422	0.342	0.278	0.226	0.184	0.150	0.123	0.101	0.083	0.068	0.056	0.046	0.018
23	0.795	0.634	0.507	0.406	0.326	0.262	0.211	0.170	0.138	0.112	0.091	0.074	0.060	0.049	0.040	0.015
24	0.788	0.622	0.492	0.390	0.310	0.247	0.197	0.158	0.126	0.102	0.082	0.066	0.053	0.043	0.035	0.013
25	0.780	0.610	0.478	0.375	0.295	0.233	0.184	0.146	0.116	0.092	0.074	0.059	0.047	0.038	0.030	0.010
26	0.772	0.598	0.464	0.361	0.281	0.220	0.172	0.135	0.106	0.084	0.066	0.053	0.042	0.033	0.026	0.009
27	0.764	0.586	0.450	0.347	0.268	0.207	0.161	0.125	0.098	0.076	0.060	0.047	0.037	0.029	0.023	0.007
28	0.757	0.574	0.437	0.333	0.255	0.196	0.150	0.116	0.090	0.069	0.054	0.042	0.033	0.026	0.020	0.006
29	0.749	0.563	0.424	0.321	0.243	0.185	0.141	0.107	0.082	0.063	0.048	0.037	0.029	0.022	0.017	0.005
30	0.742	0.552	0.412	0.308	0.231	0.174	0.131	0.099	0.075	0.057	0.044	0.033	0.026	0.020	0.015	0.004
31	0.735	0.541	0.400	0.296	0.220	0.164	0.123	0.092	0.069	0.052	0.039	0.030	0.023	0.017	0.013	0.004
32	0.727	0.531	0.388	0.285	0.210	0.155	0.115	0.085	0.063	0.047	0.035	0.027	0.020	0.015	0.011	0.003
33	0.720	0.520	0.377	0.274	0.200	0.146	0.107	0.079	0.058	0.043	0.032	0.024	0.018	0.013	0.010	0.002
34	0.713	0.510	0.366	0.264	0.190	0.138	0.100	0.073	0.053	0.039	0.029	0.021	0.016	0.012	0.009	0.002
35	0.706	0.500	0.355	0.253	0.181	0.130	0.094	0.068	0.049	0.036	0.026	0.019	0.014	0.010	0.008	0.002
36	0.699	0.490	0.345	0.244	0.173	0.123	0.088	0.063	0.045	0.032	0.023	0.017	0.012	0.009	0.007	0.001
37	0.692	0.481	0.335	0.234	0.164	0.116	0.082	0.058	0.041	0.029	0.021	0.015	0.011	0.008	0.006	0.001
38	0.685	0.471	0.325	0.225	0.157	0.109	0.076	0.054	0.038	0.027	0.019	0.013	0.010	0.007	0.005	0.001
39	0.678	0.462	0.316	0.217	0.149	0.103	0.071	0.050	0.035	0.024	0.017	0.012	0.009	0.006	0.004	0.001
40	0.672	0.453	0.307	0.208	0.142	0.097	0.067	0.046	0.032	0.022	0.015	0.011	0.008	0.005	0.004	0.001
45	0.639	0.410	0.264	0.171	0.111	0.073	0.048	0.031	0.021	0.014	0.009	0.006	0.004	0.003	0.002	0.000
50	0.608	0.372	0.228	0.141	0.087	0.054	0.034	0.021	0.013	0.009	0.005	0.003	0.002	0.001	0.001	0.000

Future value of annuity factors for €1 compounded at i% for N periods

N	1%	2%	3%	4%	5%	6%	7%	8%	9%	10%	11%	12%	13%	14%	15%	20%
1	1.000	1.000	1.000	1.000	1.000	1.000	1.000	1.000	1.000	1.000	1.000	1.000	1.000	1.000	1.000	1.000
2	2.010	2.020	2.030	2.040	2.050	2.060	2.070	2.080	2.090	2.100	2.110	2.120	2.130	2.140	2.150	2.200
3	3.030	3.060	3.091	3.122	3.153	3.184	3.215	3.246	3.278	3.310	3.342	3.374	3.407	3.440	3.473	3.640
4	4.060	4.122	4.184	4.246	4.310	4.375	4.440	4.506	4.573	4.641	4.710	4.779	4.850	4.921	4.993	5.368
5	5.101	5.204	5.309	5.416	5.526	5.637	5.751	5.867	5.985	6.105	6.228	6.353	6.480	6.610	6.742	7.442
6	6.152	6.308	6.468	6.633	6.802	6.975	7.153	7.336	7.523	7.716	7.913	8.115	8.323	8.536	8.754	9.930
7	7.214	7.434	7.662	7.898	8.142	8.394	8.654	8.923	9.200	9.487	9.783	10.089	10.405	10.730	11.067	12.916
8	8.286	8.583	8.892	9.214	9.549	9.897	10.260	10.637	11.028	11.436	11.859	12.300	12.757	13.233	13.727	16.499
9	9.369	9.755	10.159	10.583	11.027	11.491	11.978	12.488	13.021	13.579	14.164	14.776	15.416	16.085	16.786	20.799
10	10.462	10.950	11.464	12.006	12.578	13.181	13.816	14.487	15.193	15.937	16.722	17.549	18.420	19.337	20.304	25.959
11	11.567	12.169	12.808	13.486	14.207	14.972	15.784	16.645	17.560	18.531	19.561	20.655	21.814	23.045	24.349	32.150
12	12.683	13.412	14.192	15.026	15.917	16.870	17.888	18.977	20.141	21.384	22.713	24.133	25.650	27.271	29.002	39.581
13	13.809	14.680	15.618	16.627	17.713	18.882	20.141	21.495	22.953	24.523	26.212	28.029	29.985	32.089	34.352	48.497
14	14.947	15.974	17.086	18.292	19.599	21.015	22.550	24.215	26.019	27.975	30.095	32.393	34.883	37.581	40.505	59.196
15	16.097	17.293	18.599	20.024	21.579	23.276	25.129	27.152	29.361	31.772	34.405	37.280	40.417	43.842	47.580	72.035
16	17.258	18.639	20.157	21.825	23.657	25.673	27.888	30.324	33.003	35.950	39.190	42.753	46.672	50.980	55.717	87.442
17	18.430	20.012	21.762	23.698	25.840	28.213	30.840	33.750	36.974	40.545	44.501	48.884	53.739	59.118	65.075	105.931
18	19.615	21.412	23.414	25.645	28.132	30.906	33.999	37.450	41.301	45.599	50.396	55.750	61.725	68.394	75.836	128.117
19	20.811	22.841	25.117	27.671	30.539	33.760	37.379	41.446	46.018	51.159	56.939	63.440	70.749	78.969	88.212	154.740
20	22.019	24.297	26.870	29.778	33.066	36.786	40.995	45.762	51.160	57.275	64.203	72.052	80.947	91.025	102.444	186.688
21	23.239	25.783	28.676	31.969	35.719	39.993	44.865	50.423	56.765	64.002	72.265	81.699	92.470	104.768	118.810	225.026
22	24.472	27.299	30.537	34.248	38.505	43.392	49.006	55.457	62.873	71.403	81.214	92.503	105.491	120.436	137.632	271.031
23	25.716	28.845	32.453	36.618	41.430	46.996	53.436	60.893	69.532	79.543	91.148	104.603	120.205	138.297	159.276	326.237
24	26.973	30.422	34.426	39.083	44.502	50.816	58.177	66.765	76.790	88.497	102.174	118.155	136.831	158.659	184.168	392.484
25	28.243	32.030	36.459	41.646	47.727	54.865	63.249	73.106	84.701	98.347	114.413	133.334	155.620	181.871	212.793	471.981
26	29.526	33.671	38.553	44.312	51.113	59.156	68.676	79.954	93.324	109.182	127.999	150.334	176.850	208.333	245.712	567.377
27	30.821	35.344	40.710	47.084	54.669	63.706	74.484	87.351	102.723	121.100	143.079	169.374	200.841	238.499	283.569	681.853
28	32.129	37.051	42.931	49.968	58.403	68.528	80.698	95.339	112.968	134.210	159.817	190.699	227.950	272.889	327.104	819.223
29	33.450	38.792	45.219	52.966	62.323	73.640	87.347	103.966	124.135	148.631	178.397	214.583	258.583	312.094	377.170	984.068
30	34.785	40.568	47.575	56.085	66.439	79.058	94.461	113.283	136.308	164.494	199.021	241.333	293.199	356.787	434.745	1181.882
31	36.133	42.379	50.003	59.328	70.761	84.802	102.073	123.346	149.575	181.943	221.913	271.293	332.315	407.737	500.957	1419.258
32	37.494	44.227	52.503	62.701	75.299	90.890	110.218	134.214	164.037	201.138	247.324	304.848	376.516	465.820	577.100	1704.109
33	38.869	46.112	55.078	66.210	80.064	97.343	118.933	145.951	179.800	222.252	275.529	342.429	426.463	532.035	664.666	2045.931
34	40.258	48.034	57.730	69.858	85.067	104.184	128.259	158.627	196.982	245.477	306.837	384.521	482.903	607.520	765.365	2456.118
35	41.660	49.994	60.462	73.652	90.320	111.435	138.237	172.317	215.711	271.024	341.590	431.663	546.681	693.573	881.170	2948.341
36	43.077	51.994	63.276	77.598	95.836	119.121	148.913	187.102	236.125	299.127	380.164	484.463	618.749	791.673	1014.346	3539.009
37	44.508	54.034	66.174	81.702	101.628	127.268	160.337	203.070	258.376	330.039	422.982	543.599	700.187	903.507	1167.498	4247.811
38	45.953	56.115	69.159	85.970	107.710	135.904	172.561	220.316	282.630	364.043	470.511	609.831	792.211	1030.998	1343.622	5098.373
39	47.412	58.237	72.234	90.409	114.095	145.058	185.640	238.941	309.066	401.448	523.267	684.010	896.198	1176.338	1546.165	6119.048
40	48.886	60.402	75.401	95.026	120.800	154.762	199.635	259.057	337.882	442.593	581.826	767.091	1013.704	1342.025	1779.090	7343.858
45	56.481	71.893	92.720	121.029	159.700	212.744	285.749	386.506	525.859	718.905	986.639	1358.230	1874.165	2590.565	3585.128	18281.310
50	64.463	84.579	112.797	152.667	209.348	290.336	406.529	573.770	815.084	1163.909	1668.771	2400.018	3459.507	4994.521	7217.716	45497.191

Present value of annuity factors (at i% per period) for €1 received per period for each of N periods

N	1%	2%	3%	4%	5%	6%	7%	8%	9%	10%	11%	12%	13%	14%	15%	20%
1	0.990	0.980	0.971	0.962	0.952	0.943	0.935	0.926	0.917	0.909	0.901	0.893	0.885	0.877	0.870	0.833
2	1.970	1.942	1.913	1.886	1.859	1.833	1.808	1.783	1.759	1.736	1.713	1.690	1.668	1.647	1.626	1.528
3	2.941	2.884	2.829	2.775	2.723	2.673	2.624	2.577	2.531	2.487	2.444	2.402	2.361	2.322	2.283	2.106
4	3.902	3.808	3.717	3.630	3.546	3.465	3.387	3.312	3.240	3.170	3.102	3.037	2.974	2.914	2.855	2.589
5	4.853	4.713	4.580	4.452	4.329	4.212	4.100	3.993	3.890	3.791	3.696	3.605	3.517	3.433	3.352	2.991
6	5.795	5.601	5.417	5.242	5.076	4.917	4.767	4.623	4.486	4.355	4.231	4.111	3.998	3.889	3.784	3.326
7	6.728	6.472	6.230	6.002	5.786	5.582	5.389	5.206	5.033	4.868	4.712	4.564	4.423	4.288	4.160	3.605
8	7.652	7.325	7.020	6.733	6.463	6.210	5.971	5.747	5.535	5.335	5.146	4.968	4.799	4.639	4.487	3.837
9	8.566	8.162	7.786	7.435	7.108	6.802	6.515	6.247	5.995	5.759	5.537	5.328	5.132	4.946	4.772	4.031
10	9.471	8.983	8.530	8.111	7.722	7.360	7.024	6.710	6.418	6.145	5.889	5.650	5.426	5.216	5.019	4.192
11	10.368	9.787	9.253	8.760	8.306	7.887	7.499	7.139	6.805	6.495	6.207	5.938	5.687	5.453	5.234	4.327
12	11.255	10.575	9.954	9.385	8.863	8.384	7.943	7.536	7.161	6.814	6.492	6.194	5.918	5.660	5.421	4.439
13	12.134	11.348	10.635	9.986	9.394	8.853	8.358	7.904	7.487	7.103	6.750	6.424	6.122	5.842	5.583	4.533
14	13.004	12.106	11.296	10.563	9.899	9.295	8.745	8.244	7.786	7.367	6.982	6.628	6.302	6.002	5.724	4.611
15	13.865	12.849	11.938	11.118	10.380	9.712	9.108	8.559	8.061	7.606	7.191	6.811	6.462	6.142	5.847	4.675
16	14.718	13.578	12.561	11.652	10.838	10.106	9.447	8.851	8.313	7.824	7.379	6.974	6.604	6.265	5.954	4.730
17	15.562	14.292	13.166	12.166	11.274	10.477	9.763	9.122	8.544	8.022	7.549	7.120	6.729	6.373	6.047	4.775
18	16.398	14.992	13.754	12.659	11.690	10.828	10.059	9.372	8.756	8.201	7.702	7.250	6.840	6.467	6.128	4.812
19	17.226	15.678	14.324	13.134	12.085	11.158	10.336	9.604	8.950	8.365	7.839	7.366	6.938	6.550	6.198	4.843
20	18.046	16.351	14.877	13.590	12.462	11.470	10.594	9.818	9.129	8.514	7.963	7.469	7.025	6.623	6.259	4.870
21	18.857	17.011	15.415	14.029	12.821	11.764	10.836	10.017	9.292	8.649	8.075	7.562	7.102	6.687	6.312	4.891
22	19.660	17.658	15.937	14.451	13.163	12.042	11.061	10.201	9.442	8.772	8.176	7.645	7.170	6.743	6.359	4.909
23	20.456	18.292	16.444	14.857	13.489	12.303	11.272	10.371	9.580	8.883	8.266	7.718	7.230	6.792	6.399	4.925
24	21.243	18.914	16.936	15.247	13.799	12.550	11.469	10.529	9.707	8.985	8.348	7.784	7.283	6.835	6.434	4.937
25	22.023	19.523	17.413	15.622	14.094	12.783	11.654	10.675	9.823	9.077	8.422	7.843	7.330	6.873	6.464	4.948
26	22.795	20.121	17.877	15.983	14.375	13.003	11.826	10.810	9.929	9.161	8.488	7.896	7.372	6.906	6.491	4.956
27	23.560	20.707	18.327	16.330	14.643	13.211	11.987	10.935	10.027	9.237	8.548	7.943	7.409	6.935	6.514	4.964
28	24.316	21.281	18.764	16.663	14.898	13.406	12.137	11.051	10.116	9.307	8.602	7.984	7.441	6.961	6.534	4.970
29	25.066	21.844	19.188	16.984	15.141	13.591	12.278	11.158	10.198	9.370	8.650	8.022	7.470	6.983	6.551	4.975
30	25.808	22.396	19.600	17.292	15.372	13.765	12.409	11.258	10.274	9.427	8.694	8.055	7.496	7.003	6.566	4.979
31	26.542	22.938	20.000	17.588	15.593	13.929	12.532	11.350	10.343	9.479	8.733	8.085	7.518	7.020	6.579	4.982
32	27.270	23.468	20.389	17.874	15.803	14.084	12.647	11.435	10.406	9.526	8.769	8.112	7.538	7.035	6.591	4.985
33	27.990	23.989	20.766	18.148	16.003	14.230	12.754	11.514	10.464	9.569	8.801	8.135	7.556	7.048	6.600	4.988
34	28.703	24.499	21.132	18.411	16.193	14.368	12.854	11.587	10.518	9.609	8.829	8.157	7.572	7.060	6.609	4.990
35	29.409	24.999	21.487	18.665	16.374	14.498	12.948	11.655	10.567	9.644	8.855	8.176	7.586	7.070	6.617	4.992
36	30.108	25.489	21.832	18.908	16.547	14.621	13.035	11.717	10.612	9.677	8.879	8.192	7.598	7.079	6.623	4.993
37	30.800	25.969	22.167	19.143	16.711	14.737	13.117	11.775	10.653	9.706	8.900	8.208	7.609	7.087	6.629	4.994
38	31.485	26.441	22.492	19.368	16.868	14.846	13.193	11.829	10.691	9.733	8.919	8.221	7.618	7.094	6.634	4.995
39	32.163	26.903	22.808	19.584	17.017	14.949	13.265	11.879	10.726	9.757	8.936	8.233	7.627	7.100	6.638	4.996
40	32.835	27.355	23.115	19.793	17.159	15.046	13.332	11.925	10.757	9.779	8.951	8.244	7.634	7.105	6.642	4.997
45	36.095	29.490	24.519	20.720	17.774	15.456	13.606	12.108	10.881	9.863	9.008	8.283	7.661	7.123	6.654	4.999
50	39.196	31.424	25.730	21.482	18.256	15.762	13.801	12.233	10.962	9.915	9.042	8.304	7.675	7.133	6.661	4.999

Index